The
Contemporary
Chinese
Historical
Drama

The Contemporary Chinese Historical Drama

Four Studies

Rudolf G. Wagner

UNIVERSITY OF CALIFORNIA PRESS
Berkeley • *Los Angeles* • *Oxford*

This volume is sponsored by the
Center for Chinese Studies,
University of California, Berkeley

University of California Press
Berkeley and Los Angeles, California

University of California Press, Ltd.
Oxford, England

Library of Congress Cataloging-in-Publication Data

Wagner, Rudolf G.
    The contemporary Chinese historical drama: four studies / Rudolf G. Wagner.

      p. cm.
    Bibliography: p.
    Includes index.
    ISBN 0-520-05954-9 (alk. paper)
    1. Chinese drama—20th century—History and criticism.   2. Historical drama,
Chinese—History and criticism.   3. Politics and literature—China.   I. Title.
PL2393.W34   1989
895.1′20514′09—dc 19   88-38075
                                         CIP

Printed in the United States of America

1 2 3 4 5 6 7 8 9

For C.

Contents

Introduction

These studies are part of a larger project exploring methods of interpreting contemporary Chinese literary texts. As a general guideline, I have followed two rules in attempting to reconstruct the horizon of understanding within which these texts operate and from within which their logic can best be understood. First, follow every lead. And second, focus on the fringe rather than on the center.

For someone removed from these texts, in terms of both time and cultural location, there is no *a priori* way to decide what form of communication the text in question may be adopting. What is being communicated may in some cases be identical with the surface text. In others, it might be discovered only if the text is read against another text, be it a political guideline or social and political reality as seen by the author, or only if it is read against another literary product by the author himself or others. Or, it might take all of these forms at the same time. Thus anything that points toward an entrance into the subtext, even if it is in the form of minute changes in the illustrations that often accompany the texts, may help in giving access to this realm. In the case of the texts studied in this volume, the political situation at the time when they were written, the former experience of the authors with the uses of history, and, in many cases, the authors' own explicit statements make it clear that writers, censors, and readers all shared the assumption that these texts must be deciphered in order for their hidden meaning to be discovered. What might seem odd in a literary study—for instance, the utilization of agricultural statistics and mortality rates, or the introduction of the internal ruminations of political leaders, or disquisitions on certain historical dates, even the introduction of *un*quoted historical records of persons alluded to in the texts—may give access to hidden meanings. To attend to such clues is all part of this still incomplete attempt to follow every lead. Our most obvious *lacuna* today is the lack of information concerning the actual performance of the plays and public reaction to them. I have tried my best to handle these problems with the available printed material, but there is no question that interviews with actors and directors, censors and spectators who actually saw the performances, and witnessed the public's reaction to it, would have been of great value.

The second guideline for my study, to focus on the fringe, has both an economic base and a theoretical superstructure. Even the simple topic of historical drama comprises an incredible wealth of material. To focus on this totality would mean to drown in material and be forced to resign oneself to a descriptive endeavor. By keeping the entire body of material in mind but focusing on a very few pieces for a detailed study, I could achieve research economy on the one hand and gain insights into the entire body of material on the other. The texts selected for study here are not the core pieces of the genre, but its fringe. To take as the center of my study *Hai Rui Dismissed from Office*, for instance, would have meant to throw myself into a battle in which the entire leadership of the country seems to have joined. Misinformation, falsification, and suppression of information are much more likely in such a core piece than they are in the pieces studied here like *Guan Hanqing* or *Sun Wukong sanda baigujing*. The structure of these latter pieces is clearer and more easily discernible. Thus, to go for the fringe in the analysis of the center is not only economical; there are also good reasons to do so. To explore the relationship between the fringe and the center, I have added a study of the *topoi* common to the new historical drama that make them a distinctive group of texts. The enterprise of these studies is thus a hermeneutical one.

As the studies all deal with the historical drama, some words may be said as to the place of the historical drama in the group of texts dominating the intellectual field and political attention between 1958 and 1966. These were years of a multifaceted crisis in China. The common aspirations that had held the leadership together before 1949 had faded to a point where the leadership had become fragmented with infighting and where political intrigue had become a primary occupation. The already-weak Chinese legal system was further eroded by the rapid collectivization after 1955, which had eliminated individual property rights. The final collapse came in mid-1957, with the Anti-Rightist campaign, when three to four hundred thousand people, mostly younger members of the elite, were shipped off from their homes and jobs for reeducation in the poorest areas of the country, without either trial or legal redress. It was an ideal occasion for weak characters to get rid of their challengers and for strong characters to bruise their heads. By 1959, the subsequent economic experiment of the Great Leap landed, through an inextricable interaction of political, ideological, and natural factors, in what scholars now call the greatest famine in Chinese history. And this with a leadership so cut off from realities that they thought China was going from one bumper harvest to the next, and massively increased grain purchases in the midst of the disaster.

The Communist government had discontinued the old imperial institution of the censor, with his duty to remonstrate with the highest leader. Sun Yat-sen had included a modernized form of this institution in his constitution under the name of the Control Yuan, but after 1949 no institution remained that had the duty of loyal remonstrance and commanded the respect due to those who take on this heavy burden. Nevertheless, many leaders of the intellectual community saw themselves in this censorial tradition, especially in times of crisis when disagreements among the highest leaders left some leeway for those further down the ladder. But even though they were concerned with the "social fabric coming apart," they were in most cases also partisans of one faction of the center or another, a circumstance that made much of their criticism both partisan and hypocritical. Given the political climate at the time, they did not use straight language but relied on a variety of sophisticated and time-honored forms of remonstrance. They "discovered" that the Ming-dynasty official Hai Rui, who became a role model for many since the late fifties, was not simply a stiff-necked judge who would proffer his head to the next villain to come along, but also a wily politician, a man who was aware of political realities and devised tactics to take them into account without compromising "the aspiration of his life." From Hai Rui and others they learned indirect forms of discussing contemporary problems.

First, remonstrance came in the form of historical scholarship. History has always served in China as a depository of precedents in the light of which the present was discussed. During the period in question, a passionate debate raged concerning the evaluation and reevaluation of such controversial historical figures as the third-century general Cao Cao, whom popular literature depicted as a crafty arch-villain, and the empress Wu of the Tang dynasty, the hen in the cock's place whose reputed murder and sex outrages had been described with glee and detail in many a yellow book. The discussion about their merits allowed for a sophisticated treatment of the strengths and weaknesses, the popular perception and the factual features of the number-one leader at the time, Mao Zedong himself. The writing of biographies of such staunch remonstrators as Hai Rui of the Ming or Judge Bao of the Song dynasty, studies of the "international relations" with the Northern ("Soviet") tribes during the Zhanguo period (475–221 B.C.), or the evaluation of such "revolutionary" leaders as Li Zicheng of the Taiping rebellion in the middle of the nineteenth century, who was said to have caved in after his imprisonment—all these were forms of indirectly dealing with the present. There was nothing conspiratorial in this. The top leaders frequently initiated the debates, which, even though they were organized by the Propaganda Department of the Party, offered rich material for the indirect treatment of contemporary problems, and all sides made use of this opportunity.

Second, *zawen*, the historical or miscellaneous essay as a form of remonstrance, became most popular after the beginning of a second Hai Rui wave in 1961. Written by historians like Wu Han, journalists like Deng Tuo, and cultural leaders like Liao Mosha, these *zawen* essays were linked with Lu Xun's use of *zawen* during the thirties. Most of them dealt with history, from which they proceeded to draw general conclusions, both historical events and conclusions being as a rule directly linked to the present. Two such series were Deng Tuo's *Evening Chats at Yanshan* (Yanshan yehua, March 1961–September 1962, in *Beijing wanbao*) and (pseud.) Wu Nanxing's (Wu Han, Deng Tuo, and Liao Mosha) *Three Family Village*, which appeared in the Beijing Party committee's journal *Frontline* (Qianxian) between October 1961 and July 1964. They were imitated or reprinted in other parts of the country.

Third, remonstrance has taken the form of historical drama. "New historical dramas" (*xinbian lishiju*) have been written since the turn of the twentieth century, and were written under Communist guidance in Yanan since the early forties. After 1949, a number of Peking operas and works in other styles had been adapted to the educative purposes of the Party. The new historical plays were to confront the "peasant masses" with the feudal tyrants; the rewritten historical pieces dealt with moral issues but not with court intrigue. A third group, to which Guo Moruo's *Qu Yuan* (Chongqing, 1942) belongs, fell into disuse, as it operated on a "united front" theme against the foreign aggressor, a situation no longer relevant after 1949 when united front policies were abandoned. The new historical drama, as well as the adapted and rewritten pieces that were staged after 1958, dealt with the court, with the intrigues between two factions, one correct and one villainous, and with an ensuing crisis of the nation. The hero, the remonstrator, would *ma huang* (curse the emperor) and, if necessary, *da huang* (trounce the emperor). Altogether this group of texts may comprise a hundred pieces. Both the critics of the Great Leap and the critics of these critics made use of the historical drama. This book deals with some of these pieces, taken from both sides of the political controversy of the Great Leap years. The last chapter treats a larger part of them in a synthetic manner. This work does not deal with all the texts; an entire group of texts dealing with the problems of Sino-Soviet relations in the early sixties is excluded, as are works dealing with the Tibetan uprising.

Fourth, there are dramas, films, and works on revolutionary history. Factions and individuals within the leadership have discussed their relative merits through literary works, dramas, or films dealing with the history of the Chinese revolution. A novel describing the "struggle in the white areas" (areas under Guomindang control) inevitably has to deal with Liu Shaoqi, who was in charge of the Party in these areas; a film about the Pingjiang uprising would be seen as a flattery for the deposed minister of defense, Peng Dehuai, as he led this uprising; and a novel about Liu Zhidan, dealing with the northern Soviet areas and not the Jinggangshan area (under Mao Zedong), would be read as a subtle reversal of verdict for the deposed Politburo member Gao Gang, who happened to have been the leading man in the northern Soviet after Liu Zhidan's death. It was with this last work, the novel *Liu Zhidan*, that literary affairs took on their secret police side in 1962, and ended in the hands of Kang Sheng, the man who had a complete network of agents and prisons at his disposal, a network not only beyond the control of any court but beyond the control of the Party itself. After 1962, Kang persecuted an "anti-Party clique" that had purportedly assembled around this work.

All four forms of remonstrance interact with each other in multifarious ways, and often the same theme or person is dealt with in different media. To this large body of material must be added the attempts to direct public perception of the works through reviews, conferences, and propaganda directives; the rich body of Red Guard material with its inside details about many of the personalities and works involved; and finally the memoirs written after 1978 by survivors and friends of the dead. The relative density and cohesiveness of the material enable us to extrapolate generally valid rules of analysis for the entire body of material from a small fraction of this material; we rely on similar phenomena in related fields for confirmation of their validity.

Research for these studies was conducted first at the John K. Fairbank Center for East Asian Research at Harvard University, where I spent the first half of 1984 as a visiting scholar, and then at the Center for Chinese Studies, University of California, Berkeley. The magnanimous support given to me by both institutions is gratefully acknowledged. Many scholars at both universities have encouraged me in pursuing these studies and have given their support by subjecting drafts of the present work to their critical scrutiny. My special thanks are due to Merle Goldman, Cyril Birch, and Roderick MacFarquhar. Professor Wu Xiaoling kindly shared his vast knowledge about Chinese operatic tradition with me and pointed out historical sources. Sally Serafim shouldered the formidable task of transforming my jolting Germanisms into a fairly smooth English road. Sheila Levine and Betsey Scheiner, of the University of California Press, also joined in the editing endeavor. I myself, and even more so the readers, owe many bows of gratitude to them. E. Schneider, Marion Betz, and Renate Schulze were of great help in finalizing the manuscript. As is customary and correct, responsibility for any mistakes rests with me alone.

ONE

A Guide for the Perplexed and a Call to the Wavering: Tian Han's *Guan Hanqing* (1958) and the New Historical Drama

When, in the twelfth century, the Jewish community had become so dispersed that the transmission of the secrets of the Torah among the initiated could no longer be guaranteed, the rabbi Maimonides set out to write his *Guide for the Perplexed*.[1] The book, according to Leo Strauss's admirable study of the *Guide*,[2] was to explain the secrets of the Torah. By explaining its secrets, however, Maimonides violated a stringent rule of this very body of laws and prescriptions—namely, that its mysteries should not be divulged to the uninitiated. Strauss argues that Maimonides solved the problem by writing a two-layered text. The text's surface would satisfy the common spirit; however, small contradictions, misquotes, and oblique parallelisms with other texts would alert the initiated to the deeper message, which all too often was the exact opposite of the proposition made on the surface. Writers in socialist countries have faced similar problems when crafting their texts, although their specific circumstances are certainly different. There

An early draft of this chapter was presented at the Workshop on Contemporary Chinese Drama and Theater in October 1984 in Buffalo. I have greatly benefited from suggestions and criticisms, but above all encouragement, from Merle Goldman and Cyril Birch. The eminent Guan Hanqing specialist Wu Xiaoling was kind enough to help me with some important historical references. To them and many other friends and colleagues who have patiently borne with me the slow development of the analysis, I bow in gratitude.
    1. ben Maimon, *Guide.*
    2. Strauss, *Persecution and the Art of Writing.*

are strict, state-enforced rules as to the structure and content of the surface text; however, in times of crisis some writers have felt compelled to articulate the realities of society in the face of a daydreaming state leadership. They have crafted multilayered texts in an attempt to "speak the truth" and survive it. In Maimonides's preface, he hinted at the true method to be followed in reading his *Guide*, to give the reader some necessary guidance to find his way into the secret code.

Strauss gave his study of Maimonides's book a title that is misleading, to say the least: *Persecution and the Art of Writing*. The book deals neither with persecution nor with the art of writing under the threat of persecution. The misleading title is for the knowing. As Strauss's preface indicates (without of course spelling it out in any way), the book deals on another level with deciphering contemporary writing from Leninist states.[3]

Much has been written about several of the "new historical plays" (*xinbian lishiju*) of the late fifties and early sixties in the People's Republic of China. Plays like *Hai Rui Dismissed from Office (Hai Rui baguan)* by Wu Han, *Xie Yaohuan* by Tian Han, and *Li Huiniang* by Meng Chao were said to be attacks by innuendo on the Party, its Chairman, and socialism in general. The criticism directed against these plays marked the first open battle of the Cultural Revolution. Scholarly attention has been focused on the relationship of these texts to the dismissal of defense minister Peng Dehuai at the Lushan Plenum in August 1959, however, rather than on the literary aspect of the drama or even on the historical plays written before Peng's dismissal.[4]

Tian Han wrote the historical drama *Guan Hanqing* in the first half of 1958.[5] It is a play about Guan Hanqing, the Yuan dynasty playwright, as he sketches, writes, and stages the play *Injustice Done to Dou E (Dou E yuan)*,[6] which itself is a historical play. *Guan Hanqing* is thus a historical play about a playwright writing a historical play. It is my first contention that it is also, like Maimonides's *Guide*, a "guide for the perplexed," to educate the knowing in the secrets of reading historical plays, and as such it is at the same time, like Maimonides's *Preface*, preface to the "new historical plays" of the coming years. It will be

3. Ibid., p. 3.
4. For a detailed discussion and bibliography see chap. 4, "The Politics of the Historical Drama."
5. Tian, *Guan Hanqing. Juben* ed.
6. Guan, *Gantian dongdi Dou E yuan*, pp. 847ff. There is an English translation by Yang Hsien-yi and Gladys Yang under the title *Snow in Midsummer*.

remembered that Maimonides and Strauss are not much more lucid in their prefaces than they are in their text. Tian Han's play *Guan Hanqing* needs deciphering, too. This is not to say, of course, that Tian Han knew that the later texts (his own included) were to come. Writing *Guan Hanqing*, a historical drama, Tian Han defined the present *ipso facto* as a time of crisis calling for this genre, and he initiated both his colleagues and the public in the arts of crafting and deciphering such texts.

THE HISTORICAL BACKGROUND

Tian Han had been writing drama since the May Fourth movement. Like many others, he had sided with the Communists since the early 1930s. After the founding of the People's Republic in 1949, he became the head of the Dramatists' Association. That group is part of the *Wenlian*, the Association of Culture and Arts Workers, which again is subordinate to the Ministry of Culture. The actual chain of command is different, however. The Propaganda Department of the Communist Party's Central Committee is in charge of culture, and all ministry decisions have to be approved by this department's representatives, if they do not originate there in the first place. Tian Han also headed the Party organization within the Dramatists' Association. Thus, as both the highest "governmental" and highest Party representative in this body, he occupied a position of considerable power. *Qua officio* he was editor-in-chief of the *Xijubao*, the Association's paper, which was a potent instrument to guide its members. Tian had a long-standing commitment to the people who stage plays, the directors and actors. He had treated their lives on stage before 1949,[7] and he cared for their personal circumstances thereafter. During the relaxation in 1956–57, he wrote an article opposing the many political classes for young actors, saying their youth was wasted by attending them,[8] and he personally intervened in favor of an actress whom he himself had attacked earlier.[9] The sociologist Fei Xiaotong was sent around the country in 1956 to visit old social scientists and to report on their lives. His report was entitled

7. Cf. Tung, "Lonely Search."
8. Tian, "Wei yanyuan."
9. Tian, "Renmin." He referred to the Henan Opera star Chen Suzhen. When she was attacked as a "rightist" he tried to intervene with a telegram in her favor, critics charged. See Zhongguo juxie geming zaofantuan, "Chedi chanchu," p. 2.

"A Feeling of Early Spring,"[10] suggesting that there were many wet and chilly days to come and that summer might still be far away. In the same vein, Tian Han also traveled and reported on the deplorable lives of celebrated old actors, advocating that their skills be put to better use.[11]

In April 1957, Tian Han took part in a meeting in Shaanxi, where he denounced *waihang* (nonprofessional) Party control over the professional dramatists as "dangerous."[12] When the Anti-Rightist movement began in June 1957, Tian Han was not only spared attacks for his role in the preceding months but was even put in charge of the Anti-Rightist movement in his Association.[13] As Roderick MacFarquhar has pointed out, there was dissension in the central leadership as to the target of attack in this movement. Politburo member and mayor of Beijing Peng Zhen and others maintained that the target should be "bourgeois rightists," that is, non-Party intellectuals and junior Party members, whereas Mao Zedong and his supporters insisted on pursuing a "rectification movement" against cadres simultaneously and with the same methods as the Anti-Rightist movement.[14] Thus Fei Xiaotong, who was not a Party member, was publicly attacked, but Tian Han, who was a member, escaped unscathed. Further still, Tian Han led the attack against the playwright Wu Zuguang(who was not a Party member) in the Association. From the published record it would seem that Tian Han kept the criticism at a rather low pitch. Even when he eventually defined the contradiction between Wu and the other Association members as one between "the enemy and us," he still maintained one should *shan yu ren*, "be friendly to," Wu as his earlier work had many merits.[15] Wu had criticized the degree of Party control over the field of drama and demanded a stronger voice for the *neihang*, that is, the professionals. Although many articles have been written on Tian Han's life since his posthumous rehabilitation after his death during the Cultural Revolution, they tend to describe him as a sturdy pine weathering the snow-

10. Fei, "Zhishifenzi."
11. Tian, "Bixu."
12. Cf. "Zai Shaanxi sheng," here quoted from "Tian Han de xiju zhuzhang wei shei fuwu," p. 10.
13. This is specifically stated only in the Red Guard source quoted in n. 9, but it was confirmed by his chairing the meetings to criticize Wu Zuguang in 1957. Cf. Tian, "Pipan"; and "Wu Zuguang."
14. MacFarquhar, *Origins*, 1:261ff.
15. Cf. Tian, "Pipan"; and id., "Wu Zuguang."

storms of political suppression and omit those phases of Tian's life that might seem embarrassing.[16] It will be recalled that Wu Han, the author of *Hai Rui Dismissed from Office* and vice-mayor of Beijing, also sharply attacked the "rightists" in 1957 and 1958, demanding stern measures against them.[17] It is hard to fathom what went on in the minds of men like Tian Han and Wu Han. The obvious contradictions in their behavior at different times can perhaps best be described with the term *ketman* as used by Czeslaw Milosz in his *The Captive Mind* to account for the difference between manifest behavior and actual thought among intellectuals in socialist states. Milosz quotes Gobineau's description of this Islamic concept. *Ketman* represents the belief that

> he who is in possession of truth must not expose his person, his relatives or his reputation to the blindness, the folly, the perversity of those whom it has pleased God to place and maintain in error. . . . Nevertheless, there are occasions when silence no longer suffices, when it may pass as an avowal. Then one must not hesitate. Not only must one deny one's true opinion, but one is commanded to resort to all [manner of] ruses to deceive one's adversary. One makes all the protestations of faith that can please him, one performs all the rites one recognizes to be the most vain, one falsifies one's own books, one exhausts all possible means of deceit. Thus one acquires the multiple satisfactions and merits of having placed oneself and one's relatives under cover, of not having exposed a venerable faith to the horrible contact of the infidel, and finally of having, in cheating the latter and confirming him in his error, imposed on him the shame and spiritual misery that he deserves.[18]

Practicing this sublime art, Sadra, the eleventh-century Persian philosopher Avicenna's faithful disciple, managed to spread his master's new philosophy throughout the lettered class without being discovered, until the time was ripe to state his beliefs in more open language. Given the contradiction that we saw above in Tian Han's behavior and, I would argue, the long tradition of literary *ketman* in China, which found optimal conditions for its further refinement in the post-1949 society, one cannot exclude the possibility that Tian Han was practicing a sort of *ketman* during the Anti-Rightist campaign, and perhaps during the Hundred Flowers period as well.

By early 1958, several hundred thousand "rightists" had been

16. Cf. Mao Dun, "Mao Dun tongzhi zhi daoci"; Xia Yan, "Daonian Tian Han tongzhi." For a bibliography of commemorative articles on Tian Han, see Shanghai xiju xueyuan xijuwenxuexi, *Tian Han zhuanji*, pp. 728ff.
17. MacFarquhar, *Origins*, 1:276.
18. Milosz, *Captive Mind*, chap. 3.

summarily dismissed and "sent down" to the country, most of them intellectuals (*zhishi fenzi*), and many among them students and school teachers. The criticisms that had been voiced during the Hundred Flowers period had been rejected as being "anti-Party, anti-socialist"; therefore, no further criticism of the tyrannical and lawless behavior of Party cadres or of their bureaucratism was possible. Although the top leaders who had chastised abuses of power remained in their seats— Party General Secretary Deng Xiaoping and Hu Yaobang, the head of the Youth League, for instance—and although even prominent back-stage advisers to the criticism movement like *People's Daily* editor Deng Tuo, who was consulted by student leader Lin Xiling by phone on every occasion before she spoke, remained more or less unscathed, their mouths were effectively shut once those from the lower ranks whom they had encouraged to speak out had been deported.

At the same time, the cadres' power had enormously increased with the collectivization of agriculture and the nationalization of the remaining private industry starting about 1955–56. The gross discrepancy between the leeway enjoyed by the people in power and that accorded critical public opinion was further increased by a serious situation in the country's agriculture subsequent to bad harvests in 1956 and 1957 (and, perhaps, to the new organizational structure, which was imposed all too rapidly).

Reactions to what amounted to a crisis situation differed. The crisis was especially keenly felt by intellectuals, whose fortunes had taken a deep dive since Mao had abandoned his earlier hope that they might be an active force in the rapid development of the economy.[19] One reaction was that of the leaders, including Deng Xiaoping and Hu Yaobang. They eventually rallied behind Mao in organizing the Great Leap, which promised to overcome the agricultural crisis on the one hand and to be the training ground for a new class of "proletarian" intellectuals on the other. Others reacted by searching for avenues to articulate public criticism of Party cadres and policies that were seen as the cause for the crisis. On March 2, 1958, Tian Han decided to write the drama *Guan Hanqing*, which eventually evolved into his own response to the crisis.[20]

19. I follow MacFarquhar's argumentation here, cf. *Origins*, 1:293f.; id., *Origins*, 2:40ff.

20. Tian Han's secretary at the time published a day-by-day account of the writing of *Guan Hanqing*: Li Zhiyan, "Tian Han," repr. in *Xiju yanjiu* 1982.9, pp. 19ff. Tian's decision is documented on p. 20.

TIAN HAN, THE WRITER

Tian Han experienced in his own person the ambivalence of the writer's role in the "new society." Not only were the authorities wary of him for defending the *neihang* people, those from his own craft, against the Party bureaucrats; the *neihang* as well as the public were wary of him for publicly attacking as an "enemy" a man of Wu Zuguang's standing and thus showing himself to be a mere Party spokesman. This same awkward position vis-à-vis both authorities and public has led many prominent writers in other socialist countries to discuss their own role through a medium more familiar to them than political essays, namely creative writing, be it fiction or drama. There, the writer can discuss in symbolic form his understanding of his own role and responsibility and try to convince the public of his honesty and integrity, while simultaneously assuring the government of his fundamental loyalty.[21]

The current crisis in China exacerbated the dilemma. Credibility was needed more than ever, but the dangers of speaking out were greater than ever. It had been the historical duty of the upright intellectual/official to speak up in times of crisis. This Guo Moruo had done in 1942 in Chongqing by writing the play *Qu Yuan*.[22] It not only dealt with the crisis of the state of Chu under threat from powerful Qin (or its modern counterpart, Japan), but also grappled with the role of the writer in such a crisis, with Guo Moruo donning the oversized robe of Qu Yuan. Guo Moruo's *Qu Yuan* also provided another precedent; the spoken drama (*huaju*) was a very contemporary genre, dealing with modern things. *Qu Yuan* is a *huaju* on a historical theme, however, that used history as a screen on which to project the pattern of the present. Tian Han's *Guan Hanqing* thus operated within a horizon of expectation made up of the public's earlier experiences with similar themes, a similar treatment of these themes, and similar situations in which these themes had been proffered.

GUAN HANQING, THE FIRST OUTLINE

The Hundred Flowers texts had used realist prose, they had dealt with immediately contemporary themes, and they had restricted themselves

---

21. Examples would include Heym, *King David Report*; Wolf, *Cassandra*; Konrad, *The Loser*; Konwicki, *A Minor Apocalypse*. Some of the Chinese texts of this type have been dealt with in my "The Chinese Writer."

22. Guo Moruo, *Qu Yuan*.

to realities accessible to the "common people." There were no higher-level Party or government leaders in the stories. With the demise of the Hundred Flowers movement, this avenue of discourse was closed for both prose and *huaju*. Not only had the writers been banned, but also the moderate tone and modest social level of these texts were inappropriate for the treatment of a perceived crisis that involved the policies of the center. Peking opera (and other opera styles) as well as the historical drama in spoken-drama form dealt with the court and, by implication, with the center. Thus, they were the genres to use, quite apart from the advantage of dealing with such dangerous matter indirectly by use of the screen of history.

The Guan Hanqing theme was not Tian Han's invention. The World Peace Council, a body of personalities with close ties to the "socialist camp," the presidium of which included on the Chinese side Guo Moruo, Mao Dun, Liao Chengzhi, and others, had decided to "strengthen democratic tendencies in the world" by honoring a number of "giants of world culture." I have not been able to locate the resolutions, but heroes whom the Council emulated in 1957 included Goldoni, Blake, Longfellow, Linné, Glinka, Comenius, and Comte; apparently only Gorky and Guan Hanqing were feted in 1958.[23] The decision to include Guan must have come on Chinese instigation and must have been made in 1956, as articles on Guan and translations of his work were published by the English-language *Chinese Literature* (Beijing) beginning in early 1957. The proposal to make Guan a world cultural giant might have come from Professor Zheng Zhenduo, and it could have been supported by the fact that translations of some of Guan's plays had been available in Europe for well over a century. Thus, Guan's inclusion among the giants of world literature would not seem to be a wanton act.[24] In view of the critical nature of Guan's

23. "Cultural Exchanges," p. 134. The Gorky Memorial was in March 1958.

24. Zheng Zhenduo was credited with the role of having taken the initiative through the placement of his article "Guan Hanqing," which had originally appeared in *Xijubao* 1958.6, at the beginning of a collection of essays on Guan Hanqing that came out in 1958. Cf. Gutian wenxue chubanshe, *Guan Hanqing*, pp. 1ff. Zheng died in the crash of a Soviet plane en route to Egypt in that year. Prof. Wu Xiaoling recalls that the proposal to elevate Guan Hanqing to a place among the world's cultural giants came from Zheng. Guan's plays *Snow in Midsummer* (*Dou E yuan*) and *Rescued by a Coquette* were translated in *Chinese Literature* 1957.1. There were many earlier translations, cf. "Doktor

drama, it would seem that he was chosen in the context of the Hundred Flowers values.

Guan Hanqing's dates are only vaguely known, but there is agreement that he lived during the second half of the thirteenth century under the recently established Yuan dynasty. Thus it was decided that celebrations of the 750th anniversary of his work should be held on June 28, 1958. The event was taken very seriously in China, because it lifted a Chinese playwright into the top group of the world's best dramatists. A substantial body of Guan Hanqing's work survives, although it does not seem to have been performed very often during the first years of the People's Republic. The nomination of Guan to a place among the world's giants brought a sudden upsurge in editions and studies. In January 1958, Tian Han received the proofs of a carefully produced edition of Guan's works;[25] in June of that year, Professor Wu Xiaoling edited an annotated text of his major works.[26] The literary supplements and journals *Wenxue yichan*, *Xiju luncong*, and *Xiju yanjiu* engaged in a lively debate about Guan Hanqing in January 1958,[27] and many theaters prepared productions of what was to become the celebration piece, Guan Hanqing's *Gantian dongdi Dou E yuan* (The Injustice Done to Dou E Which Moved Heaven and Shook the Earth, which I will abbreviate as *Dou E yuan*).

Tian Han's *Guan Hanqing* was to interact with Guan Hanqing's *Dou E yuan*. To my knowledge, for no other dramatic text written after 1949 in China can the genesis and development be documented in such detail as *Guan Hanqing*. Not only are no less than three differing printed editions available, but also many articles and discussions about the play have been published. In addition, a day-by-day protocol of the creative process of *Guan Hanqing* was written by Li Zhiyan, who was then Tian Han's secretary.[28] The development of *Guan Hanqing* is not only of historical interest; it offers the possibility to study both the interaction between a writer's creative process and his political

---

Ching und seine Base, oder Der Yadisspiegel" and "Die Ehen des Fräuleins Schmetterling," both in Rüdelsberger, *Altchinesische Liebeskomödien*.

25. Wu Xiaoling, Li Guoyan, Liu Jian (eds.), *Guan Hanqing juqu ji*. Officially, this came out in April 1958, but Tian Han received an advance copy on January 27, 1958; cf. Li Zhiyan, "Tian Han," p. 20.

26. Wu Xiaoling et al., *Da xijujia*.

27. The articles have been included in the collection mentioned in n. 24.

28. Cf. n. 20.

and social analysis, and the strange laws of resonance between the past and the present.

Tian Han was mandated in January 1958 to give the speech commemorating Guan Hanqing on the occasion of the anniversary in June, at a meeting at which Guo Moruo was to preside. When Tian set out to study Guan's works and the historical material about him, he had no plan for a play on the topic.

Tian Han was first impressed with Guan's female character Dou E, having read an article about her by his friend Cheng Yangqiu.[29] Cheng had praised Guan for attributing to Dou E virtues that were a rarity in China in late 1957, when Cheng wrote his article. Dou E was "relatively outspoken, pungent [*pola*], and dared to resist evil forces. . . . Unto her death [she] did not submit; [she] dared to question heaven and earth and to utter her three vows; with biting words she assailed the feudal rulers of her time."[30] Tian Han had already read the biographies of two favorites of Khubilai Khan, Ahmad and Bo Yan. They would be the villains of his play. However, in the description of Li Zhiyan, which seems plausible, Tian was more impressed by the heroism exhibited by Dou E and Guan Hanqing than by the vileness of the villains.[31] He needed a hero whom he himself could emulate in the dangerous enterprise of writing his play, one who would use the stage to call on the spectators to live up to his own courage. Guan Hanqing was to be that person.

Tian was to turn sixty that year, and his friends had commented on his white hair and the absence of new plays from his hand.[32] He was incensed. On March 2, he read in Guan Hanqing's song *Bufu lao* (Not Bending to Age) what Guan wrote about himself: "I am a resounding bronze bean that steaming won't soften, boiling won't cook, beating won't flatten, and frying won't brown."[33] Guan describes himself

29. Cheng Yangqiu, "Tan Dou E," pp. 238ff of the collection mentioned in n. 24.

30. Ibid., p. 238, Tian Han referred to these phrases, cf. Li Zhiyan, "Tian Han," p. 20.

31. Li Zhiyan, "Tian Han," p. 20. Tian made Guan Hanqing say the same, that he "wanted to depict an extraordinary woman" and not "simply revile someone." *Guan Hanqing, Juben* ed., p. 11.

32. Li Zhiyan, "Tian Han," p. 20.

33. Ibid. He included it in *Guan Hanqing*, when Guan confronts the spy Ye Hefu in prison; it is included since the second edition (June 1958), which I quote from *Zhongguo lishiju xuan*, p. 270.

modestly as a small bean; though small, it is made of hard bronze, and no culinary (or political) violence can soften or change it. And Guan is not silent, but *xiang dangdang*, "resounding like a bell" for everyone to hear. Tian Han saw a need for this attitude in 1958 in view of both the political situation and his own advanced age. Guan, furthermore, was *qiaomiao*, "clever and forceful" in his battles against reactionary forces, Tian felt; "even when he sings about the wind and harps about the moon, he battles against [things present] in reality."[34] In Guan Hanqing, Tian Han found a congenial character. After reading Guan's depiction of himself as a "bronze bean," he said: "Guan Hanqing is truly a man of iron. Apart from writing the memorial talk about him, I will write a play about him." Three days later, Tian publicly announced that he would join in the Great Leap Forward and write ten new plays. On March 11, he sketched out the plot of his Guan Hanqing play to the (woman) director of the Experimental Huaju Theater in Beijing, Sun Weishi. Li Zhiyan was asked to write the sketch down in his own words. In the following text, the italicized passages are verbatim from Tian Han; the others were written by Li Zhiyan.

> *Guan Hanqing will be the chief protagonist of the play. I will not describe his biography, but one single phase of his creative life, his writing* Dou E yuan. *The characters, localities, and plot of the play I have already pretty much figured out.*

They were to be as follows:

> *The play's first act will take place in today's Peking Kunqu Theater. On one side of the stage will be the "spectators" looking at the play, simultaneously discussing the play and* [its playwright] *Guan Hanqing.* One of the "spectators" says that this play presents a great tragedy, and although it describes something from history [i.e., from the Han dynasty], *the incident looks much like something from the Yuan dynasty.* Another spectator says: "As it is a story describing a filial girl from Donghai during the Han dynasty, how can anyone misrepresent it to the point of saying it is a contemporary play dealing with the Yuan dynasty?" A third says: "Neither of you gets the entire picture; although it is a historical play, the spearhead of attack in Guan's writing the play is pointed at the reactionary rulers of the Yuan dynasty." After this they also discuss the ending of the play: would it be better to have [an optimistic] end [as in] a comedy, or a tragic denouement? While this discussion is raging, an elderly gentleman urges them: "Please, gentlemen, don't get into a fight; the play that is about to start will answer your ques-

34. Li Zhiyan, "Tian Han," p. 20.

tions." Tian Han said further: *This is the play's "xiezi"* [prelude], *or pro-logue; it is a play within a play; the "spectators" are all actors. The second act goes into Yuan history. The place is the capital* [Cambaluc, today's Bei-jing] *seven hundred years ago. In a corner of the town there is a roadhouse, where the great playwright is with a courtesan* [Zhu Lianxiu] *in her apart-ment, sighing with her about the misfortunes that have befallen the people and expressing his resentment at the troubles that the Yuan rulers have brought upon the people. He wants to take a stand and speak out for the people* [wei min qingming]. *Guan Hanqing's aspirations to resist greatly move the courtesan, and she expresses her wish to join him in his fight.*

The third act is some days later. Guan and the courtesan come by the Cishikou execution ground and see executioners dragging a young woman toward it. The people surrounding the grounds are all shedding tears for this girl, who is about to die because of an unjust verdict. The courtesan also is choked with tears. When Guan sees [their sorrow], *he asks the courtesan for further information, and she tells him that though the young woman is from a good family, because of penury her parents had been forced to sell her as a child bride. Wanting to possess her, a villain killed her husband, poisoned her mother-in-law, and then accused her of her mother's murder; the reck-less officials and corrupt functionaries accepted bribes, and, without permit-ting her any detailed explanation, condemned her to death. The courtesan also tells Guan Hanqing of other incidents in which people from the lower reaches of society have been unjustly killed. When Guan hears this, his grief and indignation know no bounds, and he decides to use his brush as a sword. He will write a play to uncover these somber realities and to depict these devilish, reckless officials and corrupt functionaries.*

In the fourth act, he drowns his sorrows in wine at a roadhouse. Under the influence of the wine he makes unguarded remarks [shiyan] *and reveals his plan to write a play that will cry out against the injustice done to the young woman. This "news" blows through the capital as quickly as the wind and the authorities pay close attention. Some of his friends from the drama world who have little courage* [danxiao] *urge him not to write plays that prick contemporary politics, and to stop rebelling against the authorities* [fanshang] *and offending the officials, in order to avoid drawing onto himself a fatal disaster. One man, with the best of intentions, even says: Hanqing, your fame already fills the capital. Even the mighty and noble of our day appreciate seeing your plays. One has to know where to stop. Don't write plays that stab at the officials. However, Guan has already made up his mind to write and he declines their advice. He and the courtesan vow that if he will write the play, she will stage it; and later if they run into trouble and are accused, they vow to hold their ground and not be afraid. In the evening, Guan stays on in the roadhouse and, wielding his brush, sets to writing, taking the Han dynasty story of the loyal girl from Donghai as a metaphor* [jiyu, lit., a lodging house] *for the reality of the Yuan dynasty. The descent, life, and fate of the lead character, Dou E, will be exactly like those of the young woman from the present dynasty who was unjustly killed.* Then com-rade Tian Han said: *Of course, the intention and method of Guan Hanqing in writing this play are to allude to the present by dealing with old matters* [yi gu yu jin]. *He sides with the unjustly executed woman, sides with the people, and comes out angrily reviling* [fennu tuoma] *those in power in his time. That is why Guan gave the title* The Injustice Done to Dou E *to the play.* Tian Han went on:

> In the fifth act, Guan has completed Dou E yuan *and it is being staged with his close friend, the courtesan, playing Dou E. This act again* [like Act 1] *is theater within the theater. On one side of the stage the mighty nobles of the Yuan look on, on the other are the common people; on the stage between them is the play* Injustice Done to Dou E. *When the play reaches the scene where Dou E scornfully reviles* [fennu zema] *Heaven, Earth, and the gods, and sings* [to her father] *"Kill all these reckless official and corrupt functionaries, share the burden with the only man* [i.e., the emperor], *and eliminate those pests for the sake of people," there is booing from the seats of the nobles. Then the reckless officials shout: Arrest the actress playing Dou E! Stop her from singing any further! She should be made the Dou E of our Yuan dynasty! In this critical moment when the singer is in greatest danger, Guan Hanqing stands up in the rows where the common people sit, and says loudly: The play was written by me. If anybody is to be arrested, it's me. I did it alone, and I alone am responsible.... Then, with awe-inspiring uprightness, he transforms the stage into a battlefield, and climbs up to the high stage. Confronting the officials, he evokes for the people the sunless darkness of Yuan society, reveals the bloody crimes of the reckless officials and corrupt functionaries, and calls on the people to rise up in resistance and battle. While Guan talks, chaos breaks out in the theater. Rough curses are yelled, and there is enthusiastic rejoicing and applause. There is great turmoil in the theater. Before the reckless officials can lay their venomous hands on Guan Hanqing, he has made off. Hidden, together with the courtesan, by the people, he flees the capital to distant parts. This, Tian Han said, was the end of the play.*[35]

From this outline, the following points emerge:

a. The first act deals with the controversy about contemporary and historical plays and themes on stage that was then raging. Many cultural leaders were pushing for more contemporary themes; in fact, this demand was the form the political battle took on the eve of the Cultural Revolution, with Jiang Qing, Ke Qingshi, Kang Sheng, and Zhang Chunqiao pushing in this direction. Zhou Enlai, on the other hand, had proposed a policy of "walking on two legs." It was eagerly taken up by writers, artists, and spectators committed to the traditional operas and looking for official permission to continue performing them. Tian Han was a promoter of *huaju*, and the *huaju* usually had modern themes. However, he was also familiar with the traditional opera and had writ-

35. Ibid., pp. 20f.

ten pieces for it. Thus, when the debate came into the open in 1963 in Shanghai, he came out in defense of Zhou's slogan.

In *Guan Hanqing*, however, the issue was more complicated. Traditional operas had been staged and rewritten during the early fifties to accord with the educational goals of the Party. Thus they were not entirely divorced from reality. With *Guan Hanqing*, Tian Han was to discover, or rather rediscover, the potential of the historical theme for a sharply critical depiction of contemporary reality that went far beyond the didactic purposes traditionally asssigned to such plays. The prologue confronts three propositions: that *Dou E* is a play about earlier history, that it is a play about the present using earlier history, and that it is both. The third proposition, being dialectical, carries the day. The debate about historical versus contemporary themes is devoid of content, Tian Han contends, because historical drama makes reference to the present. Tian Han later spelled out this notion in an article of farewell to the Canton Opera troupe when it traveled to North Korea to perform an adaptation of his *Guan Hanqing* in 1959.

> For a long time an opinion has existed in drama circles that only contemporary themes are capable of reflecting actual [i.e., present-day] struggles, and that because historical themes can reflect only historical truth they have no relationship with actual struggles. Thus the contemporary play, in contrast to the historical play, is called a "realistic play." . . . In fact, many historical plays are written for the people of today. . . . The importance of such plays in terms of actual life is extraordinarily great. . . . Guo Moruo's *Qu Yuan* describes events 2,500 years ago, but when it was first staged in Chongqing, the spectators knew that King Huai of Chu referred to Chiang Kai-shek. Qu Yuan represented the common fate of the revolutionary cultural workers at the time. . . . The historical drama can thus reflect present-day, actual struggles and furthermore, under certain circumstances, can evoke a strong, real-life meaning. One should not put it into opposition to the drama dealing with contemporary matters (*xiandaiju*).[36]

In the prologue, an elderly gentleman finally intervenes in the debate of the spectators to announce the content of the coming play, saying, "the play that is about to start will answer your questions." Within the "drama within the drama," "the play that is about to start" would refer to *Dou E yuan*. However, in fact the public in the audience, not the public on stage, is being addressed. The audience is about to see not Guan Hanqing's *Dou E yuan*, but Tian Han's play about Guan Hanqing writing *Dou E yuan*. Tian Han's *Guan Hanqing* thus sets out to

36. Tian, "Song *Guan Hanqing*," p. 7.

enter into the debate. As a historical play about the writing of a historical play, we can expect it to decry the hubbub about the necessity to treat "contemporary themes" as only ignorant sloganeering.

b. The play was to explore the creative process of writing *Dou E yuan*. Seeing the execution of the young woman, Guan will use a historical precedent to "make his brush into a sword" and speak out against this unjust verdict. He will hide his true intention in the "lodging house" of historical precedent. But there is no question that he will have such an intention, as he will spell it out when inebriated. Tian Han had practically no historical material on Guan Hanqing and his play on hand. Thus the background and motive for writing *Dou E yuan* as given in *Guan Hanqing* is extrapolated from the surviving *Dou E yuan* text itself. *Guan Hanqing* is a study in the social and political reading of historical drama.

c. *Guan Hanqing* was to be a *huaju*, a spoken drama, as opposed to an opera. Within the Western tradition of spoken drama, historical drama focusing on the political center, the court, was no rarity. Among the authors emulated by Tian Han, Shakespeare—and more important, Schiller, whose *Maria Stuart* Tian had admired in Moscow in 1957— come to mind.[37] Far from setting the *huaju* against the opera on the issue of historical versus contemporary themes, Tian stresses the appropriateness of historical themes for the *huaju*.

d. At this early stage in Tian's creative process, the plot is directed against "injustice," that is, the absence of due legal protection. The typicality of the case of the young woman is emphasized through references to similar cases. The "rulers" and the "people" confront each other on the issue of the rule of law; their representatives are without diversity, the rulers are villains, the people pure and heroic, well in tune with the traditional Marxist depiction of class confrontation in the "old society." Their battle is waged around the Dou E play. The dramatist speaks out for the people and eventually spells out the message in a political sermon, much in the fashion of propaganda plays during the Anti-Japanese War.

e. With the innovative prologue and the "romantic" ending, the play is still conceived as a *gushi ju*, a feature play that tells a story. Tian does not attempt to "combine historical and artistic truthfulness," which is the purpose of a *lishi ju*, a historical play. Tian was to change his conception of the plot later.

37. Tian, "Guanyu *Guan Hanqing*," p. 181.

f. Casting the plot in this form matched the intentions of the World Peace Council, which, as a "non-communist" body, came out in support of democratic opposition to tyranny and oppression. The heroes' roles were given to "democratic personalities" from literary circles, which were the majority among the World Peace Council members. The World Peace Council framework provided an ideal "lodging house" for presenting heroes and values not much esteemed after the beginning of the Anti-Rightist campaign. Intellectual heroes had made a short appearance on the literary stage during the Hundred Flowers period, but then they were sent for reeducation to the countryside, and the cadres, workers, peasants, and soldiers took over again.[38] If an intellectual did appear, it was as a bourgeois rightist. In *Guan Hanqing*, the intellectual hero—the dramatist Guan Hanqing himself—makes a glorious comeback. It is he alone on whom the people depend for the articulation of their grievances and their scorn.

Written during a time when "bourgeois law" was sternly denounced as reactionary, the play established a legitimate level of discourse by transferring the action to the Yuan dynasty's suppression of the people and offering a "contemporary" reading through reasonance with the experience of Communist intellectuals under Guomindang rule. Whereas to present the intellectual as hero challenged the official status of the intellectual class at the time of the writing, to make use of a historical screen with a contemporary application was at this stage uncontroversial and orthodox. Tian Han's friends from dramatic circles and historians could thus discuss the play freely and suggest materials and technical improvements. Professor Zhou Yibai, for example, pointed out to him a passage in the Yuan legal code that banned "wanton composition of *ci* poems and *qu* plays for the purposes of rebelling against authority and producing slander."[39] This provision echoed similar Guomindang laws but also *could* echo the situation in 1958. Tian Han decried this "blatantly reactionary policy" of the Yuan and resolved that he "had to base [his] play on this paragraph." Thus, the idea for the persecution of Guan Hanqing for sedition in the play resulted from this suggestion of Zhou Yibai.

Jian Bozan, a Beijing University historian, applauded the intention that "a dramatist write about a dramatist" and wisely referred to Tian's "sorrowful life before liberation when he was suppressed by the

38. See my *Inside a Service Trade*.
39. Li Zhiyan, "Tian Han," p. 21.

Guomindang" as the experience on which *Guan Hanqing* was based. He provided Tian with the historical materials about Yuan actresses from which both Guan's beloved, Zhu Lianxiu, and Sai Lianxiu, a blind actress, emerged. For Sai, Tian was to write one of the play's most dramatic scenes, the gouging out of her eyes by the henchmen of the chief villain.[40]

GUAN HANQING,
THE FIRST VERSION OF THE TEXT

On March 15, 1958, Tian withdrew to the idyllic guest house of the Association of Cultural and Art Workers in the Chang'an temple at Badachu in order to write his play. He learned about the official hierarchy of the Yuan, in which the *ru* (scholars), in whose tradition modern intellectuals see themselves, appeared as number nine in a ten-step scale, right above beggars. "Stinking number nine" became the general term for intellectuals during the Cultural Revolution, althogh they were then at the end of another scale, one that began with counterrevolutionaries and landlords, and their status on that scale meant that they were considered the least noxious in this outlaw crowd. The difference between the two scales is one of evaluation, and not really of social status. The number being the same, critics could refer to the Yuan scale and thereby express their outrage at this low estimation, whereas activists in the Cultural Revolution could imply that all intellectuals were a part of the "class enemy." In this ambivalence, "old number nine" has become a popular expression for the intellectual as a social type in China. The stock intellectual in a caricature series of the Overseas Edition of the *People's Daily*, for instance, is called *lao jiu*, Old Number Nine. Popular ditties refer to the peasant as *lao a*, Old Ah; the worker as *lao wu*, Old Have Nothing; and the intellectual as *lao jiu*, Old Number Nine. In this ambivalence, the term Old Number Nine represents another lively interplay between China's past and present, and illustrates that the status of intellectuals as class enemies was first defined during the Anti-Rightist campaign, long before the general onslaught of the Cultural Revolution.

On March 21, Tian Han started to write his play. After the prologue, the action begins: the young woman is dragged to the execution ground as Guan witnesses the scene while standing amid the people.

40. Ibid., p. 22.

The theme—the role of literature and the writer in opposing injustice and repression—is thus stated at the outset. Tian decided to bring out the *ganzuo ganwei* (dare to act, dare to do) character of Zhu Lianxiu. When Guan Hanqing muses about the impotence of literature in society, she tells him that his brush is his "sword," and she promises that she will stage the play if he dares to write it. Tian introduced a "running dog," a "literary spy" of the authorities into the realm of literature;[41] Li Zhiyan does not indicate to what specific experience Tian Han might refer.[42]

Tian changed the last act: there is no romantic "realm of freedom" to which Guan can flee.[43] Instead, Guan and Zhu are imprisoned, undaunted. After finishing the first draft on March 31, he immediately set out to revise it, finishing the second draft on April 5. A day later, the draft was presented to a group of *neihang* people, directors, actors, and actresses, namely Jiao Juyin, Ouyang Shanzun (later to direct the premiere), Shao Guangtan (to play Guan Hanqing in the premiere), and Shu Xiuwen (later to play Zhu Lianxiu). This meeting is echoed in the play itself, where Guan Hanqing confers with the actors, actresses, and musicians, who make suggestions for improvements in the play. The group meeting at Chang'an temple to read the play was peculiar not because of who was there, but because of who was not. No government cultural leader sat in. I do not know why Li Zhiyan left out the name of the single "comrade from *Xijubao* (Drama Journal)."[44] The *neihang* colleagues suggested that Tian Han improve the stature of Guan Hanqing, as Zhu Lianxiu was still a "much more moving" character, that he put more emphasis on the *neihang* communication, as "there is [too] much talk about politics [in the play], and [too] little about the life of the artists," and that he eliminate the prologue. True to his hero, Tian Han accepted all three suggestions. In the next revision, which he wrote during the following days, he strengthened Guan Hanqing, who now

41. In the first outline, his statements were put into the mouth of just weak colleagues. In the first draft, he has become a "shameless beast" and Guan is only "incensed that he cannot eat his (i.e., Ye's) flesh." *Guan Hanqing, Juben* ed., p. 22. One has the feeling that particularly unpleasant experiences during the writing of *Guan Hanqing* might have prompted those changes.

42. The other sources are usually less rich for this period. See Wei Qixuan, "Tian Han tongzhi"; and Ma Chaorong, "Lun Tian Han," here quoted from the reprint in *Xiju yanjiu* 1982.11, pp. 67ff.

43. This is Tian's own argument, Li Zhiyan, "Tian Han," p. 24.

44. The unnamed colleague from *Xijubao* was probably Wei Qixuan, who wrote an article for his paper.

became the "national leader" of drama circles of his time,[45] thus directly interacting with Tian Han's own position and role. Tian also linked Guan Hanqing to Guan Yu, an upright hero of the Sanguo (Three Kingdoms) period who had become a god in popular religion. The fact that Guan Yu was born in the same locality as Guan Hanqing and that both shared the same name Guan suggested to Tian Han that both came from the same clan. Guan Hanqing had in fact written two plays about Guan Yu,[46] and Tian Han had him claim this descent.[47] Guan Yu's last words had been the famous phrase, "You can grind jade to dust, but you cannot make it lose its whiteness; you can burn bamboo but you cannot eliminate its regular joints." In this revision, the conflict with the "literary spy" has been exacerbated to show more of Guan Hanqing's daring independence, and, when the dramatist is exiled in the end, he is seen off not only by his *neihang* colleagues but also by some peasants, to stress the popularity of his work with common folk and his close contacts with them.

Second, Tian Han inserted new scenes highlighting the ease, cooperation, and mutual support among the *neihang* people, which is epitomized in the love between Guan Hanqing and Zhu, his lead actress. Guan Hanqing is willing to accept all suggestions coming from this group, but he adamantly refuses to change a word when threatened by the "literary spy."

Third, Tian eliminated the prologue. When he changed the last act from a romantic to a "historical play" ending, the dramatic context for the very innovative first act disappeared, as it did not fit into the classical code of realism. However, in this first act the original purpose of the play, that is, to "answer the questions" about the purport of historical drama, had been spelled out. Although the act was cut, the purpose remained intact. The text eventually answers questions that are no longer spelled out.

But he made other, and more important, changes. Originally when the stress had been on the depiction of the daring intellectual heroes, the state side remained bland, crass, and dull. There is no indication in

45. Tian Han, *Guan Hanqing*, *Juben* ed.

46. Guan Hanqing wrote two plays about Guan Yu, *Dandao hui* and *Guan Zhang shuangfu xishu meng*; see *Guan Hanqing juqu ji*, pp. 1ff. The passage about his indomitable spirit that Tian Han quotes is from the scene of Guan's death in *Sanguo yanyi*.

47. Guan Hanqing is to claim this descent in *Guan Hanqing*, *Juben* ed., p. 23.

Guan Hanqing's original draft that the unjust verdict against the young
woman was handed down by a judge with links to a network of villains.
Tian had now read the story of Ahmad's faction, and of his eventual
assassination, in the "villainous ministers" section of the *Yuanshi* and
the *Xin Yuanshi*,[48] and he made the link between the unjust verdict and
Ahmad's clique. He also read Marco Polo's description of the event.[49]
Ahmad had been the personal favorite of Khubilai Khan. He built up a
large faction, helped by many of his twenty-five sons. He controlled the
law courts, amassed immense riches from bribery, and persecuted his
opponents ruthlessly. During his lifetime no one in the top leadership
dared oppose him. An officer named Wang Zhu and a Buddhist monk
named Gao eventually assassinated him. Tian Han dramatically raised
the stakes (and heightened the risks) of his play by linking the unjust
verdict against the young woman to the misdoings of Ahmad's faction,
and thus to highest government authorities.

Reading Marco Polo provided Tian with a link to the theme of the
oppressed women: Polo mentions "there was no beautiful woman
whom he [Ahmad] might desire, but he got hold of her. . . . Whenever
he knew of any one who had a pretty daughter, certain ruffians of his
would go to the father, and say: 'What say you? Here is this pretty
daughter of yours; give her in marriage to the Bailo Achmath . . . and
we will arrange for his giving you such a government or such an office
for three years.'"[50] This line is the source for a scene in Act 1 of *Guan
Hanqing*. With this change, the play moved into an entirely different
realm. The crisis was now caused by a particular faction in the center,
at the head of which sat a personal favorite of the Emperor (and Chairman) himself. The crisis necessitated action, even assassination, and
the writer called upon the audience to overthrow this faction by any
means, fair or foul.

The most important change, however, in the second draft was the
introduction of a "correct" faction in the center. Khubilai Khan had
been ignorant of his favorite's misdeeds. When eventually informed
about them, he declared that Ahmad's assassination had been justified,
and ordered the expropriation of Ahmad's family as well as the execution of over seven hundred members of his faction. He put Horikhoson

---

48. Wang Yi, *Yuanshi*, *Ershisi shi* ed., ch. 205, pp. 28874ff.; Ke Shaomin,
Xin Yuanshi, *Ershiwu shi* ed., ch. 223, pp. 7025c ff.
49. Yule, trans., *Marco Polo*, vol. 1, pp. 370ff.
50. Ibid., p. 371.

in charge of this persecution, as well as of government affairs. With the introduction of this more correct official at the top, the traditionalist confrontation in the first draft of people versus rulers disappears. There is a serious if modest reform potential in the political center, and the chairman, if properly informed, is willing to support it.

Tian Han thus saw an end to the crisis through a change in the factional control of the center. Ever since the campaign against the film *The Life of Wu Xun* right after the establishment of the People's Republic, the official line had been that reformist characters (of which Wu Xun was one) would merely try to "mollify" class conflicts; thus they objectively contributed to the maintenance of the existing reactionary rule and prevented the real solution—revolution. In a letter to Guo Moruo in 1958, Tian Han says of Horikhoson exactly this.[51] His text, however, does not support this interpretation. True, Horikhoson does not free Guan Hanqing after having earlier saved him from death at Ahmad's hands, but he does send him into exile together with his beloved, and to the pleasant city of Hangzhou. And the worst outrages committed by Ahmad and his gang are righted. Nowhere in the entire text of the second draft is the legitimacy of Mongol rule itself challenged. Guan Hanqing's revolutionary appeal has vanished from the concept. All this still might seem a change within the purview of the normal, but it drastically changes the contemporary references and parallels of the play. For a PRC audience and a Communist author, there was no echo for Horikhoson in the Guomindang leadership, no correct faction that should have been supported. With these changes, the original possibility to read the play innocuously as an anti-Guomindang piece is eliminated. The play now deals with a fundamentally legitimate government under a basically enlightened ruler; this government has fallen into the hands of a faction of villains who came to power as personal protégés of the emperor, from whom they withheld knowledge of their crimes and of the ensuing crisis of the country. As a consequence of popular action stimulated by the dramatist, a correct faction is installed in the center. This structure of the play had but a single possible contemporary resonance, the situation in the People's Republic in the year 1958. Evidently, things become more interesting. There is no reason to assume that Tian Han had planned this development from the outset; it is even highly improbable. It rather seems that he was pushed in this direction first by the historical material brought to his attention by many eager and help-

51. Tian, "Guanyu *Guan Hanqing*," p. 184.

ful hands and second by the inner dynamics unleashed by his choice of the genre of historical drama. Surely he would have retreated from this choice in horror had he ever spelled out to himself all the consequences it engendered.

Time pressed; on April 14, Tian sent the text to *Juben*, which published it on May 3. Obviously a higher decision had been made to concentrate all resources on rapid publication, since the play was to be a national event. Guo Moruo wrote to Tian on May 4 after having read the piece; he recommended that Sai Lianxiu's eyes be gouged out on stage, not behind the scenes.[52]

The two leading national drama journals, *Xijubao* and *Juben*, jointly convened a meeting on the new play on May 6, with Guan Hanqing scholars like Zhou Yibai, Wu Xiaoling, Cai Meibiao, and Dai Bufan, directors and actors like Ouyang Shanzun and Shu Xiuwen, and cultural officials like the vice-minister of culture, Liu Zhiming, attending. As he was ranked highest, Liu summed up the discussion and laid down the line in the end.[53] In the discussion, everyone used *ketman* language. No one mentioned the contemporary meaning of the play, which in fact was the only topic of the discussion, the language was that of "historical materialism," and the core problem seemed to be the "historical truthfulness" of the play. Apart from suggestions to check data and use more archaic language to convey historical depth, the main problem was rightly seen as the play's depiction of the political center. Cai and Wu warned against muddling the basic conflict between "people" and "rulers" by presenting Horikhoson in too positive a light, a point that was also taken up in Liu Zhiming's concluding remarks. "Horikhoson is not a good person," said Liu, but his willingness to let Guan and Zhu go

---

52. Guo Moruo, "Guanyu *Guan Hanqing* de tongxin," p. 180.

53. "Zuotan Tian Han xinzuo," pp. 14ff. Other articles at the time were Xia Yan, "Du *Guan Hanqing*," which starts with a letter from Xia Yan in which he says, "it had already been a very long time since [he] had been that intoxicated" by a play. Xia maintained that the past had nothing to do with the present, and that only bad characters make associations between the two. "Historical drama from the pen of an author will always be suspected of innuendo, and people will say that this resembles the reality of today. At the same time, historical drama by an auther is time and again thought to distort, and people say that this does not well accord with the historical record." He wrote this in Chongqing in defense of Guo Moruo, and felt it was still true. What also was true, however, was that after 1949 Guo took great pride in the clever ways in which he had used historical drama to attack Chiang Kai-shek; for details, see my "The Chinese Writer in His Own Mirror." The quote from Xia is on p. 4.

to exile together is a ploy by "the enemy" to "mitigate class conflict." The fact that Guan Hanqing, apart from being a dramatist, was also a doctor, treating high and low, blurred class lines. It was suggested that the play should de-emphasize the classlessness of the doctor and stress Guan's class background.[54] In the same manner, Tian was advised against letting Guan Hanqing appear to sympathize with Han-Chinese bureaucrats who were against the non-Han Mongols and their allies, the Semu: they together were the ruling class. Since, in the version in their hands, there was no indication of any "nationalist" resistance against the Yuan, this argument may be the "lodging house" for another. Any indication of an "anti-imperialist" stance of the play would have decreased its potential for the treatment of contemporary internal affairs.

Liu Zhiming commended the play's heroes for "daring to fly into a rage, daring to speak out, daring to get going, daring to act." He was quoting a Great Leap slogan, but he said "daring to fly into a rage" (which was appropriate against the feudal rulers) instead of the Great Leap's "daring to think" about new shortcuts into an ever-brighter future.

Tian acknowledged the suggestions, and answered in the same vein: "This tragedy helps people to understand what bitter days our forefathers lived through, what moving and tragic struggles they went through, so that everyone sees the contrast to the happy days we have now, and treasures even more our new China, which we have paid for in steel and blood."[55] Two days later, he answered Guo Moruo's letter in the same style. He reminisced about when they had met in Japan, and set themselves up as the Goethe (Guo) and Schiller (Tian) of young China. He added, in what might be fine irony, that Guo "had had some achievements in literature and scholarship that were not much inferior to those of Goethe. But most of all, in his political caliber he had already surpassed by far this minister from the literary retinue of the Weimar Court," a wording implying that Guo was now in the literary retinue of the Party center.[56] Guo Moruo would soon reply in kind to Tian Han's *Guan Hanqing* with his own historical drama, *Cai Wenji*. Tian Han modestly set out to "learn from" Schiller, whose *Maria Stuart* had greatly impressed him. He acknowledged Guo's proposal concerning the gouging out of Sai's eyes, and defended his handling of Horikho-

54. Cf. Cai Meibiao's remarks in "Zuotan Tian Han," p. 15.
55. Li Zhiyan, "Tian Han," p. 28.
56. Tian, "Guanyu *Guan Hanqing*," p. 181.

son on the basis of the *Yuanshi*, not with a political argument. It had been suggested to him, he wrote, to leave out Horikhoson altogether. Obviously, all sides of the controversy knew what was at stake with this figure. The elimination of Horikhoson would have brought the play back into the old people-versus-rulers confrontation. Tian Han wanted to deal with different contemporary matters, and thus he tenaciously clung to retaining Horikhoson. Had the play retained the lineup of the first draft, it could have been satisfactorily read as an anti-Guomindang piece. As such, it would have been noncontroversial, and dated. The lineup with two factions in the center under a capable if misinformed top leader had only one possible resonance board, the situation in the PRC with its factional battles, as seen through the eyes of a sympathizer of the "correct" faction. *Guan Hanqing* thus becomes the first PRC literary work to deal with the battles in the center and uphold that "at present," that is, in the present tense of the play, the villains hold the levers of power.

In June 1958, his newly revised text came out in a separate edition.[57] In its first scenes, it elaborated on the cooperation and solidarity among the *neihang* people in the creation of the text, much in tune with the actual experience of Tian, who had come to see *Guan Hanqing* as a collective effort. It contained three new scenes. In the first, Guan treats Ahmad's mother in her sumptuous home and secures the release of the daughter of Mrs. Liu, the inn proprietress who had told Guan about the girl who was to be executed. Mrs. Liu's daughter had been abducted by Ahmad's henchmen (in the way described by Marco Polo). The second added scene takes place in Horikhoson's office, where a ten-thousand-signature umbrella petitioning for the release of Guan Hanqing and Zhu Lianxiu "magically" reappears three times on Horikhoson's desk (with the help of his servant, who is by now the husband of Mrs. Liu's daughter and grateful to Guan Hanqing). In this scene Horikhoson says he is personally acquainted with the assassins, and that he is grateful to them, but that he cannot do anything to secure Guan's release. When the signature umbrella has resurfaced for the third time, however (here Tian is quoting *Dou E yuan*, where Dou E's spirit reshuffles the judge's papers three times to draw attention to her case), Horikhoson assumes

57. This second edition, in twelve acts, is quoted here from *Zhongguo lishiju xuan*. Most of the English translation published in 1961 by the Foreign Languages Press in Beijing is from the same text, but the translators include the ending of a later version, for which see *infra*.

this to be the work of the god Guan Yu, for whom he has set up an altar in his office. The third new scene unfolds in prison; Guan confronts a man from the people who is to be killed for resisting the abduction of his wife. The condemned man knows Guan and his work and draws strength from it; his short appearance on stage serves to emphasize Guan's popularity.

The first dress rehearsal for the play, based on the *Juben* edition, was held on June 15 in the Renmin Yishuyuan (People's Arts Hall). That night, Tian wrote a poem:

> Guan [Han]qing long ago was a poor scholar.
> Rather than turning to the pleasure quarters, he reviled the debauched officials.
> How can one say his intention to redress [injustice] is of an age long gone?
> [His] flute resounds down to the chill of the fifth watch.
> For [Zhu] Lian[xiu] it was easy at first to speak her mind with daring,
> From the prison's floor calmly to attack the villain was hard.
> In the end the two butterflies fly together as they wish,
> They wipe their red tears, and mount the saddles for their voyage.[58]

Quite apart from the slightly surrealist final image of butterflies wiping red tears and mounting horses, the poem makes Tian's intention clear: that both Guan and Zhu were out to redress injustice, revile debauched officials, and attack villains. Although written at the beginning of the Yuan, Guan's *xueyi* (intention to whiten, that is, to redress injustice), retained its meaning through the centuries; the poetic voice of his plays sounds through the night of old society until the very last watch, the fifth, which is followed by the dawn of revolution. The risk incurred by the two heroes is now much higher; they are made to face death for sedition, and do not flinch. Tian Han had become aware of the potential of his theme, and of the risks involved in taking it up. He changed the plot accordingly. Probably the poem also tried to give guidance to the director and the actors who had failed to bring out these points strongly enough.

The Guan Hanqing commemoration was held on June 28 in the auditorium of the People's Political Consultative Conference to mark the celebration's "united front" character. Secretary of State Chen Yi presided.[59] On the rostrum were Guo Moruo, as chair, Tian Han

58. Li Zhiyan, "Tian Han," p. 29.
59. A copy of Chen Yi's original handwritten short remarks is reproduced in *Xijubao* 1958.12, p. 10.

and Zheng Zhenduo, who made the reports, Zhou Yang, representing the Propaganda Department of the Party, and Vice-Minister Liu Zhiming, representing the Ministry of Culture, and prominent representatives of the theater world such as Mei Lanfang and Ouyang Yuqing. The only person there with no visible institutional or professional link to the celebration was Politburo member Kang Sheng. Some years later it was he who led the campaign against the new historical drama and declared Tian Han a counterrevolutionary. At this time, he probably supported the campaign for contemporary themes on the stage and was there as a threat and an announcement that he would take a keen interest in dramatic affairs. In his report, Tian Han described the dark times during which Guan lived, Guan's uses of the drama to speak out for the muted people, and his combining realism and romanticism as the latest slogan in China demanded.[60] There also were local commemorative events in other parts of China and in the Soviet Union. Over fifteen hundred opera troupes performed Guan's works, and many staged adaptations of Tian Han's *Guan Hanqing* to local opera styles.[61] If anything was needed to support the traditional theme on the stage, the Guan Hanqing affair seemed ideal.

Guan's work was very much in the Hundred Flowers spirit. Linking his name to the activities of the World Peace Council prevented the shelving of the commemoration. In terms of safeguarding the legitimacy of the traditional theme, and of keeping one of the hundred flowers alive during the hard times after the Anti-Rightist campaign, the Guan Hanqing commemoration gave optimal protection and a national sounding board. *Dou E yuan* was unanimously described as Guan's best play, and the one most frequently staged. Tian Han's *Guan Hanqing* could operate as an interpretive companion to it, reinforcing the theme of the necessity to fight back and reverse unjust verdicts. If ever there was a national theatrical event after 1949, the premiere of Tian Han's *Guan Hanqing* was it. Tian's use of this occasion to advance his own analysis of the nation's crisis guaranteed it a wide audience both with the public and indirectly through reviews; it was a clever move worthy of Guan Hanqing himself. The premiere of *Guan Hanqing* was

60. Tian, "Weida."

61. *Guan Hanqing* was instantly adapted to the Beijing opera style and performed simultaneously with the *huaju* version; it was played as a *yueju* in Shanghai. Other performances included Wuhan, Chengdu, and Canton. See the report in *Xijubao* 1958.11. The number fifteen hundred is given in "Quanguo gedi jinian Guan Hanqing."

held in the evening after the commemorative meeting, with Zhou Enlai and Chen Yi attending, along with a host of government and cultural leaders from the capital. As might be expected from Kang Sheng's presence, there was some opposition to the implied political message. First, although Tian Han and others proclaimed that *Dou E yuan* was Guan's most important piece, and although a performance of the play would have been most appropriate on the commemoration because Tian Han's *Guan Hanqing* had its premiere on the same evening and the two would have made a good pair, this was prevented. Instead, another of Guan's plays was staged. Second, the *Renmin ribao* (*People's Daily*) printed the talks of both Guo Moruo and Tian Han but made a pungent comment on the utter inappropriateness of the entire exercise by cramming three other articles onto the same page. The three consisted mainly of headlines that loudly demanded that plays were "to reflect present-day reality," obviously an effort to control the "damage" done by Tian's play and the many new stagings of Guan Hanqing's work.[62] Third, in internal discussions not reported in the slightly idyllic picture given by Li Zhiyan, Tian was accused of "vulgar sociology" for extrapolating from Guan's work the political and social issues addressed there. As this criticism went to the heart of his *Guan Hanqing* and would have buried the piece had it remained uncountered, Tian Han used the opportunity of his speech at the commemoration to defend himself.[63] With perfect timing, he had also completed his second Great Leap Forward play, which he dedicated to the Party's birthday, which was two days after the commemoration of Guan Hanqing. The premiere was on June 30. The play dealt with building the Ming tomb reservoir and the enthusiasm of the working classes toward this project.[64]

Guan Hanqing's defiance of the ban on texts critical of tyrannical bureaucrats provided a superb historical screen for criticizing the bureaucrats in 1958 when such criticism was banned as "anti-Party." Tian Han enjoyed broad support in the intellectual community in this

62. The other articles were "Rang juqu gengduo genghao di fanying xiandai shenghuo" (Let Drama Still More and Better Reflect Present Day Life); "Juqu biaoxian xiandai shenghuo xingcheng zhuliu" (Dramas Depicting Present Day Life Have Become the Mainstream); and "Juqu biaoxian xiandai shenghuo de chuantong" (The Drama's Tradition of Representing Present Day Life). All are in *Renmin ribao* June 28, 1958.
63. See n. 60.
64. Tian Han, "Shisanling shuiku changxiang qu."

endeavor, and he made sure that his play and report reflected the aspirations of his peers. The Guan Hanqing debate in scholarly circles since late 1957 had provided many opportunities to extol virtues and issues that could no longer be extolled in plain text. Guan's plays on Judge Bao thundered against the corrupt legal system. His plays on Guan Yu praised an upright and popular figure who would not bend to threats and intrigue. His heroines, with their strength and wit, could be read as paeans to the "people" in their opposition to tyrannical government. The *Dou E yuan* play epitomized all these features, and its focus on the reversal of unjust verdicts resonated with a demand popular among intellectuals during the Anti-Rightist campaign. The careful editions, sumptuous stagings, and academic discussions of Guan's plays thus created a realm and a language in which issues that in open discourse were anathema could be handled.

Tian Han absorbed as much from these discussions as possible. His play quotes from Guan's various works, integrates the proposals of colleagues, and tries to give concentrated expression to the assessment this group had of the present situation of the country and the government, of the "people," and of the group's own role in this situation. The historical and drama community in turn came out in Tian's support by providing him with materials, joining discussions about the play, and making sure that the discussions were published, and thus drew public attention to the premiere. As Yin Bing said in the discussion organized by the journals *Juben* and *Xijubao*, "Once the play was out, it sent a shock through the dramatic world,"[65] and it "intoxicated" even Xia Yan,[66] another well-known playwright who had sympathized with the Hundred Flowers activists.

The issue in the controversy raging in early 1958 about "historical" versus "contemporary" themes was a political one. Contemporary plays were expected to extol the achievements of the new heroes in the new society, show the new victories, and proclaim the new values. Historical plays were at best patriotic in theme, and, with their emphasis on the traditional values of *qing* (clean) government and justice, were ill-fitted for class struggle, socialism, and the Great Leap Forward. Zhou Enlai, Chen Yi, and Zhou Yang had all advocated the legitimacy of the "historical" theme in the preceding months,[67] and they all showed up at the premiere of *Guan Hanqing*.

65. Yin Bing, quoted in "Zuotan Tian Han," p. 14.
66. See n. 53.
67. Zhou Yang, "Yong liangtiao tui."

From Li's report and other sources it seems clear that Tian Han did not approach the writing of *Guan Hanqing* with a clearly defined political purpose in mind. It seems rather that in the process of writing and rewriting, he gradually discovered the potential of the theme to interact with the present; this discovery in turn led him to look for appropriate historical materials. It might not be unjustified to say that Guan Hanqing taught Tian as much about the present as the present helped Tian to understand Guan Hanqing. We have now two editions of the text in hand, the *Juben* edition in nine acts from May 1958 and the separate book edition in twelve acts from June. Let us turn now to an analysis of the play itself.

THE METHOD

In his study of Machiavelli's *Prince*, Leo Strauss suggests a method of reading Machiavelli's books: "We must read them according to those rules of reading that he regarded as authoritative. Since he never stated these rules by themselves, we have to observe how he applied them in reading such authors as he regarded as models. His principal author being Livy, we must pay attention to the way in which he read Livy. His manner of reading Livy may teach us something about his manner of writing."[68] Tian Han was not bound by any specific factual information in his reconstruction of Guan Hanqing's motives for writing the play, the problems in the creative process, the staging, and the reaction of government leaders. Only one phrase in the *Yuanshi* deals with this dramatist. We know nothing about his life; even his life dates are conjecture. Tian Han's play deals with Guan writing *Dou E yuan*. Although there certainly is some historical information on the social and political life of the time, no historical record exists linking it with any of Guan's plays. Tian Han's play is thus an exercise in inductive method. His main source is the literary work. From the leads it contains, he establishes links to situations, events, and individuals in the social world. In the context of Strauss's methodological suggestion, *Guan Hanqing* is an ideal text for the study of Tian Han's craft, being both the source for the method and the object of its application.

Tian Han is not the first or the only person to extract the life, views, and politics of a writer from his surviving work. Guo Moruo had

68. Strauss, *Thoughts on Machiavelli*, p. 29. Amazingly, this author has not been much quoted in literary scholarship.

pioneered this endeavor with his *Qu Yuan* in 1942; he was to continue in the same direction in *Cai Wenji* (1959) and *Wu Zetian* (1960), the latter containing his analysis of the poems by Shangguan Wan'er. Tian and Guo employ the same methodology, and it can be said that their method is, albeit on a higher level of sophistication, the standard political reading technique in contemporary China. In the case of both Guan Hanqing and Cai Wenji, the writers dealt with are considered "progressive." While this assessment makes for some suppositions about their relationship with the "people," their treatment is only a variant within a methodology also applied to "reactionary" writers.[69]

I have dealt with *Qu Yuan* elsewhere,[70] so here I will first try to extract the rules governing Tian Han's reading method from his treatment of Guan Hanqing's *Dou E yuan* in his play about the dramatist.

> RULE A. The motive for writing the play is an immediate social conflict; this conflict can therefore be reconstructed from the play itself and its protagonists.

In the play, Tian Han has Guan witness a young woman on her way to be executed. Then, within days of that event, Guan writes and stages the play *Dou E yuan*.

> RULE B. The characters of the play are "typical" and live in "typical" circumstances.

Tian Han brings out this typicality. The young woman has had to flee from the countryside because her parents' land was taken away. Her fate is replicated by that of Zhu Lianxiu, the actress who eventually plays her on stage, and in Sai Lianxiu, a young woman who is sold to the playhouse by her impoverished family. Outside the city gates are pleasure quarters housing twenty-five thousand women under "inhuman conditions. Some among them are trying to survive but don't make it, and seeking death don't find it," as Zhu Lianxiu tells Guan.[71] Immediately after Guan leaves in the first act, the innkeeper's daughter is abducted. Unjust verdicts by judges are also no rarity. In the first edition when Guan hears about the court procedures against the young

---

69. The interpretive method used by Yao Wenyuan, Liu Housheng, and others in their criticism of the new historical plays is the exact replica of the method employed by Guo Moruo and Tian Han in their plays.

70. R. Wagner, "The Chinese Writer," pp. 186ff.

71. *Guan Hanqing, Juben* ed., p. 6.

woman, he volunteers "that there should be such dog officials who trample on human life as if on grass!"[72] He seems to regard them as something of an exception. In the second edition, however, he has learned more, and says instead: "They *all* are such dog officials who trample on human life as if on grass."[73] And a passage is added that gives one of his friends from the stage the opportunity to say: "Today, nine out of ten judgments are unjust verdicts."[74] Tian Han knew of an investigation ordered early in the fourteenth century that discovered more than fifty-seven hundred unjust verdicts during the Dade reign period (1297–1308) alone.[75]

> RULE C. Drama, and literature in general, is essentially realistic; "historical" social realities given within the play are but allusions to broader social phenomena prevailing at the time of the writing.

In his studies of the Yuan materials, Tian Han looked for and felt he found references to problems addressed in the play: to the huge pleasure quarters outside the city walls with the despondent crowd of women in it, the laws regarding "plays rebelling against authority," the huge tracts of land appropriated by the Mongols as grazing ground for their horses, the low status accorded to literati, and the commonness of unjust verdicts. These materials convinced him of the highly "realist" nature of Guan Hanqing's writing; for him, Guan directly alluded to social realities.

> RULE D. Historical drama, like the historical novel, may have both "typical" and "historical" characters, the former mostly from the lower orders, the latter from the leadership. Specific features given to high-ranking individuals in Guan's drama refer to particular historical persons, recognizable to contemporaries.

Tian Han presupposes a highly personalized power structure. Ahmad, for instance, is the favorite of Khubilai Khan, and as such has the freedom to act as he wishes without institutional constraints. This highly personalized power structure being the rule in China, attacks through the medium of historical plays can be assumed to have been directed not so much at grand general problems or institutional arrangements, but against networks of individuals under some chief

---

72. Ibid., p. 4.
73. *Guan Hanqing, Zhongguo lishi xiju xuan* ed., p. 210.
74. Ibid., p. 211.
75. Cf. Li Shusi, "Guan Hanqing de *Dou E yuan*," p. 203.

villain at the top the removal of whom would bring improvement. Protagonists in the historical drama thus do not stand for an issue or a conflict, but for a historical person or group of persons. *Dou E yuan* introduces a judge in the role of *chou* (clown). When he enters court, he bends his knee before the litigants, saying: "Any party to a lawsuit who supplies me with food and clothes is as dear to me as my parents." Tian Han reads this and another incident as an *ad personam* satire of Ahmad's son Koshin. Nothing in the historical record directly supports this claim, but we are dealing with rules, not facts. For Tian Han any specific feature of this kind contains an attack on a specific person or group. For contemporaries, Tian assumes, the attack was perfectly evident, and all—the public, the government spy, and the victim of the attack himself—understood quite well against whom the attack was directed. Judge Koshin complains to his father about the scene. Wang Zhu kills Ahmad—a historical fact—after seeing Guan Hanqing's play denouncing this villain's coterie—Tian Han's interpolation.

> RULE E. The genre used by an author indicates the leeway accorded to public opinion at the time. The historical play is the last recourse in a time of heavy repression.

The time in which *Dou E yuan* is set is not quite clear. Both through the protagonist's name and through the plot structure it is directly connected to a case related by Fan Ye in the *Hou Hanshu.*[76] *In Dou E yuan*, however, Dou E's father refers to this precedent as an earlier event.[77] Scholars listing Guan Hanqing's "historical plays" do not include *Dou E yuan*.[78] To Tian Han, it seems to be set in a not-clearly-defined "earlier time." He has Guan Hanqing say that he "wrote about a historical event [*lishi gushi*]."[79] Tian Han infers that he used this form because repression was so heavy that a direct treatment of the case of the young woman whose execution Guan had witnessed would have been impossible. Thus in the situation he presents in *Guan Hanqing*, people do not even dare to show their tears for the young victim, and

76. Fan Ye, *Hou Hanshu*, ch. 114, p. 0895a; Gan Bao, *Soushen ji*, ch. 16; cf. Wang Jisi, "Guan Hanqing he tade zaju," p. 65, n. 1.

77. Guan, *Gantian dongdi Dou E yuan*, p. 868.

78. See Tan, *Yuandai xijujia Guan Hanqing*, p. 26; and Zhao Jingshen, "Guan Hanqing he tade zaju," p. 71. From the latter paper it also emerges that the Shanghai Branch of the Dramatists' Association established a "Guan Hanqing study group" at the first conference of which this paper was presented.

79. Tian, *Guan Hanqing, Juben* ed., p. 15.

they warn each other to watch their words.[80] When the news makes the rounds that Guan wants to write this play, Ye Hefu, who in the second edition has become a veritable cultural spy of the government, as well as other "cultural leaders" threaten Guan with the loss of his fame, with troubles, with prison, and eventually with death if he does not recant. A sentence from *Dou E yuan*, "Because the officials do not respect the orthodox laws, the hundred families, although they have mouths, cannot speak out," is repeated time and again in *Guan Hanqing*; to stress the point still further, Tian Han adds another quote in the second edition: "It is as if arrows are stuck through the geese's beaks; no one dares so much as cough." The quote, from another early Yuan play, had been dug up by Wu Xiaoling and quoted in the discussion about Guan Hanqing referred to above. Wu introduced it with an ambivalent "This is [or was; the time is not fixed] a time when. . . ." and then introduced the quote.[81] This could refer both to the early Yuan, and to 1958.

RULE F. Given the sensitivity of the issues addressed in a historical play, the author will rigorously deny that there is any link between the play and contemporary affairs.

This follows from the preceding rule. Spelling out the contemporary meaning of such a play would reduce the already small leeway. When Wang Zhu, Ahmad's future assassin and thus a "friend" of Guan's cause, says to Guan Hanqing: "Let me be so bold as to ask you whether this play was motivated by the case of Zhu Xiaolan [the woman executed some days before]," Guan answers, "very embarrassedly," as Tian's directive says, "Eh, no, I have only written about an event in history." Wang Zhu gets his point quickly, and answers in the same *ketman* style: "True. You really should describe more such historical events."[82] When Ye Hefu claims that Guan has personally attacked Ahmad's son Koshin (the judge) in his play, Guan bluntly disclaims: "I don't understand what you are talking about. What has my play to do

---

80. See the stage directions in the first act of *Guan Hanqing*, ibid., p. 1, and the statement of Mistress Liu on p. 4.

81. Wu Xiaoling quoted this telling phrase in the discussions about the first printed version of *Guan Hanqing*; see "Zuotan Tian Han," p. 15. The phrase is from the Yuan playwright Ma Zhiyuan's *Po youmeng guyan hangong qiu*, p. 398. Professor Wu was kind enough to point out this reference to me. Cf. Tian, *Guan Hanqing, Zhongguo lishiju xuan* ed., p. 221.

82. Tian, *Guan Hanqing, Juben* ed., p. 15.

with Ahmad?"[83] From Guan's discussions with his friends, however, it is clear that he refers to the execution and to Ahmad and his sons, although in a "typified" manner. When Wang Zhu, motivated by the play, actually kills Ahmad, Guan maintains when talking to Ye Hefu that his play has nothing to do with the murder. But when talking with his beloved Zhu Xiaolan he is elated that his play contributed something after all.[84] The disclaimer, sophistry, and open lie of the author are to be expected, and are necessary under the circumstances.

> RULE G. The faction ruling in the "present" of the text indicates the writer's assessment of the leaders dominating the center in his own time.

In the present of *Dou E yuan*, a vile faction is in power, and the woman is executed. From these events Tian Han infers that in Guan's time, the villains were running things. Searching in historical material for a faction of villains who could have been alluded to, he found Ahmad; he then dated the writing of *Dou E yuan* in the year 1281, the year before Ahmad was assassinated.

> RULE H. The pitch of the voice, the vehemence of the attack, and the dissimulation needed in launching it indicate the status of the problem handled in the play, the urgency of its treatment, and the stature and caliber needed by a writer to take it up.

A host of problems such as the decline of the moral stature of women, the selling of girls as brides, and the like are addressed in *Dou E yuan*. By focusing the play's conflict on an unjust verdict, Guan made a statement on the immediate relevance and urgency of the problem of the absence of legal redress. By comparison, the other social problems are less pressing. From the intensity of Guan's accusing voice and the daring it must have taken for Guan to stage such a play in the very face of the accused, Tian inferred that there was a great urgency in treating this topic, and that in a national crisis where the people had no redress it would be the responsibility of the nation's leading dramatist to speak up, as he was in the best position to do so. The aspect of urgency is emphasized again by Tian Han by having the performance of the play a few days after the execution of Zhu Xiaolan, with Guan Hanqing working through the nights. The responsibility of the nation's dramatic luminaries in such crises is ever more strongly emphasized in the later

83. Ibid., p. 11.
84. Ibid., pp. 21 and 22.

versions of *Guan Hanqing*, where Guan is explicitly referred to as "the national leader in dramatic circles" even by Horikhoson himself.

> RULE I. An important indicator of an allusion to touchy contemporary issues is a change imposed on the record of the past so that it matches the present.

In *Dou E yuan*, the judge does not go through the mandatory process of securing higher approval of the heroine's death sentence, but instead has her executed the very next day. During the Han dynasty, this approval process was the rule. Its omission is read by Tian Han (upon the suggestion of colleagues) as an implied criticism of court proceedings under the Yuan, which were so depraved as to execute without any review process. Tian Han spells this out from the second edition on, by having Yang Xianzhi pointing out this legal inaccuracy to Guan. "Not only was she denied the legal procedure known as the 'three appeals and six hearings,' but the sentence was not even submitted to the Ministry of Justice for approval. Now, if you want to present this as a historical play, won't it be obviously contrary to the customary practice in China?" Guan answers: "That is a good question. But tell me, under this great Yuan dynasty, does the trial of a capital crime necessarily go through 'three appeals and six hearings' and have to be approved by the Ministry of Justice? Is it not a fact that, in the case of [Zhu] Xiaolan, she was granted only one hearing by Koshin and executed the very next day in the most hasty manner?" Yang: "Oh, I see. If that is what you mean, I have nothing to say."[85] Changes imposed on the plot that are not supported by historical evidence are to be considered loaded.

> RULE J. From the urgency of the problem, the popular pressure on the writer to take it up can be inferred.

Given the widespread abuses of the legal system, and the rigid control over the public realm exercised by the villains in power, Tian infers that much pressure must have been brought to bear on Guan to deal with this topic on stage. He translates this pressure into the demands by Mrs. Liu and her daughter that Guan should do something about the case. Once it is performed, Tian shows the common people rejoicing in the play, hearing about it, and acting upon it. Even among the enlightened members of the ruling circles, some, like Wang Zhu, are moved to action. The writer is thus under popular pressure, and will receive popular support if he does what is expected of him.

85. Tian, *Guan Hanqing, Zhongguo lishiju xuan* ed., p. 232.

RULE K. From the status and clout of the group or individual attacked in a text as the cause of the core problem, the degree of repression that will come down on the text can be gauged.

Dou E yuan attacks in no uncertain terms debauched officials in the courts. Tian Han considered that such attacks must have resulted in heavy repression, and his play brings this repression to life. The villains attacked in the play are present in the audience; they proceed to indirect and direct action.

RULE L. From the political consistency of the text in its critical stance toward most bureaucrats, the resistance of the writer to government interference and censorship can be inferred.

The text of *Dou E yuan* does not contain mollifying statements about the Great Yuan or other laudatory matter. Given the sharp attack on the courts in the play, Tian Han infers that Guan Hanqing must have resisted efforts to have him change the text. Ye Hefu and finally Ahmad himself demand such changes in *Guan Hanqing*, but Guan refuses to change so much as a word.

RULE M. The fact that plays, and literary works in general, become the most important avenues of political criticism implies something about the status of intellectuals and scholars at the time.

The dramatic form of *Dou E yuan*, the *zaju*, was a lowly and despised form, fit only for the markets and the pleasure quarters. That intellectuals and scholars of the stature of Guan Hanqing, Yang Xianzhi, and Liang Jinzhi should write plays, and even act themselves, indicates for Tian that other avenues of advancement, employment, and public remonstrance were not open to them. Tian adduces outside sources to confirm this. The scholars (*ru*) ranked ninth in the Yuan social scale. In fact, during the early years of the Yuan there were no state examinations; thus the door through which literati customarily entered government service was closed to them. A part of the national crisis thus is that those who were best qualified to run the administration had to yield to a faction of villains. The fact that people with the qualifications of a Guan Hanqing had to resort to writing such lowly things as *zaju* drama is interpreted by Tian Han as an indication that the best are kept out of responsible positions, and thus have to look for a place to live and articulate their aspirations. Ahmad is made to spell this out. Sitting in the audience of the *Dou E yuan*, he says, in a most vulgar Chinese, appropriate because most of the Mongol and Semu leaders at the time spoke no or little Chinese:

> The Han Chinese who have read a couple of books have no examinations under our dynasty; they can't make a name for themselves in the manner of number two or number three on the examination list, so they've all turned their minds to this stuff here. In fact, that's not even bad. Hasn't His Majesty asked us to think of a way how these people could have a place to fritter away their knowledge and talent? That's why I often come to see their shows; for one thing, it's entertaining and I also find out what they really think.[86]

RULE N. From the evaluations implicit in the play's plot, characterization, and language, the writer's social and political standpoint can be inferred.

Guan sets Dou E up as the heroine. She implores heaven and earth to fulfill her three wishes, whereupon her blood indeed does not soil the floor, but spurts up to the white streamer on top of the flagpole at the execution ground; it snows in mid-summer, and there is a drought for three years. This shows that the heavenly authorities recognize her claim that she has been unjustly executed. Eventually, the vile judge is dismissed, and the unjust verdict righted. Tian Han extrapolates from this that Guan Hanqing sided with the "people" in the figure of the young woman, and joined them with his text in their opposition to lawless tyranny, nearly getting himself killed in the process.

RULE O. From a comparison of one text with others by the same author, a sequence can be established. The stance of a later piece will show the author's attitude toward his earlier work.

Tian Han regards *Dou E yuan* as representing the height and coming at nearly the end of Guan's known and surviving work because it comes out most vehemently against injustice.[87] From this Tian infers that Guan had a critical opinion of some of his earlier work, and a negative opinion about some other parts. In a discussion with Ye Hefu, who recommends soft and pleasant pieces that will offend no one, Guan maintains that his earlier plays on Judge Bao and Guan Yu had also "spoken out for the people" and attacked social ills. However, the implication is that

86. Tian, *Guan Hanqing, Juben* ed., p. 18.
87. Wu Xiaoling put *Dou E yuan* at the end of his edition of Guan's works. This sequence is exclusively based on internal evidence. Tian Han had this edition in hand, and obviously he must have felt that *Dou E yuan* marked both the high point and the end of Guan's career.

the present work goes much further in this respect. In discussions with his disciples, Guan flatly rejects some of his earlier work, such as the lines, "to till your own land, to retire into the mountain—in leisure and quiet one can brood over what came to pass. My rival may be wise; I may be a fool. But why should I fight?" In the second edition, he advises his friends not to teach those lines: "It is no good at all. My rival is not necessarily wise, and I am not necessarily a fool. We've got to fight it out to see who is wise and who a fool, to decide what's right and what's wrong."[88] He is helped in this reevaluation by his new experiences, and by the "people's" criticism. Mrs. Liu has this to say about the powers of literature, when her daughter implores Guan for help against the execution of the young woman: "Child, Uncle Guan is a doctor. He can only help people when they have colds and coughs. What can he do when heads are cut off?" When the cannon sounds, announcing that the execution is over, Guan muses, "can I really only help people against colds and coughs?"[89] The usual medicaments for such mild ailments were peppermint and licorice root, and reference to them quickly became a cliché in the historical drama. Guan, confronted with the new and threatening reality, feels that some of his earlier work was but licorice root, and he rejects this now as inappropriate. The intensity of *Dou E yuan*, with its celebrated aria "I accuse Heaven, accuse Earth, accuse the Gods" sung by Dou E, rejects the political attitudes of some of his earlier texts.

> RULE P. From a comparison of the text with contemporary texts by other authors, the playwright's political stance and daring can be inferred.

No other text of the period rises to the same pitch as *Dou E yuan* in its accusation of the ills of a corrupt legal system. Guan Hanqing can thus be seen as the most daring among his colleagues, and it can be inferred that the better among them will emulate his example. Tian introduces this idea into the scene in act 5 of the second version where Yang Xianzhi, another famous playwright of Guan's time, decides to rewrite the end of his *Kuhan ting* (The Bitter Cold Pavilion).[90]

> RULE Q. From textual variations in different editions of the same play, inferences can be made about political and artistic discussions and other considerations that prompted the changes.

88. Tian, *Guan Hanqing, Zhongguo lishiju xuan* ed., pp. 211f.
89. Tian, *Guan Hanqing, Juben* ed., p. 4; the second phrase by Guan is in the second version, *Zhongguo lishiju xuan* ed., p. 210.
90. Tian, *Guan Hanqing, Zhongguo lishiju xuan* ed., p. 233.

In act 5 of *Guan Hanqing*, Yang Xianzhi proposes that Guan make a change in an aria by Dou E. This change is in fact a variant transmitted in the Zang and Meng manuscripts of *Dou E yuan*.[91]

RULE R. From the literary consistency of the text and its adaptation to the needs of performance, the nature of the relationship of the author with the theatrical community can be inferred.

Guan was an innovator in dramatic terms. From the fact that he adopted a more diversified dramatic structure, Tian infers that he closely cooperated with musicians and actors. He translated this assumption into scenes where Guan discusses his play with these *neihang* companions. Their suggestions are accepted practically without exception (the sole exception being a political change),[92] and in one case the musician changes a line in the text while Guan is asleep. When Guan reads it later, he agrees to it. The solidarity among the *neihang* is thus contrasted with the playwright's complete intransigence toward the government's demands for changes in the play.

RULE S. From the relative proportions, quantitative and qualitative, of representatives of different segments of society in the play, inference can be made as to their actual weight (or the author's assessment of it).

Within *Dou E yuan*, a villainous judge is later matched by a correct judge, who is Dou E's father. There are thus two groups in the leadership, and they take turns holding power. The faction in power will suppress the other. Dou E, on the side of the people, is confronted by a man who charges her with a murder he himself has committed in order to force her to marry him. The people on his side share in his villainy, although he is the worst of them. The people on Dou E's side, such as her mother-in-law, share her positive features, although they are no match for her purity. These proportions in Guan's play are read by Tian Han as an analysis of the pattern of early Yuan society. The two judges come back as the two big factions in court, led by Ahmad and Horikho-

91. Tian, *Guan Hanqing, Juben* ed., p. 9. Cf. Guan, *Gantian dongdi Dou E yuan*, p. 860; the variant is given in n. 110 on p. 902.

92. Suggested by Yang Xianzhi, who felt that Dou E's mother-in-law should not be painted in such ambivalent colors, as a usurer on the one hand and loved by Dou E on the other. Tian Han here refers to the elimination of "middle characters" from literature, insisting on their necessary presence. The controversy came into the open some years later, in 1961, when Shao Quanlin advocated the readmission of such middle characters to the literary stage. Cf. Tian, *Guan Hanqing, Juben* ed., p. 9.

son respectively. The villains from among the people (the Han Chinese) are linked to the vile faction. Donkey Li, the accuser of Zhu Xiaolan, is an underling of a Semu commander and thus linked to Ahmad. In the literary leadership the same structure is repeated. The man who provides a theater for the staging of *Dou E yuan* is a Han Chinese linked by ties of friendship to Guan Hanqing. Ye Hefu, on the other hand, a Han Chinese but a villain, is linked to Ahmad.

> RULE T. From the characters that appear in the play(s), the writer's own social connections can be inferred.

In his plays, Guan often portrayed common folk, especially women, and showed his familiarity with the pleasure quarters of Cambaluc where his plays were performed. His apparent familiarity with the upper spheres of society enabled him to handle high officials like Judge Bao. Tian Han extrapolates from these facts something about Guan's social connections. According to one historical source, Guan was a physician in official employment. Tian Han makes him a physician at the Royal Medical College. This profession, which Tian metaphorically links to his literary endeavor, as shall be shown later, gives Guan access to all layers of society; he treats both Ahmad's mother and later the mother of his prison guard. He frequents both Mrs. Liu's modest inn and the elegant quarters of Zhu Lianxiu. As a physician at the College, Guan Hanqing's *danwei*, or institutional slot, in the contemporary term, is a government office, albeit a lowly one. Only such a position could give him access to high dignitaries, and thus a relatively complete picture of society. As a doctor, he is in a way a wild card in the social game, alone capable of moving through all the ranks and colors, and alone familiar with the entire picture of society.[93]

> RULE U. From the "realistic" and the "romantic" parts of the text, it can be inferred what is a fact and what is a hope.

The realistic parts of *Dou E yuan* concern her framing and execution. The romantic part is her return as a ghost to get her unjust verdict righted and her eventual success, which take place in the free world of magic and ghosts and in the future. Tian Han grafts the structure of *Guan Hanqing* on that of *Dou E yuan*. Horikhoson, the more or less "correct" minister, finds the petition for the release of Guan Hanqing and Zhu Lianxiu three times back on top of his desk, in same the man-

---

93. For this aspect, see my "The Chinese Writer."

ner in which, in the play within the play, Dou E had the papers of her father reshuffled to draw his attention to her case. Thus the events that follow the staging of *Dou E yuan* in *Guan Hanqing* are part of the "romantic," hopeful speculation about the future.

> RULE V. The outcome of the plot indicates whether the author hoped that the social cataclysm could be overcome, and what is needed by way of heroic virtue and popular action to achieve this end.

Dou E does not bend under torture; she confesses to a crime she has not committed, but only to save her mother-in-law. The extremes of virtue and bureaucratic villainy thus clash. Dou E is executed, but eventually her unyielding spirit gets revenge, and in the "romantic" part, which speculates about long-term future developments, she will win out. The bureaucratic villains, Tian infers, are so entrenched that immediate relief from them cannot be secured. Guan Hanqing is unable to save Zhu Xiaolan. But unyielding virtue and resistance will have their impact in the romantic end. The reshuffling by Dou E's ghost of the legal papers in order to attract the judge's attention to the unjust verdict is read "materialistically" by Tian Han. He sees the scene as symbolic; the virtue and unyielding resistance of Dou E were known to the people and the public, and, in fact, it will not have been Dou's ghost but one of the court scribes or the judge's secretaries who assiduously replaced Dou E's dossier on top of the pile of papers, thus drawing the judge's attention to it. Dou E arouses the best elements of public opinion, and in the long run people will have her wrong righted. Tian gives this interpretation through a replica of the reshuffling scene, in which a servant of Horikhoson, whom Guan has helped to get his fiancée out of Ahmad's clutches and to marry her, reshuffles Horikhoson's papers three times so that the petition for Guan's and Zhu's release reappears on top. Guan and Zhu managed to influence public opinion with their play. Tian Han goes much further in his interpretation of this aspect. He has Guan Hanqing complain to Zhu Lianxiu about how impotent politically is the writer's brush, when compared to the swords wielded by the heroes of the *Shuihu* (Water Margin) when they raided an execution ground. Zhu answers that even Li Kui, who raided the execution ground, did not do it alone: "Isn't your brush in fact your sword? Is not this play [*zaju*] in fact your sword? In your plays you upbraided [*ma*] Lord Yang, upbraided Ge Piao, and upbraided Lu Zhailang, and everyone who saw these plays hated as much as we do these men who have no morals, persecute the worthy, and terrorize the people.''[94] The theatergoers are thus turned into a sworn band, akin to the valiant *Shuihu* heroes, by the dramatist. The man who later killed Ahmad, according to Tian Han, was in the audience at the premiere of *Dou E yuan*. Virtue and resistance to villainy achieve their aims through their stimulating influence on public opinion.

> RULE W. From the relative proportions of accusation and praise, the educative intentions of the author can be inferred.

In *Dou E yuan*, Dou E occupies center stage throughout. The play focuses on praising her in her selfless purity, on the one hand—she sacrifices herself for her mother-in-law although she is critical of the latter's morals—and her undaunted spirit in the face of repression, on the other. The focus is not on bureaucratic abuses, but on the resistance to them and the legitimacy of this resistance. Tian Han has Guan Hanqing spell this out. When Ye Hefu charges hat *Dou E yuan* serves no purpose but to attack Ahmad and his retainers, Guan answers: "First, you all say that my plays put a woman into the leading role; although this play [*Dou E yuan*] is not too similar to the others, it also is about a quite extraordinary woman; her self-sacrifice for the benefit of others has moved me so that I had to write about her, and [my play] is not at all [written] only to revile some particular person."[95]

Obviously, a further batch of such rules could easily be extracted and adorned with Greek or Cyrillic letters. The above group, however, seems to me to be of immediate relevance for this study, and as this is a methodological exercise and not a taxonomy, I will break off here.

TIAN HAN'S *GUAN HANQING*, THE ANALYSIS

The situation of Strauss in his study of Machiavelli was unique; he could extract the rules for reading from the same text to which he would apply them. Normally, two separate texts would be used.

In the case of Tian Han's *Guan Hanqing*, too, both requirements are satisfied at the same time. *Guan Hanqing* is both Tian Han's sophisticated exploration of *Dou E yuan*, and the literary text studied here. *Guan Hanqing* belongs to a select group of texts from socialist countries that explore the secrets of their craft through this kind of device. Perhaps the most refined example is by Stefan Heym of East Germany, *The King David Report*, a work that reconstructs the compilation of the

94. Tian, *Guan Hanqing, Juben* ed., p. 6.
95. Ibid., p. 11.

chapters dealing with King David in the books of Samuel and Kings from contradictions and cracks in the text in a superb, and of course silent, parody on Stalin's *History of the Communist Party (Bolsheviks), Short Course.*[96]

In *Guan Hanqing*, Tian Han gives to the interpretive technique outlined in the preceding section the name *cai* (guessing, to guess). Zhu Lianxiu immediately guesses the implication of the name given by Guan to the upright female, *zhengdan*, role of Dou E; she relates it to the case of Cao E of the Han with just a change in the family name but most elements of the plot intact. Guan confirms: "That is exactly what I had in mind; *ni cai de dui* [you have guessed correctly]."[97] The term *cai* denotes thus a reading technique. It normally is used for "solving" or "cracking" riddles. This presupposes a textual structure that contains and hides some deeper meaning, and guides the searching mind through cracks in the surface of the text. *Cai* is a legitimate exercise among friends. In the play, however, the government spy Ye Hefu is the lone master in this technique. He is denounced, but in fact he does get all the implications of the *Dou E yuan*, although he sees the play only as slander against the government, and disregards its focus on the virtues of Dou E.

I now propose to apply the rules that I have extracted from Tian Han's *Guan Hanqing* concerning the reading of historical plays, to the play itself, and to do unto *Guan Hanqing* what Tian Han had done unto *Dou E yuan*. To do so would not seem to be a capricious imposition. *Guan Hanqing* is an educative exercise in the interpretation of historical drama, and it calls upon us to apply to the text what we have learned from it. Tian Han has dealt with the problems involved in this activity. Two kinds of persons do the guessing (*cai*) in the play, Guan's friends and his enemies. Both are perfectly capable of getting his points. His friends spell them out in private talk or relish them silently. His enemies, however, spell them out openly and proceed to suppress the play. There is no place for the sinological scholar in this scenario. Being no match for either the heroes or the villains of the play, we will have to don slimy Ye Hefu's methodological cap, and cannot even be sure that no contemporary Ahmad will make use of our results.

Rather than going through the entire list of rules one by one, we will refer to them as need be.

96. Heym, *King David Report.* Heym, much as Tian Han, used much historical scholarship on the passages in Samuel and in Kings, which pointed at the contradictions in the historical records given there.

97. Tian, *Guan Hanqing, Juben* ed., p. 7.

THE HISTORICAL PLAY

As a matter of principle, the historical play makes reference to the immediate present, here, the year 1958, when Tian Han wrote *Guan Hanqing* (Rules a, c, g). Tian Han, by writing a historical play, is thus indicating that at this time no other avenues of serious talk were open (Rule e). He easily squares the remoteness from the present pretended by the historical play by not writing a simple historical play, but a historical play about a dramatist writing a historical play. What seems doubly remote comes back twice as fast, since the play thus contains an education for the dramatists and the audience in the art of writing, seeing, and discussing such plays. Ahmad is correct when he spells out to Horikhoson the contemporary meaning of the historical play: "These monkey bastards, though, are damn hard to cope with. There never is a time when they keep in place, if they don't compare former times with the present or point at the mulberry to revile the ash, he [*sic*] will do exactly what you just told them to stop doing. Didn't you just hear how he needled us officials?"[98] What *Dou E yuan* does for the early Yuan rulers, *Guan Hanqing* does for the leadership in 1958.

THE HISTORICAL SCREEN

Tian Han describes the early Yuan as an appropriate screen for the discussion of China's situation in 1958. What, then, is the situation in 1281? A small minority composed of Mongols, Semu, and other non-Han peoples rules the country. It has exclusive control over the levers of power, relegating the Han Chinese intellectuals to the status of "stinking number nine." At present, a faction of villains is in power, led by Ahmad. This faction has gained control over the courts and reduced them to a sham, and it exercises control over public opinion even to the point of controlling gestures and words said in private. With public opinion stifled, the people are like "geese with arrows stuck through their mouths," and "although they have mouths, they cannot speak out." Within the ruling group there is another faction of more "correct" leaders, which is grouped around Horikhoson. Beyond the factional struggles is Khubilai Khan.

The relationship between the Han Chinese and the Yuan rulers resonates with that between the "masses" and the Party. The Party is a

98. Ibid., p. 18.

self-perpetuating minority which rules over the former. In fact, the level of control exercised by the imperial courts over the local judiciary and public opinion was no match for what came into being after 1949. But in the same way in which Guan changed the pattern of the past to match the present (Rule i), Tian changes the pattern of the Yuan. Even in their private homes and in inns, people do not dare make critical remarks anymore. The material at hand would have offered an option of an "anti-imperialist" reading. This reading seems to have been adopted by the Japanese troupes who staged *Guan Hanqing*, directing it against American "Mongols."[99] Within the Chinese context, to do so would have been anti-communist, which was certainly not Tian Han's intention. Thus there is a striking absence, a stunning lacuna in the play: at no point is anti-Mongol sentiment expressed in any manner. The Yuan are the dynasty in force, and neither Guan Hanqing nor any other hero of the play speaks out against their rule as such. The Guomindang option has been discussed above.

In his later play *Xie Yaohuan* (1961), Tian Han uses the timing of the "present" for the specific purpose of setting a date. *Xie Yaohuan* takes place some four or five years after Wu Zetian set up her own dynasty, the New Zhou, which replaced Tang rule. With these dates Tian Han refers to the taking of power by a clique that was personally obliged to Wu Zetian (Mao Zedong) around 1956 or 1957.[100] We thus have reason to check the dates in *Guan Hanqing*, especially as there is no indication within *Dou E yuan* itself that suggests any specific date of composition. The Yuan took power in 1280, Tian Han places *Dou E yuan* in 1281, *Guan Hanqing* is written in 1958, and we are thus back at the same date, 1956 or 1957, for the villains to take power in China. This is further stressed through the introduction of Wen Tianxiang, who had been prime minister under the Southern Song but was imprisoned after the demise of that dynasty. Tian Han has Guan Hanqing read a poem that Wen composed in prison, "The Song of Righteousness Prevailing" (*Zhengqi ge*).[101] Wen Tianxiang has become a symbol of

---

99. The play was staged by three troupes in Japan and shown in many cities beginning in January 1959; see the letter by the play's Japanese director to Tian, quoted in Li Zhiyan, "Tian Han," p. 30. See also the articles "*Guan Hanqing zai Riben*" and "*Riben gedacheng shangyan Guan Hanqing*." For the anti-Americanism, see Tian, "Preface," p. 5.

100. See the study of *Xie Yaohuan* in chapter 2 of this volume for details.

101. Wen Tianxiang, *Wen Wenshan wenji*, pp. 75f. See his biographical sketch by H. Huber in Franke, *Sung Biographies*, vol. 3, pp. 1187ff.

loyalism in Chinese historical thinking. According to Tian Han's interpretation, however, he extols *zheng* (righteousness or correctness) in this song, not an ethnic Han Chinese dynasty; consequently, he refuses to serve the Yuan because their ruling clique is not righteous. There are thus people of rank and standing who are loyal to a more righteous situation prevailing a year or two before, and who have been imprisoned for this. Guan Hanqing reads and likes the poem, which is "underground literature," an example of *samizdat* in the early Yuan. Guan shares Wen Tianxiang's values, without, however, making public that he does so. Again, there is a curious echo in *Xie Yaohuan*. Yuan Xingjian, with whom Xie falls in love, is the son of an official slandered for "counterrevolutionary activities" some years before and executed. His father, like Wen Tianxiang, is the victim of the "Anti-Rightist campaign" and is imbued with the more correct spirit that prevailed before it.

THE PROBLEM

In *Guan Hanqing*, a twin problem plagues society: First, injustice is perpetrated on a grand scale, and people cannot speak out against it. The figure of the young woman, the victim of the villains, is a familiar symbol that is equated with the "people"; it is imbued with the best qualities of selflessness and undauntedness, but it is also "female," that is, helpless and weak. The same symbol is used time and again on the twentieth-century stage, and Guo Moruo's play *Qu Yuan* contributed to make it a standard symbol. Tian Han adds to it a second, although subordinate point: economic expropriation. Guan Hanqing's Dou E is given to the family of her husband because her father cannot pay his way to the examination; in this case there is no expropriation. However, Zhu Xiaolan, the young woman whose execution, according to Tian Han, prompted Guan Hanqing to write the play, came to Cambaluc from Xiangyang (Hangzhou) because the Mongol lord Alihaiya "grabbed a large tract of grazing land for his horses. He not only enclosed the whole piece of land that belonged to Xiaolan's family, a total of several *mu*, but also demanded the service of her father as a stablehand." Whereupon her father ran away. Her fate is replicated not only in that of actress Zhu Lianxiu, who plays the Dou E role, but numerous other women in order to stress "typicality." To fit his present purpose, Tian Han is willing to change the information provided by Guan Hanqing.

The loss of the economic rights entails and reinforces that of civic rights. We are forced to assume that Tian Han is referring to the "upsurge of socialism in the countryside," the rapid collectivization of agriculture that occurred a few years after land reform had given "the land to the tiller." The peasants, whose land had been collectivized, were then expected to go on working it, running cooperative pigsties and the like. The dramatic increase in the population of cities like Shanghai and Guangdong after collectivization attests to the fact that peasants fled in substantial numbers. A replica that reinforces this interpretation is again found in *Xie Yaohuan*. Here Rules a through c and i apply.

The collectivization of agriculture reappears thus in *Guan Hanqing* as the expropriation of land by mighty Mongol and Semu lords. This policy is directly linked to the faction of villains in de facto power in the government. In the second edition of mid-1958, Tian Han adds a passage according to which after Horikhoson's advent to power and Ahmad's assassination the land would be given back to the peasants.[102] The elimination of property rights in the countryside and the elimination of civic rights with the Anti-Rightist campaign combine into a national crisis, which is expressed as the rape and slaughter of young women in the text, including such phrases as "These days to kill a Han Chinese is less of a crime than to kill a donkey."[103] On stage "these days" or "today" refers to the early Yuan, but for the audience, which is living in the present "today," the two time levels are readily confused. Tian Han thus pioneers a technique of making scathing and very generalized statements about the contemporary situation in the form of phrases that start with a "today" or "nowadays," and retain their innocuousness by being uttered by a historical personage in a stage time of an earlier dynasty. As the technique was much copied later, I will give a list of such statements here. They need no comment.

GUAN:	Today, there are only few officials who are not corrupt [*bu zei*]. (2d ed.)[104]
XIE [musician, friend of Guan's]:	Today, nine out of ten judgments are unjust verdicts. (2d ed.)[105]
GUAN:	However, nowadays this kind of unjust imprisonment is again being handed out

102. Tian, *Guan Hanqing, Zhongguo lishiju* ed., p. 289.
103. Tian, *Guan Hanqing, Juben* ed., p. 4.
104. Tian, *Guan Hanqing, Zhongguo lishiju xuan* ed., p. 209.
105. Ibid., p. 211.

	[referring to *Cao E* of the Han, the precedent for Dou E/Zhu Xiaolan].[106]
GUAN:	Today regardless of whether someone is from a good family or is an actress [2d ed. adds: all are suppressed and trampled on], all are slaves.[107]
QIAN [musician, friend of Guan's]:	Nowadays the hundred families are like "geese with arrows through their beaks: not a single person dares to cough."[108]
GUAN:	Since I read Prime Minister Wen [Tianxiang]'s "Song of Righteousness Prevailing" I realize that even today there are such bounds of the earth and pillars of heaven who don't have to be ashamed of those who lived earlier, and this has greatly increased my courage.[109]
GUAN [in a song composed in prison for Zhu]:	During the last few years winds and clouds have changed the color of the rivers and mountains [an image for the dramatic worsening of the political climate].[110]
PRISONER [in same cell with Guan]:	Among playwrights nowadays there is not even a handful of people like Guan Hanqing who dare to "rebel against authority and speak evil words."[111]
ZHOU FUXIANG [Mrs. Liu's son-in-law]:	What is most severely banned by today's laws is rebelling against the authorities. (2d and 3d eds.)[112]
PEASANT [praising Guan]:	The ways of these times are vile indeed: the bad ones can live on to no end, while the good ones are killed off one after the other.[113]

All of the statements are made by Guan and his friends, and, in the context of the play, are thus "true."

106. Tian, *Guan Hanqing, Juben* ed., p. 10.
107. Ibid., p. 6; *Zhongguo lishiju xuan* ed., p. 218.
108. Tian, *Guan Hanqing, Zhongguo lishiju xuan* ed., p. 221.
109. Tian, *Guan Hanqing, Juben* ed., p. 12.
110. Ibid., p. 24.
111. Tian, *Guan Hanqing, Zhongguo lishiju xuan* ed., p. 283.
112. Ibid., p. 279.
113. Tian, *Guan Hanqing, Juben* ed., p. 25.

The protagonists of *Guan Hanqing* profit from this crisis, suffer from it, ignore it, or tolerate it. Who will be the heroes to overcome it?

THE PROTAGONISTS

The People   The people appear on stage through a variety of representatives: as the innkeeper and her daughter in the first act, as the popular side of the audience of *Dou E yuan*, as prisoners and prison guards, and as peasants in the last act. "The people" furthermore figures as a symbol in many statements about the "hundred families." According to the general statements the *baixing*, hundred families, are "trampled upon like grass" by the officials[114] and are "suppressed."[115] A phrase from *Dou E yuan* is repeated ten times in *Guan Hanqing*: "the officials do not care for the orthodox law, so the hundred families, though they have mouths, cannot speak out." To this, the second edition adds the quote from another *zaju* about geese with arrows through their beaks. The *baixing* are in a passive situation; they are appalled at the way things are going but cannot do anything about it. They collectively show their support when Guan Hanqing stages *Dou E yuan*, collectively sign the petition for his release, and rejoice when their fields are returned to them. But they are in dire need of a hero to speak out for them and to galvanize their strength.

The Villains   In the People's Republic, the presence of a few individual cases of Communist officials who relapsed into old-style habits and turned into bad eggs or else had always been bad eggs and sneaked into the Party has always been admitted. Tian Han's *Guan Hanqing* takes issue with this assessment, however, through an interpretation of *Dou E yuan*. Tian Han identifies the judge as Koshin, Ahmad's son; Donkey Li, who falsely accuses the young woman of murder, has a letter of recommendation from a Semu commander, Sa; towering above them all is Ahmad. In fact, when Zhu Lianxiu encourages Guan Hanqing to attack judge Koshin with the play, Guan answers: "But there are not just one or two of these monsters [*gui dongxi*], there are many, many of them [*haoduo haoduo de*], and they band together to eat men. How can one manage to draw up the ghost masks [*guilian*] of all of them [for all to recognize]?" Zhu answers: "If there are too many of

114. Ibid., p. 4.
115. Ibid., p. 6.

such monsters, select the vilest among them for depiction."[116] They are thus not just a few individuals, but a well-organized network linking people at all levels. And they are not just the dregs of the "old society" but people who emerge and thrive under the present conditions. Ever since Lu Xun's *Diary of a Madman*, the notion of *chiren*, man-eating, has been used to characterize "old society." But, as Tian Han is not writing the orthodox Marxist historical drama with its confrontation between people and rulers, he uses the term "man-eating" not for this society as a whole, but only for the villains. Tian Han's interpretive step—making the judge into Ahmad's son and thus imputing that Guan Hanqing's *Dou E yuan* is a veiled attack on a historical personality and its faction—in turns forces us (Rules d and g) to look for contemporary individuals attacked in Tian Han's *Guan Hanqing*. Tian Han installs Ahmad as the secret target of *Dou E yuan*, and he has Guan Hanqing say that the purpose of his play is "not only to upbraid an individual," which means that besides taking up broader social issues, it is *also* to upbraid a particular person in power. As to do so is a touchy matter, the hints are subtle.

What does Tian Han tell us about Ahmad? From short characterizations in the list of protagonists in *Guan Hanqing* we learn that Ahmad is "the favorite [*chongchen*] of the emperor," Khubilai Khan. In the text, this is not repeated, but his power does not depend on either his orthodox qualities or his institutional rank, but on his personal relationship with the emperor. Within socialist literature in general, and the historical drama of this period in particular, the highest official within the text is always read as a reference to the chairman (Stalin, Mao, etc.) if he is the top person within the unit mentioned, like "first secretary," "district head," et cetera. For this reason, villains in the Hundred Flowers texts as well as in the texts written after 1979 are usually vice-heads. Khubilai Khan must thus be read against Mao Zedong. Ahmad, as his personal favorite, prevails over the more correct members of the center. Ahmad controls the courts, is responsible for the land-grabbing, and is ruthless in his handling of the "masses" of Han Chinese. He tortures people, throws them into prison for what they say, and eventually, in the second version (upon Guo Moruo's proposal), even has Sai Lianxiu's eyes gouged out right on stage for criticizing him. He furthermore takes a keen interest in the field of literature, knowing that this is the "outlet" for unemployed Han Chinese "intellectuals" to vent

116. Ibid., p. 6.

their grievances, more often than not through writing historical plays. In the analysis of Tian's later play, *Xie Yaohuan*, we will be forced to conclude that Tian Han attacked Kang Sheng in the person of the empress's secret police chief. A first check seems to confirm the hypothesis that Kang Sheng is also attacked through the figure of Ahmad. Kang Sheng[117] was in charge of a separate police and prison system since the rectification movement in Yan'an, the Social Welfare Department, and had been reinforced in this position after the Gao Gang–Rao Shushi persecution in the early years of the Republic. This prison system was greatly expanded later during the Cultural Revolution, when innumerable people were incarcerated there, and many were tortured and shot.

There are rumors among people who were in Yan'an during the early forties charging Kang Sheng with using torture against intellectuals to force them into false confessions, and with having ordered the execution of Wang Shiwei, the author of "Wild Lily." Kang Sheng was a member of the Politburo, and although he was demoted to alternate member at the Party Congress in September 1956, scholars are unanimous that his power did not diminish[118] and in fact greatly increased after the beginning of the Anti-Rightist campaign.

After Kang Sheng was singled out as the chief Maoist villain by the leadership installed after the Third Plenum in December 1978, there were revelations about his earlier doings. Posthumously excluded from the Party, he was also designated in due order as a lifelong Trotskyist and Guomindang agent. But the information about him has to be used with great care, and internal evidence must strongly support our contention before we can link Tian Han's attack to this person. PRC authors have never linked the Ahmad of *Guan Hanqing* to Kang Sheng.

In his preface to *Guan Hanqing*, Tian Han mentions among the important sources for his play Ahmad's biography in the *Yuanshi* and Marco Polo's account of his travels. Perhaps we are well advised to follow this lead and share the information given there. According to the

117. The history of Kang Sheng's prison system has not been published if indeed it has been written. When he was posthumously expelled from the Party in 1980, an internal document was distributed by the Discipline Commission. To my knowledge this document has not become available. The most detailed study of Kang Sheng, the author of which obviously had access to secret files of the Taiwan secret police concerning the mainland, is by Fang Jing: "Dui Kang Sheng," pp. 41ff.

118. Cf. MacFarquhar, *Origins* 1:148.

Yuanshi, Ahmad became a favorite of Khubilai Khan through his association with and support for Khubilai's wife, Jamui Khatun, to whose court he had been attached before her marriage. We are told in *Guan Hanqing* that Ahmad was in favor already for over twenty years. In 1937, Kang Sheng returned from the Soviet Union, where he had studied Berija's political prison system, which at the time was certainly leading in the world. Although he was associated with Wang Ming, who had been sent to replace Mao in the leadership of the Communist Party, he linked up with Jiang Qing—both were born in the same place —and helped in getting the Party's consent for her marriage to the Chairman.[119] In this way he won the latter's confidence. His "problem" with Wang Ming notwithstanding, Mao put him of all people in charge of running the secret police side of the Rectification movement, which was designed to weed out Wang Ming's adherents.

Reading Marco Polo's description of Ahmad, the resonance cannot be overheard.

> You will hear further how there are twelve persons appointed who have authority to dispose of lands, offices, and everything else at their discretion [which would be the Yuan Politburo]. Now one of these was a certain Saracen named Achmath, a shrewd and able man, who had more power and influence with the Grand Kaan than any of the others; and the Kaan held him in such regard that he could do what he pleased. The fact was, as came out after his death, that Achmath had so wrought upon the Kaan with his sorcery, that the latter had the greatest faith and reliance on everything he said, and in this way did everything that Achmath wished him to do.

Ahmad derives his power not from his economic but from his political position. He is defined, in *Guan Hanqing,* in terms not of "class" but of "bureaucratic power," which improves his resonance with the present. Marco Polo's report continues:

> This person disposed of all governments and offices, and passed sentence on all malefactors; and whenever he desired to have anyone whom he hated put to death, whether with justice or without it, he would go to the Emperor and say: "Such an one deserves death, for he hath done this or that against your imperial dignity." Then the Lord would say: "Do as you think right," and so he would have the man forthwith executed. Thus when people saw how unbounded were his powers, and how unbounded the reliance placed by the emperor on everything that he said, they did not venture to oppose him in anything. No one was so high in rank or power as to be free from dread of him. If anyone was accused by him to the emperor of a capital offence, and

119. Fang Jing, "Dui Kang Sheng," p. 48.

desired to defend himself, he was unable to bring proofs in his own exculpation, for no one would stand by him, as no one dared to oppose Achmath. And thus the latter caused many to perish unjustly.[120]

Reading the reports about Kang Sheng's role some years later during the Cultural Revolution and the innumerable people who died in his prisons or were executed on his direct orders, as well as the casual remarks by Hu Yaobang and Deng Xiaoping that his policies had directly "affected" 100 million (according to Hu) or 200 million (according to Deng) people,[121] there is some basis for a retroactive assumption that Kang Sheng had followed similar policies, although on a much smaller scale, in the years before.

There is, however, more. After having described the popular rebellion and eventual assassination of Ahmad, Marco Polo says that the latter belonged to a specific sect. "These circumstances called the Kaan's [Khan's] attention to the accursed doctrines of the Sect of the Saracens, which excuse every crime, and even murder itself when committed on such as are not of their religion. And seeing that this doctrine had led the accursed Achmath and his sons to act as they did without any sense of guilt, the Kaan was led to entertain the greatest disgust and abomination for it. So he summoned the Saracens and prohibited their doing many things which their religion enjoined." Ahmad was thus not just a villain, but found encouragement for his doings in his sectarian beliefs, which permitted all kinds of actions as long as the victims were not of his sect.

Kang Sheng was newly in charge of the Higher Party School when *Guan Hanqing* was written, and was thus a leading dispenser of ideology. We cannot ascertain his ideological positions at the time as there seems to be no published record, but from his stance a year later, it is clear that he advocated the elevation of Mao Zedong Thought above the Marxist-Leninist classics and was the first to describe Mao as the greatest Marxist of our time.[122] Although it is dangerous to credit politicians with any beliefs retroactively, there seems to be a certain consistency here. He had also shown his willingness to go to great lengths with police methods to eliminate "rightist" tendencies in the Party. The Semu (Saracens) and Mongols were the two big groups in the Yuan leadership, and Tian Han reserved the acts of grossest villainy

120. Yule, *Marco Polo*, pp. 370f.
121. Fang Jing, "Dui Kang Sheng," p. 47.
122. Ibid., p. 42.

to the Semu, that is, to "leftists" who shared Kang Sheng's beliefs, if my identification is correct. Finally, Kang Sheng took a great interest in the theater, being himself a devotee of *kunqu* opera. He seems to have invited himself to the Guan Hanqing commemoration, and the scene in *Guan Hanqing* where Ahmad himself sees the play that attacks him and his faction was nicely repeated by Kang Sheng sitting in the audience at the premiere of Tian Han's new play. It was Kang Sheng who organized from the center the attacks against the historical drama in 1964, it was he who denounced *Hai Rui baguan*, *Xie Yaohuan*, and *Li Huiniang* as "anti-Party, anti-socialist," and it was he who eventually hounded Tian Han to death in the first years of the Cultural Revolution, in effect saying that Tian had "done this or that against [the emperor's] imperial dignity," if we may quote Polo's rendering of Ahmad's words.

As there was no echo from Kang Sheng, no reference is made to Ahmad's being in charge of finances at Khubilai Khan's court.

As might be expected from the line of polemics followed here, the villains pride themselves on the people's love for them. Koshin the judge, from the second version on, loves to have people present him with ten-thousand-signature umbrellas, and he gets very annoyed if they don't come forth.[123] Ahmad and his faction refer to themselves as "father and mother of the people."[124] Not content with being oppressive, they also require jubilation. Similar PRC scenes come easily to mind.

There are elements where I am less confident. Is Ahmad's gross and primitive language—after all Chinese was a foreign language for him—an allusion to Kang Sheng's "uneducated" Shandong dialect? Is there more than historical truthfulness in Tian Han's taking up Marco Polo's charge that for Ahmad "there was no beautiful woman whom he might desire, but he got hold of her?" The *neibu* biography of Kang Sheng published by Hongqi Press after his ouster from the Party relishes in details of his going off to the Soviet Union not with his wife, but with his brother's, who eventually committed suicide; Hu Yaobang claimed that "everyone knows" about Kang's private relationship with the Chairman's wife, and rumors circulated that he was indeed after young women. But again, this charge is standard in political denunciations of

123. Tian, *Guan Hanqing*, *Zhongguo lishiju xuan* ed., p. 209. It is interesting to see how the allegorical potential of these characters slowly unfolds in subsequent editions.

124. Tian, *Guan Hanqing*, *Juben* ed., p. 5.

opponents. Ahmad's Semu seem to be responsible for the Yuan "collectivization," but what was Kang Sheng's role, if any, in that of the fifties?
When he was expelled from the Party in 1981, the Party Discipline
Commission distributed an internal dossier about him. This is not
accessible to me; perhaps more information could be gleaned from it.

The identification of Kang Sheng as the innuendo object of Tian
Han's attack certainly is of some importance, but it is not crucial. There
is a chance that Tian had another leader in mind. What is crucial is the
methodological point that he definitely had a particular person and his
claque in mind.

The worst appendages to the villains' faction are the Han Chinese
who run their errands. They appear in two exemplars, Donkey Li,
associated with a Semu commander, and Ye Hefu, Ahmad's cultural
spy. Whereas the Semu ideological villains are hated, these creatures are
merely despised. Ye Hefu poses as a *neihang*, one of the theater people;
he is knowledgeable and exceedingly skilled in *cai*, interpretation. He
advises Guan to seek fame and wealth, and to entertain the rulers with
his work. After Wang Zhu has assassinated Ahmad, Ye brings (from the
second edition on) a proposal from Koshin, Ahmad's son, that Guan
should denounce Wang Zhu for attempting to slaughter a loyal minister
of the government. This scene echoes the exercises in which Chinese
intellectuals were forced to denounce a Party politician who had fallen
from favor or one of their colleagues. Tian Han said "under these conditions there must have been such people as Ye Hefu" because such
people were around in 1958. The description of Ye Hefu seems so lively
that a real-life counterpart probably existed. When Tian Han set out to
write his *Guan Hanqing*, he might have received exactly the advice Ye
gave to Guan.

The Emperor   The emperor, Khubilai Khan, does not come onto the
stage. A year later, this barrier was overcome; the Chairman himself
appeared on stage in the form of different emperors and of Empress Wu.

Given the sensitivity of the subject, all remarks about the emperor
have to be read with care. Ahmad is his favorite, but Khubilai Khan is
ignorant of his villainy. When he learns of it after Ahmad's death, he
does not hesitate to declare Ahmad's assassination to have been justified, and to persecute Ahmad's faction and ideological ("religious")
line. Ahmad can quote him on the policy concerning Han Chinese intellectuals as referred to above, and Khubilai Khan's attitude is cynical, but
not brutal. Ahmad's action to control the intellectuals crosses that

threshold. Mao Zedong too had by early 1958 given up the intellectuals as a core group for the modernization. They had been given some leeway in the previous two years and had quickly forgotten that they had been called upon to accelerate economic development, not to claim democracy. Now, a new crowd of technicians and poets was to be produced from the "proletariat" during the Great Leap. The status of the "bourgeois intellectuals" was thus lowest. Khubilai's comments agree with Mao's utterances at the time.

Finally, the emperor is referred to in the Wen Tianxiang affair. As Wen refuses to serve the Yuan, he may be executed. A poem is quoted in *Guan Hanqing* asking the emperor for Wen's release, but a friend of Guan's remarks: "Do you think the emperor is really that broad-minded?"[125] The Chairman will not tolerate someone who refuses to serve the administration because he thinks righteousness is not prevailing there.

The overall assessment of the emperor is not unfriendly. He is not a member of Ahmad's faction, and ignores his misdeeds. But his favoritism prevents him from getting a true picture of the state of the country.[126] There is never a thought that he and the dynasty should be overthrown or replaced. On the stage, Dou E as a ghost asks her father to "eliminate the vile officials" and by doing this "share the burden with the only human [a term for the emperor] and rid the ten thousand com-

125. Ibid., p. 10.

126. Another possible silent text might be quoted here, the evaluation of Khubilai Khan in the *Xu Tongjian gangmu*; it is translated by de Mailla in *Histoire de l'Empire Chinois*, vol. 9, pp. 459f. and is also included in Yule's commentary to his Marco Polo translation on p. 375: "Hupilai Khan must certainly be regarded as one of the greatest princes that ever existed, and as one of the most successful in all that he undertook. This he owed to his judgement in the selection of his officers, and to his talent for commanding them. He carried his arms into the most remote countries, and rendered his name so formidable that not a few nations spontaneously submitted to his supremacy. Nor was there ever an Empire of such vast extent. He cultivated literature, protected its professors, and even thankfully received their advice. Yet he never placed a Chinese in his cabinet, and he employed foreigners only as Ministers. These, however, he chose with discernment, always excepting the Ministers of Finance [like Ahmad]. He really loved his subjects; and if they were not always happy under his government, it is because they took care to conceal their sufferings. There were in those days no Public Censors whose duty is to warn the Sovereign of what is going on: and no one dared to speak out for fear of the resentment of the Ministers who were the depositaries of Imperial authority, and the authors of the oppressions under which the people laboured. Several Chinese, men of

moners of these evils."[127] This is the moment when Wang Zhu cries "Rid the ten thousand commoners of these evils"; indeed, he does so shortly by killing Ahmad—for the only human.

The Members of the Ruling Tribe Afflicted with a "Pain in the Heart"
The main representative of the "correct" faction is Horikhoson. Like Ahmad, whose network extends down to Han Chinese villains like Donkey Li, Horikhoson has his own social base. He is personally acquainted with the two people who later assassinate Ahmad. His secretary, "though a Mongol," is kind-hearted and tries to secure Guan Hanqing's release from prison. Horikhoson's servant is the son-in-law of Mrs. Liu, the innkeeper who tells the story of Zhu Xiaolan in the first scene. Horikhoson intervenes in favor of Guan Hanqing when Ahmad wants him executed in the playhouse. There are others who show some concern and kindheartedness, like Superintendent He, who organizes the birthday party for the prime minister's mother at which *Dou E yuan* is staged. Tian Han says that the members of this faction suffer from a curious disease, *xintong*, "pain in the heart." As a doctor, Guan Hanqing has specialized in this ailment.[128] Horikhoson, who suffers from it, saves Guan.[129] Superintendent He, who suffers from it,[130] procures an opportunity to stage *Dou E yuan*. Ahmad's mother, a fellow-sufferer,[131] releases Mrs. Liu's daughter, whom her son had abducted. Prime Minister Bo Yan's mother, another sufferer, is moved to tears by *Dou E yuan*, and wants to adopt the actress who plays Dou E, Zhu Lianxiu. Horikhoson finally adds: "[Guan Hanqing] is an expert in curing pain of heart. I myself have taken the medicament he prescribed, and indeed it is a drug that makes the disease [pain in the heart] disappear. At court there are quite a few people with this same disease. . . ."[132] The leaders with "pain in the heart" are the opposite of

letters and of great ability, who lived at Hupilai's court, might have rendered that prince the greatest service in the administration of his dominions, but they were never intrusted with any but subordinate offices, and they were not in a position to make known the malversations of those public bloodsuckers." This is a suggestive statement indeed about Mao Zedong.

127. Tian, *Guan Hanqing, Juben* ed., p. 15.
128. Ibid., p. 19.
129. Ibid.
130. Ibid., p. 14.
131. Ibid., p. 7.
132. Ibid., p. 19.

the "officials without a heart for the righteous law" (*wuxin zhengfa*). The faction in power has no heart. The males who are temporarily out of power and the females, who are always out of power, retain a heart, which hurts at the sight of the sufferings inflicted by the other faction. *Guan Hanqing* is written in great haste, and Tian Han did not manage to integrate this disease with his other medical metaphors, and with the role of Guan Hanqing as both a writer and a doctor. Thus one could argue that Guan's plays would increase the pain in the heart of this faction, but then Tian assures us that Guan is in fact curing this political disease and making the pain disappear. The type of medicaments/texts that Guan now repudiates are termed "peppermint" and "licorice root."[133] Again, he relates neither of them to the heart disease. There is thus much disconnected wordplay on the association between literature and medicine, but the references are scattered and not unified. Each element has to be read with a separate meaning.

The faction of the sufferers from pain in the heart belongs to the ruling tribe. Their internal ("heart") suffering indicates that they don't vent their frustrations in public. In fact, the picture given of this faction becomes ever more gloomy in the subsequent editions. In formal terms, Tian Han was reacting to the admonitions of critics who argued in the dialect of historical materialism that he should emphasize the utter vileness of the ruling class as a whole, differentiating between neither Ahmad and Horikhoson nor Han Chinese bureaucrats and their Mongol and Semu masters. Tian followed that suggestion but with a result quite different from the original intention. He indeed darkened the image of Horikhoson and his group, but retained the important factional difference between Ahmad and Horikhoson. His changes were thus a reflection on the leeway and the actual motives of the "correct" faction in contemporary China, and not a return to a people versus ruling class contradiction, which would allow the entire Communist crowd to easily associate itself with the "people."

There are important changes in Horikhoson's attitude toward literature, as reflected in his attitude toward Guan Hanqing's release. In the first version, Horikhoson comes on stage with Ahmad to see the second performance of *Dou E yuan*. He says: "That play is quite good." When Ahmad points out to him that the play attacks "us officials," Horikhoson remarks: "Yes, I heard that. His criticism of corrupt officials is quite strong, but what has that to do with us?" Ahmad

133. Ibid., p. 6

answers: "Great Preceptor, you are too honest and tolerant. If they can revile them [the corrupt officials], they can revile [*ma*] us." Replies Horikhoson: "Not necessarily; furthermore, 'He who speaks, commits no crime, and he who listens is sufficiently admonished.'" Ahmad then says: "No, one cannot allow them to speak. Once you relax controls, they will rebel against authority [*fan shang*] and create disturbances, and there will be nothing to stop them. Just imagine how terrible!"[134] In the second edition, written some weeks later, the last exchange has been altered. Horikhoson now says after Ahmad's "they can revile us": "Let them revile us as much as they want [*mama*], that even has some advantages for strengthening the social fabric [*zhengchi jigang*]."[135] The earlier version enunciated the principle that such criticism should be allowed; the later version pointed at the tactical advantages such criticism would have in keeping officials on the right path. When Ahmad proceeds to incarcerate Guan and Zhu and to have Sai Lian-xiu's eyes gouged out, Horikhoson does not interfere, but leaves.

According to the first version, Horikhoson "holds power" after Ahmad's death, and is *chengxiang*, Prime Minister. It is said that he was "well disposed" toward Guan Hanqing and that he "had a fight with others about the Guan Hanqing affair."[136] When Guan is sent to exile, the forces demanding his execution for *fanshang* (rebellion) are not strong enough to have him executed, but neither do the forces of Horikhoson suffice to have him set free altogether. Horikhoson sends a flattering note together with the permission for Zhu Lianxiu to join Guan Hanqing in exile: "Guan Hanqing is the most important writer of this generation; he dares to resist villains in power. Although he is ordered to leave the capital, he will continue to be recognized as the cultural leader [*batuo*] of the capital."[137] The second edition demotes Horikhoson to *you chengxiang*, Junior Prime Minister, but adds a special scene in Horikhoson's office. In dramatic terms, this scene is an interpretation and adaptation of the scene in *Dou E yuan* in which Dou E's ghost reshuffles the legal papers. Here, the people's petition to have Guan set free is reshuffled so that it comes out on top. Horikhoson admits that he personally knew Ahmad's assassins and rejoices at what they have done, but avers that he saw to it that they were executed,

134. Ibid., p. 18.
135. Tian, *Guan Hanqing, Zhongguo lishiju xuan* ed., p. 258.
136. Tian, *Guan Hanqing, Juben* ed., p. 27.
137. Ibid., p. 29.

while he is "grateful to them in his heart," because they eliminated his competitor. Now, Horikhoson has nightmares, and sees the assassin Wang Zhu in his dreams.

Horikhoson is a politician. He has a likeness of the dark-bearded god Guan Yu hanging on the wall, and thus he shares some basic values with Guan Hanqing himself, who is described as Guan Yu's relative and descendant. However, he comments on the petition in favor of Guan Hanqing: "The text is very moving, but the signatures are merely of little commoners from the city and peasants from the outskirts. If the ministry would consent to react to such popular scribbling there would be no end to it." As a politician, he decides to bow to a rising new villain, Lord Bor, who heads the military. Bor argues that Wang Zhu assassinated a high-ranking official, which was a rebellion independent of the crimes that Ahmad had committed, and that Guan Hanqing rebelled with the word against the authorities, and therefore had to "be severely dealt with." Horikhoson decides to associate himself with this view because he is not strong enough to oppose it. When the petition appears for the third time on his desk thanks to the agile hands of Mrs. Liu's son-in-law, Horikhoson believes that it is a sign from Guan Yu, and bans Guan Hanqing instead of having him executed. Only public opinion pressures him into this attenuation. Otherwise, he would have "looked at the water while the boat drifts by," which is what Dou E accuses heaven of doing while she was killed.[138]

From the indications given in the text, we can hardly avoid the conclusion that Tian Han is dealing with Zhou Enlai in the person of Horikhoson. He grants him a commitment to hard work, and to orthodox moral values symbolized by Guan Yu's picture on the wall. He has a heart pain, and is willing to intervene personally to save an intellectual here or there. But while he may admire Wang Zhu, and be grateful to him, he has him executed because otherwise his position with the emperor would be endangered. His own standing depends on the actions of people like Wang Zhu and Guan Hanqing who represent popular feeling, but as a politician he dissociates himself from them if the association seems too dangerous. The first version still shows him as

138. Tian, *Guan Hanqing, Zhongguo lishiju xuan* ed., pp. 285ff. Mrs. Liu's son-in-law's fear that Horikhoson would not do a thing has prompted his decision to present the umbrella with the signatures; see ibid., p. 278. The phrase about "looking at the water" is taken from Dou E's remonstrance against Heaven for not interfering against the injustice done to her; Guan, *Dou E yuan*, p. 860 has a slightly different formula.

a "correct" hero who merely lacks strength. The second makes him the least noxious among the government leaders below the emperor, and a man who continues to see some merit in the public denunciation of the abuses of officials. As we shall see, the real-life counterpart of Horikhoson was to intervene to change this figure even further in the third edition.

The other members of the ruling tribe are dealt with just as gingerly. Prime Minister Bo Yan's mother, on whose birthday the play *Dou E yuan* was performed, sheds tears and gives rich presents to Zhu Lianxiu; the latter is saved from instant execution at Ahmad's hands when it is hinted that an execution would leave a bad impression since the old lady has taken a liking to her. But the old woman's tears are as political as the correctness of Horikhoson. When Guan Hanqing suggests to Zhu Lianxiu that she write a letter to the old lady to secure the latter's help in her efforts to be released from prison, she rejects the idea in a dogmatic tirade. "She took a liking to me only because the girl I played entertained her. She has not really understood our play, and she weeps at the play only to make other people remark how compassionate she is. In fact when Prime Minister Bo Yan today butchers the inhabitants of a city, and tomorrow puts to the sword people who have already capitulated, not half a tear rolls from her eye. I hate this kind of woman, and I should implore her? Not for the death of me!"[139]

In fact, on both sides tactics prevail. Guan Hanqing and Zhu Lianxiu use the conflicts between the pain-in-the-heart faction and the heartless faction to find a public space for their performance and thus mobilize the "masses"; the faction with the pain in the heart uses them to weaken and eliminate Ahmad in order to strengthen their own position. But whereas Tian Han refuses to make the mandatory sharp delineation between the "people" and the "ruling class" because to do so would greatly impair the suggestiveness of this arrangement for the present, he also does not forget that Guan belongs to the "people," the Han. Horikhoson, even though he frequently espouses Chinese ethics, remains a member of the ruling non-Han tribe.

The identification of Horikhoson with Zhou Enlai, which is confirmed by the role attributed in later historical plays to the leader of the benevolent faction in the center, does not serve to reduce the historical figure of Horikhoson to a simple replica of Zhou. Rather, it points out a continuity. Time and again in Chinese history there have been leaders in

---

139. Tian, *Guan Hanqing*, *Juben* ed., p. 23.

the highest positions in the center who personally felt bound by rules of correctness but as politicians would play the game of power, operating not on principle but on pragmatism. They justified doing so with the argument that if they were removed from power for a rash act of principle, things would become much worse. Zhou Enlai fits this traditional pattern all too well. Neither Guan nor Zhu Lianxiu criticizes Horikhoson for reasoning thus.

The Heroes   The title of the play proclaims Guan Hanqing to be its hero. By 1958, the intellectual community had experienced as dramatic a drop in its social status as their thirteenth-century peers had with the advent of the Yuan dynasty. To set up an intellectual, a playwright, as the hero of a piece in mid-1958 required daring; it also required some bolstering of one's own courage by setting up oversized heroes of the past as the true forerunners and models of modern intellectuals. In the ideological universe of Chinese socialism, Guan Hanqing could not be allowed to draw his motivation, energy, and faith from his wavering intellectual self alone. Intrinsically, Guan is a medical doctor. The theme of the writer as a doctor has some tradition in China.

Lao Can, the hero of Liu E's novel *Lao Can youji* (Lao Can's Travels), which was published around 1903, is a physician.[140] This social role is defined by humanist ethics: the doctor treats the sick whether they are rich or poor, and this is what both Lao Can and Guan are doing. Moreover, traditionally doctors were migrant in China. They went about from place to place dispensing advice and drugs; in addition, they also would pick up news and rumors, transporting information where no other channel for horizontal communication was open. The imperial government saw their social, and especially their geographical, mobility as a threat, and time and again it tried to curtail and control their movements.

The image of the writer as a doctor thus also carries an ethical implication: doctors are no devotees of class struggle, and Guan treats not only Ahmad's mother but also the mother of his own prison guard. To be a doctor implies wide-ranging social contacts at all levels. A play-

140. Guan Hanqing, who was all too familiar with Cambaluc's pleasure quarters, had to be much purified before he would fit the stature of a hero. Tian Han has Guan's wife die to prevent him from having an affair with Zhu Lianxiu, who herself has lost all similarity to the elegant courtesan of the capital. Guo Moruo had done the same with Qu Yuan during the war, and he did an even more energetic job with Wu Zetian some years later.

wright friend of Guan's, also a doctor, manages to visit even Wen Tian-xiang under house arrest, and to smuggle his "Song of Righteousness Prevailing" out for underground circulation. Guan, as a nationally re-nowned playwright and equally renowned member of the Royal Academy of Medicine, has access to all walks of life, to people who otherwise are separated from each other by high walls. Such access is crucial for a "realist" writer. It enables him to give a many-sided picture of reality, drawn from both the talk in the tavern and that of the Prime Minister's private study. This double role of confidant of high and low enables him, quite independently of his writing, to help several indi-viduals get redress for their grievances in a society where other avenues are closed. Guan cannot save Zhu Xiaolan's life, but he saves Mrs. Liu's daughter from being forced into the bed of Ahmad's twenty-fifth son. In the same manner, Lao Can used his contacts to cure social ills and injus-tices. There is, however, a tension between the role of doctor and that of writer, between the humanitarian impulse to cure physical and social ills and the painful insufficiency of individual therapy in times when the entire country is under the sway of tyranny. Lu Xun's reaction to a film clip in Japan that showed the execution of one of his compatriots and his subsequent decision to give up medicine and turn to literature are well known. Tian Han himself studied medicine for some time, then became a writer. Guo Moruo did the same.

The conflict is not just one of symbolism, but of real life. In literature, it goes back to the European antecedents of the political novel. Dumas's *Joseph Balsamo* tells the story of the years immediately preceding the French Revolution.[141] Balsamo, as his name implies, represents the soothing balms and herbs, and tries to bring about the inevitable change by peaceful and unbloody means. His approach contrasts that of Marat, a surgeon not only in life but also in politics. In its Japanese translation, Dumas's novel became one of the standards for a new genre, the political novel, called in Japanese *seiji shōsetsu*, and in Chinese *zhengzhi xiaoshuo*.[142] In *Guan Hanqing* we have the con-flict between Balsamo and Marat echoed in that between the licorice root and the sword. Guan sees his own work as but "peppermint and licorice root." He finds himself criticized by the very people with whom he sympathizes, and says to Zhu Lianxiu: "How much would I hope for a 'blue sky' like Judge Bao to appear and fill up that abyss of injustice!

141. Dumas, *Joseph Balsamo*.
142. Yanagida Izumi, *Seiji shōsetsu kenkyū*, vol. 2, p. 119.

But what appears before our eyes are only man-eating leopards and wolves, and against them our hands are tied and we are without recourse. Mrs. Liu said quite rightly 'Guan Hanqing is a doctor and can help people only when they have colds or coughs.' She gave me quite a dressing down, but she was right. I am just a doctor specialized in handing out peppermint and licorice root. Li Kui [one of the rebel band in *Water Margin*], who could not read a word, dared to raid the execution ground in Jiangzhou—but me? I can only stand behind the throng of people and repress my anger, swallow my ire, and look on with my hands hanging down. That is me, Guan Hanqing, who thinks himself to be quite out of the ordinary. I really despise myself."[143]

Guan Hanqing is appalled at the powerlessness of literature in the face of the villains who run and ruin the country. Although he makes up his mind on his own to write a play about the young woman, he doubts that his play would ever be performed even if he wrote it. Each time, it is Zhu Lianxiu who helps him over his doubts and fears. To Guan's despondent statement quoted above, she replies ("holding his hand to calm him down," according to the stage direction): "True, Li Kui was courageous, but he could not have raided the execution ground all alone. That was all well prepared by the heroes from Liangshanbo. When you perchance encounter some injustice on the street, what is there for you to do?" Guan: "In olden times when people saw an injustice perpetrated on the street they would draw their swords and come to help. But I have no sword; I only have a brush." To which Zhu answers with the decisive line: "Isn't the brush your sword? Isn't the drama (*zaju*) your sword?"

And to his second problem she answers that she is perfectly willing to stage the play: "If you dare write it, I dare stage it." Guan: "If you dare stage it, I will definitely write it, and furthermore finish it quickly."[144]

Who is Zhu Lianxiu, that she is able to guide Guan Hanqing and give him the strength necessary for his endeavor? The young woman unjustly executed bears the family name Zhu, and so does Zhu Lianxiu. Zhu Lianxiu plays the young woman's counterpart on stage, Dou E, and when she is dragged to prison by Ahmad's guards, she still wears the clothing Dou E wore on the execution ground, which she keeps during the prison scenes in *Guan Hanqing*. On the symbolical level, she is identified with the young woman. This is reinforced by her biography. Zhu

143. Tian, *Guan Hanqing, Juben* ed., p. 6.
144. Ibid.

Xiaolan and Zhu Lianxiu are both from "good families" (*liangjia*). In both cases, their parents were deprived of their livelihoods by Ahmad's gang, and the young women were then shipped off to the city by their destitute parents. Zhu Lianxiu quite explicitly identifies with the fate of the other young woman. "Now, for the sake of Zhu Xiaolan, and for that of all the women nursing a bitter sense of injustice and being oppressed, I will surely play this role well."[145]

The general symbolism Tian had written into the part of Dou E as the suppressed, virtuous, and upright people is "now" invested in Zhu Lianxiu. Her personal experience of the sufferings of injustice common to "the people" enables her to give guidance and strength to Guan Hanqing, a fairly orthodox construct. The love between Guan Hanqing and Zhu Lianxiu then serves to indicate the eventual unity of heart and purpose of the "people" and the "progressive intellectuals" in the traditional manner of the political novel. Guan Hanqing does not remain unchanged by this experience. He rises to the occasion, and in the second and third versions of *Guan Hanqing* he is eventually willing to "risk his life" for his duty to "speak out for the people."

Finally, Zhu Lianxiu and Guan Hanqing together move into the real-life roles of Dou E. The second part of *Guan Hanqing*, dealing with events after the staging of *Dou E yuan*, is written as a replica of the second part of *Dou E yuan*. In the latter, the ghost of Dou E appears to her father and has him right the injustice done to her. In *Guan Hanqing*, public opinion pressures Horikhoson to release Guan Hanqing and Zhu Lianxiu from prison. The reversal of unjust verdicts thus operates through public opinion. Therefore, the "ghost" of Dou E lives on in the very community that operates on the public mind—the dramatic community represented by the playwright Guan and the actress Zhu.

In a more cumulative procedure indicative again of the great haste with which the play was written, Tian Han further buttresses his heroic couple. They live in a time of political crisis due to all-pervading injustice. In this situation, the national leader of the drama world is challenged. Lesser lights would be easily disposed of. Guan Hanqing is thus made into something like the Yuan dynasty head of the Chinese Dramatists' Association (which Tian Han himself headed in 1958), and he is well aware of the special duties incumbent upon him. In the later versions, Guan's role as the national leader of drama both in terms of craft and of political daring is even more emphasized.

145. Ibid.

In the first version, Guan only "hopes" for another Judge Bao; in the second edition, this wish is fulfilled. His friends are invited to stage one of his plays in a village, and Guan Hanqing himself will play the role of Judge Bao.[146] His stage turns into the court of this stern judge, since the official courts have been taken over by the villains. His beloved Zhu Lianxiu is allowed to resonate with a still-taller figure, Qu Yuan. When Zhu hears about the threats uttered by Ye Hefu, Ahmad's literary spy, she says heroically: "Let me use a phrase by Qu Yuan: 'Even though I should die nine deaths, I would not regret it.'"[147] In the background was still another echo. Tian Han's friend Cheng Yangqiu had rewritten *Dou E yuan*, and in his version Dou E's verdict is reversed by none other than Hai Rui,[148] which put Guan Hanqing in the role of another celebrated judge who also dared to stand up to the mighty villains. From the advertisements for *Dou E yuan* on the occasion of the Guan Hanqing commemoration, it is difficult to ascertain which version was presented, but, given the fame of Cheng Yangqiu, it is probable that many troupes used his version. As in the case of the medical metaphors, this cumulative procedure indicates the stress under which Tian Han wrote the play. All too often the intention carries the day, and we are faced with emblems, not characters. To serve the same purpose, the walls of Guan's study and Zhu's living room are both hung with symbolical freight, a musical instrument (which refers to the opera) and a sword (with which to mete out righteous judgment through public opinion).

Tian Han characterizes the dramatic community in his play by an idealized *neihang* spirit. Instead of the envy, cliquishness, and petty badmouthing that in fact are so common in the world of the theater, all *neihang*, all professionals of the theater, communicate with openness, warmth, and ease. They are willing to risk their lives for the good of the people. Tian Han followed the suggestions made by his first group of discussants and included some scenes depicting the life of the theatrical community. He portrays a community that can solve all of its internal problems, be they personal or artistic. The strong historical, ideological, and symbolical buttressing of the heroic community as embodying the best interests of the people and inheriting the best of the past was a necessary condition for the vehement rejection of government

146. Tian, *Guan Hanqing, Zhongguo lishiju xuan* ed., p. 220.
147. *Guan Hanqing, Juben* ed., p. 12.
148. Cheng Yangqiu, "Tan Dou E," p. 249.

interference into the creative process, both in its artistic and its political aspects. This interference comes from the two arch-villains of the play, Ahmad and Ye Hefu, and is therewith denounced as something that only such people could think of. Horikhoson does not interfere.

Expressing the deepest aspirations of the people, the dramatic community is able to bring about a sworn brotherhood of the public akin to the "heroes from Liangshanbo." In *Guan Hanqing*, the process is not only announced, but shown. Public opinion identifies in the theater the villains who are attacked on stage. It brings forth the real "sword," Wang Zhu, to eliminate the top bureaucratic villain, and it intervenes in a highly organized form with a ten-thousand-signature petition.

In a scene added in the second version but eliminated for artistic reasons from the third, Guan Hanqing encounters a prisoner, Long-Life Liu, who is to be executed the next day. Liu asks the playwright, as his last wish, to "tell everybody that if only we all dared to fight back, good days could be coming." To which Guan answers: "You are right."[149]

In contemporary terms, Tian Han deals with his own role and responsibility in the person of Guan Hanqing. The analysis of the circumstances surrounding *Dou E yuan* becomes a screen on which to project what is going to be the probable fate of *Guan Hanqing* and its author, Tian Han, if he dares to bring it on stage. Tian Han had much support from the dramatic community, and in *Guan Hanqing* many scenes directly evoke the discussions about *Guan Hanqing* as described by Tian's secretary. In the person of Zhu Lianxiu and the other characters, Tian shows the great importance of their support for the work, both in artistic and in psychological terms. The direct interference into artistic creation of government leaders and "cultural spies" was a sorry fact since the founding of the People's Republic, and especially in the hysterical days of the Anti-Rightist campaign. Tian Han denounces it in the characters of Ahmad and Ye Hefu. Though Tian had publicly criticized Wu Zuguang for speaking out against the Party's control over theatrical matters and advocating a stronger role for the *neihang*, and had even described Wu as an "enemy," in *Guan Hanqing* he repeats the very argument made by Wu. Artistic and political matters of dramatic production are to be handled exclusively by *neihang* people, and the wiser government leaders respect this. One might read Tian Han's reference to Wen Tianxiang as an apology to Wu Zuguang. Wu

149. Tian, *Guan Hanqing, Zhongguo lishiju xuan* ed., p. 284.

Zuguang had, in the thirties, written a play entitled *Wen Tianxiang*; its alternative title was *Zhengqi ge* (The Song of Righteousness Prevailing), the name of the very poem quoted in *Guan Hanqing*. This would well explain the awkward position of the Wen Tianxiang episode. Tian Han would in fact link up with Wu Zuguang in this way, the unexpectedness and awkwardness of the episode attracting the attention of those "in the know" to this entry into the subtext.

In the "present" crisis, the only avenue open for talk is the symbolical language of literature. The stage is the only court where the "abyss [or, more accurately, "ocean"] of unjust verdicts can be filled up," where the injustice of the mass deportations of the Anti-Rightist campaign can be reversed. *Guan Hanqing* sets out to do so. Through the play, Tian Han came out with a self-criticism of his earlier work, describing it as being but "peppermint and licorice root," palliatives and mild laxatives, which could be read as a safe reference to his romantic writings of the twenties, which he had repudiated in an earlier self-criticism,[150] but also to his recent, more subdued texts. The Chinese dramatic community, both friend and foe, never doubted the identification between Tian Han and Guan Hanqing.[151] A well-established tradition already with Guo Moruo's *Qu Yuan*, the tradition was to continue in later historical dramas written by members of both factions. Tian Han "risked his life" to mobilize public opinion against the unjust verdicts and the faction that meted them out. He demanded and arrogated independence from outside interference for this bold action, which in tactical terms he linked as well with Guan Hanqing's commemoration, just as Guan had, in his own play, linked *Dou E yuan*'s premiere with Prime Minister Bo Yan's mother's birthday. The differences between Dou E, Zhu Lianxiu playing Dou E, and the actual fate of Zhu Lianxiu and the theatrical community become

150. Tian, "Women de ziji pipan," pp. 17ff.
151. The rebels in the Dramatists' Association quote Zhang Xin as saying at the time that the longer he looked at *Guan Hanqing*, the more Guan seemed to him like Tian Han. Tian is said to have smiled when he heard it. Zhou Yang is reported to have said in 1964 that "the play only shows Tian Han's mood of self-expression" and "*Guan Hanqing* just inordinately exaggerates the role of the intellectual and the playwright." The rebels themselves assumed the same thing; see the source cited in n. 9 above. More recently, after Tian's rehabilitation, the same argument was repeated by Ma Chaorong in his article quoted in n. 42. In a poem on the Canton Opera version of *Guan Hanqing* written in July 1959, Tian himself seems to have made this association; see Li Zhiyan and Qu Xiwen, "Tian Han xiju shici jicui," p. 53.

blurred, as does the difference between the symbolical "sword" in the form of public opinion and the very real instrument in Wang Zhu's hands. In prison, Zhu Lianxiu tells Guan, in another phrase containing the word "now": "Now I truly don't know whether I am living normal life or on stage. I want to be as I am when facing the thousands of theatergoers—without a speck of cowardice."[152] Tian Han and the theatrical community gave a national spectacle with *Guan Hanqing*, and to survive the expected ordeal, they acted as if all eyes were still on their every movement.

THE PLOT

Briefly put, the plot translates into 1958 language in the following manner. The peasants have been deprived of their land, many having fled rather than work for the new overlords. The same faction that is responsible for the land policy also runs the legal system, and an "ocean of injustice" has been created, in which nine out of ten judgments are wrong verdicts. The same faction has established tight control over the public sector so that even tears have to be hidden. The people are reduced to the pure uprightness of a weak young woman. The villains in power are not a landlord class but owe their might to their "bureaucratic" position in the center. Their chieftain is the chairman's confidant; he ruthlessly persecutes his critics, while demanding a show of devotion from the people.

Guan Hanqing/Tian Han, the national leader (*batuo*) of the drama world, throws in his lot to reverse the unjust verdict and get the country out of the gutter; he is joined in this by the performing artists. They use the contradictions within the ruling tribe to have their play performed in public, and they mobilize the public so that one of the spectators kills the chief villain and many of the others petition to have Guan and Zhu released. The fate of the lovers seems to follow that of their heroine, Dou E. Dou E gets justice only after her death, however, in the realm of romantic fantasy, and only after heavenly intervention. As, in terms of time, the staging of *Dou E yuan* within *Guan Hanqing* corresponds to the staging of *Guan Hanqing* in the summer of 1958, the developments after the staging belong to the same realm of romantic speculation about what might and hopefully will happen. *Guan Hanqing* is to contribute to the demise of the villains.

152. Tian, *Guan Hanqing*, *Juben* ed., p. 23.

One small scene of high dramatic power, which was added by Tian
Han to the second version upon Guo Moruo's suggestion, brings out
the high pitch of aggressiveness between the villains and the dramatic
community, the causes of the crisis, and the hopes encoded in staging
the play. Ahmad has been frustrated in his efforts to vent his anger on
Guan Hanqing and Zhu Lianxiu, as both are protected by people "with
heart pains." He has Sai Lianxiu, who played Dou E's mother-in-law,
brought before him. She had added a phrase of her own to her text:
"When finally will Heaven open its eyes and have these greedy officials
skinned alive?" When asked whether she has a *laitou* ("background"),
too, she does not understand the slang expression, which refers to some
higher protection, and thinks she is being asked about her family background. She answers: "I was born the daughter of a peasant living west
of the capital. The few *mou* of land belonging to our family were all
seized by a servant of your lordship. My father had no means left to eke
out a living and sold me to the entertainment house to learn singing."
Ahmad: "And you hope that Heaven will open its eyes and give you
revenge, don't you?" Sai: "How could a young woman like me have
such thoughts?" Ahmad then has her eyes gouged out. Then, he asks
her: "Sai Lianxiu, you still think of vengeance?" Sai: "How could a
young woman like me get vengeance?—I have only one request: I only
ask you to hang up my gouged-out eyeballs on the city wall of Cambaluc." Ahmad: "Hang them up on the city wall—what for?" Sai: "To
hang there and see your lordship's downfall."[153] The pitch of *Guan
Hanqing*, with its very harsh language and acts including political assassination, was obviously still insufficient to express Tian Han's rage, so he
added this bloody scene and the no-less-bloody words. In the ensuing
"romantic" speculation, the heroes do not cave in to threats and tempt-
ing offers, the public is mobilized, and its mighty action will operate on
the internal contradictions within the ruling tribe's leadership to bring a
more correct politician to power and have Guan and Zhu released from
prison because people again dare to write petitions. The peasants get
back their land, which has been communalized, and they labor on it
with a will as we are told in the last scene since the second version.
Again Tian Han operates with cumulative symbolism to make his most
important point. In the last scene, we are told it is early spring. This had

153. Tian, *Guan Hanqing, Zhongguo lishiju xuan* ed., p. 264. Sai's wish is a
quote from Wu Zixu, a hero of Zhangguo times, who predicted the invasion of a
neighboring country if his advice were not followed. He had his eyes hung up on
the city wall to see the neighbors coming. Which they did.

been a familiar symbol in the early phase of the Hundred Flowers period, indicating that there was hope but icy days were still to be reckoned with.[154] The political climate thus remains unstable, even after all the changes that have taken place. Guan Hanqing and Zhu Lianxiu are not freed, but sent to exile together, on another level the same statement. The judgment is not really reversed; the verdicts against the playwright and the lead actress are only attenuated. With their next piece they may again be jailed or killed for *fanshang*, rebelling against authority. Horikhoson is only the junior Prime Minister. Lord Bor of the military high command demands severe punishment for Guan, because although Ahmad was a brute, he was still a leading politician, and to rebel against him was still, in principle, to rebel against authority. The third symbolical arrangement that points to the fact that despite the change in the chief villain, nothing in fact has been solved, comes with a speculation about time. The peasants mention in the last scene that it had "been dry the year before, and now there was too much water. How should we survive another inundation?" Thus we know that there have already been two years of natural disaster; in actuality, bad weather and probably organizational changes had led to bad harvests after 1956; the ensuing shortage in staple foods then led to the plan for a "Great Leap Forward" to solve this problem. However, in her last words, Dou E had implored Heaven to cause a drought of three years as a proof that the verdict against her was wrong. The verdict is not really revised, as Guan and Zhu are not freed but exiled, and thus Dou E's imprecation is still operative. The end of the play leaves all the questions and problems open.

There remains a difference between the "old society" in which Dou E lives, and the "new society" of Guan Hanqing. Dou E is killed, and only later will she be rehabilitated. Guan Hanqing and Zhu Lianxiu are no longer killed, but only sent to exile. They "thank" Horikhoson for his magnanimity. The prospective scenario in the "romantic" part of *Guan Hanqing* serves to educate the public in the possible forms of resistance, from shouting consent in the theater to filling umbrellas with ten thousand signatures, to instill it with the hope that its reaction and action would count, and to dampen idealistic expectations about the singularity of villains and the morality of "correct" politicians.

154. In fact, the stage directions for the prison scene (act 8, later cut) read that "although in early spring, weather still seemed very cold." Tian, *Guan Hanqing, Zhongguo lishiju xuan* ed., p. 264.

AFTERMATH

A drama remains present if it is printed, which was the case with both versions of *Guan Hanqing* studied hitherto. But it comes into its own when staged. Zhou Enlai had been present at the premiere in June 1958. In mid-June 1959, the Premier returned from a visit to Guangzhou, where he had seen the Canton Opera adaptation of *Guan Hanqing* three times, with the celebrated Hong Xiannü in the female lead. Later, at a banquet in the Ministry of Foreign Affairs, Zhou told Tian Han that this performance had been excellent, but that the end had been changed to a tragedy and the two lovers could not go together into exile. In Beijing on June 19, Hong Xiannü visited Tian Han, and sang some of the songs of the Canton *Guan Hanqing* to him. She told Tian Han that the Premier himself had suggested that the end be changed. Tian Han inquired what his exact words had been. She said in substance, according to Tian's secretary: "The Premier said to conclude with Bo Yan and Horikhoson letting Guan and Zhu leave together is in the specific situation of that time impossible. 'I suggest you change this to a tragic end, and don't let Guan Hanqing and Zhu Lianxiu leave together, which would be "separated fly the butterflies" [instead of the song "Together fly the butterflies" in the text].' The Premier also said that changing it to a tragic end has, in the present new situation of the national struggle and class struggle, a meaning full of actuality [*xianshi yiyi*]." These mysterious words do not become any clearer from Tian Han's reaction. "Tian Han listened silently, constantly nodding his head."[155] Obviously there is a subtext that he understood. Zhou had not suggested the change a year earlier, but now there was a "new situation." In July, the Canton Opera troupe came through Beijing on its way to perform *Guan Hanqing* in North Korea. Tian Han saw the play three times, and on July 20 he wrote a poem dedicated to Ma Shiceng (who played Guan) and Hong Xiannü. Referring to the new end, he concludes: "The waves roar under the Lugou bridge, to bid farewell to the traveler going south [Guan]. Why must there be sadness in parting, for a thousand autumns these hearts will stay together."[156] On July 30, Tian Han decided: "This change of ending of the Canton Opera has been proposed by the Premier. This is well changed, and has a positive meaning with regard

155. Li Zhiyan, "Tian Han," p. 30.
156. Tian, "Song *Guan Hanqing*." Another poem on the same occasion has been recently published. See Tian, "San kan," in the collation by Li Zhiyan and Qu Xiwen mentioned in n. 151, p. 53. It is dated June 1959.

to history as well as the actual anti-imperialist struggle. The end of my *huaju* (spoken drama) will also be changed. To let them fly off together as two butterflies seems to have too much of a romantic coloring." Early in May 1960, Tian Han made this change. He remained ambivalent, however, and left it to the discretion of directors whether to have an optimistic or a tragic ending.[157]

All of these statements are made in strict *ketman* style. Zhou Enlai had spoken of both the international and the domestic scene in his proposal. Tian Han spoke only of the "anti-imperialist" struggle. It seems to be a reference to the Taiwan Straits crisis of 1959. The hopes for a rapid unification between the Mainland and Taiwan had faded, and both parties were bombing each other. It is a remote possibility that the separation of the lovers was meant to refer to this situation.

Within the play, Horikhoson seemed to be the very person resonating with Zhou Enlai. Now the real-life protagonist rearranges his likeness on stage. He does so by direct interference, sure that the word will get around. Zhou does not propose to depict Horikhoson in brighter colors but argues that it was impossible that Guan and Zhu would be permitted to go in exile together. Even Horikhoson's leeway is not that wide. He has to stay in power for the common good, and has to separate the lovers as long as he can keep them alive. Was Zhou Enlai using this complicated maneuver to indicate publicly how little leeway of action he enjoyed? And did Tian Han understand the message that even in his very ambivalent ending, he had been "too romantic?" The Canton Opera version was made into a film for national distribution, and was thus codified as the official text.[158]

In the rewritten ending, Horikhoson's flattering statements about Guan Hanqing's ongoing role as the head of the capital's literary circles have vanished. Now Zhu Lianxiu writes to Bo Yan's mother asking her to help them to be exiled together. She refuses. Zhu has read her letter of refusal, but she does not tell Guan its contents. Rather, she takes leave of him with a very moving song, "The Intoxicating East Wind." In late

---

157. Li Zhiyan, "Tian Han," p. 31. In Tian's preface to the third version, dated May 28, 1960, he deals with these different endings, saying that both have their strong points. The third edition, however, has the tragic end, as has the English version published in 1961 by the Foreign Languages Press.

158. This version was published as *Guan Hanqing*, in *Yueju congkan*, adapted by the Art Office of the Guangdong Yueju Institute and the Guangzhou Branch of the Chinese Dramatists' Association by Guangzhou wenhua Press in 1959.

1961 when many of the new historical dramas were staged in Beijing, *Guan Hanqing* also reappeared. Tian Han's romantic prediction of events had indeed been wrong. The "unjust verdicts" were not reversed; the land was not returned. Instead, the People's Communes had been formed, and a new campaign against "right opportunism" had added new victims to the old ones. But in one respect, he had been all too far-sighted. History provided a new and powerful resonating board for the play. When Dou E sings just before her execution, "I am truly dying an unjust death. When I am gone, this district shall suffer a drought for three consecutive years," she was speaking now to an audience that had been through three consecutive years of disasters both natural and social. There was famine in the country; swollen bellies were a common sight. The dark words of a play seven hundred years old must have struck a responsive cord. In the historical plays written by Tian Han and others after *Guan Hanqing*, what was a subtheme in the latter, the seizing of land, comes to the fore as a compounding cause, together with injustice, for a social cataclysm.

In 1963, *Guan Hanqing* was restaged as a *huaju* in the new tragic version. Tian Han is reliably quoted as having said to Jiao Juyin during the Guangzhou meeting in 1962 that *Guan Hanqing* should be staged to interact with the other historical plays like *Hai Rui baguan*, *Li Huiniang*, and *Xie Xaohuan*.[159] Jiao in fact was the director of a new staging of the play in August 1963 in the Beijing Renmin Yishu Juyuan.[160] Li Zhiyan, Tian's secretary, wrote a review (under the pseudonym Li Yan) attempting to defend the play against charges that were in the air already. He stated that it had been written shortly "after the Anti-Rightist struggle," a statement that implied that it had been a part of it.[161] For the performance, reference was made to a "directive" from Zhou Enlai to "do it well," evidently a casual remark raised to a directive to secure the Premier's protection for the performance. The direct link between Zhou Enlai and *Guan Hanqing* prevented the play from being mentioned in the increasingly vituperative attacks against Tian Han that followed Kang Sheng's speech in mid-1964. The focus was on Tian's *Xie Yaohuan*, and in this context much of Tian Han's earlier work was attacked. In the early phase of the Cultural Revolution, only unofficial Red Guard papers included *Guan Hanqing* in their

159. Zhongguo juxie geming zaofantuan, "Chedi chanchu."
160. Li Zhiyan, "Tian Han," p. 31.
161. Li Yan, "Xuexi *Guan Hanqing*," p. 61.

criticism, probably with the intention of getting at Zhou Enlai. The authors of the "Revolutionary Rebel Group of the Chinese Dramatists Association" who wrote in the *Xiju zhanbao* (Drama Battle News) in June 1967 had a field day with *Guan Hanqing*, to be sure.[162] They counted no less than ten times in *Guan Hanqing* in which Tian Han had repeated the phrase, "the officials have no heart for the correct law, so the hundred families, though having mouths, are hard put to speak out." The play emphasized three concepts, they said, *yuan* (unjust verdict), *hen* (hatred), and *fan* (rebellion). The first referred to the feeling of the bourgeois rightists who felt wronged by the Anti-Rightist campaign, the second to their hatred "for the proletariat," and the third to their attempt at counter-revolution. It is remarkable that they did not miss any of the hints that identified Ahmad with what emerged then as the Cultural Revolution Group under Kang Sheng's guidance, and bluntly identified the attacks on Ahmad's policies as an attack on the "dictatorship of the proletariat." They read the political assassination of Ahmad, which eliminated his entire faction from power, as advocacy of counterrevolution. They quoted many statements by Tian Han and others about the meaning of *Guan Hanqing* that have been adduced above, and they described the play quite accurately as the harbinger of a new set of tactics that was dictated by the tight situation of the Anti-Rightist campaign. They admitted the popularity of the play by saying that "no small number among the masses were deceived by the play," and they judged it to be "anti-Party" and "anti-socialist."

As insiders in the Chinese Dramatists Association, the authors knew that Zhou Enlai had intervened to change the ending of *Guan Hanqing*. By explicitly including this change among their other charges, they indirectly jabbed at Zhou Enlai, who had come out for "walking on two legs" with regard to the historical-versus-contemporary-theme controversy. Their attacks are not really wanton slander; they are based on a careful reading of the play and some background material, with their strong language (charges of "counterrevolution," etc.) a reply in kind to Tian Han's ("let them be skinned alive," etc.). Their charges are wrong in one essential aspect, however. Tian Han attacked a faction within the Party, and was mildly critical of the Chairman for choosing an Ahmad as his favorite, but he never opposed Mongol rule as such.

For all his criticisms, Tian stayed within the realm of accepted

162. Zhongguo juxie geming zaofantuan, "Chedi chanchu." *Guan Hanqing* is also listed as an anti-Party poisonous weed in "Wenyijie," p. 3, col. 3.

polemics against bureaucratic tyrants, although the violence of both his language and many elements of the plot, and the fact that he did not glorify the "correct" faction, must have considerably weakened his support from this side.

In March 1971, just before the demise of Lin Biao, and three years after Tian Han had died in prison, *Guan Hanqing* was not only mentioned, but finally attacked in the official press. A full-page article appeared in the *Renmin ribao*, entitled "On the Counterrevolutionary Tactics of Tian Han—Tian Han's Anti-Party Crimes by Means of New Historical Dramas Seen from His *Guan Hanqing*."[163] The article repeats the arguments already outlined. It quotes Vice-Chairman Lin Biao as an authority on the importance of such literary battles: "The barrel of the pen and the barrel of the gun—the seizure of political power relies on these two barrels." *Guan Hanqing* had made the same point and also discussed the transformation of the pen into the sword. The article ends by emphasizing the necessity of an "all-out dictatorship over the bourgeoisie in the superstructure, including all realms of culture." These words are set in bold type, as they are a quote from Mao Zedong. Tian Han had indeed been too romantic in his assessment that in the "new society" Dou E's fate would not have to be reenacted verbatim by Guan Hanqing and Zhu Lianxiu. He died for this and his later historical plays, and anticipated his own death in the fate of Xie Yaohuan, as we shall see. It would be another decade after his death before the faction that he had (tactically) supported came to power, reversing the "unjust verdict" against him and the "bourgeois rightists," and against *Guan Hanqing* and *Dou E yuan*, and proceeding to put his critics on trial.

CONCLUSION

The relationship of *Guan Hanqing* to the Hundred Flowers texts as well as to the later historical drama is treated in another chapter of this book. The conclusions suggested here refer only to the analysis of the play itself.

a. *Guan Hanqing* draws on elements in the Western *huaju*, spoken drama, tradition that resonate with the high pitch and high degree of

163. *Guan Hanqing* is already mentioned as a poisonous weed in "Chedi qingsuan Tian Han de fandang cuixing (Radically Expose the Anti-Party Crimes of Tian Han)," in *Guangming ribao*, Dec. 6, 1966, col. a. But there seem to be no long, detailed diatribes. The 1971 article is Xin Wentong, "Ping Tian Han."

typification and exaggeration of the Chinese opera, most directly probably Schiller's historical dramas. Tian Han had a clear precedent in Guo
Moruo's *Qu Yuan*. This genre allowed for an ambivalence in his text;
were the harsh language and the extremes of hatred and passion part of
the genre, or were they unmediated expression of political sentiment?
The choice of this genre was certainly motivated by a feeling that it was
most appropriate to render the actual political sentiments about the
situation in 1958, but it also operated a dynamic of its own, "producing" characters, actions, and words "in style."

b. *Guan Hanqing* serves a double function. As a play about the writing of another play, it provides a lesson in the art of reading innuendo
drama. As an innuendo drama about the playwright's role and duty in
times of the national crisis of 1958, it invites the spectator to apply to
this very play, *Guan Hanqing*, the methodological devices sketched
through its characters and plot.

c. *Guan Hanqing* presents the ruling tribe as a self-perpetuating
minority with two factions in the center. The villains are in power due
to the favors shown by the Chairman to the chief villain, who is ideologically motivated and responsible both for the tyranny of the courts
and for the seizing of lands from the peasants. The rule of this tribe
is presented as a given; it is nowhere suggested that it should be
abolished. Popular resentment is directed against the villain in power.
But there is no enthusiasm for the "correct" leader. The action of the
dramatic community and the people is directed against the villain.
Eventually this action engenders a change in the factional balance, and
the more correct faction is strengthened. But already the next Ahmads
are coming to the fore.

d. *Guan Hanqing* presents the "present" as plagued by a complete
disregard for the law by the faction in power. Economic problems are
kept in the background. In this situation of national crisis, the leader of
the nation's dramatic community has to take and takes the daring step
of welding public opinion into a "sword" to eliminate the villains in
power. The best virtues of the nation are embodied in the artistic
community of intellectuals. This community, as a body, speaks out for
the people.

e. *Guan Hanqing* "speaks out for the people" and sets out to establish a public mind as coherent and strong as the Liangshanbo rebels.
The strategy of getting as many public performances of *Guan Hanqing*
as possible was no vain seeking for glory. Theater is a collective
medium. It gives the public a chance to voice its feelings anonymously

in the face of its rulers, who, as in *Guan Hanqing* itself, have remained eager theatergoers. The collective experience and reaction furthermore could enhance the feeling of solidarity and strength that the play itself intended to promote.[164] The heroes presented on stage as well as the actions by members of the public, as a matter of "education," set up models of behavior so that "everyone would dare to strike back." The guiding light remains the intellectual. In this sense, the purpose is that of political propaganda.

    f. The play is divided into a realistic part and a romantic part, replicating the heroine Dou E's real life and her ghost existence. The events in *Guan Hanqing* after the staging of *Dou E yuan* are Tian Han's reflections about the possible fate of his play and himself, as well as instructions to the public as to proper action.

    g. In the scenes of *Guan Hanqing* that depict the dramatic community, interference by *waihang* leaders from the center in the political and artistic creative process is rejected as a part of Ahmad's activities. The dramatic community operates well as a self-determining unit of *neihang* professionals of the dramatic trade. "Art is to serve politics," Tian Han stated in the preface to his second edition of *Guan Hanqing*. The dramatic community claims freedom from *waihang* interference not in order to pursue art for art's sake but to fulfill its social responsibility to speak out politically against abuses by the very people who control the center.

    h. In terms of values, criticisms, and demands, *Guan Hanqing* continued the Hundred Flowers tradition. As a historical drama, however, it reacted to the political climate of the Anti-Rightist campaign by attacking indirectly. At the same time it greatly heightened the pitch of the conflict and the emotions and actions accompanying the conflict on both sides.

    i. *Guan Hanqing* is part of a rich and growing body of literary texts on writing, its role, and its fate in socialist states as written by prominent authors in these very states. *Guan Hanqing* shares with these texts a

---

164. This collective aspect of the theater experience has always been stressed in PRC course materials on drama; see Beijing shifan daxue wenyi lilun zu, ed., *Wenxue lilun xuexi cankao ziliao* (1956), pp. 801ff. The excerpts there from the work of B. Chekhova seem to be the source for Zhou Enlai's statements in 1961 on the same matter; see Zhou Enlai, *Guanyu wenyi gongzuo de sanci jianghua*, pp. 32ff. Zhou's remarks in turn have been incorporated into the new course materials in Beijing daxue zhongwenxi lilun jiaoyanshi, ed., *Wenxue lilun xuexi ziliao* (1980), vol. 2, pp. 136ff.

critical attitude toward the author's earlier propagandistic writing, a high assessment of the writer's social role in these states, an emphasis on the writer's unique social mobility as a source for his rich knowledge of society, and a need to explain to both government and public the writer's basic commitment. Guan Hanqing throws in his lot for *Dou E yuan*, and this pathetic stance prevents him from modestly reflecting on human weaknesses such as those displayed by Tian Han in attacking Wu Zuguang. In *Guan Hanqing*, as in Guo Moruo's *Qu Yuan*, there is a complete absence of self-irony, which becomes all the more evident when contrasted with the attitude of the text from another socialist country whose method most closely resembles that applied in *Guan Hanqing*, Stefan Heym's *King David Report*. In the latter, the authorial voice lives with and articulates its own weakness.

j. *Guan Hanqing* interacts with real life in a most intriguing and often tragic manner. The real-life counterpart of Horikhoson talked back, and wanted darker colors. The three years of natural disaster threatened by Dou E indeed came. Kang Sheng obliged to do what Ahmad had done, and jailed Tian Han. History, it seems, was eager to add its own interpretation to Tian Han's. In the play, the levels of past, present, and future become blurred as much as the differences between the stage and life itself.

Tian Han's Peking Opera
Xie Yaohuan (1961)

Tian Han's *Xie Yaohuan*[1] is one of three historical plays the criticism of which set the stage for the Cultural Revolution, the other two being Wu Han's *Hai Rui baguan* (Hai Rui Dismissed from Office)[2] and Meng Chao's *Li Huiniang*.[3] All three were published and staged in 1961. Among Western scholars, considerable attention has been given to Wu Han's play,[4] much less to Tian Han's, and very little to Meng Chao's. Even in the case of *Hai Rui baguan*, however, scholars have been mainly interested in the immediate political implications and repercussions of the play in terms of the politics of the center. Although translations of *Hai Rui baguan* have been published, most scholars have chiefly

Research for this chapter was conducted in the context of my work as a research linguist at the Center for Chinese Studies, University of California, Berkeley. I am exceedingly grateful to the Center for its active and ongoing support. My thanks also go to the library of the Center, the East Asiatic Library at Berkeley, the Hoover Collection in Stanford University, the Staatsbibliothek Stiftung Preussischer Kulturbesitz in Berlin, and the library of the Harvard-Yenching Institute at Harvard University.

1. Tian, *Xie Yaohuan, Juben* ed. There is an additional scene in Tian, "Tian Han tongzhi laihan," pp. 94f. A slightly revised version including the additional scene appeared as a separate volume in 1963: Tian, *Xie Yaohuan* (Xi'an: Dongfang wenyi Publ., 1963), from which the edition in vol. 10 of *Tian Han wenji* (Beijing: Zhongguo xiju Publ., 1983) is taken.

Merle Goldman referred briefly to the play in her stimulating article "Party Policies," pp. 293ff. The most detailed analysis I have found is in a paper by Elizabeth Jeannette M. T. Bernard entitled "T'ien Han's 'Reactionary Works': 1956–1962." Ms. Bernard has used much of the material in the polemical arti-

analyzed not this drama but other texts Wu Han wrote on Hai Rui. Thus the rich potential of this drama, with its dense texture and its layers of silent or half-mute text, has hardly been tapped. It is my hypothesis, first, that the study of the texts of the historical dramas themselves might yield the best results, and second, that these dramas go far beyond a simple criticism of the Chairman, of the dismissal of Peng Dehuai, and of Great Leap policies.

I will test this hypothesis with *Xie Yaohuan*, for reasons outlined in the Introduction. For this purpose I must reconstruct the horizon of perception and expectation within which the play appeared. I will follow the leads to the more esoteric levels of the text. In addition, I will compare the play to the absent and unspoken texts of the demands on literature made by various segments of the political class at the time.

To facilitate the analysis proper, I will first give a short, factual sketch of the different parameters within which the play is situated.

THE NETWORK

THE NEW HISTORICAL PLAY

Xie Yaohuan appeared amid a wave of new historical plays. Tian Han himself had greatly contributed to this fashion through his *Guan Han-*

---

cles against *Xie Yaohuan* written in 1966 and has identified many of the direct allusions to contemporary events. This study has drawn many suggestions from her work. Of great use has been the two-volume set of materials on Tian Han edited by Shanghai xijuxueyuan xijuwenxuexi, *Tian Han zhuanji*, published in 1980. It contains a very useful bibliography not only of Tian's works but also of articles dealing with his work, including criticisms in official papers immediately prior to and during the Cultural Revolution. A selection of such works and articles is reprinted there. Sadly, the bibliography does not include the articles dealing with Tian Han written in the so-called Red Guard papers, which contain a wealth of important information.

2. Wu Han, *Hai Rui baguan.*

3. Meng Chao, *Li Huiniang.* The three are treated together in many articles in 1966; see Liu Housheng, "Fandang fanshehuizhuyi gongtongti, *Li Huiniang, Hai Rui baguan, Xie Yaohuan* zonglun," in *Xijubao* 1966.3, which is translated as "Co-workers against the Party and Socialism—a General Discussion of *Li Hui-niang, Hai Jui Relieved of His Office,* and *Hsieh Yao-huan,*" in SCMM no. 528, June 13, 1966, pp. 25ff.

4. See the bibliography in Fisher, "'The Play's the Thing,'" and the treatment in MacFarquhar, *Origins*, vol. 2, pp. 207ff.

qing in 1958,[5] which was quickly followed by Guo Moruo's *Cai Wenji*.[6] In early 1959, the new historical play received a boost. After seeing a rewritten traditional *xiangju* opera, *Shengsi pai* (Life and Death Tablets), in which the "southern Judge Bao" (i.e., Hai Rui) intervenes courageously to save a young woman from being wrongly condemned to death upon the instigation of a local representative of the chief villain at court, Mao Zedong was quoted to have said in substance: "One should not emulate the imperial concubines [in one's speech and deeds], but learn from the indomitable 'spirit of Hai Rui.'" A spate of articles, essays, and historical plays dealing with such figures as Hai Rui, the Tang minister Wei Zheng, and the Warring States loyal remonstrator Wu Zixu were thus written under direct guidance of the top cultural leadership in 1959 through 1963. The factional divide was apparent in these works, too, with both factions making ample use of the historical play.[7]

These works took a variety of forms. Some were entirely new texts, such as *Hai Rui shangshu*,[8] *Hai Rui baguan*, and Guo Moruo's *Wu Zetian*.[9] Others took the form of adaptations from earlier texts—for instance, *Xie Yaohuan*, *Li Huiniang*, and *Danjian pian*[10]—the changes, however, being so substantial that it is sound policy to treat them as new texts. Although set in one or the other of the traditional opera forms, they were often also adapted to the other styles by local companies.

The use of the historical play for the purposes of remonstrance is no novelty. The Peking opera traditionally used historical themes with a more or less direct bearing on contemporary affairs. Even the spoken drama, the *huaju*, the hallmark of the "modern," and often leftist, dramatists of the twenties and thirties, used historical themes when political or literary issues called for doing so. Tian Han, although committed to the promotion of the *huaju*, wrote operas with historical themes be-

    5. Tian, *Guan Hanqing, Juben* ed. For a detailed study see the first chapter of this book.

    6. Guo Moruo, *Cai Wenji*.

    7. For details see chapter 4 of this book.

    8. Shanghai jingjuyuan, with Xu Siyan holding the pen, *Hai Rui shangshu*. The writing was supervised by and the play written for the opera star Zhou Xinfang.

    9. Guo Moruo, *Wu Zetian*, *Renmin wenxue* ed.

    10. Cao Yu, Mei Qian, Yu Shizhi, with Cao Yu holding the pen, *Danjian pian*.

fore 1949. As we saw in chapter 1, he resumed this tradition with *Guan Hanqing*, a *huaju*, which had its eventual success in the form of a Cantonese opera.[11] Since Yan'an days, the Communists had promoted the writing of "new" historical plays to promote their cause. The new historical play as well as the rewritten traditional historical play had a modest place on the stage during the fifties. The rewritten version of *Qin Xianglian*, which took the newly risen Communist cadres to task, many of whom strove to exchange their wartime women for young women students more compatible with their new status, was one of these. Other rewritten plays chastised bureaucratism or the contempt of the military men, the *wu*, for the better educated specialists, the *wen*.[12] Within the Communist movement, the historical play thus had clear connotations of dealing with the present on a historical screen. This "present" could be either the social situation of the time or the power struggles in the political center, with direct references to specific leaders (as in Guo Moruo's *Qu Yuan*).[13]

The relative status of the historical play in the field of literature had radically changed by 1959. "Realistic" prose, in vogue during the Hundred Flowers period, had spent its force, with most of the important writers silenced or exiled to labor camps. The new forms that occupied center stage—the historical play, the historical essay, and the *zawen*—all used esoteric forms of communication with a much greater variety and richer texture of meaning. The importance attached to these texts can be gleaned from the inordinate attention given by Mao Zedong and his circle in 1963 and 1964 to the Shanghai and Beijing model performance festivals, which were designed to promote plays on contemporary themes about contemporary heroes. Jiang Qing's rise to power was brought about by her taking into her own hands the reform of the Peking opera, the leading genre.

As a historical play, *Xie Yaohuan* thus was entering a well-defined and critical field, one in which certain coding techniques were as much the custom as routines in their deciphering. Tian Han himself had written the instruction handbook for this type of text in his *Guan Hanqing*.

11. The *huaju* version was changed to a *yueju* (Canton opera) jointly by Guangdong yuejuyuan yishuzhi and Zhongguo xijujia xiehui, Guangzhou division, in the series *Yueju congkan* in 1959.

12. See Zhao Cong, *Zhongguo dalu de xiqu gaige, 1942–1967*, pp. 66ff., 101ff., 129ff., 136ff.

13. Guo Moruo, *Qu Yuan*. For more details about this play, see my "The Chinese Writer."

Given the prominence of the historical play at a time of intense in-fighting among party leaders, it is not surprising that many leaders tried to steer the plays and authors to their purpose. It will be recalled from chapter 1 how Zhou Enlai changed the end of Tian Han's *Guan Han-qing* into a tragedy;[14] a year later, Zhou and He Long had Tian rewrite the entire *Wencheng gongzhu* (Princess Wencheng), which dealt with Sino-Tibetan relations during the Tang, a touchy theme in view of the contemporary Tibetan uprising.[15] Peng Zhen personally intervened to have *Hai Rui baguan* published rapidly and nationally. Kang Sheng intervened in the choice of what dress Li Huiniang was to wear. In 1964 this Soviet-trained head of the Secret Service and later the "adviser" to the Cultural Revolution Group, characterized *Xie Yaohuan* as a "anti-party, anti-socialist poisonous weed." Sources from the Cultural Revolution as well as personal memoirs published since 1979 have revealed the extent of this top-level political interference. In a recent article, the young writer Zeng Liping described such government inter-ference as a common phenomenon in Communist China. Writing in the Beijing publication *Xiju yishu* in 1981, he said: "Much of the creative work in historical drama since the founding of the People's Republic follows the directives of some leader or bases itself on the requirements of the policies of a given moment or short-term political purposes. It treats history as a dough that can be kneaded into any form and wan-tonly fabricates coincidences. The result is historical dramas in which real historical persons appear in made-up events, in order to come up with footnotes for today's politics or a policy just enacted, to prove [the rectitude of] the present on the basis of the past, or to jubilate about the present with the help of the past."[16] Zeng apparently wanted to restrict his remarks to writers such as Guo Moruo, with his painful paeans to Mao in various historical guises, but the same case can be made for most other authors, including those with assessments quite different from those of Guo.

14. See Li Zhiyan, "Tian Han." Li, who was Tian's private secretary at the time, gives a day-by-day account of the writing and rewriting of *Guan Hanqing* on p. 30 of the reprint ed.

15. Tian, *Wencheng gongzhu*. For Zhou Enlai's role, see Dai Ping, "Han Zang ruchao kan jiangpa"; and He Yantai and Li Dasan, *Tian Han pingzhuan*, p. 207.

16. Zeng Liping, "Ping lishiju chuangzuo zhong de fanlishizhuyi qing-xiang," pp. 67f.

THE SILENT DIALOGUE

Early Cultural Revolution–period critics like Liu Housheng and He Qifang have convincingly demonstrated the many similarities in structure of what were termed the three "most poisonous" plays.[17] These range from similarities in plot structure to the character of the hero or heroine, from the repetition of slogans to the fact that all three authors found it necessary to write a preface, adding yet another layer of meaning to the enterprise. In each case, I would hypothesize, the play engages in a dialogue with the other plays of the time, a dialogue that heightens the profile of some otherwise seemingly innocuous features. What these early Cultural Revolution critics failed to point out, however, is that there is also a dialogue with the plays coming from the opposing faction—in Tian Han's case, from Guo Moruo. This dialogue had been going on for quite some time. The harshly critical messages of Tian Han's *Guan Hanqing* were answered some months later by Guo Moruo's *Cai Wenji*. Its plot centers on a poetess of the same name who marries a Hun and years later is bought back from the Huns by the Wei emperor Cao Cao (A.D. 155–220). Cai Wenji has heard rumors about Cao's recklessness and crafty ways.[18] However, it turns out that he is a sincere adherent of the mass line, life is gorgeous after his taking the throne in Wei, and she ends up singing his praises.[19] In Guo Moruo's play, Cai Wenji returns home to Central China, leaving her husband and children. In his effort to deal with his own return from Japan in 1937 to join in Mao's enterprise, Guo ended up writing a chauvinist plot, because the Huns, in contemporary parlance, were "national minorities," and therefore life among them would be quite acceptable for an educated Chinese woman.[20] Tian Han's reply to this play came several months later in the form of his *Princess Wencheng*. His Tang princess is married off to a Tibetan (for the grand purpose of cementing the eternal friendship between the Han and the Tibetans in the year 1959). In a pointed departure from Guo's plot, Tian has the princess decide, from

---

17. Liu Housheng (n. 3 above); He Qifang, "Ping *Xie Yaohuan*," pp. 18ff.; Yun, "Tian Han de *Xie Yaohuan*."

18. Guo Moruo, *Cai Wenji*, p. 16.

19. Ibid., pp. 54ff.

20. In 1980, articles by minority members appeared that were bitterly critical of Guo's chauvinism in this play. See "Guanyu lishiju *Cai Wenji* de taolun," pp. 84ff.

the very beginning, to stay in Lhasa and never look back. The same type of silent dialogue thus was going on even before the appearance of *Xie Yaohuan*.

THE WU ZETIAN THEME

Xie Yaohuan is a play on the theme of Wu Zetian. Known in the West as the Empress Wu, Wu Zetian (625–705) controlled China's fortunes for over forty years at a time when the power and prestige of the Middle Kingdom were at their height. Ruthlessly eliminating her potential rivals, the empress eventually replaced the Tang with her own dynasty, the Zhou, and the ruling Li family with her own, the Wu. The very idea of a woman occupying the emperor's throne infuriated Chinese historians of a later age, when the position of women greatly deteriorated, to such a degree that the Zhou dynasty, and Wu Zetian's rule of it, was expunged from the list of accepted dynasties. Occasionally, however, historians would be liberal enough to admit Wu Zetian's intellectual and political acumen.[21]

The traditional opera had reviled Wu Zetian as a "crowing hen," decrying her persecution even of her own children and relatives and alluding to her sexual debauchery. In the twentieth century, however, this sharp-witted, ruthless, and beautiful woman on the dragon throne presented an ideal subject to aspiring dramatic authors from the left; at a time when women's emancipation was the order of the day, the historical dimensions of women's roles in China could be explored in the fate of Wu Zetian. Her challenge to male domination could be projected on the screen of the present; at the same time, traditional assumptions of the public and the scholarly world about women in general and about Wu in particular could be challenged on the stage.

In 1939, the dramatist Song Zhidi, who some years later was to write the first directly Communist-inspired historical drama in Yan'an,[22] wrote his *Wu Zetian*.[23] Song's pioneering play contains superb scenes,

---

21. Guo Moruo was elated to hear of the discovery of a local Five-Dynasty cult devoted to her near her home village in Sichuan. See Guo Moruo, "Wo zenyang xie *Wu Zetian*?" p. 115.

22. Song Zhidi and Jin Ren, *Jiujian yi*; cf. Zhao Cong (n. 12 above), p. 67. There is a biographical note on Song in Li Liming, *Zhongguo xiandai liubai zuojia xiaozhuan, sub nomine*; and in Eberstein, *Das Chinesische Theater*, p. 113, n. 50.

23. Song Zhidi, *Wu Zetian*, pp. 151ff.

each of which alone would surpass later efforts to deal with the same subject. But, though the play created a storm at the time, it has not received the scholarly attention it deserves. Oscar Wilde's *Salomé* set the tone for Song's exploration of Wu Zetian, both in its scenic management and in its characterization.[24] Half a dozen translations of Wilde's play had already appeared in Chinese, the best known by none other than Tian Han himself (1921).[25] Wilde's technique of introducing his heroine Salomé through conversations between secondary characters is used by Song in nearly every act. Like *Salomé*, *Wu Zetian* does not focus on action and plot but explores the underlying theme of the female situation in the male political world. In Song's play, Wu the "seductress" takes vengeance on men, who are portrayed as weak and fragile, in the way that women would normally be portrayed. She has her lovers' faces powdered and painted; one of them is even ordered to stand facing the wall (*mianbi*) while she walks off to her inner chambers with another. When criticized for her behavior, she laughingly replies that no one finds fault with emperors for assembling thousands of concubines. She is adamant toward other women. As an educational exercise, she takes the prospective husband of her woman friend and attendant as a lover, reducing him to ridicule as a powdered, drunken braggart in a theatrical general's uniform. Fighting to survive at the top, she mercilessly kills the empress, her daughter-in-law, and the emperor's favorite. In the end, her son and her last (and strongest-willed) lover turn against her and plot to put a man on the throne. Now "alone"—although supported by the women, even by the ghost of empress Wang, whom she killed—she collapses upon learning that her minister and lover have gone to do homage to the dauphin. The play, Song said, does "not set out to reverse the verdict on Wu Zetian."[26]

Wilde's Salomé too was very much a woman in the world of politics. Jokanaan the prophet reviles Salomé's mother for the latter's loose conduct but not her stepfather Herod for his fratricide.

Using her seductive charms, Salomé takes revenge on both Herod and Jokanaan. And when Jokanaan's head has been severed, and his mouth silenced, she kisses him. Her Chinese counterpart is modeled on the same pattern. The play's ending and much of its content were

24. Tian, *Shalemei*.
25. This argument is justly made by Guo Moruo, "Wo zenyang xie *Wu Zetian?*" p. 110.
26. Song Zhidi, preface to *Wu Zetian*, p. 150.

a disturbing provocation to Song Zhidi's friends from the left, who, quickly realizing the dramatic substance of the subject, proceeded to defuse its unorthodox elements.

Wu Feng, an associate of Tian Han, seems to have done the first rewriting; I have not seen this text. Tian Han then rewrote Wu Feng's version in Guilin in 1944.[27] At the same time, Tian also wrote *Baishe* (White Snake), whose theme is the battle between a woman's genuine feelings and the dead, old forms, represented in the play by a man with the telling name of Fa Hai (Ocean of Laws). Tian Han's *Wu Zetian* was never finished, although the first part alone runs to well over a hundred pages. It was staged in Shanghai in 1948 as a *pingju* opera. Tian Han tried to plant some seeds in what he described as the *juben huang*, the "desert of [new] drama scripts" at the time. Although Tian's *Wu Zetian* still sports feminist slogans ("If I were emperor, I would take vengeance on the men, I would make men into my 'three palace [gentlemen],' 'six court [gents],' 'nine [male] concubines,' and 'eight beauties.' After my death I would have them locked up in a monastery and ask them to remain chaste!"),[28] the exploration of the specifically female response to the political world *à la Salomé* has been replaced by a strongly didactic description of the dynamics of political action; the fact that Wu is a woman is only a further complicating factor. Tian retains the loose scenic sequence of Song but with the theme of emancipation loses the logic of this arrangement, and successfully eliminates all dramatic scenes on the way.

Tian's play reverses the verdict on Wu Zetian as a politican, though not on her as a woman. She is presented as a political reformer. Even though she spies, and persecutes, and kills, this is the hard logic of political survival, and the victims are her opponents in the ruling class, who would do her in were she not the first to get them. The people enjoy "open avenues of talk," and a scene is added where she personally sets two citizens free who have dared to discuss her reform program in public. When the man who advocated her becoming the new empress starts to sell offices and abduct women, she charges him with "undermining the social order of the court" and dismisses him. Her defense of the interests of the common people, her persecution of the old guard of ministers who oppose her and her reforms, and her problems with corruption among her own retainers are portrayed in Tian's version and

27. This information is based on Tian Han's preface to his *Wu Zetian*, written in Jan. 1947. Tian, "*Wu Zetian* zixu," p. 435.

28. Tian, *Wu Zetian*, p. 33.

would remain standard ingredients in the Wu Zetian plays of the 1950s and 1960s. In its extant form, the play ends not with her collapse, but with her victory over minister Shangguan Yi and her own husband, who plot to depose her on the basis of charges reeking of superstition.

In his reversal of the verdict on Wu Zetian, Tian combines praise for her reform program with admiration for the hard hand with which she controls her underlings. The first scenes of the play deal with her celebrated program to break a stunning but stubborn horse sent as tribute to Emperor Taizong from Central Asia. Asking for a metal whip, spurs, and a hammer, she explains that if the first two instruments do not suffice to break the horse, the last will be used to kill it. Even a stunning horse or a highly qualified minister must bend to the reins or else be killed. This scene gives Taizong occasion to draw a political lesson: "This indeed is also the way to bring order to a land in disarray."[29] China during and after the Second World War was certainly a land in disarray (*luanguo*). Thus the "forces of progress," we are told, arc right in using all the ruthlessness of Wu Zetian both against their enemies and against the bad eggs in their own nest. Ruthlessness is legitimate as long as it serves the ultimate purpose, "the people," whose representatives are also given a chance to express their support for Wu Zetian's measures on stage. The play is much more politicized than Song Zhidi's in dealing with immediately contemporary matters, but its references to the present are general. There seems to be no evidence that it makes any direct allusion either to specific persons on the political stage or to specific acts. Tian's play is, however, the first attempt to define Wu, her supporters, and her opponents in terms of "class" and "progress" in the traditional historical-materialist sense.

In 1959, the two playwrights' different attempts to come to grips with Wu Zetian were suddenly republished, with Song's and Tian's plays appearing in their respective selected works. In June, a *yueju*, on the same theme, entitled *Zetian Huangdi* (Emperor [Wu] Zetian), by Wu Chen, Meng Yundi, and the actress Wang Wenjuan (who played the lead), was selected for the Shanghai theater festival.[30] I have been

29. Ibid., p. 12.
30. According to an article in the Shanghai newspaper *Wenhuibao* of June 5, 1959, p. 2, the play was selected to be shown. The same paper reported on June 14 that the play received an award. On the same day the paper carried Fu Junwen's article "Tan yueju *Zetian Huangdi*." Shortly thereafter, the historian Jian Bozan and Lü Zhenyu discussed the relationship between the play and historical reality. Jian Bozan and Lü Zhenyu, "Lishi de zhenshi yu yishu de zhenshi," in *Xijubao* 1959.4, pp. 18ff.

unable to locate the text, but from reviews we can reconstruct that it took material from both Song and Tian and added some new scenes. The play again presents scenes from Wu's life, showing her "democratic spirit," her imposition of reforms against the opposition of the privileged class, her victories over various and invariably male rebels, and her willingness to listen to the loyal remonstrance of Di Renjie. Her capacity to gain the devotion of the young female poet Shangguan Wan'er, even after having killed the young woman's grandfather and father for their opposing her, is also shown. In the end, however, Wu despairs. There is no one to take over from her and carry on her "revolution." With the words *"wo shule"* (I've lost) she finally hands over the throne to her dull-witted son.

It would be risky to attempt to analyze the political import of the play in detail without having the actual text. Some things can be said with a degree of confidence, however. The play took the purpose of "reversing the verdict" very seriously, omitting all elements from the historical record that might detract from this purpose. The historian Jian Bozan wrote at the time that he agreed with the representation of Wu as a positive character but felt that the play should have explicitly answered the charges made against her in the past, such as her use of spies, her killings, and her lecherous thirst for men. As for the killings, he said that she did not kill simple folk, but only members of the nobility and their spokesmen. As for her lust for men, he said that it was certainly no match for most emperors' lust for women.[31] Jian further claimed that the play had analytical weaknesses. Wu, he said, had made her most important contribution with her relentless battle against the top nobility, that is, the leading families from the preceding centuries and the newly risen nobility of the Tang. The play failed to depict this.[32] In another article, Lü Zhenyu defined Wu's "class struggle" even more narrowly, saying that she "corresponded to some interests of the peasants."[33] The power of the old nobility had weakened, and thus Wu's main opposition came from the new nobility of the Tang founding fathers. The political potential of the latter construct would become evident once the equation between Wu Zetian and Mao Zedong had been made more clearly; then it would mean that the main problem obstructing further progress lay in the "founding fathers" of the PRC.

31. Jian and Liu, "Lishi," p. 19b.
32. Ibid., p. 18a.
33. Ibid., p. 20a.

Both scholars argued at the time that the social base for Wu's purge was the support of middle and smaller landholders. Objectively spoken, Wu had thus "won," because the nobility never recovered from her onslaught. Jian said that the play's pessimistic ending was based on the residual feminist elements in the play, which he saw as an obstacle to a truthful depiction of history's essence. He felt that the play's emphasis on Wu's political reforms was thus misplaced, and that these reforms had not been introduced in their political context. Wu's policy of opening the avenues of talk (*kai yanlu*) was not a result of her devotion to democratic principles but was a political stratagem to encourage telling secrets (*gaomi*) about the doings of her political opponents. In its praise for Wu, the play had her personally judge a case in a lower *xian* court and determine that a young woman had been unjustly convicted. With a pointed reference to the present, Jian argued that the reversal of individual verdicts was of no great significance: "It is much more important to make use of the legal system in order to protect the interests of the broad masses of the people." This then marks the introduction of the theme of legality into the Wu Zetian complex.[34]

It is quite evident that the play was a reaction to discussions going on at the time. The introduction of the character Di Renjie, a stern and loyal remonstrator, for instance, was a clear reaction to the promotion of similar figures (Hai Rui, Wei Zheng) as positive historical precedents for contemporary behavior. The most important example of the "reversal of verdicts" at the time was that of Cao Cao, the founder of the Wei dynasty, whose ruthless cunning had earned him in folklore a name as low as that of Wu Zetian. Defending his own policies, Mao Zedong had praised Cao Cao in a poem shortly before, and Guo Moruo had been quick to join the ensuing movement to reverse the verdict on Cao Cao with his play *Cai Wenji* and several articles. Lü Zhenyu explicitly linked the case of Wu Zetian with that of Cao Cao in the 1959 article quoted above.[35] This now-explicit connection brought about a new interpretive dimension. Guo Moruo, by linking Cao with Mao, implied that slanders were rife about the Chairman. And, by punning his *Cai Wenji* on Mao's relationship with him as the intellectual, Guo set out to refute these slanders. This precedent would suggest that the authors of *Zetian Huangdi* were aware of this possible interpretation of their treatment of Wu Zetian and would explain the "stiffness" of the Wu Zetian charac-

34. Ibid., p. 18b.
35. Ibid., p. 20b.

ter decried by Jian Bocan, the denial by simple omission of all the "slanders" leveled against her, and the emphasis on her willingness to listen
to the remonstrance of Di Renjie. These, however, are but suggestions.
At this early stage in the development of the Wu Zetian theme, things
probably were much in flux. The two levels of argument—the
"historical-materialist" analysis of things past and the veiled treatment
of contemporary affairs through the discussion of presumable historical
precedents—had not yet been reduced to and amalgamated into tactical
cant.

A few months later, when Guo Moruo came out with his own Wu
Zetian play, this transition was complete. He finished the draft of *Wu
Zetian* in January 1960, and it was published in May of the same year.
Guo had carefully read the earlier plays; he mentions in the preface
Song Zhidi (but not Tian Han), and had taken the lessons from the
historians' criticisms of *Zetian Huangdi*. In a technique Guo had employed already in *Cai Wenji*, the "slanders" circulating about Wu Zetian are all spelled out, to be refuted one by one. Those who articulate
them, the new nobility of the "founding fathers," condemn themselves
because their perspective is only based on preserving their own privileges. The battle is on for the conversion of Shangguan Wan'er. A
poetess and thus an intellectual, she hails from one of the most prestigious founding families of the Tang. Her father and grandfather have
both been killed by Wu Zetian. She has inherited their best—literary
talent—but was born after her father's execution and has thus escaped
his bad class influence; furthermore, she is a woman and thus in terms
of literary symbolism less class distinct. All these factors combine to
make her a nice image for the old intelligentsia under the new regime.
Guo Moruo adds some grand symbolism to make her the "scale" on
which Wu's merits are to be balanced against her faults. As is to be
expected, Wu's support comes from the lower officials and the common
people, the former advancing on the basis of "merit only," the latter
having bumper harvests due to political stability. In desperation, the
founding fathers stage a rebellion, a theme introduced in *Zetian Huangdi*. Shangguan Wan'er, a familiar figure from both Tian Han's play and
Zetian Huangdi, becomes instrumental in the undoing of this band of
class enemies. True, Wu has a hard hand, but only against class enemies; with them she is implacable, even if they are her own sons. Shangguan Wan'er ends up applauding the execution of her father and grandfather by her new mistress. The message, thinly veiled, is that the main
problem confronting the progressive side—made up of the Chairman,
who unconventional ways are represented by his depiction as a

woman, the common people, and the "bourgeois" intelligentsia, with
its mandatory wavering—is the "founding families" of the new state,
who are afraid of losing their privileges because of Wu's reforms. This
struggle is a class struggle, and all methods, including an extensive
espionage network operated by Wu, are used and permitted. Danger-
ously, the "new bourgeoisie" is able to pull to its side some intellectuals
who are stupid enough to write bourgeois propaganda without noticing
that they will be the first to be eliminated by their bourgeois friends.
This fate awaits the intellectual Luo Binwang, who furthermore is of
lowly origin and is thus more easily tempted by the entreaties of the
great lords. Guo eliminates the loose assortment of "scenes from Wu
Zetian's life" of the earlier plays and shows her in a situation of acute
crisis. The crisis, however, is not that of the land: All-Under-Heaven is
happy and peaceful. Rather, it is a struggle in the political center, with
the "new nobility" trying to take power and plunge the country into a
new cataclysm of suffering and poverty for the many while granting
privileges for the few. Importantly, the economic base of great noble
families is in large landholdings, thus corresponding to the orthodox
notion. Their power is not based on their role in the state apparatus—
that is, it is not a "bureaucratic" power. Guo Moruo thus denounces, in
1960, criticisms of the Chairman as but hypocritical masks for alien
class interests; he defines the main problem as the attempt of the new
nobility to restore old ways at a time when the people are happy with
the rich results of the new ways. The play is his way of dealing with the
Lushan Plenum, which appears in the guise of the abortive revolt of Xu
Jingye.

All of Wu's actions are in the Tang emperor's name, for his sake,
and eventually supported by him. Gaozong, the Tang emperor in this
play, is a weakling who studies the *Laozi* (a text made into a new classic
by the Tang). He is carried around when he is not lolling in his bed,
which is right on stage. With the strong resonance between Wu Zetian
and Mao Zedong, this figure Gaozong becomes the general symbol of
"the Party," in whose name Mao was operating and which lamely and
reluctantly gave its consent to the Chairman's daring deeds. This interpretation is aided by the linguistic pun between *Tang* (the name of
the dynasty) and *dang* (meaning "the Party"); the same pun is common
in the *Xiyou ji* play (to be discussed in chapter 3) and the Wei Zheng
plays already referred to.[36] Guo Moruo's assessment of the Party of the

---

36. For other evidence see the analysis of Guo Moruo's poem on the Sun
Wukong play on p. 148ff. of this book.

time as a bedridden, bookish weakling is not exactly flattering. But when Wu Zetian finally has undone all the secret machinations of the founding families, who operate in unison with the crown prince, even the decrepit emperor is roused and for once dispenses a box on the ear (*erguang*) to his son.

Guo's play thus presented a challenge at a time of widespread criticism of Mao Zedong. Tian Han did not invent the resonances between Wu Zetian and the Chairman but used an established pattern to state his own views. The pattern was not only established on the mainland, but was shared by Communist and anticommunist authors. In 1957, Lin Yutang published his *Lady Wu*.[37] Basing his account on the rich lore of bizarre and often gruesome detail about her life, he depicted her expressly as the Stalin of the Tang dynasty, with the implication that her modern counterpart was now running the mainland. Communist authors have found merits in the most gruesome tyrants of former times, from Ivan the Terrible (in Eisenstein's "historical" hymn on Stalin), to Count Dracula (Vlad Tepes, whom the Ceaușescu government made into the Rumanian national hero, even making a three-hour film showing the merits of his government), to Qin Shi Huangdi in China and Frederic the Great of Prussia (in East Germany), defending on the way as "objectively necessary" the harsh measures and dismissing the rest as calumniation and fabrication. Anticommunist writers tended to identify the historical monsters with the present Communist rulers without questioning the accuracy of the historical record. Basing their research on completely different criteria from what the Communists used, Western scholars have in the last two decades published their own "reversal of verdict" on Wu Zetian, praising her efforts in institution building, her successes in the military control of neighboring lands, and the rapid increases in (registered) population due to stability and peace.[38] They were, however, certainly not implying that these successes reflected on the merits or demerits of the chairman of the Communist Party of China.

A decade or more later, interpretative disaster befell Guo's play; political changes prompted a radically different identification of the protagonists. Jiang Qing began praising Wu Zetian in the early seventies,

37. Lin Yutang, *Lady Wu*.
38. See Fitzgerald, *The Empress Wu*; Guisso, *Wu Tse-t'ien*; see also the articles by Guisso, Twitchett, and Wechsler in Twitchett, *The Cambridge History of China*; and Forte, *Political Propaganda and Ideology*.

the Chairman himself was by now bedridden, and the play was (and unjustly so) reread as a paean on Jiang Qing's control of the center in Mao's name and using "class struggle" methods. Later the PRC reprinted Lin Yutang's *Lady Wu*. A scholar from Henan sighed, writing a rather desperate defense of the play in 1982: "For a variety of reasons . . . *Wu Zetian* has become a forbidden area for literary criticism; the critics all avoid it and don't talk about it. But in fact, Jiang Qing is Jiang Qing, Wu Zetian is Wu Zetian, drama is drama, and the borders between all of them should be clearly drawn."[39]

Thus, in taking up the Wu Zetian theme, Tian Han was responding to the challenge implied in the earlier works on the same theme—especially in Guo Moruo's *Wu Zetian*—and he responded to it on the same grounds. The relevant identifiers remained intact, and he could now give his public a fine tour of multiple readings, with each word, scene, and character engaging in a silent dialogue with the other texts.

THE PRECEDENTS FOR *XIE YAOHUAN*

In his introduction to *Xie Yaohuan*, Tian Han briefly describes the precedents on which his play is based. Touring Shaanxi province in the disaster year 1960, he saw a play entitled *Nü xun'an* (The Inspectress). It dealt with the palace lady Xie Yaohuan's being sent by the Tang empress to inspect abuses of bureaucratic privilege. It was a recently rewritten version of a Qing-dynasty puppet play by Li Shisan (var. Li Fanggui) entitled *Wanfulian* (the precedents of which I will treat elsewhere). The *Nü xun'an* version seen by Tian Han is not available to me, but Tian himself and some of his critics have given some indications of the changes he wrought in it. The critics based themselves on the reasonable methodological assumption that Tian Han's changes must be considered "loaded" and then proceed to handle this load in the most wanton manner.[40] *Wanfulian* curses Wu Zetian as a ruthless

---

39. Gao Guoping, "'Fan'an hefang fufen duo,'" p. 22.
40. Tian, *Xie Yaohuan*, preface, *Juben* ed., p. 6; Yun, "Tian Han de *Xie Yaohuan*"; He Qifang, "Ping *Xie Yaohuan*," pp. 2ff.; Wen Siye, "*Xie Yaohuan* de maotouci xiang nali?" p. 2; Yin Bing, "Manhua *Xie Yaohuan*," p. 6; Gao Qili, "Cong *Nü xun'an* dao *Xie Yaohuan*, jiantan *Xie Yaohuan* juben gaibian de chengjiu," vol. 2, pp. 585ff; *Wanfulian* was internally published in *Shaanxi zhuantong jumu huipian, Huaju*, collection 1, probably around 1959. See also Wen Qing, "Cong *Nü xun'an* dao *Xie Yaohuan* de gaibian kan *Xie Yaohuan* de fandong benzhi." I have not seen this article.

tyrant, and a sex maniac to boot. In this play, Wu Zetian has killed the
father of the court lady Xie Yaohuan. Xie seeks revenge and conspires
with Di Renjie and other upright ministers to dissolve the New Zhou
dynasty that was set up by Wu Zetian and to restore the glory of the
Tang. To establish these contacts, she makes use of her appointment in
the service of the empress. A coalition comes about between Xie Yaohuan, who speaks for many whose family members have been killed by
Wu Zetian; the upright courtiers Di Renjie and Zhang Jianzhi; Sun
Tianbao, a rebel from a band at Lake Taihu; and Yuan Hua, a scholar
who refuses to serve under this empress although he has the degrees to
do so. In the end the empress is forced to resign; her son Zhongzong
becomes emperor again in 705, and the members of the coalition are
ennobled. Xie and Yuan presumably marry.

In the context of the "reversal of verdicts" on Wu Zetian, Yu Xun
and Huang Junyao from the Shaanxi Province Drama Research Institute rewrote the puppet play in 1959, renaming it *Nü xun'an*. They
placed the action in 684 during Zhongzong's first reign. Xie opposes
not Wu Zetian, but Zhongzong's wife Wei and the dissolute government over which the couple presides. Although Xie Yaohuan is not
opposed to the court in principle, she is calumniated by Wu Zetian's
nephew Wu Sansi as a rebel, and, being threatened with persecution
and death, she escapes with Yuan Hua, her lover, to join the rebel band
at Lake Taihu. The various transformations of the play all make use
of the "woman inspector in man's clothes" ploy and the dramatic
potential it offers for the love affair between Xie Yaohuan and Yuan
Hua. Both *Wanfulian* and Yu and Huang's *Nü Xun'an* end on an optimistic note: the lovers find each other.

Tian Han, who first thought rewriting would be a matter of days,
found himself in a difficult position given the sensitivity the treatment of
this topic now had. His *Xie Yaohuan* switches the time back to Wu
Zetian's Zhou dynasty, and makes Xie a supporter of Wu; it ends on a
somber note, with Xie being executed and her lover withdrawing to the
lake in bitterness, the empress's entreaties notwithstanding. The plot
structure of the play's two precedents and Tian Han's changes will give
insights into what Tian saw as the potential of the subject for his own
purposes.

TIAN HAN'S EARLIER WORK

Xie Yaohuan also has a place within Tian Han's own oeuvre, and not
only with regard to the earlier treatment of the Wu Zetian theme. Tian

belongs to the old generation of writers who spent their formative years long before leftist ideologies had any sizable effect in China. Inspired by such Western playwrights as Strindberg, Wilde, Baudelaire, Hugo von Hofmannsthal, Georg Kaiser, and Ibsen, he went on a "lonely search into the unknown"—as Constantine Tung entitles his essay on Tian's early plays.[41] Tung sees a turning point in his development around 1929, when he adapted the *Peony Pavilion*, with its happy ending, to become the "Tragedy on the Lake," which ends with the eternal separation of the lovers. "This play shows the tragic failure in search of a lost dream," writes Tung. In a conscious and perhaps desperate decision, Tian Han joined the League of Left-Wing Writers in the following year. During the next twenty-five years he ardently supported the Communist cause in his work, becoming after the founding of the PRC a high-level cultural official in charge of the Dramatists' Association, the reform of the Peking Opera, and even the Party Committee in the Dramatists' Association and the political purge of the Anti-Rightist campaign. He is seen as an associate of the literary overlord of the 1950s, Zhou Yang.

Tian Han had not, however, grown up in a socialist society. He had seen governments come and go, had seen the new state emerge, and had seen the problems it inherited and produced. He had joined the Communists in the hope and belief that they would be able to give a purpose and perspective to the country, improve the material and spiritual lot of its people, remove the shackles binding women, and give the dramatists' and actors' craft its due attention, honor, and importance. He was willing to toe the official line both in his speeches and in his literary production throughout the fifties and early sixties on key issues, writing the appropriate "Great Leap Forward" piece in 1958,[42] and the appropriate "Tibet and China are eternally one" piece at the time of the Tibetan uprising in 1959. However, his assessment of the state of the nation and of the treatment given to theater people in the PRC took a dramatic turn for the worse with his *Guan Hanqing*. In the original version it still had some light at the end: the lovers were at least sent to exile together. But the 1961 version was even more somber after the Premier's odd intervention.

With *Guan Hanqing*, Tian Han had struggled to define the social and analytical framework for the new historical drama.[43] *Xie Yaohuan*, which from the outset had a tragic ending, deftly operates within

41. Constantine Tung, "Lonely Search." See also his "T'ien Han and the Romantic Ibsen."
42. Tian, "Shisan ling shuiku changxiang qu."
43. This point is well made by Bernard, "'Reactionary Works.'"

this now-established framework. With both pieces, Tian eventually returned to the mood if not the style of his plays of the late twenties.

SOCIAL AND POLITICAL REALITY

There is an interpretive consensus in the PRC that literary texts and artistic creations are to be perceived in the immediate context of the times and circumstances in which they were written. This certainly does not imply that such works are "realistic" in the traditional meaning of the word. A political directive easily covers entire realms of reality with the veil of oblivion or gives it a surprisingly new coloring. "Reality" might enter as a mood, or through the back door as its own caricature.

During the last decade our knowledge about political developments in the center during the years 1958 through 1962 has been greatly advanced, both through the work of Roderick MacFarquhar and others and, since 1979, through the publication of much memoir material. The picture of social and economic development, however, is still rather confused. The available material on the life of the population as a whole and its segments is little more than scanty. Recently published PRC population statistics indicate that mortality increased during the Great Leap period by 30 million and fertility declined by the same number.[44] It was the greatest famine in this century. At the same time, little is known to this very day about the human tragedy and the political and social dynamics of this man-made disaster. A few things have been learned from letters sent by peasants to relatives in Southeast Asia during the time.[45] Another source is short quotes from the statements of politicians who were criticized during the Cultural Revolution for "slandering" the Great Leap Forward.[46] Further evidence comes from short stories published in recent years.[47] I suggest that the historical

44. Ashton et al., "Famine in China," p. 614. A study by the World Bank shows significantly stunted growth in children who were in their first years of life at the time, indicating widespread famine. Jamison et al., *China: The Health Sector*, pp. 29ff.

45. Richard Walker, *Hunger in China*; and id., *Letters from the Communes*.

46. A great number of such statements have been published in the Red Guard press but these were never systematically collected; others appear in Mao's talks, the Peng Dehuai dossier, and the *Gongzuo tongxun* of the Red Army.

47. Thomas Bernstein has gone further by including some interviews and recent short stories among the sources for his "Stalinism." The guarded attitude

dramas of the period, *Xie Yaohuan* included, be added to this small body of evidence.

THE TEXT

The printed text of *Xie Yaohuan* is substantially longer than the staged version, no print version of which is available. The edition in *Juben* of July/August 1961 was only minimally changed some months later through the addition of one small scene (act 7 in the book edition) and minor corrections.[48] The 1963 book edition is thus basically the same as the 1961 text. Some adaptations based on local opera forms changed the ending to a happy one.[49] The outline of the plot is as follows: People in the Jiangnan area have fled after the expropriation of their land and assemble at Lake Taihu with the intent to rebel. The time is the Zhou dynasty set up by Wu Zetian. Wu Sansi, the empress's nephew and prime minister, advocates quick military suppression of the rebellion. He is supported by Lai Junchen, a censor in charge of the secret service and prisons. In fact, the younger relatives of these two are the ones responsible for appropriating the land, bending the law, and running roughshod over the people. They are immune from persecution due to the position of their elders.

A court lady, Xie Yaohuan, proposes to eliminate the cause of the grievances by giving the land back and reestablishing the rule of law. Wu Zetian appoints her inspector (*xun'an*) for Jiangnan. She is charged with investigating the local situation and invested with the right to judge and even execute recalcitrants, including those from big families. Xie is indirectly supported by the censor Xu Yougong, who advises her to be careful.

Xie is given a new, and male, name, Zhongju, by the empress and proceeds to her assignment in male disguise, arriving at the Wu Zixu temple near Suzhou. There, she meets Yuan Xingjian whose father was an official executed by another secret service leader, Zhou Xing, on the false charge of having joined an antigovernment conspiracy. Yuan Xingjian has avenged his father by killing this official; he then changes

---

of the post–Hua Guofeng Chinese leadership with regard to the Great Leap and to the human tragedy of this time becomes evident from James Boswell's study, "A Tragedy of Good Intentions."

48. See n. 1 above.

49. Tian, preface to *Xie Yaohuan*, *Juben* ed., p. 7.

his name to Ruan Hua to evade persecution. On his way to see his friend Li Decai, the leader of the rebels at Lake Taihu, he witnesses the abduction of a peasant girl by Wu Hong, the prime minister's son, and Cai Shaobing, a more distant relative of the censor Lai. Having devoted himself to the emulation of Wu Zixu, an intrepid hero of old, Yuan intervenes against the bullies. Xie Yaohuan, still incognito, prevents the two parties from coming to blows and prompts them to bring their claims to court. Wu and Cai assume the court, now under Xie, will be at their beck and call. To them, Yuan Xingjian's intervention and his chiding their behavior is equivalent to rebelling against the government. Yuan in turn charges them with land-grabbing, setting themselves up as the law, even requesting people to give up their copper and iron from household utensils and agricultural implements to serve as raw material for a column praising the new dynasty. Xie rules that the land is to be given back and that the peasant girl is to be returned to her home. She also jails one of Wu Hong's underlings. Incensed, the two bullies overturn the judge's table and start a brawl in court. Xie thereupon has Wu Hong immediately executed, and vows to eliminate those despots, *haoqiang*.

She invites Yuan Xingjian, who protected her during the brawl, to her office, and encourages him to seek an official position, as Wu Zetian employs people solely on the basis of their talents. He refuses, however, pointing to the ongoing suppression of the people. While still in disguise, Xie, who has fallen in love with him, proposes they should become sworn brothers, dismissing the murder that he committed as justifiable vengeance. Meanwhile, a race for time is on. The big government clans, fearing the dismantling of their economic and political power, conspire to have Xie dismissed and condemned as a rebel. Xie in turn has sent a secret report stating her case to Wu Zetian. She also sends another man from the Wu clan, a local official, to Lake Taihu to encourage the people to return to their fields, which will be restored to them immediately. Once the people would have returned to their fields, she reasons, the charge that she was fostering rebellion would be without substance. Meanwhile Yuan Xingjian overhears a conversation between Xie Yaohuan (in female garb) and her woman attendant in which she expresses her love for him. Xie knows her life to be in jeopardy and wants to "give herself to the state" without personal considerations. The two marry secretly.

At court, the two vile ministers Lai Junchen and Wu Sansi conspire to have "misunderstood" an order from the empress. In their version, it orders them not to "wait until she had thought it over" but "to execute [Xie] on her behalf." The two ministers hasten south. Meanwhile Xie's emissary, back from Taihu, reports that the people are rejoicing but still hesitate to commit themselves without a written promise. Aware of the impending disaster, Xie sends the emissary and her lover back with the writ. The two ministers arrive and torture Xie right on the stage. They are unable to extract a confession, but Xie dies in the process. The empress, meanwhile, has received Xie's secret report and discovered the plot of her two ministers. In person, she hurries to Jiangnan and has censor Xu Yougong try them. Secret Service Chief Lai is executed, and Wu Sansi demoted to commoner status. In the final scene, Yuan Xing-jian, on his way to Lake Taihu, sees Xie in a dream and learns about her death. The empress sends word that he is expected in the capital to receive a reward. He refuses the reward, however, and the play ends with his warning the empress that "there will be much turmoil in the country if again she trusts vile officials and destroys the loyal and good." Yuan then joins the people at Lake Taihu.

ANALYSIS

THE TIME

Xie Yaohuan is set in Wu Zetian's Zhou dynasty, in the later years of her rule. Each time negates another. Guo Moruo's *Wu Zetian* was set in Wu's prime (around 684), during the Tang dynasty. This setting again rejects others, and other historical dramas written at the time, which used the very early years of the Tang as a screen, and held up Tang Taizong's counselor Wei Zheng as the hero in the mold of Hai Rui. In these other plays the founding fathers of the People's Republic were portrayed not as counterrevolutionaries, but on the screen of the founding fathers of the Tang, and Wei Zheng's blunt and open criticism of Taizong as well as the latter's willingness to listen to it were emphasized. Guo showed the founding fathers as already having turned into a new nobility, with Wu Zetian, the chairperson, fighting a desperate battle against their coup d'état attempts. But Wu is still shown serving the Tang dynasty, represented by the bedridden Gaozong. In allegorical form, *Sun Wukong sanda baigujing* (Sun Wukong Three Times Beats the White-Bone Demon) takes up the same theme, with Tang Seng, the muddle-headed "monk from the Tang," eventually submitting to the guid-

ance of the sharp-witted Monkey.[50] The Tang dynasty is a preferred
screen for the present, both because of the easy pun between the name
Tang and *dang* (the Party), and because of the flattering association
between the present and a time when China was at the peak of its power
and prestige. Tian Han had in fact used this screen two years before in
his *Weicheng gongzhu*, where he dealt with Chinese-Tibetan relations
in 1959 in terms of a Tang princess going to Lhasa to marry.

The time setting of *Xie Yaohuan* thus emphasizes that the proper
screen is neither the time of the camaraderie of the founding fathers nor
the time of "counterrevolutionary" activities of the founding fathers at
the peak of Wu Zetian's reign. No, we see her late in her life, and the
great achievements of the "former dynasty" (i.e., the Tang/*dang*), with
its equal distribution of land and high moral caliber of the cadres, are a
thing of the past. Wu Zetian has set up her own dynasty, the Tang/*dang*
is out, and Wu's "family" and confidants are running the country. The
original plot of *Wanfulian* had advocated the overthrow of the Zhou
and the return to Tang rule. In terms of political implications, to do so
was evidently going a bit far, but Tian selected this piece at the time
exactly because it evoked these associations. As a deleted element, the
"restore Tang rule" tendency remains visible to the knowing, especially
as the secondary props remain in place. There are, for instance, flattering references to the preceding dynasty, and a complete absence of di-
atribe against it on the part of the heroes. There seems to be no qualitative change for the heroes in *Xie Yaohuan* between the Tang and the
Zhou, but a gradual transition, which is characterized by Wu Zetian's
self-elevation to the world savior Maitreya on the one hand and an
acute and deepening social crisis on the other. Perhaps the dates give a
clue to what Tian had in mind. The action takes place in the "fortieth
year" of Wu Zetian's ascent to power. Since she became empress in
655, we are thus in the year 694 or 695. The Zhou dynasty was officially founded in September 690, four or five years preceding the time of
the action in *Xie Yaohuan*. In terms of the present, this would bring us
back to the year 1956 or 1957—indeed the time when the "transition"
to socialism was considered to have been completed and a new phase
started in economical, legal, and political terms. (The dates in *Guan
Hanqing* also point to a fundamental change in the same year.) In terms
of communication on the stage, there would be no need for Tian Han to
let Wu Zetian inform the public that it is forty years since she became

50. See my analysis referred to in n. 36 above.

empress, if not to permit the above calculation, which fits all too well into the rest. Historically, the public knew, the Zhou hinged on Wu's person. Eventually, and perhaps with her consent, the Tang/*dang* was restored.

The immediate present of the action is characterized by two facts: "for every happy family there are ten thousand in distress," and "the administration is falling apart and the social fabric is dissolving."[51] People have fled after being robbed of their land, being deprived of legal redress, and having suffered their daughters to be abducted and raped— all this by government officials. The play opens with the news that the people have now congregated around Lake Taihu. The underlying threat is that they will take up arms, as this is a traditional rebel haven. Indeed, the empress feels that it is a national crisis. She reminds herself of the Tang emperor Taizong's warning to forestall a situation where "the water that carries the boat will overturn the boat," the "water" being in the traditional metaphorical canon the "people," and the "boat" the court and government.[52] The temporal setting of Tian Han's play shares key features with that of plays like *Hai Rui shangshu* and *Hai Rui baguan*, and the contrast to Guo Moruo's play is perfect. In Guo the present is one of abundance, and the people show no support whatever for the conspiracy against Wu Zetian. In *Xie Yaohuan* the crisis has changed in quality from that of *Guan Hanqing*. In the version of 1958, the crisis was mostly political and legal; the later versions increasingly stressed the economic crisis. In *Xie Yaohuan*, the people suffer under a legal as well as economic crisis, the two aspects being invested in the two chief villains. No detailed reasons are given within the play to explain how this state of affairs came about. Wu Zetian herself volunteers the explanation that bureaucratic ossification may be the natural cause: "When times of peace last long in a state, dereliction [by officials of their duties] easily comes about."[53]

THE PROTAGONISTS: WU ZETIAN

Xie Yaohuan is a fictitious character, both in history and on the screen of the present. Not so Wu Zetian. She comes on stage under her imperial title *Jinlun shengshen huangdi*, "Golden Wheel Saint and Holy

51. Tian, *Xie Yaohuan, Juben* ed., p. 8.
52. Ibid.
53. Ibid.

Emperor." When the play was performed, this was probably communicated to the audience through the ministers shouting her title in salute.
The extravagant name is due to her being proclaimed as the incarnation
of the world savior, Buddha Maitreya.

The Golden Wheel, historically the title given one of the four world
kings in Buddhist doctrine, is an allegory to the sun. The sun has also
been the standard image for Mao Zedong since the late fifties, when he
was praised as rising as the sun in the East.[54] Zetian, Wu's personal
name means "modeling oneself after Heaven" and echoes with Equal-
to-Heaven (*Qitian*), the honorific of Monkey, Sun Wukong (see chapter
3). Wu comes on stage confused. Immediately she spells out the conflicting messages she has received from heavenly portents and secret
reports:

When I arrived in the Rising Sun Palace for a promenade,
Tens of thousands of Red Birds danced about the palace's towers,
Is it not true that when the winds are in harmony, the rains are in season, and
    the people live in peaceful abundance,
The multicolored phoenix and the auspicious unicorn turn toward the imperial
    crown?
The hundred-foot-high Heavenly Pivot has recently been completed,
Pillars of iron and plates of copper sing the praise of the Great Zhou.
[It is] only that different palace officials and commoners sent up
    many secret reports,
[Saying] that for every happy family there are ten thousand in distress.[55]

The lines are reminiscent of the opening scene of *Hai Rui shangshu*,
where the emperor is surrounded by his Taoist magicians, who are con-
cocting an immortality pill from (appropriately) red cinnabar under the
picture of Laozi, who shares with Marx the fate of having a white beard
and having written a classic. The scene is a fine satire on the slogan
"Ten Thousand Years for Mao Zedong Thought," and on the Chairman
himself. The difference is that in *Hai Rui shangshu* the Jiajing emperor

54. Mao was so often compared to the sun and described as the "deliverer"
in Maitreya fashion that critics took up that point. The *Renmin ribao* quotes
Chen Mingshu in this manner on July 15, 1957, although the motive of this
publication probably was different; cf. MacFarquhar, *Origins*, vol. 1., pp. 283
and 397, n. 63.

55. Tian, *Xie Yaohuan, Juben* ed., p. 8. The line about rains, winds, and
abundance might have sounded too cynical when the play was staged in places
where there were indeed floods and famine. The later edition changed the line to
"that compassion and virtue moved Heaven has often happened since of old, /
[then] the multicolored. . . ." Cf. the edition in *Tian Han wenji*, p. 333.

is perfectly oblivious of the state of the country, which he learns only from the fanciful heavenly favors brought in by a stream of Taoist quacks; Wu Zetian in *Xie Yaohuan* is aware of the different messages from above and from below. She reads the secret reports and believes them, but she is also convinced of Heaven's special favor toward her. In the airy, higher realm things look well: the birds that flutter around the Palace of the Rising Sun are red and numerous. In fact this had been so since the founding of the dynasty. "Formerly [when it was founded]," says Wu, "the phoenixes came to offer their homage, and congregated on the Wutong tree of the Mingtang [the place where the sacrifice to Heaven, the highest sacrifice, was performed], and just now, when I came to the palace of the Rising Sun I again saw these tens of thousands of red birds dancing around its towers. This truly should let people rejoice." But after the ministers present have proffered their congratulations, she continues with her morose reflection about the consequences of long peace on a state, the administration's limbo, and the dissolution of the social fabric, ending "my heart is much concerned about this." Conflicting news was indeed in the air at this time. In the field of ideology, the government was engaged in a lively polemic with the Soviet Union about "revisionism," and had started to proclaim itself the revolutionary center of the world. The papers reported the unending wonders of the Great Leap Forward. At the same time, Mao himself was quoting reports about refugees fleeing famine areas, about edema, and questioning the accuracy of the notoriously inflated figures transmitted to higher levels.

The empress is ignorant of the crimes committed by some of her ministers, and would oppose them if she knew about them. They are her "family" and supporters, and so they are in fact in power at the center, while Xie is but a palace lady from lowly stock. In Guo Moruo's play, the empress does the acting and talking; here, Xie Yaohuan takes over, and the empress remains passive until Xie is killed.

With his charge that despotism prevailed in Wu's later years, Tian Han took up a familiar theme. Mao himself had said in Lushan in 1959: "You say I have 'reached Stalin's later years,' am 'despotic and dictatorial,' and refuse to give you 'freedom' and 'democracy.' I am also 'vain and fond of credit' and 'biased in view and faith.'"

The empress's own ambivalence and confused mixture of family loyalty and support of progressive things are extrapolated onto the persons surrounding her. Tian Han leaves no doubt about his intentions: "Xie Yaohuan represents Wu Zetian's spirit of fighting against the

mighty families and the nobility," which is characteristic of her earlier
years, but now her own crowd, her family and her supporters, "trod
again onto the old way" and thus represent her later tendency.[56] The
proportion between the two tendencies is expressed through the power
each of them has. Xie is a palace lady suddenly made inspectress by
Wu's doing. Wu Sansi and Lai are top ministers with their own networks of power and influence. Although the empress personally dislikes
their politics in certain respects, she retains them in office for long years
while they commit crimes in her service and fawn on her.

Guo was able to retain much of the colorful image of Wu Zetian for
his panegyric on Mao. Guo's play reacted to the Hai Rui wave. There,
the emperor was the dull-witted ignoramus and was upbraided and
enlightened by the *qingguan*, the upright official. Guo "reverses the verdict" and portrays the much-calumniated Wu Zetian as the true hero.
"It is unavoidable that in reversing a verdict one should add a bit too
much rouge," he commented on criticisms of the work.[57] Tian Han
moved in the opposite direction, reversing Guo's judgment. Certainly,
Wu Zetian in *Xie Yaohuan* is a regent far superior to the Jiajing emperor
in *Hai Rui shangshu*, but she is quite different from the idol set up by
Guo Moruo. The stress of this second reversal of verdicts is visible in
the work. Wu has lost all her female charms and goals as well as her
sharp wit. Her language is reduced to political sloganeering, quite different from the often lyrical and moving language of *Guan Hanqing*. Tian
accepts the basic line that Wu and her modern counterpart had great
merits in the past and still have many. Nonetheless the country's crisis
has not been brought on by natural disasters or the like,[58] but by the
actions of those people who were the props of her power, and were
protected by her. This responsibility is mitigated only by the fact that
when she hears of the true state of affairs in the land, she comes to the

---

56. Tian, *Xie Yaohuan*, *Juben* ed., preface.

57. Guo Moruo, "Zai Kunming kan yanchu huaju *Wu Zetian*," p. 17.

58. The dispute over proportions—how much of the Great Leap disaster
was to be attributed to external causes such as the weather and the withdrawal
of the Soviet advisers, and how much to internal causes such as Party
mismanagement—is still going on today. At the time, Liu Shaoqi was reported
as saying that the human (internal) factor was 70%, the external 30%; see
Zhongguo juxie zaofantuan, "Liu Shaoqi shi zenyang baobi Tian Han de daducao *Xie Yaohuan* de." In *Xie Yaohuan*, a much more radical position is taken.
The entire disaster is caused by "human factors," i.e., the tyrants' thirst for
power.

support of Xie Yaohuan against her high ministers, much as Mao Zedong did time and again.

THE PROTAGONISTS: THE VILLAINS

Xie Yaohuan being a *pièce à thèses*, Tian Han makes no efforts to individualize his villains. The two chief villains, Prime Minister Wu Sansi and Minister Lai Junchen, thus come as flat characters representing the two most pressing scourges of the country. Minister Wu stands more for economic suppression, his clan having led the field in grabbing land from the peasants. Lai, in traditional opera fashion, is given a chance to introduce himself:

> [My] career is due to my framing others,
> [my] rise to power rests on torturing [others to give confessions].

As the person in charge of secret police and prisons, Lai has established a reign of terror. The play does not tell us why he occupies such a lofty position at Wu Zetian's court. But the opera is addressed to an audience that knows something about history and can savor the fine allusions. Tian Han portrays Wu Zetian's rise to supreme power as relying in good part on Lai's ruthless persecution of her potential and actual opponents. The character Lai seems to be a newcomer among the protagonists of the Wu Zetian plays; the secret police theme had been introduced by *Hai Rui shangshu*. Both ministers control a network in the provinces, here specifically in Jiangnan. Minister Wu's son and Censor Lai's nephew are the overlords at the local level. The interaction between the two scourges is shown first in the friendship of the ministers at the top, who share the pleasures of a singing girl from Suzhou while discussing their dark schemes, and second in their young relatives' prowling together for women. The pedestal of their power is not wealth and land, but political status and network. It is thus a bureaucratic power. Guo Moruo defined his villains as the rich landed gentry into which the founding families had turned; they were a traditional class, the power of which rested on their economic standing. Wu Zetian there became a populist revolutionary fighting the big landlords. We thus have the Tang/*dang* led by Wu/Mao battling against the new aristocracy/bourgeoisie.

In Tian Han's play, the problem is in the family itself; although the top leader has good intentions, villains are in power at the center. The same constellation prevails in *Guan Hanqing*, where the Party is depicted as a separate ethnic group, the Yuan Mongols, versus the "masses" of Han Chinese. Again there is a top leader, Khubilai Khan, who has good intentions but lacks judgment and is ill informed; thus his "favorite" Ahmad and Ahmad's underlings can tyrannize the country. Tian Han abandons the traditional "class analysis" concept, which is singularly ill adapted for socialist states; he has the villains right in the center/court, living off the absolute powers arrogated by the new dynasty and being therefore all the more dangerous and destructive.

Lai Junchen, who not only brags about his fancy instruments of torture but applies them on stage to extract a confession from Xie Yaohuan, represents a powerful indictment of the system of secret police and prisons in the PRC. Lai is not shown mistreating common mortals; instead, the long list of cases he has handled consists exclusively of officials, of "cadres." While the courts are generally serving the villains in power, Lai Junchen specializes in dealing with his enemies, who are either his competitors, like Zhou Xing, or upright cadres threatening to bring the true state of the country to the empress's attention.

From what we know of *Guan Hanqing* we may assume that here also Tian Han had one specific leader in mind, and there is some evidence that one such leader found a resemblance to himself in Lai Junchen— namely, Kang Sheng. Kang Sheng's special police system has been mentioned, and its victims typically were Communist officials.[59] He clearly belongs to the "new" dynasty set up in 1956.[60] He fawned on the Chairman,[61] attacked Peng Dehuai after the Lushan Plenum, and later served as the chief adviser of the Cultural Revolution Group around Jiang Qing. It was he who publicly defined *Xie Yaohuan* as "anti-Party, anti-socialist" in 1964 in an important but unpublished speech.[62] This

59. There is now an extensive if insufficient literature about Kang Sheng. See "Problems Concerning the Purge of K'ang Sheng," pp. 74ff.; Lu, "Ping Kang Sheng"; You Lin, "Ping Kang Sheng"; Yu Ming, "Kang Sheng yu Jiang Qing"; Fang Jing, "Dui Kang Sheng," pp. 41ff.; Zhong Kan, *Kang Sheng pingzhuan*. The last-mentioned work has been withdrawn from even internal circulation. Although it is an extensive biography, it omits references to Kang Sheng's police system and Mao's use of it, presumably because the system is still in place.

60. See his biography in Klein and Clark, *Biographic Dictionary*.

61. MacFarquhar, *Origins*, vol. 2, p. 319.

62. Kang's talk, given around or on June 23, 1964, is mentioned in the papers at the time; see "Zhou zongli jiejian jingju xiandaixi guanmo yanchu renyuan," p. 3. Kang in fact seems to have given two talks, the second one, given on July 30, being ranked only "important": see "Mao Zedong sixiang de guanghui shengli shehuizhuyi xinjingju xuangao yansheng," p. 15. There he

charge was quite probably based on the play's very negative depiction of Wu Sansi, as the Prime Minister, and Lai Junchen as Kang himself.

As the text strongly suggests real-life counterparts for the other historical figures, the question naturally arises whether Wu Sansi also has such a counterpart. Tian Han's criticism, it is true, is more general, but, given the high degree of personalization in Chinese politics, the readers and spectators at least are used to *ad personam* criticism. Wu Sansi is high up in the center, has his power base in Jiangnan, instigates the casting of the "iron pillar," promotes "land grabbing," fawns on the empress, defines all criticism in terms of "rebellion" to be suppressed by military means, and builds travel palaces for the empress. I have no evidence to suggest who was behind the building of the travel palaces for Mao, which were built during the Great Leap and criticized by Peng Dehuai at the Lushan meeting.[63] The person who comes to mind for every other of these points, however, would be Ke Qingshi. He was in the Politburo since the Fifth Plenum of the Eighth Party Congress in 1958, and thus was of the new ruling family. His power base was "Jiangnan" (lit., south of the [Yangzi] River) indeed, as he was the mayor of Shanghai. He, as Mao said, instigated the steel drive, and was among the most feverish promoters of the People's Commune movement ("land grabbing"). He fawned on the Chairman, and, though he

---

attacked *Hai Rui baguan*, *Li Huiniang*, and *Xie Yaohuan* as anti-Party and anti-socialist in a talk given to the entire body of participants. See for *Xie Yaohuan* the Red Guard source *Xiju zhanbao* mentioned in n. 58 above. Kang is quoted as having said the play "has very substantial problems" in He Yantai and Li Dasan, *Tian Han pingzhuan*, p. 195. Kang Sheng is usually referred to not by name but as "that 'theoretician' within the Party" or "that 'theoretician' who is closely linked to the 'Gang of Four.'" Under the former appellation, the article announcing the rehabilitation of *Xie Yaohuan* in 1979 quotes him as proclaiming *Xie Yaohuan* an "anti-Party, anti-socialist poisonous weed," which implied that Tian Han was to be an object of class struggle; see Li Chao, "*Xie Yaohuan* de fusu." For the references concerning the other plays, see the last chapter of this book.

63. According to "Excerpts from P'eng Te-huai's talks at the meeting of the Northern Group of the Lushan Meeting," p. 4, the marshal charged: "Many provinces have built villas for Chairman Mao. This was after all not done at Chairman Mao's bidding." Within *Xie Yaohuan*, to be sure, Wu Zetian expressly denies that the travel palaces were built by Wu Sansi on her orders; Tian, *Xie Yaohuan*, *Juben* ed., p. 28a. I don't think it necessary to conclude from this that Tian was linked to Peng Dehuai. Peng only stated what everybody had already heard about.

had supported Mao early in the Anti-Rightist movement in favoring fairly lenient treatment, even then he was already persecuting people directly.[64] Liu Binyan felt that his own persecution had been handled by Ke Qingshi.[65] In political terms, Ke was close to the group later denounced as the "Gang of Four," three of whom had risen to prominence in Shanghai. Ke also came out heavily against the historical drama in the early sixties. Half a year before the big Peking drama festival in 1964, when Shanghai had had its own festival for the support of "revolutionary" pieces, Ke had given the keynote speech. It was published in *Hongqi* once all the leadership had attended the performances of these plays in Beijing.[66] It seems that Ke and Zhang Chunqiao were both well aware of the target of attack in Tian Han's play, because at the Shanghai festival, they had attacked him, and he eventually left the festival.[67] When Jiang Qing, Kang Sheng, and others pondered who should write the article criticizing *Hai Rui baguan*, the article signalizing the actual beginning of the Cultural Revolution, they saw Ke Qingshi as one of the potential authors.[68] As for the travel palaces, I can only adduce the evidence that Mao traveled extensively with Ke during the Great Leap, and it might be that the proposal to set up accommodations for the Chairman was made by Ke at that time. Ke died in 1965, however, so he failed to become the fifth (or sixth, or seventh, or eighth) member of the group later denounced as the Gang of Four. The interpretative argument, needless to say, does not hinge on this identification.

Among the villains, there is one more intriguing force, the military. The military's function within the play is exclusively the organized repression of the populace, never the defense of the country or other aims. The villains seem to have control of the military. Xie Yaohuan and Yuan Xingjian speak only with horror of the potential use of the military against the people. It is probable that there were cases during the Great Leap when the military was called in to search for hidden grain reserves or household and farm implements; the military are known to have been widely used against the minorities at the time. The play makes an "unnecessary" detailed reference to the devastating use

64. See his treatment in MacFarquhar, *Origins*, vols. 1 and 2.
65. See my "Liu Binyan and the *texie*."
66. Ke Qingshi, "Dali fazhan he fanrong shehuizhuyi xiju, genghao di wei shehuizhuyi de jingjijichu fuwu."
67. See He Yantai and Li Dasan, *Tian Han pingzhuan*, pp. 192f.
68. See the last chapter of this book for details.

of military force against the local population in Bozhou (Shandong), Hebei, and in Zhao and Bei (Shanxi), but I do not have specific sources detailing events there for the Great Leap period.[69] In each case, the commander leading the troops is named; this fact might be of importance.

The two top villains depend in their "bureaucratic" power on ingratiating themselves with the empress and preventing her from perceiving the real state of the nation. They reinforce her self-aggrandizement and belief in her divine mission. They also dispel her uneasiness about reports of local disaster and unrest by affirming that these reports are only designed to prop up the efforts by some bastards from the Li family to restore Tang rule. The theme is familiar in this group of plays. Ahmad, in *Guan Hanqing*, is the personal favorite of Khubilai Khan, and a band of spooky ideologues crowd around the Jiaqing emperor and flatter him in the basest terms, assuring him that the sky is rosy with portents of his immortality while they quite unabashedly go about filling their pockets and suppressing the common folk. In *Hai Rui shangshu*, the Jiajing emperor's ministers debase themselves to the point of singing his praises in chorus, while the land is in shambles. Tian Han, in both *Guan Hanqing* and *Xie Yaohuan*, operates on such a high pitch of crisis-conscious seriousness that he merely states the fact of favoritism without making use of the great satirical potential of the theme.

"Bureaucratic" power would normally mean power that rests on a position within the state machinery. Tian Han, however, is not dealing with such broad, general issues as the structure of the socialist state. On both screens of history and present, power emanates to a large extent from the "chairperson," not from an anonymous institutional setup. It is characteristic of the new dynasty that its own institutions and laws are not respected.

THE PROTAGONISTS: THE HEROES

When *Xie Yaohuan* was rehabilitated and restaged in 1979 after being denounced as "counterrevolutionary" earlier, the *Renmin ribao* claimed that Tian Han had written the play in response to the Party's call to "overcome subjectivism and metaphysics" and to "learn not from the concubines of the tyrants, but from the upright and indomi-

69. Tian, *Xie Yaohuan, Juben* ed., p. 24a.

table 'spirit of Hai Rui.'"[70] The claim is justified but exaggerated. Tian
had written *Guan Hanqing* well before Mao had proposed in early
1959 to "learn from the spirit of Hai Rui." On the other hand, Wu
Zetian herself comes on stage (Khubilai Khan had not done so in *Guan
Hanqing*), is intrigued about the conflicting information, and supports
Xie Yaohuan—the embodiment of Wu Zetian's earlier and purer
aspirations (from the time of Tang-rule). Xie, like most of the Hai Ruis
on stage, remains emblematic throughout the play, bland in her purity
and commitment. In the historical play, both historical and fictitious
characters will normally appear. A traditional technique of PRC
fiction—to inform the public about the moral essence of a character by
giving, like an opera mask, a telling name—would thus be applicable
for fictitious characters only. Xie is given both types of names. When
investing her with her office, Wu Zetian gives her the male name *zhongju*, which is an easy pun on *zhongju*, "recommended by the masses,"
indicating that she indeed is the official the masses, who are not Party
members, would like to see. There is no precedent for this name in the
earlier versions of the play, it seems. Xie is a palace lady in Wu's favor;
how could she be the choice of the masses, remote as the palace is from
their lives and problems? The reason is her lowly class background. She
sings: "Your servant [I] was originally registered in Jiangnan. My late
father was a village teacher there."[71] Her father (who laid down his life
thus saving Tian Han from the need to write a scene of an encounter
between father and daughter, but in this version is not slaughtered by
Wu Zetian as he was in *Wanfulian*) leaves her a letter in which he
details the situation in Jiangnan. The letter gives her an independent
access to reality, a feature to which we will return. Her class background is an important communication to the public. Guo Moruo has
Wu Zetian herself come from such lowly origins; thus the interests of
the "people" are invested in her.

Xie introduces herself when she arrives in Jiangnan:

> A snow plum in the Luoyang palace,
> and now in charge of the Jiangnan inspectorate.
> May torrential rains and fiery winds here rage,
> a clear sky and blazing sun are bound to come.[72]

70. Li Chao, "*Xie Yaohuan* de fusu."
71. Tian, *Xie Yaohuan, Juben* ed., p. 9a.
72. Ibid., p. 13.

The snow plum symbolizes Xie's indomitable uprightness and capacity to withstand trial. The last lines show an optimism that she will, once out of the narrow confines of the center, be able to turn things to the better. Her "indignation" or "ire" is roused by the sufferings undergone by the people at the hands of the local bullies, and eventually she casts aside all warnings to be "careful" and "watch out" and has the son of the prime minister executed. Her commitment is not to the empress or the Wu family, but to "the court" and "the people." The point is brought out clearly in the following exchange, which attacks the arrogance of children of high cadres:

<blockquote>

XIE: This court of law is run by the government's [*chaoting*] inspector.

CAI: And which family's is this government?

WU HONG (WU SANSI'S SON): Indeed, you are but an official of our Wu family, and you must manage things in the interest of our family. . . .

XIE: You really are too brazen, Wu Hong! This court of law has received orders to inspect the Jiangnan area. Above, it acts on behalf of the government [not the Wu family]; below, it gives the hundred families relief from their problems.[73]

</blockquote>

To mark the difference still further, Xie contrasts the good laws of the government with the licentious behavior of Wu and Cai, demonstrating that her court is an independent institution that is bound by the laws and provides avenues of redress for common people even against the powerful and mighty—things that the courts most certainly were not in China in the late fifties and early sixties of the twentieth century. As the conflict sharpens, the pitch of her voice rises. Warned that the top villains are ganging up against her, she vows:

Let them denounce me. When I received the directive, I already knew that this would be an ugly battle. I rely on her majesty's wisdom; as she has enrusted me with this mission outside the palace, she must have in mind that I have some capacity. I furthermore give myself to the state, and have long given up any consieration of life or death, happiness or misfortune. (Sings:)

Since receiving her majesty's orders to battle against the mighty tyrants,
I have made Jiangnan the battleground.

73. Ibid., p. 16a.

> Life and death, misfortune and happiness I nowhere consider,
> My red heart is all in the service of the empress.[74]

Her engagement is for the state and the people; her fervor is not for the empress as an individual, but for the leader who is giving a directive that finally is correct and can help stop the abuses; and her actions are controlled by due process of law. She is fervently loyal to state and government; her loyalty is not blind, however, but rests on many and well-defined conditions. Her own political program: "Secure the people's peace; bring malefactors to justice; promote the worthy."[75] Before returning to the practicalities of the last point, let us consider the first two, which link her directly with the Hai Rui figures.

To show this link, Tian Han inserts a short scene of great symbolism. The fiancé of the abducted young peasant woman has run into terrible weather on his way home, a climatological echo of the political tyranny reigning there. He presses on toward the court where Xie Yaohuan is to decide his fiancée's case, ending his song with the line "What a violent wind and storm this late in spring" and, battling against wind and rain, with his umbrella held high, he exits.[76] This scene, some eight lines in length and showing a lone figure fighting the elements with an umbrella, reeks of symbolism.

Indeed, in *Hai Rui shangshu* the umbrella was used as the general symbol for Hai Rui's protecting the people's interests; in the end, a triumphant Hai Rui upon his release from prison holds a huge umbrella over the entire stage and the "masses" assembled there. Tian Han's scene is a subtle quote, linking Xie's functions to those of Hai Rui.

In the Hai Rui plays the officials depicted are lower officials, but in this play Xie Yaohuan is portrayed as only a palace lady, there to adorn the center with her beauty. Given the juxtaposition between Xie Yaohuan and Shangguan Wan'er in Guo's play (the poetess of noble class background that reflects on Guo Moruo himself), it could be hypothesized that Xie may be a reflection on the *persona* of the author, an emblem of a particular kind of literature. The hypothesis receives some support from the fact that the hero of *Guan Hanqing* is, of course, Guan Hanqing, a writer, who alone can articulate the people's grievances. Further support for the hypothesis comes from the job given to Xie Yaohuan. The empress makes her an inspector, a *xun'an*, and tells

74. Ibid., p. 19b.
75. Ibid., p. 13b. There is a misprint of *nü* (woman) for *an* (peace).
76. Ibid., p. 13.

her: "Wherever you go, investigate the good and evil of officials and common people [i.e., cadres and masses], observe what is wholesome and what deficient in customs and habits, investigate and inquire after hardships, give relief to the hungry and destitute."[77] She enters Jiangnan not only disguised as a man but incognito as well, in order to be able to make firsthand observations. The kind of social investigation (*shehui diaocha*) performed by Xie Yaohuan is indeed the duty of the writer within the socialist order of things. The official line at the time, to emulate Hai Rui and bring the facts of the crisis gripping the land to the attention of the authorities, further emphasized this point. Both Tian Han and Wu Han made extensive trips through the country in 1960 and 1961 to familiarize themselves with the situation. The trips were suggested and approved by the cultural leadership. As we noted earlier, it was while making such a trip in 1960 that Tian Han saw the antecedent to *Xie Yaohuan*, *Nü xun'an*. The guarded protection Xie receives from Xu Yougong in the center in the play is consistent with Tian's relationship with Zhou Enlai in real life. In addition to her investigative duties, however, Xie receives from the empress an official sword, which gives her the right to mete out death sentences. Her court thus is not only to be an instrument of investigation, but also of judgment. Tian Han had previously dealt with the potential punitive powers of literature in *Guan Hanqing*. Where Guan's beloved tells him that his "brush" is to be his "sword"—the very real sword of Wang Zhu, who sees the play and then metes out judgment to Ahmad—illustrates that she was not talking metaphors.

The play itself is Xie Yaohuan's inspectorate. True, there are secret memoranda that go to the Empress and the leadership, but Xie's court is open to the public, like the theater in which the play is staged. Only here the true facts can be heard, which are in all ways deformed when they go through internal channels. The sword in Xie's hands shows the power of literature to pass judgment, the fact that she never gets at the chief culprits shows the limits of literature's power, and her torture and death anticipate the fate of literature and the author in this power constellation. Already in the Hundred Flowers texts, the writers often dealt with their own social station and role through a persona in the text. Tian's *Guan Hanqing* is in this tradition, a tradition that is both followed and reinterpreted by Guo Moruo with his "Cai Wenji c'est moi," taken from Flaubert's celebrated (and misundertood) statement about

77. Ibid., p. 10a.

Madame Bovary. Thus, the public was accustomed to and prepared for seeing Xie Yaohuan in the same tradition, and furthermore the text itself gave good reasons for doing so. The charge made in later years, that Tian Han had depicted (and glorified) himself in Xie Yaohuan, is no empty slander.

Xie Yaohuan is elevated to her position "by the masses" and shares with them or "the people" a core of symbolical features. Both she and the raped young woman in the temple who stands for the "people" are symbolical females. Both are upright and pure, but young and weak as they lack the institutional powers of males.

Institutionally, Xie Yaohuan as the emblem for literature is attached to the center, but from the (hopefully) enlightened top leader she has the mandate to do critical investigation. With her high social and geographical mobility she mediates between the leader and the people, speaking out for the latter in the court and for the former among the lowly crowds in Jiangnan. Up to this point, we have been stressing the symbolical lore that *Xie Yaohuan* has in common with other historical plays of the time; now let us look at the differences.

It is a common feature of "unbending remonstrator" plays since *Guan Hanqing* to add depth and power to the lead by adding a supporting character—Zhu Lianxiu in *Guan Hanqing*, Hai Rui's mother in *Hai Rui baguan*, the student in *Li Huiniang*, and Yuan Xingjian here. Yuan, however, has a somewhat independent function.

Yuan enters the stage bearing as much programmatic and emblematic weight as the Statue of Liberty. His late father's name, for instance, is Yuan Leshan, the *leshan* being a sad pun on *leshan* (with a different second character), making it "Yuan Who-Rejoices-In-The-Good." Yuan Leshan's death was instigated by Zhou Xing, who, together with Lai, had managed the secret service. Zhou Xing, after having tortured and persecuted thousands of public servants, himself ends up as a victim of his own outfit, being first boiled in a cauldron by his colleague Lai (a form of torture Zhou had pioneered), whereupon he confesses his crimes—a fate that has been repeated in some form or another by all too many Party cadres in China. On his way to banishment, Zhou Xing is killed by Yuan Who-Rejoices-In-The-Good's son, Yuan Xingjian. The latter thus bears the hat of a "counterrevolutionary" family; and, having committed a political murder, he is unable to get redress from the courts. Tian had defended political murder under duress in *Guan Hanqing*, certainly less as an appeal to such action than as an appeal to resistance expressed in the ecstatic language of the opera. In terms of

contemporary events, the persecution of Yuan's father would seem to
refer to the Anti-Rightist movement of 1957 and 1958; it was then that
Tian Han had written his *Guan Hanqing* even while being in charge of
execution of the Anti-Rightist line within the Dramatists' Association.
Yuan Xingjian's name is a new creation in this play, and means (with
different characters) "Intent-On-Constructive-Work." Yuan's peaceful
bent is reinforced by his pseudonym, which has been changed from
Yuan Hua in the original *Nü xun'an* to Ruan Hua. Thus it makes a pun
on *ruanhua*, to "win over by soft tactics." His adopted name is Huai-
jing, "Cherishing Peace." There is an allusion to the medical profession
of Tian Han himself and Guan Hanqing, Yuan having studied the
"soft" Chinese pharmacology. He is no revolutionary surgeon, but a
principled fellow. His committing a political murder and his peaceful
bent are not in contradiction. He is introduced with a statement
expressing his abhorrence for the local bullies and his friendship with Li
Decai, the leader of the people at Lake Taihu. He then sings two lines
that set the tone for his role:

> With a blade three feet long, a pouch full of poems, and a breast full of guts,
> I have roamed for some years north of the pass and south of the River.[78]

The mention of his blade is a reference to his killing one of the worst
oppressors of the people, his poems show his education, and his guts
would seem to predestine him to a valiant role in the service of the
nation; but he has roamed: there is no place for him. Arriving at the Wu
Zixu temple, he sets himself up to emulate this hero of old, whom the
people regard as a protective river spirit and also invoke against unjust
verdicts. The historical Wu fled after losing his father and brother;
eventually he achieved the destruction of the king who had put them to
death. A minister in the state of Wu, he had excelled because of his loyal
remonstrance and was eventually forced to commit suicide.[79] Tian had
quoted him in *Guan Hanqing*;[80] Wu was also a standard figure in the
many historical plays in the early sixties dealing with the relationship
between the states of Wu and Yue and extolling the Wu king Gou
Jian's self-reliance and bravery. Wu Zixu belongs to the Hai Rui group,

78. Ibid., p. 11a.
79. On Wu Zixu's life and cult, see Rudolph, "Wu Tzu-hsü"; David Johnson, "The Wu Tzu-hsü Pien-wen and Its Sources"; cf. id., "Epic and History in
Early China: The Matter of Wu Tzu-hsü."
80. In a scene added in 1960, he has the young woman whose eyes are
gouged out by Ahmad quote Wu indirectly; see chapter 1 of this book, p. 70.

so Di Renjie of the same group spares his temple, despite having razed 1,500 others that he considered superstitious.[81] Immediately after a woman from the people prays to Wu Zixu to help her daughter's fiancé to a speedy return and save the girl from the gang around the prime minister's son, Wu Zixu's embodiment, Yuan Xingjian, indeed saves the girl. Although Yuan's father was a minor official he claims descent from peasant stock (*hongnong renshi*), thus sharing, for the PRC audience, Xie's high credibility. "Since my youth I have studied books and learned to handle the sword, I was concerned with the advances and sufferings of All-Under-Heaven, and I even thought of pacifying the borders and serving the state and not contenting myself with an ordinary life," Yuan relates, but adds that since the death of his father he has roamed around "and achieved nothing," to his great shame. After this confession he weeps, but when Xie tries to draw him into state service, he instantly declines: "Nowadays, even though her majesty [Wu Zetian] is on the throne, the mighty officials monopolize power and use it perversely [*zhuanheng*]. They violently plunder the hundred families, while their oppressive underlings are reckless and brutal. Thus valiant men are cool in their hearts [toward the idea of serving the empress]. Therefore I, Ruan Hua, would prefer to be drifting and homeless among the lakes. I have no intention of seeking a rank in the world."[82] His political experiences have instilled in him a nearly cynical mistrust against the government of his time, and he does not heed Xie's appeal that his very criticism should prompt him to support Wu Zetian's latest efforts. The best don't enter public service anymore, although they are willing to cooperate with those few honest souls like Xie who find favor with the Empress.

Yuan's friend, the leader of the people at Lake Taihu, never comes on stage. His name, Li Decai, characterizes him sufficiently; it is a pun on *decai*, signifying that he has both "moral virtue" and "talent." With this name, Tian Han alludes to discussions of the Hundred Flowers and the Anti-Rightist movement. In the former, some people had publicly criticized the Party for basing its recruitment not on *cai*, talent and qualifications, but on *de*, moral stance (meaning political beliefs); they had demanded a reversal. During the Anti-Rightist movement, it was affirmed that political beliefs were indeed, and justly so, the basis for

81. This is specifically mentioned in the play, Tian, *Xie Yaohuan, Juben* ed., p. 11a; cf. De Groot, *Sectarianism*, pp. 17–26 for Di Renjie's action.

82. Tian, *Xie Yaohuan, Juben* ed., p. 18a.

recruitment. The Chairman kept out of the controversy by advocating a combination of both; he was supported in this stance by Tian Han in this play.

THE PROTAGONISTS: COALITIONS

The heroes and villains of *Xie Yaohuan* do not enter the stage as individuals but as part of networks and coalitions. The villains have power in the center and protect their local relatives and friends. The bases of their alliance, in which there is no conflict, is, first, the blood link; second, the hunger for wealth and power; third, a willingness to go to any end of flattery to the empress and brutality toward the people to achieve that wealth and power; and, finally, moral depravity in the form of lechery. The pattern of *Guan Hanqing*, with the top villain Ahmad as the king's favorite, and his twenty-five sons to man the lower levels, is repeated. Ahmad and his underlings are at least witty or well-satirized rascals; the villains in *Xie Yaohuan* are a sorry lot in literary terms, being just very, very bad.

The side of the heroes is more complex. Despite Xie's weak institutional and gender standing, she is not alone; she receives guarded support from Xu Yougong in the center. Xu Yougong, however, never ventures his own opinions. He will give her a platform to speak out and support her when he feels the empress might be convinced. Xu's treatment of Xie is of great importance, as he is one of the three top leaders (under Wu Zetian) on stage. His attitude is strikingly similar to that of his counterparts in the other Hai Rui plays, for instance, of Horikhoson in *Guan Hanqing* and Xu Jie in both *Hai Rui shangshu* and *Hai Rui baguan*, both of whom are high-ranking ministers who reflect the Premier's attitude. Xu Yougong, outnumbered two to one at the top, has a local counterpart, a member of the Wu family who cooperates with Xie and passively opposes Wu Hong and young Cai. Thus not everyone in the Wu clan is bad. These men, however, don't risk their lives; the only one to do so is Xie, a young palace lady in man's clothes with an official appointment, a character whose existence is fictional in a twofold sense. The dynasty/Party does have a sprinkling of honest characters. The coalition of these honest characters is no faction: they have no network of mutual protection. Xie Yaohuan's local supporter from the Wu family has not been appointed by Xu Yougong; there seem to be no links between Xu and Xie beyond their agreement on some political issues. Within the court/Party the coalition of heroes is weak and only loosely held together. They truly adhere to the Party rule banning factions.

The intentionality of Tian Han's procedure is best visible in his treatment of Xu Yougong. Historically, Xu openly and strongly opposed the secret police system set up by Lai and Zhou, and dared to do so in the face of the empress who relied on them. There was the potential of a historical figure in a top position who could resonate with someone in the present, had there been one. There was, however, for Tian Han, no force in the center that could live up to the high standard set by Xu Yougong, and Xu Yougong had to suffer it by being degraded to a fairly weak backstage supporter of humane considerations once he was confident that they enjoyed the support of the empress. Xu had to be compressed into Zhou Enlai's shape.

The mainstay of Xie's group—Yuan Xingjian, the male lead—is not in government service, and even refuses to enter it. Being forced by government persecution into the lower reaches of society, he is familiar with the life of the people, and he knows their aspirations much better than the palace insider Xie. Although Yuan is a wanted man for his assassination of the secret police chief, Xie seeks an alliance with him, first as his "sworn brother," then as his love and wife. Though she may sympathize with the suffering refugees in Lake Taihu, they still distrust her because she is part of the government—a self-critical comment on the public perception of literature. However, Yuan can mediate, and in his independent manner is willing to do so. The fourth member of this weak coalition is thus the people—wary, reluctant to believe Xie's promises, but finally coming out in force to support her when she is tortured to death.

The role of the people in this play is a touchy subject. Many books and plays about peasant rebellions have been written since 1949; in them, however, the rebels were the forefathers of the modern Communists, and thus imbued with glory. But in Tian Han's play the Communist government is dealt with on the screen of the traditional government, i.e., the court, and the "people" become what in the PRC is referred to as the "masses"—a term not referring to their numbers but to the fact that they are not Party members. The actions of the people in the play thus represent the attitude of the "masses" toward the Party. Whereas in a play glorifying peasant resistance to a tyrannical government, a great deal would be made of the peasants arming themselves and not relying on petitions, to do so in the present case would imply a glorification of and thus a call for armed resistance against the Communist government. The stress of this possible reading is felt in the text of *Xie Yaohuan*. The people flee to Lake Taihu, which is the traditional place where rebels find a safe haven from which to oppose the government. But Tian Han, aware of the implications of this scenario, carefully avoids any mention of armed resistance, which at the time was being reported only in Tibet and the adjacent provinces of Yunnan, Sichuan, and Qinghai.[83] The only line that can be read as a direct *military* threat is said by Xie Yaohuan. When young Cai brags "we have awe-inspiring power and are known to be ready to kill [*weifeng shaqi*]; why should we fear that they [i.e., the people] would raise the standard of revolt?" Xie counters "It is only to be feared that the awe-inspiring power and readiness to kill [*weifeng shaqi*] of the hundred families is immeasurably higher than yours."[84] In the edition of the play completed a few months later, Tian toned down even this indirect reference, and Xie's answer to Cai becomes "Haha, don't you know that the hundred families, too, have awe-inspiring power and a readiness to kill?" This change did not prevent critics during the Cultural Revolution from charging Tian Han with inciting the people to armed rebellion against the dictatorship of the proletariat.

The Empress is linked to both coalitions. Tian Han again uses romantic means to deal with her link to Xie Yaohuan. Most of the harshest phrases about the situation in the country and the dangers for her "boat" are put into the mouth of the empress, including a self-criticism for employing and listening to the villainous ministers (a traditional technique first used by Sima Xiangru [d. 117 B.C.] in his *fu* on the hunting park, where Sima has the Han emperor himself propose what he, the poet, wants him to do, that is, to do away with the huge park to give the people more land to plant). Wu Zetian's trip south to rescue Xie and her bestowal of a reward on Yuan Xingjian are so evidently out of tune with historical reality that they must be called fictional hopes.

The constellation Wu Zetian/Xie Yaohuan refers to and rejects that between Wu Zetian and Shangguan Wan'er in Guo Moruo's play. There, the empress eventually convinces the young woman of noble stock that her actions, including the execution of Shangguan Wan'er's

83. L. Cheng, *The Politics of the Red Army*, pp. 13 and 190f.
84. Tian, *Xie Yaohuan, Juben* ed., p. 15.

grandfather, were justified, "progressive," and in the interests of the "people." Here, it is Xie Yaohuan, with the prestige of her lowly origin, who proves to the empress that the empress is to blame for the disaster of the nation, and awakens the dormant progressive elements in her majesty's mind.

Two coalitions thus confront each other. The first consists of the corrupt and greedy top officials who control the military and secret police and arrogate privileges; they are a faction in every sense, secret meetings included. The basis of their power is their link to the empress. The second consists of the upright and virtuous "people," the offspring of correct officials who have been killed by the villains, and the palace lady, symbol of investigative literature. If the second coalition is strong enough and can win the favor of the empress, it will gain a powerful and careful ally, Xu Yougong. In short, Tian Han presents a fairly detailed analysis of the power and coalition constellations in 1961 as he saw them, and made it quite clear which side was right and deserved support.

THE SETTING

The play is set in the center, that is, the court, and in Jiangnan. Guo Moruo in *Cai Wenji* and *Wu Zetian* had done much to make the court an acceptable setting for the new historical drama. The focus in *Xie Yaohuan*, more so than in *Guan Hanqing*, is on politics and society, with the empress herself and the highest ministers coming on stage. By selecting these two locales, Tian Han employs a traditional device for handling typicality. Often, typicality is stressed though multiplication, as in the case of the women in *Guan Hanqing*. Here it is stressed in a qualitative manner. If things are bad in the court, under the very eyes of the Empress, they must be much worse in provincial and local governments and courts.

The same holds true for Jiangnan. "Jiangnan," says Xu Yougong, "is a rich and populous area where the hundred families [the people] all just want to live in peace and enjoy their station." People in this area have no inclination to rebel. If things are bad here, they must be that much worse elsewhere. Other historical dramas of the time like *Hai Rui baguan* and *Li Huiniang* employ the same device. Jiangnan also provided an easy way to deal with the "Maoists" in Shanghai, a city situated in the Jiangnan area. The play claims that it portrays the problems of the land in their mildest form.

THE PROBLEM

The first problem plaguing the country, the play avers, is land-grabbing. "The preceding dynasty [i.e., Tang/*dang*] has promoted the *juntian* system [of equal distribution of land]," says Xie Yaohuan, referring to the early Tang reforms and the land reform in the early days of the PRC. This policy is held up as the ideal. Quoting the letter from her father, Xie sings on:

> In recent years these excellent laws and good intentions have largely become invalid.
> The rich and noble annex land
> forcing the hundred families to wander far from home in utter poverty [*dianpei liuli*].
> How should the number of those who fled stop at one out of ten,
> to mountain crags and the sea shore they take their children and bring their wives.[85]

The communalization of land is thus described as the "annexation" of the land by the mighty and the abandonment of the healthy earlier measures. The number of those fleeing in destitution from China's key agricultural area is higher than ten percent, "one out of ten." We know of a sharp increase in the number of refugees in Shanghai, Canton, Amoy, Hongkong, and Macao at the time, as well as movements of large numbers of people from national minorities into Burma, India, and the Soviet Union.[86] There are mentions of refugee problems in contemporary political speeches[87] as well as the dramatic depiction in the recent story "Fanren Li Tongzhong de gushi" (The Story of Li Tongzhong, the Criminal).[88] Here, in *Xie Yaohuan*, we get a description and even a quantitative assessment from a man who traveled a lot during these hard times and was willing to listen. Right in the preface to *Xie Yaohuan*, there is an ominous list of Tian Han's actor friends in Xi'an who were all "sick" for the entire month he was there and thus could not perform, a reference to the effects of malnutrition.

The charge of the "annexation" of land is often repeated in the play. Thus large tracts of land are accumulated under the villains' control, no less than 1,200 mu in Wu Hong's case. These are fields in permanent

85. Ibid., p. 9a.
86. Kumari, "China Tribesmen Flee into Burma and India."
87. Cf. MacFarquhar, *Origins*, vol. 2, p. 149.
88. Zhang Yigong, "Fanren Li Tongzhong de gushi"; cf. T. Bernstein, "Stalinism," pp. 363f.

possession of the family which are not to be sold, or *yongyetian*; nonetheless, they are bought for a pittance. As Wu's majordomo explains, many of these fields have been given "voluntarily," in the sense that joining the people's communes had been voluntary. An exchange occurs:

MAJORDOMO: There are even people who don't want a single copper. They just glue the land deeds to the doors of our mansion, take their families, and run off.

XIE: So, they fix their land deeds to the door, take their families, and run off?

MAJORDOMO: Yes, that's what they do.

XIE: If that is so, they must dance, [they must be] beside themselves with joy.

MAJORDOMO: Dance they may, but we don't have people to plant the fields for us.

XIE: (Laughing) After giving you the land they should still plant it; that's how you would like it.[89]

Dancing with joy, *yongyue*, is a reference to the exuberance of peasants when they joined the collectives and gave up their land, which, of course, they were expected to till thereafter. The *yue* in the binom also might refer to the *dayuejin*, the Great Leap Forward. The passage is a satire on cadre reports about the founding of the communes. The land of the young woman's mother is taken by Wu Hong to enlarge the Imperial Garden he built to honor the Empress, a reference to the wave of park and garden building during the Great Leap. Liu Binyan reports that in the village to which he was exiled in 1958, where people had meat perhaps once a year, they planned to have a zoo.

The economic deprivation caused by the villains does not stop there. In imitation of the huge, iron Heavenly Pillar that Wu Sansi has had erected in the capital to glorify Wu Zetian, Wu's son has a similar monument built in Suzhou. Since there is no historical record of this local monument, the reference is fraught with meaning. Yuan Xingjian charges: "Under the pretext of erecting in Suzhou a 'Heavenly Pillar to Praise the Virtue (of the new dynasty)' for which not enough copper and iron was around, [Wu Hong] requisitioned agricultural implements from the people, so that the peasants were unable to till and plant, and joined together to flee to the Taihu area." This requisitioning is mentioned frequently as a major crime. The reference is to the requisitioning,

89. Tian, *Xie Yaohuan, Juben* ed., pp. 14b f.

during the Greap Leap, of household iron and copper ware as well as agricultural implements. They were used for the communal fields and kitchens, but more relevantly for the present passage, as raw material for the "Heavenly Pillar in Praise of the Virtue" of the Chairman and the Great Leap, that is, the huge campaign of backyard steel furnaces, the output of which, the play charges, was about as useful as if it had been literally wasted on a public monument. The methods used in the requisitioning were often violent and generally coercive. The two most visible economic ingredients of the Great Leap, the people's communes and the steel campaign, are thus denounced as a grand and systematic robbery, which deprived the people of the means to produce their livelihood and were perpetrated by a well-wrought hierarchy of villains whose highest rung was in charge of the government. Similar charges are made in the other plays of this group. It is important to notice that the crimes by Wu Hong and young Cai are not presented within the play as reprehensible exceptions and deformations of a basically sound policy but as the rule.

The second problem the play points out is absence of legal protection. Legal protection, like land distribution, is portrayed as having been well established under Tang/*dang* rule. Xie Yaohuan can constantly refer to Tang/*dang* legal rules and proscriptions against the forced marriage of women, privileged treatment of officials in the courts, and so on. The reference is to the general principles of the PRC constitution, which would, if applied, provide some protection. The earliest miscarriage of justice mentioned in the play is the framing and subsequent execution of Yuan Xingjian's father by Zhou Xing for "rebellion" or counterrevolution. It is a turning point in the life of the surviving son, who loses faith in the legal system of the state, and in state services in general. Another example of this theme is that the two local villains are known even to the censor Xu Yougong to "act arbitrarily without respect for the law"; this is mentioned not to encourage Xie to engage in battle with them, but to warn her to be "somewhat careful."[90] Their crimes are known even to Xu, but he dares not mention them to the empress. They are only too willing to appear in court against Yuan Xingjian, secure in their belief that no court will dare to oppose them. A third example of the theme occurs when Wu Hong enters the stage singing, "I'm born into the first family of the present dynasty," and demands that the court handle things "in the interests of

90. Ibid., p. 10b.

the Wu family." He refuses to bend his knee in respect for the court of law. When Xie reminds him "princes and commoners are to be treated alike for infractions of the law," he laughs at this empty phrase, asking, "Have you really ever seen anyone strike at a prince?" Indeed, cadres have been immune from the law in most times since the founding of the PRC. In a questionnaire about the merits and defects of the Shanghai play *Jiaru woshi zhende* (1979, banned), in which higher Party cadres are shown as witnesses in court (although they should have been the defendants), one person noted that the play was unrealistic, because cadres never appeared in court.[91] The approximately 400,000 citizens who were classified as rightists in 1957–58 and deprived of their civil and political rights were summarily handled by the "authorities" and never saw a court. The same was true for the large number of people purged after the Lushan Plenum in late 1959 for being "right opportunists." The emphasis on the law has been noted as an especially "reactionary" feature of Tian's play by critics, law being a "bourgeois" institution cutting into the "dictatorship of the proletariat." When Xie upholds the word of the law against the two villains, Lai Junchen's nephew says: "Third Wu, stop the chatter. If this court does not handle matters in our interest, let's tear it down." They then overturn the judge's table and almost succeed in grabbing Xie's credentials.

To make it quite clear that these were not merely local excesses, but rather local examples of activities also being performed by top leaders in the center, Tian Han introduces evidence from the top level. Wu Sansi and Lai Junchen, intent on removing Xie after she orders the lands to be given back, conspire to fake the empress's directive (*zhi*, the very term used, by the way, for Mao's directives), confident that she will take little offense. They thus bend the directives of the empress to fit their personal interests, and to eliminate the dangerous person who has awakened the positive elements in the empress's mind and threatens the very hinges of their network. They then proceed, on stage, to hold a kangaroo court, complete with torture, showing how the "evidence" for rebellious plots and counterrevolutionary activities is produced now as then. The result of all this is that the villains "have set themselves up as the law,"[92] "that they commit, relying on the power of their elders, each and every villainy, while the people of Suzhou have no appeal when injustice is committed, and a difficult time finding help when they

91. "Zuotanhui chaiji," p. 97c.
92. Tian, *Xie Yaohuan, Juben* ed., p. 14a.

suffer calamity."[93] Deprived of their land and their rights, they flee in destitution. The symbolical individual suffering from both economic and legal deprivation is the familiar pure young woman, as might be expected, and her plight is again expressed in her being kidnapped by villains. She and her fate are familiar from *Guan Hanqing, Dou E yuan, Li Huiniang,* and other pieces. In fact, the image is more than symbolical. There are reports from the early sixties of cadres using their powers to force themselves on peasant women, and of bride sales by destitute parents increasing in frequency. In *Xie Yaohuan,* Tian Han has the young woman's mother sign the contract selling the girl to Wu Hong "voluntarily." But when she is able to speak out openly in Xie's court, she shows the wounds the villains inflicted on her body in the process of convincing her. By this time in the action her daughter has already been transformed into the emblem of the suffering nation; her appearance on stage as the brutalized people is purely symbolical.

The consequence of the above situation in the eyes of the heroes, and eventually the empress, is that the villains "corrode public morality, and damage the confidence in the court"[94] (i.e., the Party). They have, as Wu Zetian finally charges, "shaken the fundaments of the state."[95] Xie in her last speech charges police chief Lai with "being tied to criminals, having calumniated the good and worthy, taken other people's wives, arrogated other people's products, destroyed families and ruined clans,"[96] so "that the souls of the unjustly slain clog the lanes." He is finally charged by Xu Yougong to have done all this with the single purpose of "rocking the court and secretly getting [his] hands on the great levers of the state."[97] Wu Zetian's own relatives and supporters have returned to "the old ways of the rich and noble" and are out to get their hands on state power. And things have come to a point where people are gathering in the marshes, are on the brink of open rebellion, and threaten to "capsize the boat" which they hitherto supported. However, even in their dire straits, they don't really "have the intention to rebel" and may be pacified.[98]

Thus in her final speech Xie Yaohuan defines the main problems "now" plaguing the country, and her assessment is supported by the

93. Ibid., p. 14b.
94. Ibid., p. 14a.
95. Ibid., p. 28.
96. Ibid., p. 26b.
97. Ibid., p. 28b.
98. Ibid., p. 9b.

facts given within the play itself. Eventually, the empress is led to see things in the same way.

Xie's opponents are not ignorant of these problems but define them in other ways and suggest different solutions. Tian Han does not lend them his brush to present a neutral and reasoned statement; all they say is immediately falsified by the facts on stage. It is a polemical presentation, and Tian Han would most vehemently object if one were to suggest, following Bakhtin's celebrated argument, that he explores a part of himself in these monsters. However, as Tian Han is engaging in polemics, the duty falls on us to extract from the clues that he gives us what Xie Yaohuan's opponents thought, and to present the opponents' viewpoint in a sober way.

The people in the Taihu marshes are led by a Li Decai. Since Li's family name is the same as that of the Tang ruling house, Wu Sansi defines the threat as an attempt at restoration by the remnants of the deposed dynasty, who have attracted rascals from among the people to their cause. The language is all too familiar. Routinely, Communist critics in China were accused during the fifties and sixties of this benighted century of attempting the restoration of Guomindang rule. The real beginning of the new era, in this view, occurred not in 1949, but only after the transition to socialism had been completed in the mid-fifties. Before then things were just a prolongation of the old capitalist system. Whereas the Tang/*dang* rule in Xie's view was the time when things were correct and glorious, in the view of Wu and his associates it was the time when the class enemy still ruled. They thus stress the radical break that came with the founding of the Zhou. It is Wu Sansi who erects the Heavenly Pillar for the Praise of Virtue, which was to celebrate the downfall of the Tang dynasty and the rise of the Zhou. Wu Zetian refers to this huge monument at the beginning of the play. Here is C. P. Fitzgerald's description of the monument:

> In 694, at the instance of her nephew Wu San-ssu [Wu Sansi] . . . she [Wu Zetian] ordered the construction of another great monument which was expressly designed to celebrate the founding of the Chou [Zhou] dynasty and the overthrow of the T'ang [Tang]. This was called the T'ien Shu [Tianshu] or Celestial Pillar, and was completed in the fourth month of 695, at immense cost. It was in the form of an octagonal column, 105 feet high, each face of the pillar being five feet wide, and the whole twelve feet in diameter. The base was in the form of a hill of iron one hundred and seventy feet round, on which were bronze dragons supporting the pillar. Fabulous beasts carved in stone encircled the column, and the top was a canopy in the form of clouds crowned by a great pearl, presumably of copper or gilded copper.

The canopy was ten feet in height with a circuit of thirty feet, and four dragons measuring twelve feet supported the pearl, which was ten feet high. About two million catties of copper and iron were used to cast this monument.[99]

While the pillar in Tian Han's eyes represents a fine satire on the megalomania, senseless waste, and ruthless exploitation of the people characteristic of the Great Leap Forward, in Wu Sansi's eyes it is seen as a glorious monument to the new crowd's ascent to power under the old leader Wu Zetian (Mao Zedong) with the Zhou dynasty. What Xie sees as a deterioration of the good traditions, Wu Sansi celebrates as the beginning of the new order. Wu Zetian's relatives and supporters, in Wu Sansi's view, had every right, historically speaking, to ward off "counterrevolutionary" rebellions with the power of the army, to amass the land in their hands in the name of collective agriculture, to expropriate people's private belongings to be melted down into monuments to their glory, and to run the courts under their dictatorship so that they would serve their interests. All the rumors about so-called real issues like hunger and destitution, refugees and oppression, torture and forced confessions, are but cunning devices used by the class enemy to stage his comeback. Criticizing the sons and nephews of high cadres for misbehavior is "rebellion," *zaofan*.[100] These are not social issues, just political ones. In caricature, but sharply drawn, Tian Han here portrays the very views that were to dominate the scene a few years later, when his own play was denounced as part of a counterrevolutionary plot to restore capitalism and bourgeois rule.

Given the glorious arrival of the new dynasty the new crowd had every reason to glorify the leader. The Heavenly Pillar is but one example; Wu Zetian loved to travel, as did her modern counterpart. Wu Sansi therefore builds travel palaces for her at great cost, as did the provinces for the Chairman during the Great Leap.[101] The palaces reinforce her inflated view of her own importance and the heavenly favors bestowed upon her, and she eventually assumes that she is indeed the reincarnation of Maitreya. We recognize this pattern only too well from the paeans to Mao Zedong. In Tian Han's presentation, there is nothing genuine about all this praise. The villains know about the genuine commitment of the empress to the people, and set out to cloud her eyes with

99. Fitzgerald, *The Empress Wu*, p. 136.
100. Tian, *Xie Yaohuan, Juben* ed., p. 13a.
101. See n. 63.

conceit. They eliminate all critics, even those installed by the empress herself, such as Xie, using brutal secret police methods, and they attempt to control the channels of internal communication.

The empress has proclaimed that anyone with a "secret report" to her should be given official means of transportation and brought to the capital with the greatest speed. Xie Yaohuan, however, sends her letter denouncing the two chief villains at court through a man traveling privately. He explains his dusty attire to the empress: "Your subject's secret memo refers to two great ministers at court. Their powers are vast. They have very many ears and eyes, and I was afraid something might happen to me on the way."[102] Tian Han does not criticize the system of "internal" and "secret" reports from below, which is common in China and in fact provides one of the rare channels of communication between citizens and top government leaders. But he indicates that only people like Xie who are willing to risk their lives in the process will dare to denounce the chief culprits.

The villains define the main problem of the country in the last phase of the Great Leap Forward as a counterrevolutionary attempt at restoration. This definition is denounced as a self-serving proposition cooked up by people in power interested in fact in nothing but following the "old ways" of the noble and rich. They do not form a class in any economic sense, and not all officials share their assumptions, but they form a network that has acquired huge powers and consists of people ruthless in the wielding of these powers.

THE SOLUTION TO THE PROBLEM

The conflict over how to define and how to solve the national crisis dominates *Xie Yaohuan*. In the very beginning of the first scene, the two factions oppose each other. Xie argues for a removal of the causes of the rebellion, Wu Sansi for a military intervention to crush this counterrevolutionary attempt and "cut out the ulcer." Understandably, Xie's proposals are given more space in the play, and, as they suggest a way in which to remedy the national catastrophe of the Great Leap years, I will present them in more detail. Since the people have fled to the Taihu area because their land was taken from them, Xie says, "when the annexation of their lands is stopped they will certainly return." Thus the main tenet of Xie's program is return the land, *fahuan tian*. The annexation

102. Tian, *Xie Yaohuan*, *Juben* ed., p. 22.

of land has created the present hunger, destitution, and threat of rebellion. The second tenet concerns strict adherence to the laws, so that the courts can give redress to people unjustly treated. Better than sending the army, Xie sings

> . . . let her majesty exude compassion and benevolence,
> Pacify the black-haired people and give peace to the altars of the nation,
> Bring the strong and mighty under strict control and strictly enforce the legal
>   provisions,
> So that the tillers have land, and the hungry have food to eat;
> Then indeed would feelings of spring spread south and north of the River,
> Songs and dances would everywhere extol these glorious times.[103]

The claim is thus made that the two core points of the "socialist transition," the collectivization of land and the removal of legal protection of the individual vis-à-vis the state, must be reversed for glorious times to arrive. Land to the tiller and legal protection for citizens from state officials are the main demands. Tian Han was not alone in making these demands, however. At the time when the play came out, the retrenchment was under way. The people's communes' size and their discretionary powers were being cut down, individual farming had been restored to a certain degree, and some property that had been taken away was returned. The Hai Rui plays and other pieces had advocated similar reforms. There were also discussions about strengthening the legal system. (Ironically, most of the reforms advocated by Tian Han in 1961 became government policy in the early eighties.)

For Tian Han the core question, in true materialist spirit, was the land question. The continuously repeated term *huan tian*, return the land, even suggests a pun on the title of the play. Xie's name is also used in the earlier versions of the play, so normally it would not mean much. Tian Han, however, changed the title of the play from *Nü xun'an* (The Inspectress) to *Xie Yaohuan*. This change attracts attention to the name, and he also adds a telling name for the "male" Xie Yaohuan that operates in the same way. There is a strong echo between the slogan *huan tian*, return the land, and the heroine's personal name, which with homophonous characters would mean "give [the land] back!" We will have more to say about this later.

For Xie Yaohuan, eliminating the root cause of the nation's crisis and preventing the boat from capsizing consists of eliminating the network of villains in the center and in outlying regions. Each side charges

103. Ibid., p. 9a.

the other with fervently desiring to restore the old rule. In fact (of the play), however, Wu Sansi and his group really walk the "old ways" of the deposed nobility, whereas Xie wants only to restore the glorious traditions prevailing under Tang/*dang* rule. Xie has historical dynamics to support her: eventually the Tang rule was restored, a "romantic" hope in the guise of historical sequence.

THE DENOUEMENT

Written during the famine of 1961, Tian Han's play is but a speculation as to what would happen if indeed efforts were made to restore the law and the land. The proposal to make such efforts comes from the persona of the writer, Xie. She daringly links up with victims of former purges (such as Yuan), and the "masses" driven to the marshes. Both her knowledge and her strength come from these sources, her official position being but that of a "tiny inspectress," as Wu Hong says. Her irregular mandate and weak support from Xu Yougong enable her nevertheless to bring out the truth, and even to pass judgment on the local bullies. Tian Han noted in 1965 in his diary that Liu Shaoqi had said that villains not only have roots below, but also above; he added, "if the roots above are not dug up, the villains cannot be eradicated."[104] Despite possessing the imperial mandate and all her righteousness, Xie is no match for the top villains. When their position is threatened, they torture her to death. This is a new element, introduced by Tian Han, and accordingly heavily loaded.

In Tian Han's version, Xie must believe that she is killed on orders from the empress as she is unaware that the two villains falsified Wu Zetian's directive. Nonetheless, in her last breath Xie Yaohuan does not curse the supreme leader, who she thinks is ignorant of the crimes perpetrated in her name.

Empress, majesty, your majesty!
Don't you know that the villains in power turn right and wrong upside down?
Ah, that I cannot return to the palace and argue truth with you,
Ah, that I cannot clear away the dark clouds so that the clear sky may again be
    seen,
Ah, that I cannot let Jiangnan resound all over with singing![105]

The person she curses is Lai Junchen. In *Guan Hanqing* Tian Han treated Khubilai Khan in a similar manner to the way he treats Wu

104. Zhongguo juxie zaofantuan, "Liu Shaoqi."
105. Tian, *Xie Yaohuan*, *Juben* ed., p. 26b.

Zetian here, thus confirming our analysis. Xie Yaohuan's death, however, is not wasted. Skillfully banking on the internal contradictions of
the empress (Chairperson), Xie supplies her with truthful information
through internal channels, giving Xu Yougong a copy, and she eventually and romantically triumphs. Wu Zetian herself finally understands
what a fool she has been to have placed her faith in vile flatterers and
torturers. Too late to rescue Xie Yaohuan, who anticipated her death
and felt that only the supreme sacrifice might awaken the empress, the
empress starts her self-criticism. The other plays of the Hai Rui tradition vent the feelings of their authors and their public by having the
hero curse the emperor (or, as in *Li Huiniang*, curse the prime minister),
but Tian Han has his heroine curse the villains, and has the empress/
Chairperson come up with a self-criticism, a fine variant on the Hai Rui
theme. Arriving in Jiangnan, Wu Zetian sings:

I have talked only about phoenixes paying homage and the red birds being seen,
And who would have thought tigers and wolves lurked in the ranks of the
    court.
The loyal and worthy, on the other hand, are framed by villainous ministers.
Where should peace for the Hundred Families in the land come from?[106]

To this mild self-criticism she adds the insight that Wu Sansi flattered
her to suit his own interests, but this insight concerns only a side issue,
the travel lodges built for Wu Zetian and Mao.

Evidently you noticed that I enjoy making inspection trips [*xunyou*] and thus
in the name of the empress you first built the Sanyang Palace on Song Mountain, and then the Xingtai Palace in Shouan in Henan, wasting several tens of
thousands of taels from the state treasury. And now you have instructed
your son to annex people's land to build something like an imperial garden
with nothing else in mind than to monopolize power for yourself and get
emoluments, and without any regard for the people who were put to destitution and flight. You, you, you![107]

However, she includes in her self-criticism neither the Heavenly Pillar nor Lai's secret police methods. Mentioning the latter is left to Xu
Yougong. In a scene full of didacticism, Xie's ambition to have the rule
of law reestablished is fufilled. Wu Zetian does not herself sit as judge,
but she demonstrates respect for the separateness of the judiciary by
having Xu Yougong judge the culprits, Xu as the chief censor being in
charge of the judiciary. The tide has been turned by Xie Yaohuan with
her battle, suffering, and death, and in the end one of the chief culprits is

106. Ibid., p. 27a.
107. Ibid., P. 28a.

killed (the secret police chief) and one is made into a commoner (Wu Sansi). Xie's last words had been:

> Even when transformed [after death] into a malign spirit, I will go on fighting against you villains and traitors [*jianzei*].[108]

This is reminiscent of the ghost plays of the time, where the ghosts of the unjustly slain return to take their vengeance. Evidently, events after Xie Yaohuan's death belong to the realm of romantic hope as they did in both *Dou E yuan* and *Guan Hanqing*. These events take the form of an appeal to what should happen. They force us into taking a third look at Xie Yaohuan's name. After her gruesome death under torture right on stage, the Xie of her family name takes on an ominous meaning. According to a suggestion by an eminent Chinese scholar, the *xie* might be read as a pun on *xue*, blood. "The blood [debt] has to be repaid" would then be the meaning of the play's title, not an inappropriate title in view of the human cost of the Great Leap and the purge of the "right opportunists."

There was a possibility, and even much pressure, to end the play on an optimistic note after the empress (Chairperson) has performed the rite of self-criticism. Xu Yougong is now in power, like Horikhoson in *Guan Hanqing*, and the villains and their network are destroyed. Thus, the people could have returned from their hideout, Yuan Xingjian could have become an official, Xie Yaohuan's woman friend and attendant could have replaced her, perhaps with an appointment further up the ladder. Within *Xie Yaohuan*, these indeed are Wu Zetian's hopes, and even Yuan Xingjian's dream. But Yuan dreams this before he learns of Xie Yaohuan's death, and Wu Zetian has utterly underestimated how much the people have suffered, how much they hold her responsible for the operations of the villains' network, and how deeply they now mistrust any government action, even if benevolent.

Instead, Xie Yaohuan's woman attendant refuses government office and decides to stay in Jiangnan to mourn for Xie. Yuan Xingjian is offered a government post by Wu Zetian. Reading the epitaph written by the empress for Xie, he exclaims:

> Let there be the richest tombstone a hundred paces high,
> My hatred [for Xie's death] spans the width of heaven and the earth!

He refuses Wu's offer, and then he ends the play with a most astonishing message for the empress:

108. Ibid., p. 26b.

Yaohuan is dead and my heart is in pieces. When you see the empress please tell her to open wide her eyes and ears, to accept loyal comments [i.e., criti- cisms], so that the Hundred Families may have the joy of beating the drums and not the suffering of mud and ashes. If again she puts her faith in the vile and cunning, and hurts and damages the loyal and worthy, it is to be feared that from then on there will be much unrest [*duoshi*] in the country.[109]

He then retires to the Taihu area. We are not told that the people return from there. At the start of the play, the people had fled to the Taihu area and there was a latent threat that "the boat would be overturned." In the end, the people have learned their lesson. Distrustful of the empress and her Xu Yougong, they remain in this area, which is an emblem of their attitude, the lake being of course a materialization of the "water" in Wu Zetian's first statement about the water [people] that can carry the boat as well as capsize it. They are joined there by the worthiest and best in the land, who no longer go into government office. The play ends with a symbolical depiction of this situation, with Yuan singing just one line, "The misty waters of the Five Lakes are yet lingering." The term *panhuan* (here "lingering," not a happy translation in terms of the metaphor) comes from the oracle classic, the *I Ching* (*Zhouyi*). Commentators interpret it as "still waiting and not coming forward." Thus the people, in their metaphorical guise as the "water" of the Five Lakes (i.e., of the nation, not just Taihu), and hard to fathom in their intentions ("misty"), remain reserved. A storm might break out at any moment, capsizing the boat of government. As the plot of *Xie Yaohuan* has shown, only this withholding and reserve can exert sufficient pressure on the palace ladies (that is, writers), and through them on the government, to force a critical self-appraisal and modest renovation.

The tragic ending of the plot thus has "great educational meaning" indeed, as Tian Han claimed in the preface. In *Guan Hanqing* the tragic ending was introduced by Zhou Enlai, but here it is of Tian's own doing. He does not return to the style of his plays of the late twenties, but the ending shows that he is back at stage one. There is no solution. In the twenties, he could make the step to join the Communists to end the tragedy; now, however, he is a high-ranking Communist cadre himself. Within the play, the hopes for a government, any government, to save the nation are gone. The saviors of yore have brought about a national crisis of major proportions. All the frail palace lady can do is throw in her own pure life.

109. Ibid., p. 30.

THE AFTERMATH

As has been suggested, Xie Yaohuan's fate is a speculation on the fate of the writer if he dares intervene, if he dares reveal the "truth" and attack the villains. Hai Rui, it was said in mid-1959, was to be emulated for "daring to fight vicious powers" and "daring to hold on to truth"; Tian Han followed this advice to the letter. All the Hai Rui plays contain reflections about the social consequences of such intervention in the contemporary scene. These consequences are heavy in *Hai Rui baguan*, where Hai Rui is dismissed from office, in *Xie Yaohuan*, where Xie is killed, and in *Li Huiniang*, where Li too is killed. The authors of these dramas were not inexperienced; they had taken part in the battles of the fifties. But they saw a national crisis in both social and political terms, and they spoke out, quite aware of the risks. In terms of Great Leap realities Tian Han's scenario is even gruesomely true. Liu Shaoqi had seen *Xie Yaohuan* in Kunming in April or May of 1963. There was much apprehension because of its explosive political content, which was not lost on anyone. The question was put to Liu whether the play should be withdrawn, and he decided it should not. Later, in the beginning of January 1964, he spoke at a Conference on Work in Literature and the Arts about *Xie Yaohuan*, saying: "In the past, during the Great Leap Forward there were problems in our work, but to depict the weaknesses after they have been corrected is self-criticism. This may be written about." Nothing about the "problems" some leaders had with the play should be communicated to the lower levels, he ordered.

Tian Han is quoted as having said about the Great Leap: "One has to write about it, and has to transmit the lessons to one's sons and daughters."[110] In the summer of 1964 at the Peking Theater Festival, Kang Sheng gave his important speech advocating "revolutionary" plays on contemporary themes. In the same speech, he described *Xie Yaohuan* as an "anti-Party, anti-socialist poisonous weed." Nevertheless, somewhat later Jiang Qing asked Tian Han to cooperate in creating "revolutionary Peking operas"; he refused to do so.[111]

Of all the new historical dramatists, Meng Chao, the author of *Li Huiniang*, had the least political clout, and therefore his play was the first to be publicly denounced, in early 1965. In November of 1965, when Yao Wenyuan's article criticizing Wu Han's *Hai Rui baguan* appeared, Wu Han had the protection of the mayor of Beijing, Peng

110. Zhongguo juxie caofantuan, "Liu Shaoqi."
111. He Yantai and Li Dasan, *Tian Han pingzhuan*, p. 195.

Zhen. A few months later, in early February 1966, Tian Han's time finally came.[112] He was the last because of his link with Zhou Enlai. Criticism meetings in Gansu, Shaanxi, Yunnan, and Guangdong followed,
and the *Jiefang ribao* (Shanghai) described *Xie Yaohuan* as a "political
manifesto."

The criticisms of *Xie Yaohuan* did not lack sophistication. Written
by experienced and knowledgeable critics like Liu Housheng and He
Qifang, they did not fail to get the analytical points and political
message of the play. As anticipated in the play itself when Xie Yaohuan
is attacked for supporting a "rebellion," the critics accused Tian of
slandering the Party and its chairman with his criticism of the Great
Leap Forward, and they challenged him to name the villains attacked in
the play. Their charge, as this chapter illustrates, is accurate if polemical
and sometimes exaggerated. Nonetheless Tian Han's description of the
national and social crisis of the country in 1961 was quite in tune with
the actual events. Tian Han's predictions in the play turned out to be all
too true. Tian himself was eventually incarcerated as a "counterrevolutionary" in a prison set up under Kang Sheng's personal control. There
he died, on December 10, 1968.[113] The play was rehabilitated, together
with its author, in 1979. A funeral ceremony was held in front of an
empty urn, and the play was restaged and then made into a film. In a
Renmin ribao article announcing the rehabilitation of *Xie Yaohuan*, the
author argued: "Today some of our leaders are polluted by the thought
and work style of the exploiting classes. They transgress the laws and

112. Yun Song, "Tian Han de *Xie Yaohuan* shi yike daducao," in *Renmin
ribao*, Feb. 1, 1966, reprinted in *Juben* 1966.1, in *Xijubao* 1966.2, and in
Guangming ribao Feb. 2, 1966. The article takes up an entire page of the *People's Daily*. Yin Mo, "*Xie Yaohuan* weishei 'qingming,'" in *Wenyibao*, 1966.2,
pp. 18ff. Wen Siye, "*Xie Yaohuan* de maotouci xiang nali?" in *Guangming
ribao* Mar. 23, 1966. Liu Housheng, "Fandang fanshehuizhuyi gongtongti—*Li
Huiniang, Hai Rui baguan, Xie Yaohuan* zonglun," in *Xijubao* 1966.3, pp. 7ff.
Shi Yansheng, "'Wei min qingming' shi Tian Han tongzhi yiguan de fandong
sixiang," ibid., pp. 13ff. Wei Qun, "Tian Han tongzhi yao ba xiju chuangzuo
yin xiang hechu?" ibid., pp. 17ff. Xu Yingshan, "Shitan 'qingguan xi' de
duhai," ibid., pp. 20ff. Other articles of this period are summarized in Ref.
Dept. of *Xijubao*, "Dui *Hai Rui baguan, Xie Yaohuan* deng de dapipan jixu
shenru," ibid., pp. 24ff.; and Zhong Ju, "Jiechuan Tian Han zhizuo *Xie Yaohuan* de fangeming qitu," *Guangming ribao* Dec. 18, 1966. Earlier reviews had
been friendly; cf. Yi Bing, "Manhua *Xie Yaohuan*," *Xijubao* 1962.3, pp. 6ff.;
and (name illegible), "Lingren nanwang de *Xie Yaohuan*," *Xinjiang ribao*, Dec.
17, 1961.

113. He Yantai and Li Dasan, *Tian Han pingzhuan*, p. 197.

flout the regulations without any regard for the interests of the people so that there are many problems indeed and we need people who dare to struggle against them. We should not forget the time when Lin Biao and the Gang of Four ruled supreme and brought such profound disaster upon the state and the people. Did they not use the very methods employed by Wu Sansi and Lai Junchen, fabricating so many wrong verdicts, trumped-up charges, and false charges, and destroying so many good and loyal people like He Long and Chen Yi?"[114] The article uses the same interpretive technique that we have seen, reading the play as an early attack on the Gang of Four and a timely warning about persistent problems; the only difference is the evaluation.

POSTFACE

In the above analysis I have been concerned with interpretation, not with evaluation. The play sustains a very close reading of open and silent texts. It is a *pièce à thèses*, and thus the author leaves little room for the character of his protagonists to unfold in any complex manner.

The play implies a fairly detailed social and political analysis of the state of the nation at the time, engaging in friendly debate as well as implied bitter polemics with other assessments, be they in literary or other form. My intention in this study is to make the voice of the play and its author better heard, and to introduce an additional voice into the few that tell us about this cataclysmic time. Certainly, to interpret Tian's play does not imply agreement with his conclusions. One might argue that purely moral categories are not sufficient to explain the dissolution of the social fabric during the Great Leap Forward, that Tian retained all too much faith in the empress, that he overtaxed the powers of the palace lady, and that he glorified his heroes too unabashedly. And finally one might take issue with the sad drainage of dramatic substance that has occurred in transforming Song Zhidi's daring piece into this dramatic litany.

Our first duty, however, is to understand what is said. In this chapter I have tried to fulfill a part of this duty.

114. Li Chao, "*Xie Yaohuan* de fusu," p. 3.

Monkey King Subdues the White-Bone Demon: A Study in PRC Mythology

Among the popular novels of earlier times informing the fantasy of the Chinese public, both literate and illiterate, the *Xiyou ji*, or *Journey to the West*, occupies a prominent place. Since the late sixteenth century it has been available in many editions. Not a few of its episodes have been adapted into the various types of Chinese operas and puppet plays, contributing to the public's familiarity with both plot and characters. It thus became part of the rich background texture of Chinese thought, speech, and behavior; it is to the present day an inexhaustible archive for role modeling, argumentative wit, and political innuendo.

One element, however, differentiates the *Xiyou ji* from other popular novels such as the *Shuihu zhuan* (Water Margin), the *Sanguo zhi yanyi* (Three Kingdoms), or the *Fengshen yanyi* (Investiture of the Gods): it shows an arduous quest for an ultimate goal. Tang Seng sets out with his disciples Sun Wukong (the Monkey King or "Monkey"), Zhu Bajie ("Pigsy"), and Sha Heshang ("Monk Sha"), for the Western Heaven, where the Buddha resides, to find Him and the teachings of the Mahāyāna, the Great Vehicle, which is great enough to carry all living beings across the sea of suffering. The basic metaphor is thus the same as in John Bunyan's *The Pilgrim's Progress*, in which the hero, Christian, battles with a multitude of demonic temptations and dangers on his way to the Heavenly City. Tang Seng's inner faculties—his mind, will, sensual nature, and the like—are transformed allegorically into real characters, with the Monkey King acting as his mind, Pigsy as his visceral nature, his horse as his will, and so forth. The *Journey to the West* thus becomes an allegory for the way of the Buddhist adept to enlightenment and deliverance from suffering, and the author takes pains to keep the reader mindful of this second level of the narrative.

The basic model of history as salvation history was absorbed into the Marxist world view from European Christian sources: in Marxism it was secularized into a theory of revolution leading to the eventual establishment, after a period of transition, of eternal communist bliss. After the victory of the Chinese Communist revolution, the *Xiyou ji* offered one of the few autochthonous and familiar plot structures able to meaningfully resonate—to use Benjamin Schwartz's term—with the revolutionary transformation.

Two parts of the plot were especially suited for this purpose—Sun Wukong's creating an uproar in Heaven and the battles between the heroes and various demons on the way to the West. The former became the image of revolution, the latter an image of the problems to be encountered in the transition period from capitalism to communism —in other words, in socialism. The focus of this study is on the latter element, but we will first deal briefly with the former, as it is of importance in making identifications between the story's characters and contemporary figures and issues.

GREAT UPROAR IN HEAVEN

To suit present-day needs, changes were made in the plots of the operas dealing with Monkey's uproar in Heaven. In the original version of the *Xiyou ji*, Monkey is subdued after many battles and incarcerated under a mountain. This ending did not fit the victory of the Revolution, and thus it was changed in the first PRC edition in 1953.[1] In that version

---

1. I use the two-volume edition of Wu Cheng'en's *Xiyou ji* published by Zuojia chubanshe in 1954 and the four-volume translation by Anthony C. Yu, *The Journey to the West*. The text of the older version of the Peking opera *Nao tiangong* is found in Zhang Bojin, ed., *Guoju daguan*, vol. 6, pp. 183ff. The revised version of *Nao Tiangong* is in Zhongguo xiqu yanjiuyuan, ed., *Jingju congkan*, vol. 8, pp. 1ff.

Another play from the Sun Wukong group, *Sun Wukong xiangyao fumo* (Sun Wukong Subdues Demons), which was popular in 1954 in the Northeast, was staged in Shanghai in 1959. It was based on the episode of the demon turning the forest into a fire wall to block the advance of the pilgrims. Evidently the episode was seen as a metaphor for the war with Japan and the KMT, so the ending was changed. Instead of the lands being left scorched, "the great earth

Monkey, steeled and tempered from battle, comes out victorious. During the mid-fifties, the most skilled of Chinese animated-film artists, Wan Laiming, started work on his own version of the story, *Danao tiangong* (Great Uproar in Heaven), by far the most successful and original use of this new medium in postrevolutionary China.[2] The film was first shown, it seems, in 1961. In tune with the revised opera versions, it developed the first seven chapters of the *Xiyou ji* into a powerful image of the triumphant Chinese revolution. As the film was shown widely to audiences down to the village level and was the piece with the greatest influence on popular fantasy, I will use it here. Without further ado, I will proceed in this short summary to the identification of characters and events, the proof for the identifications coming with the consistency of the match between the two levels.

The opening scenes of the film relate how for hundreds of years, cosmic forces have interacted to imbue an egg-shaped stone on a mountaintop with life. From this stone springs Monkey, a being of magical powers. Joining up with other simians, he becomes their leader and they find a haven secure from their enemies on Flower-Fruit Mountain. There, Monkey trains his kin in the martial arts. Social harmony prevails on their mountain, and they lead a modest but happy life under his enlightened guidance. However, Monkey lacks a weapon suited to his powers. The heaviest halberds just break in his hands. He travels to the bottom of the Eastern Sea, where the Dragon King points to a giant yardstick used by Great Yu of old to determine the depth of the rivers and oceans. Monkey contemplates this huge pillar, which is now without luster and encrusted with shells like an old ship. From his mind rays emanate; the crusts peel off, revealing a shining golden rod. As the earth trembles Monkey wrenches the pillar free, and with his magic powers he transforms the unwieldy monster into a fighting rod whose size he can reduce at will to the length of needle, which can be stored in his ear when it is not needed.

These scenes offer a fine parable on the early stages of the Chinese revolution, as seen from the perspective of the late fifties. This was a time when the Mao cult reached its first heights, and the Central Party

---

returned to spring and all things came to life again," a change that was to illustrate developments after 1949. See *Wenyibao* Aug. 6, 1959.

2. See Jay Leyda, *Dianying*, pp. 291 and 384. See also Zhongguo dianying zihaoguan and Zhongguo yishu yanjiuyuan, dianying yanjiusuo, eds., *Zhongguo yishu yingpian bianmu*, vol. 1, p. 610.

School decided to make Mao into the greatest living Marxist-Leninist. The magical birth of the chairman in China was described in a song that was much publicized at the time. "The East is red, the Great Sun rises, China has brought forth Mao Zedong," it began. "The East is Red" replaced the national anthem during the Cultural Revolution. The song's political and magical imagery is repeated in the first scenes of the film, which show the birth of Monkey; indeed Mao and the Monkey King were seen to mirror each other in the following decades. Flower-Fruit Mountain was an easy allegory for the "liberated areas" in the inaccessible regions of China's Northwest, and the search for the proper weapon echoed the Chairman's search for the ideological instrument with which to beat down all enemies. Like Monkey, Mao is confronted with an old, encrusted, unwieldy, and rusty thing—orthodox Marxism. Using his brain (the rays emanating from his head), he clears it of rust and debris and transforms it into an invincible handy fighting rod, which is stored where Mao Zedong Thought is stored, in his head. His weapon is thus a mental, an ideological weapon.

In another scene in the movie, the assembled heavenly authorities conspire to win Monkey over, or subdue him. He is put in charge of the heavenly stables, but when he sees horses standing, short-tethered, in their mud, he sets them free. Taken to task for this crime, he wrecks the stables and leaves in a huff. The authorities make him another offer, this time to be in charge of the garden where the peaches of immortality grow. But he discovers that his rank on the heavenly hierarchy is so low that he is not even invited to the Peach Banquet of the Queen Mother. After eating all the peaches, he leaves on another rampage and brings the peaches of immortality to his little people. The authorities in the heavenly superstructure now decide to subdue him with violence. They come with the most modern arms and much bragging, but Monkey and his witty and well-trained simian army use guerrilla methods to beat back these attacks. Eventually, Monkey is caught by magic and put into Laozi's cauldron, where the old sage normally manufactures his immortality pills. Unexpectedly, however—in a completely new element in the story—Monkey is not pulverized but emerges steeled and tempered.

The scenes I have just described offer a parable for the war years. The main confrontation is the one between Monkey and his simian kin, on the one hand, and the authorities in the superstructure of state and ideology, on the other. The Marxist notion of the superstructure finds a lively counterpart in the "Heaven" of the *Xiyou ji*. The change in the ending allows for a pun on the present: the emergence of a victorious

Mao. Other elements that lacked an echo in the present were changed, too. In older versions Monkey refines his powers early in his career by studying under the Buddhist Patriarch Subodhi. The motive for these studies is his fear of ending in Yama's realm, death. This episode was cut as well.

The identification of the Monkey King Sun Wukong with Mao Zedong is no flat innuendo. The figure of Sun is fully developed in the film and not just a stand-in for Mao Zedong. The implied argument is, rather, that Mao Zedong embodies in the present world all the characteristics that made a popular hero of Sun Wukong, who, as is asserted time and again, represents the most lively and progressive elements of the Chinese people.

SUN WUKONG DEFEATS THE WHITE-BONE DEMON

Wan Laiming's film was a paean to the Chinese revolution and Mao Zedong. In the meantime, however, China had in its own terms become a socialist state on its way to Communism, with new and complex problems. Happily, the *Xiyou ji* provided further illustration for these problems, and even the contemporary counterparts for Sun and the magic rod could remain the same. The Great Leap Forward had ended in human suffering on a massive scale. The many disastrous decisions made then showed that the leadership had a severely distorted picture of the country. Mao Zedong himself was strongly identified with the Great Leap, and thus he was in for criticism, especially during the renewed frenzy subsequent to the Lushan Plenum in late 1959. The focus of scholarship and polemics has been on literary works and essays containing this criticism, such as the Peking opera *Hai Rui baguan* (Hai Rui Dismissed from Office),[3] but no attention has been paid heretofore to the fact that both sides, supporters as well as critics of Mao, were using the pen and the stage for their purposes. The publication of the fourth volume of Mao's *Selected Works* in 1961 was clearly intended as a reminder that Mao had been mostly right in his judgments during the crucial phase between 1945 and 1949 and that most of his present critics had been wrong.[4] But this era also produced other, literary, works.

In the spring of 1960, leaders from the Cultural Bureau of Zhejiang Province spotted a plot traditionally played by the Shaoxing Opera

3. See chapter 4 for details and bibliography.
4. The point is made by Joffe, *Between Two Plenums*, pp. 22ff.

Troupe of that province. The cultural leaders felt the play had "great educational meaning" for contemporary affairs. Tao Junqi directs us to the original play.[5] The original title was *Huangbao gui* (The Monster with the Yellow Robe), var. *Baoxiang guo* and *Qing mei Houwang*; the plot had been rewritten by Li Shaochun into *Zhiji mei Houwang* (Arousing Monkey King with Wit), var. *Guloushan Houwang ji humo* (On Skull Mountain the Monkey King Attacks the Specter Demon), which then had been made into a Shaoxing opera entitled *Da baigujing* (Beating the White-Bone Demon). The only edition available to me is *Zhiji mei Houwang*, which was published in Beijing in 1958.[6] The core elements of the later plot are already assembled here. In the play, Tang Seng, Sun Wukong, and the others are going through the wastelands on their journey to the West to find the holy scriptures. On the way lurks the Yellow Robe Monster. To trap the pilgrims, the monster transforms itself into a young woman bringing food to her father in the fields and offers the food to Tang Seng. Sun Wukong arrives in time to kill the monster and throw the food on the ground, where it is transformed into demonic refuse. The monster then transforms itself into the mother of the young woman, only to be killed by Sun. What is left is again demonic refuse. Although this proof materializes where the body should have been, Zhu Bajie and Tang Seng are outraged, and the latter dismisses the Monkey King. Led by Zhu Bajie, the pilgrims end up in the trap and Tang Seng is caught by the monster. In a valiant attempt, Zhu Bajie and Monk Sha try to free their master, but Sha is caught and Zhu barely escapes. He hastens to Sun Wukong's Flower-Fruit Mountain to ask Sun for help. Sun Wukong remembers Zhu Bajie's earlier words, which led to his being dismissed by the master, and prepares to have Zhu tortured. In a desperate attempt to convince Sun, Zhu finally charges that Sun Wukong is afraid of the Yellow Robe Monster and if he dared to show up in front of the monster, the latter would ridicule him as a "red-assed monkey." Incensed at this suggestion, Sun is, as the title announces, "aroused through [Zhu's] wit," and he joins in the battle to free the master. The battle ends in success after a lot of fighting in the dark on stage, and the pilgrims' journey can continue.

The Zhejiang "cultural leaders" were not entirely without orientation when seeing this play. Not only had the film *Great Uproar in Heaven* already made the story of the Monkey King into a familiar

---

5. Tao Junqi, *Jingju jumu chutan*, p. 162.
6. *Zhiji mei Houwang*, pp. 33ff.

image for the revolution, the *Journey to the West* itself had also received its contemporary interpretation.

In a talk given in March 1958, Mao had given his interpretation of the contemporary meaning of the *Journey to the West*. There, he said:

> Pilgrim Sun respects neither law nor Heaven, why don't [you] all learn from him? He is against dogmatism; he dares to act and dares to do things. Zhu Bajie is liberalism, but with some revisionism; he always thinks about getting demobilized. Of course that Party was no good. It was the Second International [of 1889], and Tang Seng corresponds to [Edward] Bernstein.[7]

Mao thus implies a link between the enterprise itself, the Journey to the West, and the revolutionary endeavor, the achievement of communism. This point is implied, because it was already familiar. As evidence of its familiarity, two earlier references in popular material may be adduced.

In late 1956, Song Tan wrote a satire in the journal *Xin guancha* entitled "*Xiyou ji* xinbian" (A New Chapter of the *Xiyou ji*).[8] In it, the pilgrims arrive at *bangzi ling*, the Peak of Clubs (that is, sticks). The local monster has stolen a judge's vermilion pencil and specializes in making hats with which it catches its victims. It catches Tang Seng with a hat that is inscribed "adventurist" (because he left Chang'an and roamed about), Zhu Bajie's is inscribed "degenerate in thinking" (because he longed for a wife), while Sha is guilty of "being nice to everyone around" *(haoren zhuyi)*, and the horse, of having a "slave mentality." This bureaucratic monster now goes after Sun with a hat inscribed "lack of organization and discipline." Even Sun is no match for these devices, and the Bodhisattva Guanyin herself has to intervene. Surprisingly, the monster turns out to be a Buddhist monk of heavenly descent. It is not killed, but is brought before the heavenly disciplinary commission. After all, since the bureaucrats are "Buddhist" monsters, it would be inadvisable to deal too severely with them even in a satire. Zhu Bajie kicks the hats around in a fury, and when the pilgrims collect them, 112 are missing; obviously they have found their way into the realm of men. The story orders its readers to bring them to the editorial board of *Xin guancha* to be returned to the original owner. The story

---

7. *Mao Zedong sixiang wansui* (1979), repr. Hongkong: Bowen Publ., n.d., p. 185. Edward Bernstein (1850–1932) was selected by Lenin as his chief reformist opponent, who wanted to "revise" Marxist doctrine on the imminent collapse of capitalism and the doctrine of Revolution based thereon.

8. Song Tan, "*Xiyou ji* xinbian," pp. 28ff.

does not differentiate very clearly between the various pilgrims, but it is clear that they together stand for the Party, led by Mao, which is obstructed on the way to communism by people of "good background" who have turned into bureaucrats.

Some months later, the vice-head of a village, in a story published in *Renmin wenxue*, casually referred to the parallel between the *Xiyou ji* and the Communist endeavor. "Our work here is pretty much like Tang Seng's quest for the scriptures. One has to go through nine times nine [i.e., eighty-one] difficulties, and then success will come all by itself."[9] Neither author saw a need to elucidate the metaphor any further.

In his talk, Mao Zedong identifies the entire pilgrim group as "the Party," albeit in the old sense of the Communist International, which in theory was organized as one single Party with national "branches." Tang Seng represents the political spirit pervading that Party— Bernsteinian "revisionism." He is qualitatively different from the other pilgrims, serving as the frame of mind of the whole. Zhu Bajie and Sun Wukong represent different currents within the Party, Sun the revolutionary "anti-dogmatic" option, Zhu a "liberal-revisionist" option. Mao does not specify who the monster represents, but there is only one slot left, "imperialism." In the original version of his "On the Correct Handling of Contradictions" (1957), which has recently become available from an unofficially printed 1967 edition of *Xuexi wenxuan*, Mao referred to Stalin's Soviet Union half satirically as the "Western Paradise" whence the Chinese cadres get their "true scriptures."[10]

Mao Zedong took a moderate line when he identified Tang Seng as Eduard Bernstein. Tang is part of the enterprise, and although he makes many mistakes, he is never dismissed in the *Xiyou ji*. Revisionism at the time is defined as a deviant current within the movement. Mao certainly was not dealing with history in an academic manner but was talking about the immediate present, in which he was taking Sun's role—that is, that of Lenin in the Bernstein case. The identification of Tang Seng with Bernstein contains a subtle hint about possible further developments. Eventually, it will be recalled, Lenin did set up the Third International and denounced Bernstein's Second for capitulating before im-

9. Bai Wei, "Bei weikun de nongzhuang zhuxi," here quoted from *Chong-fang de xianhua*, p. 306.
10. Mao Zedong, "Guanyu zhengque chuli renmin neibu maodun de wenti," p. 196. I am indebted to Roderick MacFarquhar for giving me access to this source.

perialism. There is thus a latent contradiction between Mao's historical allusion to Bernstein and the fixed plot of the *Xiyou ji*, in which no such development is envisaged.

Seeing that *Sun Wukong sanda baigujing* could aptly illustrate Mao's current assessment of revisionism, imperialism, and himself, the Zhejiang Bureau set up a "small group" to revise the play. The group was under the direct "guidance of the leading comrades concerned," the group's head wrote in 1962.[11] As revised, the plot put strong emphasis on the growing conflict between Tang Seng and Sun Wukong, reflecting the growing differences with the Soviet leadership, which were more and more openly expressed.[12] Late in 1960, the Zhejiang Provincial Opera troupe was invited to Shanghai, and there the play received a dramatic boost. It was not only adapted to the Huai and Peking opera styles but made into a children's dance drama. Furthermore, a film version was begun. It was to be a color film for national distribution, the highest category of films.[13] These activities surely involved a high-level decision from cultural and political leaders in Shanghai. The mayor, Ke Qingshi, was very close to Mao at the time, and he had been instrumental in pushing many of the Great Leap policies. One of the City Committee members was Chang Chunqiao, who took care of many cultural activities. The details of the rapid promotion of the opera are not known, however.

A year later, in early October 1961, the troupe made it one step higher, being invited to Beijing, where it gave six public performances of the Sun Wukong play.[14] One of those who saw it was Guo Moruo, the "national poet" and president of the Chinese Academy of Sciences.

---

11. Wang Guming, "Gaibian *Sun Wukong sanda baigujing* de tihui," pp. 1ff.

12. Evidence is the review by Bao Shiyuan and Gong Yijiang, "Kan Shaoju *Sun Wukong sanda baigujing*," p. 21, where they talk about a "step-by-step deepening of the conflict between Tang Seng and Sun Wukong." The article, written in late 1960, deals with the first revision. Furthermore, see Guo Moruo, "Yuyou chengqing wanli ai," col. 1. Guo there maintains that when he saw the play in 1961, "the figure of Tang Seng on stage made people really hate him."

13. See Bao and Gong, "Kan Shaoju." That it was a color film is inferred from the advertisements for it in *Beijing ribao* Oct. 16, 1961, where this is mentioned.

14. See the advertisements in *Renmin ribao* on Oct. 6 and in *Beijing ribao* on Oct. 16 and 19.

He had by then written two plays, *Cai Wenji* and *Wu Zetian*, to defend Mao and to counter what Guo saw as the ill winds blowing in the field of "new historical drama."

Guo quickly discerned what he assumed to be the "educational meaning for contemporary affairs" in the play, given the high pitch of polemics against Soviet "revisionism" in the newspapers at the time. He saw the play on October 18, and, asked by members of the Zhejiang troupe to give his critical advice *(yijian)*, wrote them a poem on the twenty-fifth. There had been no review of the play in the Beijing papers—they might have disagreed with the political line of the piece— but Guo got his poem and a summary of the play published in *Renmin ribao* on November 1.

Wu Han's *Hai Rui baguan* was just being staged in Peking, Zhou Xinfang's *Hai Rui shangshu* had guest performances in the capital, Tian Han's and Meng Chao's plays *Xie Yaohuan* and *Li Huiniang* had just been published. All of these were more or less critical of the Chairman and the Great Leap, all the greater reason for Guo to advertise the Sun Wukong play and its lessons. Guo's poem, entitled "Seeing 'Sun Wukong Three Times Beats the White-Bone Demon,'" ran as follows:

Humans and demons he confounds, right and wrong he confuses;
toward enemies he is merciful, toward the friend he is mean.
His incantation of the "Golden Hoop [Contracting] Spell" was heard ten
    thousand times,
while a demonic escape of the White-Bone Demon he let happen three times in a
    row.
A thousand knives should cut Tang Seng's flesh to pieces,
One pluck—how would it diminish the Great Sage's hair,
This timely teaching may be highly praised,
even Zhu Bajie's insight surpassed that of the fools.[15]

The first four lines are unambiguous. Guo attacks Tang Seng for his ideological muddleheadedness and for showing Buddhist mercy to his enemies, the various transformations of the Demon, while being mean to Sun Wukong, who helps him. Tang recites the spell that makes the band around Sun's head contract, causing unbearable pain, and thereby contributes to the Demon's escape. Eventually he even dismisses Sun. For this he deserves to be cut to pieces. The next line, however, is more intricate, as there are, and quite intentionally so, two readings. It runs

15. Guo Moruo, "Kan *Sun Wukong sanda baigujing* shuzeng Zhejiang sheng shaojutuan," p. 6. For a translation of this poem, see *Ten More Poems of Mao Tse-tung*, p. 29.

yiba hekui dasheng mao. Word for word this means: One pluck (or "one dismissal")—how would it be a loss to the Great Sage Mao (or, as Mao's name means "hair," to the Great Sage's hair).

With this fairly tortuous grammatical construction, Guo, who has been among the most unabashed panegyrists for Mao, manages to slip in the expression *dasheng mao*, the Great Sage Mao, equating Mao Zedong with Sun Wukong, whose grand title is *Qitian dasheng*, Great Sage Equal to Heaven. Other scholars also have noted this point.[16] If Sun is Mao, who are the other pilgrims? Amazingly, the poem hardly refers to the White-Bone Demon, instead focusing its attack on Tang Seng.

Tang Seng capitulates to the Demon; he also suppresses Monkey. In a later article, Guo Moruo explains that Tang Seng corresponds to Nikita Khrushchev.[17] The "modern revisionists" under Khrushchev, Chinese polemicists charged at the time, had capitulated to imperialism. When Guo wrote the poem, the Soviet Party just held its Twenty-second Congress. Khrushchev proclaimed "peaceful transition" to Communism to be the goal, and "peaceful coexistence with (U.S.) imperialism" to be the base line of Soviet foreign policy. He said that the country was now entering the first stage of Communism after having achieved the socialist transition. The Soviet Union would rapidly leave behind the Western economies, and then the attraction of its social system would be irresistible; therefore, "peaceful transition" to socialism could replace revolution in the other states.

In Guo's view of the world, the problem was not imperialism, the White-Bone Demon. That was a familiar monster. The group of pilgrims represented the international Communist movement. Tang Seng/Khrushchev was suppressing the "revolutionary" forces who were out to "kill" the Demon and were best embodied in Mao Zedong himself, the great Chairman "equal to Heaven." For this Tang Seng deserved death. Guo even tried to read the term *sanda*, the beating down of the three transformations of the Demon, as a reference to the experience of the international Communist movement.[18] Finally, who corresponds to Zhu Bajie? Zhang Xiangtian has suggested that in another poem by Guo (given below), Guo refers to himself in this image.[19] Zhang's sug-

16. Zhang Xiangtian, *Mao*, vol. 4, p. 122.
17. See Guo, "'Yuyou.'"
18. Ibid.
19. Zhang Xiangtian, *Mao*, p. 125.

gestion seems valid for this poem, too. It is modest self-reference. Even he, the muddleheaded Guo Moruo, eventually proves to be more intelligent than the "stupids," which as Mao's reply to the poem suggests would refer to Tang. Zhang suggests that Zhu may correspond to those fooled by Khrushchev, that is, the European Communist leaders, but there is nothing in the poem to substantiate this.[20] I tend to support the Chairman's view in this matter. In the play Zhu Bajie realizes the true nature of the imperialist Demon when the Demon shows its true face and catches the pilgrims. Zhu fights his way out of the Demon's grotto to implore Sun Wukong, whom he had earlier repressed, to come back, save them from disaster, and take the lead again. One might read this as a self-critical reference to Guo's role as a member of the Soviet-dominated World Peace Council. Within the poem, Guo pledges his allegiance to the *dasheng Mao*, the Great Sage Mao.

His proposal for action against Tang Seng is contained in the line "one pluck—how would it be a loss to the Great Sage Mao [or 'the Great Sage's hair']." Tang Seng "should" be cut to pieces. Short of this, he should be "plucked out" and dismissed. To do so would also include a purge of his followers in China (as in the campaign against "right opportunism" then going on). Given the sage's millions of hairs, all of which can be transformed into miniature editions of himself, one pluck would hardly detract from his furry appearance.

Sadly, Guo Moruo, who had been quick to identify the "educational meaning" of the play and had done all he could to make it more widely known, had completely missed the point. True, the play had suggested this interpretation, and he had truthfully expressed this alignment in his poem, but he had failed to notice that the political situation had evolved. What the Chairman had indicated by talking in 1958 about the Second International—that a split would develop, that Eduard Bernstein would capitulate to imperialism and try to get at the revolutionary forces, and that eventually Lenin would "have to" set up his own International—had now happened again. Historical development had exploded the historical screen which he had used in 1958, and which had been the basis for the play and Guo's interpretation. Guo, who evidently was familiar with the passage in the 1958 talk, had tried to be obedient and follow the Chairman's directives verbatim. But the Chairman was no Maoist; he could change his assessments more easily. After Guo's poem was published on November 1, his interpretation became a

20. Ibid., p. 122.

matter of public record on an extremely sensitive political issue. The Chairman was to take interpretive matters into his own hands.

Premier Zhou Enlai returned to Beijing on October 24, 1961, from Moscow's Party Congress. There had been bitter exchanges, both political and personal, between him and Khrushchev. Mao personally went to the airport with flowers to congratulate Zhou for his antirevisionist stance.[21] Zhou must have spent a substantial part of the time before he left for Moscow reviewing the Sun Wukong play. The actor who played the part of Monkey recalls that the Premier went "four times" and then recommended it to the Chairman.[22]

There had been six public performances, on October 8 and 9 in the Beijing Workers Club, on the eighteenth and the nineteenth in the National Palace (Minzu gong), and in the People's Theater (Renmin juchang) on the twenty-first and second. If Zhou had seen it four times before he left for Moscow on the sixteenth, there must have been internal performances for the leaders. No review appeared in the *Renmin ribao*, the *Guangming ribao*, or the *Beijing ribao*. The Chairman went, congratulated the actors, and, after Guo's poem had appeared, he spelled out on November 17 the new, true, and only interpretation in a poem, "Reply to Comrade Guo Moruo." One day before, Khrushchev had pronounced the program of his recent Congress the "true Communist Manifesto of our times."[23] Mao's poem ran as follows:

Once when from the great earth a thunderstorm arises
there also will be a demonic coming to life of white-bone heaps.
The Monk[s] is [are] stupid and ignorant, but nevertheless can be instructed.
The Demon is treacherous and malicious, and by necessity will wreak disaster.
The Golden Monkey impetuously raises his thousand-*jun* rod,
and the jadelike firmament is cleared of dust for ten thousand miles.
When today Sun the Great Sage is acclaimed,
this is only because demonic vapors are on the rise again.[24]

This is a serious rebuttal of Guo Moruo's poem. Mao sets the plot into a larger perspective. The acceleration of life's intensity, once the thunderstorm of revolution arises on the great earth, is such that even the dead and decayed white-bone heaps of the rotten ideas of the old ruling classes are momentarily revived. This time, however, they are in the very heart of the thunderstorm of revolution. Incidentally, the

21. See the photograph in *Guangming ribao* Oct. 25, 1961, p. 1.
22. Liuling Tong, p. 77.
23. Zhang Xiangtian, *Mao*, p. 100.
24. Mao Zedong, "Qilü," p. 1.

White-Bone Demon is but such a heap of white bones. Within the Marxist and Maoist perception of the world, such a "revival" occurred after every revolution before and since the emergence of Marxism; in his notes on this poem, Guo Moruo referred to the struggles confronting Marx with Bukharin, Engels with Ferdinand Lassalle and others, Lenin with the Mensheviks, and now Mao with "modern revisionism." Guo pointed out later that he himself had identified the White-Bone Demon as "imperialism," while Mao in his poem correctly identified it as "opportunists who capitulate to imperialism," which had been the standard charge against the "revisionist" currents mentioned above.[25]

Mao thus operates a fundamental change in the interpretation of the play. Khrushchev's revisionism is not embodied in Tang Seng, but in the White-Bone Demon himself. In analytical terms, this indeed fits the substance of the play. The White-Bone Demon comes in all sorts of disguises, all of which are "Buddhist" (Marxist), but in fact it is only out to "eat" Tang Seng's flesh. The notion of "modern revisionism" fits the image of the White-Bone Demon much better than the traditional notion of saber-rattling imperialism.

In the play, there are two kinds of contradictions, those between "us and the enemy" and those "among ourselves." Mao had written much about the difference between the two. He saw his theory of the two kinds of contradictions as one of his main contributions to revolutionary doctrine. The White-Bone Demon is in essence "treacherous and malicious" regardless of outward appearance, and therefore will "by necessity" try to wreak disaster. Between the Demon and Tang Seng's group the contradiction is defined as "antagonistic," whereas Tang Seng, although he was stupid and dull-witted, "can be instructed." He remains "one of us." The general tone goes on with the following line. The Golden Monkey clears the air fouled by the Demon, using his magic cudgel. Historically, this would refer to Marx/Engels and Lenin excluding their ideological opponents. Guo Moruo assumed later that now the "third" beating down was to come. The last line in Mao's poem brings history up to the present. "Demonic vapors are on the rise again," he writes. They are "demonic" because they don't appear openly, hiding their essence in a disguise. When Mao's poem was published together with a commentary and another poem by Guo in January 1964, the *Wenyibao* editorialist wrote about these vapors:

25. Guo, "'Yuyou.'"

It is not at all surprising that within the world communist movement reactionary currents should rise. "Demonic vapors" will time and again recur and the jadelike firmament will eventually have to be cleansed. The main link is to hold up the banner of revolution, develop the spirit of struggle, and make clear the differences between ourselves and the enemy, and then in the end the people's victory will be certain.[26]

Vapors rise "within the world communist movement" and, of course, this refers to "Soviet revisionism." The contemporary incarnation of the Demon is thus Khrushchev. (Red Guards would later also read it as a reference to the "right opportunism" of Peng Dehuai, the inner-Chinese "revisionist" current.)[27]

Less than a month before Mao wrote his poem, Zhou Enlai was still maintaining in Moscow that the differences between the Chinese and Soviet parties were those among "fraternal parties or fraternal countries," which "should be resolved patiently in the spirit of proletarian internationalism."[28] The very congress, however, witnessed Khrushchev's transmutation, and the *Xiyou ji* was to bear the consequences.

Wan Laiming's film, the many Monkey plays, the Shaoxing opera, and Guo's poem all had come out with paeans for Sun the Great Sage. Mao does not repeat the flattering identification of himself as being the modern incarnation of Sun Wukong, but nothing indicates that he rejected it. The sudden rise in fervor toward him that he sees in some circles in 1961, he modestly adds, is due not to any personal attachment, but to the fact that the "demonic" and threatening vapors of Soviet revisionism are rising. That is the time when he is most needed.

Who then is Tang Seng? In the *Xiyou ji*, Tang Seng has *chujia*, left his family, to join the community of Buddhist believers. He is characterized as a man devoted to and specializing in "religion." He is the only monk to appear, and his features are bland and generalized, as is the name by which he is called in the story and the opera: Tang Seng, "the Monk from Tang" (China).

It is my hypothesis that Tang must now be read as a pun on *dang*, the (Chinese Communist) Party. Here I will only adduce some formal proofs; in the analysis of the play itself, there will be further discussion. This identification precludes any open discussion of this issue, but, needless to say, proofs *ex absentia contrarii* are not admissible either.

26. *Wenyibao* Jan. 1964, p. 1.
27. Beijing shi, "Jiekai."
28. Zhou Enlai, "Speech," p. 1053.

In a letter to Guo Moruo about Guo's poem, Mao spelled out his new identification of Tang: "'Thousand knives should cut Tang Seng's flesh to pieces' is not right. Toward the middle-of-the-roaders [*zhong-jian pai*] it would be better to pursue a united front policy."[29] Mao defines Tang Seng as a middle-of-the-roader. In his commentary to Mao's poem, Guo volunteers the explanation that they "stand between the White-Bone Demon and Sun Wukong, and have been deceived by the White-Bone Demon. Of such people there are relatively many."

Any attempt, however, to put Tang Seng and his companions on par does damage to the structure of both the opera and the *Xiyou ji*. In Tang Seng the ultimate purpose of the journey is invested, and to him belongs Sun's ultimate loyalty. Only the Party fits this image. Mao's statement about middle-of-the-roaders thus has to be read as a description of the Party's state of mind. The majority of the Party, that is, the majority of the leadership of it, belongs to the middle-of-the-road faction, but it can and should be saved. The "educational meaning" of the play (or the *potential* educational meaning, because the 1958 line was still being forced on a plot better suited to Mao's new line) was to give a scenario of what would happen to members of the Party if they were to go on failing to see the rightness of Sun Wukong's definition of the deadly nature of revisionism.

The name Tang Seng opened the way for the wordplay on *dang*. There would have been a wide variety of options for referring to the pilgrim; he could have been called by his "real" name, Xuan Zang or Sanzang (Tripitaka). In the historical drama of the time, the Tang dynasty, in which the *Xiyou ji* is set, provided a fairly common historical screen for the present, first because of the Tang/*dang* pun, second because the Tang had been a great period in Chinese history. Guo Moruo used it in this way in his *Wu Zetian* in 1960, and so did Tian Han in his reply to Guo, *Xie Yaohuan*. The identification between Tang and *dang* seems so strong that in contemporary short stories (*xiaoshuo*), people rarely have the family name Tang if they are not supposed to represent the Party. In Wang Meng's "Loyal Heart," Tang Jiuyuan is the Party leader, for instance.[30]

There is thus some foundation for the Tang/*dang* hypothesis. It will be recalled that already in Mao's 1958 talk, Tang Seng as Bernstein represented the current "state of mind" of the Party. Mao's criticism

---

29. Mao Zedong, "Letter to Guo Moruo."
30. Wang Meng, "Youyou cuncao xin."

was not lost on Guo Moruo. Mao's poem was not published at the time, but like everything that had to do with our opera, it was dealt with at the Politburo level. As Guo wrote in his commentary, Politburo member Kang Sheng "showed" Mao's poem to him (he did not "give" it to him) on January 6, 1962, in Guangzhou, whereupon Guo experienced "*henda de qifa*," supreme enlightenment. As detailed elsewhere in this book, Kang Sheng was instrumental in moving the battle of the factions from the stage to the prisons. Though he had come out strongly against the historical plays that were critical of the Chairman like those by Zhou Xinfang, Tian Han, Wu Han, and others, he seems to have supported the Sun Wukong play because of its political line.

Kang Sheng's gesture called for a speedy reaction. Guo instantly wrote a new poem to convey his updated insights to the Chairman.

> Due to the thunder rolling through the sky
>   [we] should not let the white bones gather in a pile.
> The Nine Heavens and Four Seas are cleared of blinding vapors,
>   nine times nine disasters will be overcome.
> The Monk suffered torment and learned bitter remorse,
>   the Pig in time got up to contribute its trifle.
> The golden pupil [eye] and the fiery glance will give no pardon,
>   why fear the monster even if it comes a hundred million times![31]

Let us examine the poem line by line. Mao had spoken out on the essence of revisionism, and with his poem had again elucidated the fundamental difference between the two types of contradictions. Based on this thunderous teaching, we should try to isolate the monster, instead of driving people into its ranks and helping it to let its white bones "gather in a pile" and become lively and strong. Now that the line is clear, the eighty-one disasters caused by various incarnations of the demon described in the *Xiyou ji* can all be overcome. The Monk made mistakes, it is true, but is essentially good; he has suffered and repented. He does not represent Khrushchev anymore, and therefore no longer should be cut to "a thousand pieces." As in the earlier poem, the "Pig" is "in time" with its change of line, and Guo still feels that he contributed his "trifle" to restoring Sun to his righteous leadership long before the Monk(s) saw his (their) mistake. The monkey, with his special faculties of the golden pupil and the fiery eye, can discern all revisionist monsters, even if they come, as Guo modestly states, "a hundred million times." They will be given no quarter.

31. Guo, "'Yuyou.'"

Mao acknowledged that Guo was now on the right path. "[Your] responding poem was all right."[32] When Mao's poem was officially published in early 1964, Guo contributed his trifle by writing a short analysis of the controversy, and included his reply poem.

However, if even the president of the Chinese Academy of Sciences was unable to understand the play's "real" and "new" meaning at first sight, it evidently would have to be rewritten to make the points clear. Based on Mao's redefinition of the play's key protagonists and the proper handling of contradictions, the little group from the Zhejiang ministry again went to work and in the summer of 1962 the final version was finished. It properly emphasized the two different kinds of contradictions. In the meantime, however, the struggle within the Party had become even fiercer, especially on stage. Thus not as much had to be changed; the play's "educational meaning" was not directed toward the Demon, which was essentially evil, but toward the class represented by Tang Seng (and Zhu Bajie) as well as toward the public, which was to observe their behavior in the real world. The film version was adapted to fit the new and slightly changed emphasis. A videotape version was available to me. The opera text was published, but neither the original edition of this text nor the first revision was available to me. In 1979, the Zhejiang People's Press published another edition, which according to the Postface slightly differs from the edition(s) of the sixties. The new editors state there that they "time and again systematically studied Comrade Mao Zedong's writings about the matter, in particular his 'Reply to Guo Moruo.' Taking guidance from Comrade Mao Zedong's literary thought we made some small changes in a few places while keeping to the principle of not greatly altering the original opera." In this version, Mao's poem is projected on a screen on the stage before the start of the opera; the difference between the various disguises of the White-Bone Demon is also stressed.[33] Apart from the videotape, we do have an earlier printed version of it, however. In 1962, a picture book based on the opera and the film was released for mass distribution;[34] it was widely used by the schools for its "educational

32. Ibid.
33. I have only this revised edition of 1979 in my hands, Zhejiang sheng wenhuaju *Sun Wukong sanda baigujing* zhengli xiaozu, *(Shaoju) Sun Wukong sanda baigujing.*
34. Wang Xingbei, text, Zhao Hongben and Qian Xiaodai, graphics, *Sun Wukong sanda baigujing.* The English version, *Monkey Subdues the White-Bone Demon*, was published by the Foreign Languages Press in 1964. There

meaning."[35] Its illustrations were directly taken from the opera performance and they closely follow the costumes, gestures, and staging. The captions are based on the opera but are not necessarily the same word for word. They were simplified in order to drive home the story's "educational" points. While the overall plot is retained, the action is streamlined, cutting, for instance, the slow beginning of the opera, in which Zhu Bajie is sent ahead to explore and promptly falls asleep under a tree, only to be discovered there by Monkey. However, for our purposes the picture book has a triple advantage. First, together with the videotape it is the oldest available version; second, it is the most widely distributed version; third, with its exceedingly skillful illustrations it presents us for this study with easily reproducible material. I will therefore use it as the primary source, and I will on occasion juxtapose passages from the opera text with captions from the picture book to enable the reader to independently assess the relationship between the two texts. The film was released for mass viewing even in obscure corners of the country. The high artistic quality of the opera, the picture book, and the film certainly contributed as much to public acceptance as the familiarity of the basic plot elements. By 1979, a newspaper would still refer to the film as "known to everyone."[36]

The picture book, which like the opera is entitled *Sun Wukong sanda baigujing*, was reprinted throughout the Cultural Revolution. The Foreign Languages Press translated it into various languages, and these editions, too, were available all during this period, a rarity of some political significance.

As the above documentation suggests, the play has received close attention from the country's top political and intellectual leaders. Its general political purport evidently was different from that of the historical dramas of the kind of *Hai Rui baguan*. In 1966, He Qifang singled it out as one of the few "historical" pieces that he deemed "correct," as opposed to the plays of Tian Han, Wu Han, Meng Chao, and others.[37]

---

were further editions in 1973 and 1976. Zhao Hongben did most of the drawing. He remained active during the Cultural Revolution, with a picture book on the Small Sword Society (*Xiaodao hui*) in 1974 and another in the context of the Shuihu campaign, *Touxiangpai Song Jiang* in 1973.

35. Unger, *Education under Mao*, p. 269, n. 9.

36. Shi Gandang, "Tang Seng he minzhu." The videotape is commercially available from Solid Video Ltd, Hongkong.

37. He Qifang, "Ping *Xie Yaohuan*," p. 23.

Nevertheless, it has received little scholarly attention despite the picture book's familiarity. The interaction of the *Xiyou ji* elements and the character of a picture book, which in our culture belongs to the trivial genre handed to children, probably discouraged a closer reading. Even a scholar as aware of the social and political implications of PRC opera as Zhao Cong has stated that *Sun Wukong sanda baigujing* was "nearly without propagandistic content."[38] Maybe he enjoyed the piece and concluded that therefore it could not be propaganda. However, as a side effect of our investigation of the background of our opera text, we have found that the politics of this obscure literary text were considered of highest institutional and political prominence, and that its implications were in fact handled by the Chairman himself (and enacted by his supporter Kang Sheng).

THE PICTURE BOOK *SUN WUKONG SANDA BAIGUJING*

THE SITUATION

We will now proceed to a close reading of the entire picture book. A considerable number of changes were made in the plot of the opera from the original novel. Such changes were politically loaded, as they were made with evident intention.

In both novel and picture book, the purpose of Tang Seng and his disciples is to "journey to the West to get holy scriptures." In the novel, the West or Western Heaven is the place where the Buddha resides, and the novel describes the gradual purification of Tang and his entourage until they arrive in (attain) this realm (state) of eternal bliss. In the picture book text, however, the meaning of "West" and "scriptures" is not further defined. The area through which the pilgrims have to pass before arriving "there" is inhospitable and lacks food and comfort; "there," however, the most felicitous circumstances prevail. The "scriptures" mark this destination as the realm of orthodoxy consummated. The combination of material plenitude and orthodoxy would give the image of full Communism, with the implication that it is from the West that both Marxism and technical modernism reached China. After Monkey's great and now-successful revolutionary uproar in the superstructure, Tang Seng and his group now traverse the dangerous and uncharted area of transition between the Revolution and the glorious state of final Communism.

38. Zhao Cong, *Zhongguo dalu de xiju gaige*, p. 185.

Indeed, the Marxist classics gave little guidance for this area, and the Soviet example was no longer in good standing in China when the opera was produced. In 1962 Mao Zedong still spoke of the "unkown realm of socialist economy."[39] Thus, in the first picture (fig. 1) there is no well-trodden way on which the pilgrims can walk; instead, they venture through uncharted lands.

The text reads: "Sun Wukong of Great Uproar in Heaven fame together with Zhu Bajie and Monk Sha protect Tang Seng on his way to the Western Paradise to get the scriptures. With Wukong taking the lead and exploring the way, all four together, master and disciples, cross mountains and wade through streams, all the time hastening toward the West."

We will return to the pilgrims' personalities later on. Here, our interest is in defining the situation, the framework of time. The journey being a metaphor for the time axis, we might be able to define the time of the reader. At what point of the narrative is the reader? Did the event being described occur in the distant past? Have all the troubles of this difficult journey already been mastered? Or are these troubles ahead, impending "now," in the reader's present?

In figure 1, the pilgrims are coming toward us out of the metaphorical past of the revolution achieved. After winning his battles against the old superstructure, the Monkey King is now leading the group through this difficult transitional period. The time is the very present of the reader; the problems confronting the pilgrims are those immediately at hand.

From the first picture on, the journey to the West is arrested. Only on one occasion do Tang and his disciples take further steps. But they do so only after Tang Seng has dismissed Monkey, and thus there is no progress in these steps; they go sidewise into a trap set up by the demon. Thus, as long as the problem presented in the text is not solved, no further progress is possible. Only at the very end can the pilgrims advance further on their way, as shown in the final picture (see figure 16). Here, Sun Wukong again takes the lead, guiding the pilgrims away from us into the future. Both he and Zhu Bajie invite the reader to join in the further advance.

The story thus offers a predictive and educative scenario of the immediately impending obstacles to further progress in the transition to communism, projecting events onto the historical screen of the

39. Mao Zedong, *Talk*, p. 21.

Fig. 1.   The Pilgrims Set Off. Wang Xingbei (text), Zhao Hongben and Qian Xiaodai (illus.), *Sun Wukong sanda baigujing* (Shanghai: Shanghai renmin meishu Press, 1962), p. 1.

Xiyou ji. Its purpose is to educate the reader to understand the situation properly and take the correct side in the coming battles. Having defined the situation, let us move now to characterize the protagonists.

THE PROTAGONISTS

In the context of the *Xiyou ji*, Tang Seng alone is given a human biography. His fellow pilgrims are explicitly identified with his various faculties and urges, Sun Wukong being his mind, Zhu Bajie (Pigsy) his visceral nature and lust, Sha his stubborn endeavor, and Tang Seng's horse his will. Tang Seng is on occasion explicitly defined as the *Dao*, the Way—that is, the human quest for enlightenment. Tang's fellow pilgrims thus are his own faculties. Monkey, fast and nervous like the mind, is able to move through space at the speed of thought, unimpeded by obstacles. His weapon can be reduced to the mere physical nothingness of a thought, and it can be stored, appropriately, in his head, where thoughts and ideas are to be found; his rod can be reduced to miniature size and stuck into his ear. The battles he fights are with the demons of heterodoxy and temptation, spiritual battles at that. Zhu Bajie is already a hog, attesting to the low value given to bodily urges in Buddhist doctrine; he carries a muck-rake with nine prongs, so he can strike the nine (male) openings of the body of any fiend and metaphorically subdue him by visceral temptation. And so on. The entire group of pilgrims represents one single human being, with Tang Seng giving the idea of the whole, and each of his companions embodying one of his key features. The inner conflicts that arise during the hard quest for ultimate truth and bliss are presented here as the conflicts between his companions and also between the companions and Tang himself. His conflicts being externalized, Tang himself is portrayed as rather bland. This basic constellation of the *Xiyou ji* has been kept in the opera *Sun Wukong sanda baigujing*. This does not mean that Tang Seng is a secondary character. The entire enterprise of the journey to the West is for his benefit, he alone is riding a horse, and he is called "master." However, neither in the *Xiyou ji* nor in opera text and picture book is Tang idealized; rather the opposite is true. But without Tang, there would be no journey to the West. As I have suggested earlier, Tang Seng represents "the Party," exalted and bland, making mistakes but being the Party nevertheless. The image is quite compelling. Time and again the Party has come under criticism from its members and leaders in China, but its ultimate function has always been upheld, and "obedience to the Party" has been stressed. Tang Seng has left his family to become a monk in pursuit of the absolute truth of Buddhism, in the same way that Party members have to "leave" their families and enter into new bonds of allegiance prescribed within the Party, devoting themselves, according to the rules, to the rapid achievement of complete communism, with Marxism replacing Buddhism as the guiding light.

What the various disciples of Tang Seng represent, thus, is the inner composition of the Party. Both in the novel and in our texts, a hierarchy exists among the disciples, with Sun Wukong ranking highest, followed by Zhu Bajie and then Sha. In the *Xiyou ji* and the earlier opera version, the horse is also counted as a pilgrim, representing the will. In the picture book it has been eliminated from that role, evidently because no present-day social counterpart could be found in the scenario that the story was to illustrate.

The exalted status of the entire group when seen as the Party necessitated some changes. In the *Xiyou ji*, the pilgrims live by begging for offerings of vegetarian food from lay people. Tang Seng constantly sends off his disciples to beg for food and shelter. But, as Buddhist mendicants are described as social parasites in PRC books about Buddhism, this feature was felt to be inappropriate as a depiction of the Party's relationship with the lay "masses"; thus the begging has been eliminated.

Although Sun Wukong is the mind and leader of the enterprise, he is also in the service of Tang/*dang*, that is, under Tang Seng's firm control. He wears a band around his head that contracts, causing him unbearable pain, when Tang Seng recites the Tight-Fillet-Spell. The Party is thus able to give the Chairman a considerable headache, and it makes use of this device. It will be remembered that in the novel the headband was put around Sun Wukong's head by the Bodhisattva Guanyin in order to give to Tang Seng some control over a monkey that had even dared to wreak havoc in Heaven. When the evaluation of the revolution changed in the PRC, the rationale for the headband disappeared. Now the headband is just there, denoting the structural relationship between the Chairman and the Party. Even when unjustly tormented by the Party, the Chairman will serve it. The dull-wit image of Tang/*dang* in both opera and picture book corresponds well with the image of the Party as the bookish and bedridden Tang emperor in Guo Moruo's *Wu Zetian*; the structural relationship in that play between the emperor and Wu Zetian finds its replica here in the one between Tang Seng and Sun Wukong.

As Sun Wukong was to act as proxy for Mao Zedong, obviously the simian nature of the Monkey King had to be changed. In the opera, Monkey never scratches himself, nor does he search for fleas, and his disrespectful remarks to Tang Seng have been cut. In the process, the necessity for Tang Seng to have some device to control him also disappeared. Liu Litong, the actor who played the Monkey role, related that he did not adopt the traditional technique, "human behaving like a monkey" (*ren xue hou*), but invented a new technique of "monkey behaving like a human" (*hou xue ren*) to bring out this new aspect of the Monkey King,[40] which was necessitated by the exalted status of Monkey's real-life counterpart. We have already seen how in Guo Moruo's and Tian Han's plays Wu Zetian had to part with her proverbial sexual appetite for the same reason.

There remains thus a link at the institutional level between Tang and Sun. Sun leads, but he serves Tang and is subject to Tang's disciplinary measures, even if they are ill-advised.

Below Sun, the chairman, we have Zhu Bajie (Pigsy) in the middle level of the hierarchy. In the novel, it is Tang Seng who constantly clamors for food, even more so than the visceral Pigsy. But in the opera this aspect of Tang's nature is entirely vested in Zhu Bajie. Zhu's devotion to the demands of his stomach is not extraneous to his politics but leads to mistaken political judgments, and even to opposing Sun Wukong's leadership. Zhu's strong bent for the good life and his abhorrence of struggle make him an easy caricature for middle- and upper-level Communist cadres. Zhu's antics notwithstanding, the *Xiyou ji* never makes him into an "enemy" of the pilgrims' progress. He never turns into a demon or the like. This conciliatory note is retained in the opera and the picture book.

Finally, there is Monk Sha. In the *Xiyou ji*, both he and Zhu Bajie carry the luggage. In the opera and the picture book, Sha alone does the hard work, an indication of his low rank and modest role. Sha is utterly devoted to Tang Seng, but in case of conflict he sides with Sun Wukong, and he constantly urges the others to follow Sun's directives. Iconographically, he is depicted with the facial features and body posture characteristic of the "working class" or "poor and lower-middle peasants." In the novel Sha was originally a river monster, and he wears the skulls of his former victims as a necklace. This detail did not befit the base-level Party members and cadres on whom this character is to play, and thus the necklace is not mentioned and is eliminated from the

40. Liuling Tong, p. 78. This has also been noted by reviewers; see Bao Shiyan and Gong Yijiang, "Kan Shaoju," p. 21.

film. Sha lacks education and sharp wit, all his devotion and loyalty notwithstanding. A line said by Sun Wukong gives a surprisingly cutting characterization of this figure: "Monk Sha, you really are loyal and devoted; it is a pity that you lack qualification [*kexi meiyou benling*]." In the opera edition of 1979, this passage has been cut. It was obviously seen as a slander of the proletariat.

In the *Xiyou ji*, all three disciples engage in battles with demons, but in the opera and the picture book, it is Sun alone who recognizes the demons and battles them to the very end. Only very late do the two others become enlightened enough to join in the struggle.

Each of Tang Seng's subcharacters has his own peculiar traits, and there is considerable contradiction among them. True to Maoist teaching about the Party, they form a unity of opposites.

This, however, is not true for the "enemy." A powerful and cunning monster, the White-Bone Demon obstructs the pilgrims' progress. This demon specializes in transforming itself and appears in four or five different guises, each with its own specific "line." Nevertheless, all are essentially the same. The fundamental difference between Tang Seng and his disciples, on the one hand, and the White-Bone Demon and its various manifestations, on the other, was stressed by Mao in his poem and indeed is encoded into the very plot of the opera.

The White-Bone Demon is the enemy, and the literary and pictorial tradition for this type of presentation of the enemy can be found in PRC depictions of "Japanese aggressors," "U.S. imperialists," and "landlords and bourgeoisie." All of these characterizations operate under the assumption that despite their seeming variety, the essential and primary urges of these monsters are the same, namely, to "eat men." The White-Bone Demon's primary interest is also to "eat men"—more particularly, to "eat the flesh of Tang Seng." In the *Xiyou ji*, the monsters living on the way to the West are looking forward to Tang Seng's arrival, because his rarefied body will give eternal life to whoever eats him. The picture book dispenses with this idea altogether. What remains is the formula "eating men," which in this century has been filled with a new meaning. In "The Diary of a Madman"(1918), Lu Xun characterized the "old society" as a "man-eating" society. The "man-eating" formula has become a standard description of imperialism. For example, the well-known *Hongqi* editorial of April 16, 1960, entitled "Long Live Leninism," which opened the bitter ideological dispute with "modern revisionism," says: "At a time when the imperialists in the imperialist countries are armed to the teeth as never before in order to protect their savage, man-eating system, can it be said that imperialism has become very 'peaceable' towards the proletariat and the people at home and the oppressed nations, as the modern revisionists claim...?[41] The charge here is that revisionists underestimate the dangers of imperialism. However, there was little echo between the *Xiyou ji* and the traditional notion of imperialism. The White-Bone Demon begins, it is true, with a frontal attack on the pilgrims, but they are immune to such crass devices. All the Demon's further transformations are erstwhile devout Buddhists who pretend to share the same beliefs as the pilgrims. "We all are no match for Monkey," the White-Bone Demon says to her underlings. "In this matter only cunning will bring success; it is impossible to counter him with strength." This is the form in which "revisionism," in its new "social imperialist" variant, was to appear in later Chinese polemics. Mao had already alluded to the revisionist threat in his poem about this opera. Revisionism thus comes on stage as a more dangerous variant of the "man-eating" system of imperialism itself, not as a Marxist current characterized by underestimating imperialism. In symbolic form, the opera and the picture book anticipate what was to become the Maoist line on revisionism years later. The most highly prized meal of this demon is the rarefied body of the Chinese Communist Party.

THE PROBLEM

At the very outset of the opera, Tang Seng depicts the pilgrims' sorry situation.

Ravines ten thousand feet deep, heart and gall cold [with fear],
[we] don't give up seeking the scriptures [but] the journey is hard,
the four directions all hazy, nowhere [is there] smoke from a human [dwelling].

This depiction does not define the problem. But Sun Wukong and Zhu Bajie now proceed to present two radically different assessments.
    Sun Wukong defines their main problem:

Calm now, master. (Stops the horse.) Your disciple thinks in these mountains ahead the cliffs are steep and the slopes abrupt, they are thick with demonic vapors, definitely demons are in and out there.

This text is from the opera, but the picture book concurs: Sun: "Master and disciples, watch out. There are monsters around here. I am afraid." No demon is in sight, but from the general characterization of the situa-

41. "Long Live Leninism," p. 851.

tion, Sun Wukong has already defined the main problem and threat. It is the contradiction between "ourselves" and "the demons," the same insight that Mao expressed in the first two lines of his poem. It is a general rule that in such a situation, demons abound. Sun then promises to devote himself to handling such monsters, assuring the frightened Tang Seng: "Master, don't be afraid as long as old Sun is around. I will chop off the roots and cut off the path of whatever demon [might come]." Sure enough, Sun soon smells a monster, and "instantly leaps up into the air to investigate," as the picture book says (fig. 2).

For Sun Wukong, the main problem is to avoid being eaten by the demons. But Zhu Bajie just sneers at this assessment. "Master, if you believe in the idle babble of Monkey you'll die of fright and fear, if not of cold and hunger, and you'll neither make it up to the Western Heaven nor ever see the Bodhisattva." Instead of going after imagined demons, Zhu Bajie suggests looking for food. Simplifying the longer dialogue in the opera, the picture book has Zhu Bajie pouting and sniggering: "Senior brother, you really are too cowardly with your suspicions about clouds and vapors." Patting his belly, he says: "Let's be on our way quickly to find what is essential—something to eat." In the opera text, Tang Seng asks Sun, "How are we going to make it through these mountains?" and Zhu Bajie interjects, "[Our] bellies are dying of hunger." For Zhu Bajie, the main task is not to avoid being eaten, but to find something to eat.

The controversy takes place in the play's "now", that is, in terms of the audience, in 1961. To illustrate it let us turn to a completely different set of graphics. By 1961, after years of slow but regular progress in agriculture, the country's attempt to overcome once and for all the latent threat and crisis by means of a Great Leap Forward had landed wide areas in famine. From recently published population data, we can reconstruct the demographic consequences of this disaster.

Table 1 shows the development of grain intake per capita for the period under review. Figure 3 shows the development of mortality rates, and table 2 shows how the birth rate changed in the period.

The total human cost of the Great Leap amounted to 30 million additional deaths, 33 million non-occurring births, and stunted growth among a large portion of those who were infants at the time.[42] As a consequence, a substantial number of Chinese leaders who had initially supported Great Leap policies asked for a readjustment in order to

42. B. Ashton et al., "Famine in China," p. 614.

Fig. 2.   Food or Demons. Wang Xingbei (text), Zhao Hongben and Qian
Xiaodai (illus.), *Sun Wukong sanda baigujing* (Shanghai: Shanghai renmin
meishu Press, 1962), p. 4.

TABLE 1.   Annual Per Capita Grain Supply and Average Daily Nutrient
            Availability, 1953–64

Year	Per Capita Grain Supply (kg/yr)	Daily Food Energy (Kcal)	Daily Food Protein (gm)	Daily Food Fat (gm)
1953	283.2	2018.1	53.3	25.2
1954	280.5	2024.2	53.5	25.9
1955	298.9	2130.5	55.8	26.3
1956	306.6	2175.6	56.3	26.0
1957	304.7	2167.0	58.5	25.4
1958	304.9	2169.6	57.4	27.1
1959	253.8	1820.2	48.8	22.9
1960	216.4	1534.8	41.7	16.6
1961	235.0	1650.5	45.1	17.1
1962	250.7	1761.2	47.9	17.6
1963	257.5	1863.7	48.4	19.8
1964	276.1	2026.1	52.3	22.6

SOURCE: B. Ashton et al., "Famine in China," p. 622.

TABLE 2.   Year-End Population and Birth Rate, China, 1955–64

Year	Year-End Population (millions)	Birth Rate
1955	614.7	32.6
1956	628.3	31.9
1957	646.5	34.0
1958	659.9	29.2
1959	672.1	24.8
1960	662.1	20.9
1961	658.6	18.0
1962	672.9	37.0
1963	691.7	43.4
1964	705.0	39.1

SOURCE: B. Ashton et al., "Famine in China," p. 614.

secure the basic livelihood of the starving population. Liu Shaoqi, Deng
Xiaoping, Peng Zhen, Tao Zhu, and others pressed for a partial restoration of family-based agricultural production and a semblance of legal
order. At the same time, important developments were also taking place
in the Soviet Union. Khrushchev had declared since 1958 that owing to
the rapid advancement of the Soviet Union, the socialist camp was growing ever stronger and the possibility was emerging that the "oppressed
peoples" would be able to make it into socialism without a bloody revolution. The key link in the acceleration of this shift was the economic

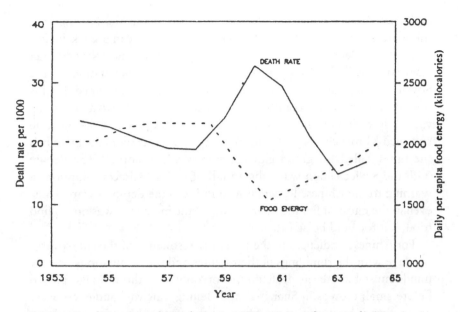

Fig. 3. Food Energy and Death Rate, 1953–65. B. Ashton et al., "Famine in China, 1956–61," *Population and Development Review* 10.4, 1984, p. 263.

development of the Soviet Union itself. Instead of focusing on fomenting revolution abroad, the Soviet Union would make all efforts to outproduce the imperialist industrial nations in the shortest possible time, making socialism's attractions irresistible in the process. The assessments of the group of Chinese leaders mentioned above and of Khrushchev coincided in one important point: both focused on the improvement of the material well-being (or simply the survival) of the populace.

Mao Zedong conceded that he had made some mistakes and reluctantly approved the measures to restore the economy. However, in 1959 prior to the Lushan Plenum, many voices in the leadership had advocated that Great Leap policies be abandoned in the face of already widespread famine. When Mao Zedong himself was imputed to be responsible for the mistakes by Peng Dehuai and others at the Plenum, he decided that a "right-opportunist" deviation (i.e., an ideological demon, not famine) was the main danger. In consequence, the country plunged into a second and more devastating frenzy after the Plenum, with the Anti-Right-Opportunist movement effectively preventing any realistic assessment of the situation. In other words, the battle between two different sets of priorities had already gone through a first round. In 1962, the immediately pressing problems of the famine slowly receded, and Mao Zedong returned to his orginal set of priorities. Having kept the issue alive by criticizing Soviet revisionism, he came back in full force at the plenum in September 1962 with the slogan "Never forget class struggle," thus upgrading the language of denunciation of the Soviet Union. In his answering poem to Guo Moruo, he claimed that his political return (Sun's recently growing acclaim) was due to a "demonic vapor" hovering on the horizon. And in another poem of the time, he ridiculed Khrushchev's penchant for petty "goulash communism" when the times called for grand global schemes and visions.[43] The debate with the Soviet Union was substantially for domestic consumption, a warning to the Chinese leaders not to fall into the demon's trap. Thus, even in the midst of famine's barren lands, the main task was not to find food, but to avoid being eaten.

For Chinese audiences of the time, the resonance of the controversy on stage with the rumblings in their bellies and the ruminations of their minds must have been deafening. Not only was the message played before small crowds in Shanghai and Beijing, but vast audiences were exposed to it by means of the film and the picture book in the villages and schools. From the high status assigned to this production, they knew that some great educative purpose was bound up with the piece.

In Guo Moruo's *Wu Zetian*, which also advocates the Chairman's line, critics of the Chair's policies are denounced as privilege-hunting landed families. Their charges against Wu Zetian have no factual basis, the storage bins are overflowing, the populace is at ease and rest. This polemical negation of the hard fact of the country's famine is not repeated here. *Sun Wukong sanda baigujing* is more sophisticated and goes one step further. The members of the Tang Seng, the Chinese Party, advocating a shift of emphasis to food production, appear in the garb of a fat, gluttonous hog, Zhu Bajie. They are allowed to make their criticism of the Chair, Sun Wukong, and Zhu ridicules Sun's obsession with ideological demons. Amazingly, Sun Wukong does not deny in the least that this transitional period is a desolate stretch with hardly a thing to eat. He answers Zhu Bajie: "Hereabouts is just a row of barren mountains; for some hundred miles around, there is neither human being nor smoke from a hearth; let [me] first go ahead to scout the mountain in search of a path, and in passing collect some fresh fruit to allay [your] hunger" (caption 6). The transition society is a barren land. To find a way through it and ward off the demons is the

43. Mao Zedong, "Nian nu jiao." The poem is dated fall 1965.

main task. The economy has low priority, as we see from the words "in passing collect some fresh fruit to allay [your] hunger." The apprehensions of the public in the midst of famine are taken up, but then they are denounced by being articulated through Zhu Bajie. The opera and picture book indeed take up the most pressing political issue of the time. The controversy between the two assessments—avoiding being eaten versus finding something to eat—dominates the entire plot. Let us now turn to the drama.

THE DRAMA

Sun now goes off to search for the demon that by necessity lurks in this barren region. But first, with his magic rod he makes a circle around Tang Seng, Zhu Bajie, and Monk Sha, "admonishing them several times to sit within the circle and wait for his return" (fig. 4). There is no precedent for this circle in the relevant chapter of the *Xiyou ji*, but it appears in a different place, in chapter 50, where it is used (unsuccessfully) to protect Tang Seng against another demon. The transfer is thus fraught with intention.

As the picture book shows (fig. 5), this demon is not alone but commands vast demonic armies and lives in splendor and high fashion. Being informed about the pilgrims' long-expected arrival, the White-Bone Demon, in the shape of a beautiful lady, ponders ways to get at Tang Seng's flesh. In the opera, she gives up the strategy of open attack after a meek attempt. In the picture book, however, she attacks openly, "imperialist style." Noticing Sun Wukong's absence, she tries to grab the pilgrims (fig. 6). Her later, more cunning attempts essentially have the same intention.

Her attempt fails, as the circle drawn by Sun Wukong's rod repels her. Against the direct and open man-eating attacks of imperialistic demons, Mao Zedong Thought effectively protects the Party. The iconographic element of the radiant circle of Mao Zedong Thought comes from the image of Mao Zedong's head as the sun. This image is evoked in many panegyrical earlier "folk songs," and it finds its ultimate expression in illustrations, posters, and lapel pins of the Cultural Revolution period in which sunbeams radiate from Mao's head.

Unable to catch the pilgrims using a direct attack, the demon now proceeds to "cunning," in the words of the opera text quoted above. In her first incarnation, the demon appears as a young woman with a basket full of dumplings, "her mouth invoking the Buddha's name" (fig. 7).

Fig. 4.   The Magic Circle. Wang Xingbei (text), Zhao Hongben and Qian Xiaodai (illus.), *Sun Wukong sanda baigujing* (Shanghai: Shanghai renmin meishu Press, 1962), p. 7.

Fig. 5. The Demon's Retinue. Wang Xingbei (text), Zhao Hongben and Qian Xiaodai (illus.), *Sun Wukong sanda baigujing* (Shanghai: Shanghai renmin meishu Press, 1962), p. 11.

Fig. 6. Direct Attack Thwarted. Wang Xingbei (text), Zhao Hongben and Qian Xiaodai (illus.), *Sun Wukong sanda baigujing* (Shanghai: Shanghai renmin meishu Press, 1962), p. 13.

Fig. 7. The First Temptation. Wang Xingbei (text), Zhao Hongben and Qian Xiaodai (illus.), *Sun Wukong sanda baigujing* (Shanghai: Shanghai renmin meishu Press, 1962), p. 16.

With his sharp wit, Sun Wukong has anticipated that a demon would most probably try to capitalize on the pilgrims' greatest distress, hunger. Therefore he warned them when he left, "When you meet someone, don't answer. When you see food, do not eat it." Sure enough, the demon comes with the dumplings of economism and lures Zhu Bajie out of the circle, away from the enclosure of Mao Zedong Thought. "Smelling the fragrance of the dumplings," Zue Bajie "could not but rejoice in his heart."

The demon comes like a true revisionist, with "Buddha's name," orthodox Marxist phrases, on her lips and the lure of a policy that stresses only food, as Khrushchev did in Mao Zedong's eyes. She is not a Communist pilgrim committing a "mistake." The opposite is true: she is a demon, using the temporary troubles of the pilgrims to lure them onto her banquet plate. Zhu Bajie, however, now commits another mistake. In his frenzy, he also pulls Tang Seng out of the circle to follow the young woman to her revisionist shrine and temple (fig. 8).

What was earlier a slight difference of opinion between Sun and Zhu as to the relative importance of demon-fighting and food, has now become a matter of life and death for the pilgrims. Monk Sha is as unaware of the true nature of the young woman as the others, but his obedience to Sun's commands persists even if he does not understand their meaning. Helplessly he runs after the others, loudly asking the woman who she is and being scolded for his lack of politeness by Tang Seng. Lin Biao was later to formulate this principle quite explicitly: "So I have always said that Mao Zedong Thought must be implemented both when we understand it and when we may temporarily not understand it."[44] But Sha is the only one familiar with this principle. For the others, the young woman both shares their faith and brings much-needed nutrition. When Sun arrives on the scene, without further investigation or analysis, he smashes the woman's head with his rod of Mao Zedong Thought.

The rapidity with which he acts leads to the second controversy, one about "revolutionary" and "counterrevolutionary" violence. Tang Seng exclaims: "Killing living beings, hurting life—an offense! an offense!" Zhu Bajie also "grumbles against Wukong," while Sha, true to his principles, says, "Wukong is good at recognizing demons and will absolutely not kill a good person by mistake." At this moment, in the

44. Mao Zedong, "Dui Aerbaniya," p. 674; trans. in *Miscellany of Mao Tse-tung Thought*, pt. 2, p. 457.

Fig. 8. Dragging Tang Seng Off. Wang Xingbei (text), Zhao Hongben and Qian Xiaodai (illus.), *Sun Wukong sanda baigujing* (Shanghai: Shanghai renmin meishu Press, 1962), p. 21.

picture book, "it was altogether unclear to Tang Seng whether [the young woman] was a human or a demon." In the original novel, immediately after killing the young woman, Sun points to substantial proof: the food in the basket has changed into maggots, frogs, and toads—in short, to traditional and unquestionably demoniacal refuse. The opera, film, and picture book eliminate this proof. Indeed, there is nothing to help Tang Seng and the fellow disciples of Sun discover the demoniacal nature of the young woman, if not the blind belief that Sun will do the right thing, whether it can be understood at the time or not.

In the polemical exchange with the Soviet leaders, the second controversy after economism had to do with the communist commitment to "revolutionary violence" as a necessary instrument of revolution, on the one hand, and the communist devotion to peace, humanism, and compassion for mankind's suffering, on the other. In 1960, an editorial entitled "Long Live Leninism" charged that Yugoslavian revisionists "deny the inherent class nature of violence and thereby obliterate the fundamental difference between revolutionary and counterrevolutionary violence."[45] In October 1963, Zhou Yang further elaborated on the relationship between Communist ideology and humanism: "They [i.e., the revisionists] say: 'Communist ideology is the most humane ideology.' They talk of humanism as the 'highest embodiment of Communism,' and they assert that 'humanism in the broad sense of the word means the triumph of humaneness.' They harp such slogans as 'everything for the sake of man and for the benefit of man,' 'man is to man a friend, comrade, and brother,' and 'long live the fraternity of all peoples and all men on earth.' They brag about 'peaceful coexistence' as the 'most humane, the proletarian method of class struggle in the international arena' and about the plan for universal and complete disarmament as the 'highest expression of humanism . . .' which in effect is 'fraternity' between the oppressor and the oppressed classes."[46]

The *Xiyou ji* has many elements that operate well as a foil for this debate. The demon next changes into the young woman's mother and charges Tang Seng with wanton killing, moving the beads of the rosary with her hands to show that she, too, is a good Marxist.

The Buddhist doctrine of compassion, of not taking human life, matches the "humanism" mentioned by Zhou Yang as being part of the

45. "Long Live Leninism," p. 848.
46. Zhou Yang, "The Fighting Task," p. 1001.

revisionist arsenal. When Tang Seng repudiates Sun in front of the old woman for the killing of the girl, she applauds him, saying, "This old gentleman really is compassionate," and tries to lure him away to get a coffin. Monkey returns, however, and with great laughter finishes her off with one blow of his anti-revisionist rod.

Again, in the *Xiyou ji* Sun had some proof. The old woman was "at least eighty," while the "daughter" was eighteen at most, a mistake in the age relationship that suggested demonic blunder. In the picture book Tang Seng, who is always drawn in close proximity to Bajie, since he is under Bajie's influence, asks Sun: "You . . . have you gone mad?" This is a strong accusation, which was also used by Khrushchev against the Chinese leadership at the time.[47] Sun answers lamely: "Master, you have been deceived. They were not mother and daughter, but transformations of one and the same demon." Sun adds that there could hardly be any humans in such a desolate area. While Tang Seng was unsure whether dumpling communism was human or demonic, he now makes up his mind that there is no difference between revolutionary and counterrevolutionary violence. Led by Zhu Bajie, who lifts up the old woman's prayer beads and says, "Senior Brother is wrong; evidently this is a human," Tang Seng quotes the Buddhist *śīla* rule that forbids killing, and he intones the Tight-Fillet Spell to discipline and punish Monkey.

Only Sha's intervention stops Tang Seng from painfully transforming Monkey's head into a long gourd. "If Senior Brother had not eliminated the demons on the way without regard for his own life, Master would have long since been gobbled up by the monsters," Sha says, and offers to take the punishment upon himself. This support from the "base level" prevents Tang Seng from dismissing Monkey altogether.

The policy differences between the Party and the being that leads it on its way, Sun Wukong, have thus exacerbated. Tang Seng is coming ever more under the influence of Zhu Bajie, and behind the scenes the cunning demon gloats as he observes the widening rift.

The demon now changes into its third, and decisive, transformation. It now appears as the father and husband respectively of the two females. He is called the *laoweng* or (in the opera text) the *laozhang*, the "senior gentleman" in the family. As he is old and male, he is the highest manifestation of the demon. This old man brings neither bread nor

47. See MacFarquhar, *Origins*, vol. 2, p. 277.

tears. The soft ways of revisionism, represented by the two females, have split the group of pilgrims. The "old man" is armed and fights Monkey, whom he "does not fear."

Both Chinese commentators on the story and imitators have always emphasized the qualitative difference between the female manifestations and the male, a difference that marks the transition from an ideological to a political struggle. To further exacerbate contradictions between Tang Seng and Monkey, the old man asks for Tang Seng's protection. Then in utter desperation, he throws himself toward Monkey and demands to be killed and thus to share the fate of his unfortunate daughter and wife.

Humanitarian postures and concerns, the reader is warned through this scene, are but the most devious of the many ruses of the man-eating demon of revisionism. The figure of the old man seems to point toward the senior male leaders. When Liu Shaoqi had mutated from an erring communist to an essentially revisionist demon during the Cultural Revolution, he was cast into this "old man" role, as we shall later see.

Without further investigation, Sun Wukong proceeds to kill the old man, yelling: "You may make a thousand changes and ten thousand transformations, but a demon still is a demon, and you are not going to dupe me!" Monkey is stopped by Tang Seng, who makes a key statement: "Disciples of Buddha take mercy as the root. Even if this should be a demon, one should encourage him to change his mind and mend his ways, but it is not permitted to hurt him!" To which Sun answers: "Master, you save him, but he will not let you go." In the more elaborate language of the opera, Tang Seng says: "Even if he were a demon, he still should be encouraged to mend his ways, [since] evidently our Buddha's compassion does save *all* sentient beings." Says Sun Wukong: "Even when saving all sentient beings one should not fail to be clear about right and wrong, nor should one blur the difference between humans and demons." But after some more heated exchanges, Tang Seng still insists, "Even if he were a demon, you should not beat him down."

During the polemics about the general line of the international communist movement of the years 1960 through 1963, the Soviet leadership accused Mao Zedong of being bellicose, a war fanatic and even a war provocateur, instead of concentrating on economic issues and peaceful coexistence. The old man in our opera voices this very view: "All you people talk about is killing. What good do you ever do, and what holy scripture do you say you are getting!" In the *Xiyou ji*, Sun

kills the old man, and then the Tight-Fillet Spell is again intoned and
Sun is sent away. Here, the order is inverted. Tang Seng first intones the
spell, causing Monkey to roll on the ground in unbearable pain. But
driven by the ardent desire to save the Tang/*dang* from being consumed,
Sun Wukong, in a scene of tragic dimensions, lifts his staff (fig. 9) and
kills the old man (see fig. 20). It is a strong image of the Chairman's
devotion to the cause of the Party even after having been wrongly
chastised by that very body.

In the *Xiyou ji*, this scene marks the end of the episode. Nothing but
a heap of white bones remains after the last blow, proving that Monkey's assessment of the true nature of this fiend was correct. Nevertheless, Zhu convinces Tang that this heap of bones was only made up by
Monkey to convince Tang Seng. Tang Seng then in effect dismisses
Monkey, who goes back to his cave at Flower-Fruit Mountain. Leader-
less, Tang and his remaining associates are caught by the Yellow Robe
Monster, which lives in a building mistakenly regarded by Tang Seng as
a Buddhist pagoda. Zhu Bajie manages to escape and is sent by the
horse to get Monkey back. After several battles, Monkey finally kills the
monster. In the opera and the picture book the scenario has been radically changed. First, the proof of the demon's nature has been eliminated. This also serves a dramatic purpose, because in the opera the
pilgrims (Sun excluded) continue to be fooled by the demon, which
would have been unconvincing had a proof materialized. The demon
now exerts complete ideological control over Tang Seng, who has even
saved the monster's life. Second, the Yellow Robe Monster, originally a
different demon, now is made into the White-Bone Demon's fourth
manifestation. It appears in the form of a piece of yellow cloth fluttering
down from the sky. This is a *fozhi*, a "directive from the Buddha" himself. Its inscription reads:

> The Core of Buddhism Is Mercy; It Absolutely
> Prohibits the Killing of Life.
> If [Sun] Wukong Stays With You, You Will Have
> Trouble Getting the True Scriptures.

For Tang Seng, this is a message from the Buddha. He therefore dismisses Sun, sending him home to his Flower-Fruit Mountain. Sun
leaves without a harsh word for Tang, enjoining both Zhu and Sha
to take good care of their master. His loyalty is unbroken, and so is his
commitment to the ultimate goal of the journey. For the time being,
he has lost the struggle with the White-Bone Demon for the mind of

Fig. 9. Painfully Monkey Does His Duty. Wang Xingbei (text), Zhao Hongben and Qian Xiaodai (illus.), *Sun Wukong sanda baigujing* (Shanghai: Shanghai renmin meishu Press, 1962), p. 55.

Tang Seng. We will now learn what happens if one does not blindly believe Sun Wukong. But before following the pilgrims further on their journey, we have to deal with the issue of Sun's "dismissal."

Much has been written about the dismissal of Marshal Peng Dehuai at the Lushan Plenum and the question of whether Wu Han's play *Hai Rui Dismissed from Office* alluded to this event and came out in the defense of the Marshal. Indeed, the idea of a dismissal of the hero, or the threat of a dismissal, is not restricted to the plays of the Hai Rui group. In the plays of this group, the hero is a junior official in whom the truth is invested, and in whom rest the people's aspirations. He or she is dismissed, imprisoned, and either tortured to death or beheaded outright for saying the truth, advocating improvements of the people's lives, and opposing villains in high places.

The opposing faction responded in kind. In Guo Moruo's *Wu Zetian*, the empress is in danger of being dismissed from her throne through a planned coup of her ministers. In *Sun Wukong sanda baigujing*, Sun Wukong is in fact temporarily dismissed. In these pieces, the Chairman (Wu Zetian or Sun Wukong) is the hero embodying all aspirations. If these heroes do not kill or dismiss those who try to get them out of the way (the White-Bone Demon, or the landed gentry in *Wu Zetian*), the entire dynasty will change color, the Tang/*dang* will collapse, and their journey will come to an abrupt end. The Sun Wukong opera was brought into the limelight from the relative obscurity of a local performance of the Shaoxing Opera Troupe in Zhejiang because of its implied polemic with the plays of the Hai Rui group. It found support from Guo Moruo and Mao Zedong (and Zhou Enlai) because it could be made into a public message countering the influence of the Hai Rui plays.

Within the group of texts to which our opera belongs, there remain differences. Sun is dismissed upon the instigation of the White-Bone Demon, an agent foreign to his group, whereas the coup against Wu Zetian is engineered by the founding fathers of the Tang dynasty, who have gone back on the ideals of their youth. They are now "class enemies," whereas in our opera even Zhu Bajie never changes into a demon—a conciliatory note that was also stressed in Mao's rebuttal of Guo's poem.

In the opera, the "directive" to dismiss Sun comes from the Buddha "himself." Indeed, in 1959 Khrushchev had "hinted that Mao should be classified as a heretic," as Roderick MacFarquhar writes,[48] and at the

48. See ibid., p. 265.

banquet of the Warsaw Pact session on February 4, 1960, Khrushchev called Mao "an elderly, crotchety person, rather like an old shoe, which is just good enough to put in a corner to be admired."[49] Both the Chinese and the Albanian parties accused the Soviet leadership of uttering "directives" to the other parties, thus interfering in their internal affairs.[50]

The historical record seems to indicate that in 1958 Mao himself had proposed his retreat from day-to-day political management into the "second line," and that he himself had proposed in 1959 to emulate the "spirit of Hai Rui." He had also voiced sharp criticisms of Great Leap policies and supported the new agricultural policies enacted since 1961. As is well known, he maintained in later statements that he had opposed these developments, that "revisionism" had made inroads into the Party and thus led to his "dismissal" in the early sixties when his star was lowest. The Sun Wukong opera shows a keen sense of the actual "dismissal" of the leader in the "present" of the plot. The dismissal is engineered by the White-Bone Demon masquerading as the highest Buddhist authority, but the ruse is only successful because Zhu Bajie is susceptible to the lure of "revisionism" and gets control over the orientation of the weak-willed and muddle-headed Party. Thus even by 1961 or 1962 it was being charged that Mao was brought down by a collusion of Muscovite directives and Chinese Party officials devoutly following their guidance.

When Sun leaves, he admonishes Tang to "distinguish clearly between good and evil," but demonic forces already extend their tentacles to Tang Seng, as the vivid illustration shows (fig. 10). Until now, the group has neither advanced nor retreated. With the dismissal of Sun, it resumes its march. As was to be expected, Zhu Bajie is now "leading the way." In terms of time, it is a predictive scenario: What will happen if Sun Wukong is "dismissed?" In the illustration (fig. 11), the pilgrims are not getting "ahead." They move away from the "progressive" way, which would bring them nearer to their goal, and move sidewise.

The political climate then takes a dramatic turn for the worse. The picture book says: "The sky darkened and the mountain wind blew, chilling the bone. . . ." They end right in front of the temple of the "Buddha" himself.

49. Ibid., p. 268.
50. Ibid., p. 265.

Fig. 10.　Monkey Dismissed from Office. Wang Xingbei (text), Zhao Hongben and Qian Xiaodai (illus.), *Sun Wukong sanda baigujing* (Shanghai: Shanghai renmin meishu Press, 1962), p. 62.

Fig. 11. Leaving the Right Path. Wang Xingbei (text), Zhao Hongben and Qian Xiaodai (illus.), *Sun Wukong sanda baigujing* (Shanghai: Shanghai renmin meishu Press, 1962), p. 63.

In a grand and triumphant gesture Zhu Bajie invites them to enter, the temple promising both orthodoxy and food. We now witness what happens to Tang Seng and his adherents once they reject Sun's assumption that the main danger is being eaten by the demons and accept Zhu's definition that the main problem is getting food (fig. 12).

In the *Xiyou ji*, the building simply "resembles" a pagoda enough to lure Tang Seng into entering it. The authors of the opera and the picture book have drawn on an entirely different episode in chapter 65 for this scene. There, Tang Seng and his disciples suddenly arrive at what seems to them to be their final goal, Thunderclap Monastery. It is but a trap set up by a mighty local demon who has installed himself on the Buddha's throne to fool the pilgrims. When they (with the exception of Sun) bow to him, he and his underlings suddenly show their true faces and take them prisoner, with the wholesome purpose of having them for dinner. Here in the opera the various demons of the *Xiyou ji* are all merged and become but manifestations of the one single man-eating White-Bone Demon, the revenant of bleached ideologies from history's garbage dump in the guise of Marxism.

We have one interesting addition here. The wall surrounding the monastery is "red," though it was not red in the *Xiyou ji*. Red, to be sure, is the color of the walls around Buddhist monasteries; red is also the color of the *hongqiang*, the wall surrounding the government quarters in the Forbidden City in Peking, the Zhongnanhai. Most important, however, is the wall surrounding the Kremlin in Moscow is red. Zhu invites his fellow pilgrims to enter. We have arrived at the Holy See of the faith, and inside we can expect to find the Buddha himself, surrounded by his Arhats and Bodhisattvas, the same Buddha who sent the directive to dismiss Sun (fig. 13). The picture forcefully (and ironically) captures the Maoist perspective of the role of the Soviet Party at the time, even down to details of physiognomy of both the Buddha and his disciples. From the seat of teaching, surrounded by the fragrances of devotion, the Buddha presides over his monks as Khrushchev did, according to the Chinese criticisms, over the meeting in October 1961 in Moscow where the first open clash occurred. Arrogating the seat at the center of the world revolution is the supreme stunt of "revisionism," and it is no wonder that many are fooled. But now, with the pilgrims disarmed and their protector dismissed, the demon shows its true face (fig. 14).

Mao was quoted in a *Hongqi* editorial in 1967 as saying, " 'Imperialism is very vicious.' That is to say its fundamental nature cannot be changed. Till their doom, the imperialist elements will never lay down

Fig. 12.   The Buddha's Temple. Wang Xingbei (text), Zhao Hongben and Qian Xiaodai (illus.), *Sun Wukong sanda baigujing* (Shanghai: Shanghai renmin meishu Press, 1962), p. 65.

Fig. 13. His Holy Retinue. Wang Xingbei (text), Zhao Hongben and Qian Xiaodai (illus.), *Sun Wukong sanda baigujing* (Shanghai: Shanghai renmin meishu Press, 1962), p. 66.

Fig. 14. The Essential Demon. Wang Xingbei (text), Zhao Hongben and Qian Xiaodai (illus.), *Sun Wukong sanda baigujing* (Shanghai: Shanghai renmin meishu Press, 1962), p. 67.

their butcher knives, nor will they ever become [real] Buddhas."[51] They can only dress up as Buddhas. The pilgrims are now in the demon's hands. Their quest is ended, and their flesh will spice the demon's meal. That is where Zhu Bajie's way—the "economism" of the agricultural reforms of the early sixties—ends, we are told. He who in this time of famine concentrates on getting food will end up being eaten by the revisionist demon. The pilgrims' only hope lies in finding Sun, asking him to help them out of the trap, and imploring him to take over the leadership again. In the *Xiyou ji*, it is this very Zhu Bajie who had been instrumental in having Sun dismissed, who now courageously fights his way out of the demon's den in order to fetch Monkey. Given the liberties the authors of the opera have taken with the original text, it would have been possible to make a change here and have Sha, for example, accomplish this service. Instead, in tune with the conciliatory line toward Zhu Bajie and his real-life counterparts expressed in Mao's poem, the original setting is maintained.

The allegorical nature of the narrative allows the authors some delightful depictions of Zhu's efforts to lure Sun back from his enforced "retirement" to help Tang escape from the revisionist demon (fig. 15).

Sun refuses to go with Zhu, remarking that the demon will not fail to be impressed by Tang Seng's compassion and set him free. It should be remembered that at the time Mao had indeed left Peking and retired to the countryside. The novel depicts Sun as thoroughly enjoying himself, although on occasion some thoughts about his master cross his mind; when Zhu arrives, Sun has him severely beaten. But in the opera, the small monkeys inform Zhu when he arrives that the "Great Sage has just been thinking about you with concern," emphasizing Sun's continuing loyalty to Tang. Zhu has to leave alone, however, heroically announcing his willingness to die for his master (a further conciliatory element not contained in the original).

The episode that follows in the picture book is not a part of the original plot, nor was it in the first version of the opera. The White-Bone Demon's underlings arrest Zhu Bajie on his way back to save his master. Without Zhu's knowledge, Sun Wukong also hurries to the demon's cave. On the way, he discovers the demon's mother, who is on her way to join her daughter to eat the pilgrims. Sun kills the mother and transforms himself into her shape. He then enters the cave and induces his "daughter" to show the stunned pilgrims the various trans-

51. Quoted in Wakeman, *History and Will*, p. 16.

Fig. 15.   Zhu Bajie Learns His Lesson. Wang Xingbei (text), Zhao Hongben and Qian Xiaodai (illus.), *Sun Wukong sanda baigujing* (Shanghai: Shanghai renmin meishu Press, 1962), p. 77.

formations that have fooled them. This element, which serves the purpose of their "education," is taken from chapter 34 of the novel *Xiyou ji*, and was an element in another opera, *Pingding shan* (var. *Lianhuadong*).[52] There Sun kills the mother of two monsters who have caught Tang Seng and enters their den disguised as the lady. As these monsters are quite independent of the White-Bone Demon, there is no precedent for Sun Wukong's didactics.

In Guo Moruo's *Wu Zetian*, however, there is one parallel that might help in the analysis of this episode. There, Wu Zetian is reluctant to condemn the leader of the coup against her and have him executed secretly. Instead, she tries to lure him into spelling out his plans and goals in public, in front of all the courtiers, so that the evidence against him is there for all to see; otherwise, the educational purpose will not be served and suspicions will remain. With some tricks she sets up a trap worthy of a Judge Di to get him to speak out. Here, Sun uses a similar technique, inducing the White-Bone Demon to show her ruses right in front of Tang Seng and his companions. This seems to tie in with Maoist thinking at the time. Mao's "Examples of Dialectics," which may date from 1959, was published by Red Guards in *Mao Zedong sixiang wansui* in 1967. In point 12 of that work, Mao observes: "There are two kinds of established opposites. One kind has originally existed in society. For example, the rightists. Whether we let them loose or not is a question of policy. When we decided to organize a frank airing of views, we let them out to serve as opposites and mobilized the laboring people to debate with them, oppose them, and knock them down. . . . We have let them loose so as to educate the people and enable the people to analyze them." And in point 13, he directly states, "It is very important to establish opposites."[53] At a later stage of my analysis, this point will be taken up again. At this time and level, Sun's ruse seems to allude to the renewed "airing of views," both in terms of the publication in China of the Soviet arguments in the polemics about revisionism, and in terms of the many essays and historical dramas that take a critical view of the chairman. "Airing of views," in the context of both Guo's play and the Sun Wukong opera, is explained as a didactic device for the benefit of the public rather than a murky political maneuver to weed out critics by first encouraging them to speak out.

52. *Lianhuadong*, pp. 271ff. Cf. Tao Junqi, *Jingju jumu chutan*, p. 162.
53. Mao Zedong, "Examples of Dialectics," pp. 207f.

In our opera, Sun even dons the cloak of a demon himself to spell out what the demons themselves are unable to discover, that is, their own essence. Zhu Bajie later comments admiringly: "You have used the method applied by the demon to deceive us for the purpose of annihilating the demon; that is really sublime!" Even at this stage of the action, Tang Seng and his companions are too "stupid"; Tang still cannot understand why the demon should make efforts to deceive him and even asks for his release, pointing out that he has made three efforts to save the life of the demon. And Sun Wukong, in the disguise of the demon's mother, drives home the point: "You are talking about mercy; we are talking about eating men. If you think about encouraging demons to do good, you are truly dreaming." Only then does Tang Seng sigh, "Wukong, I should not have sent you away," and the old mother resumes the shape of Wukong, and quickly ends the demon's life. Tang Seng does not criticize Sun anymore for killing the demon and her mother. On his knees, Sun receives the master's welcome, an action that strongly emphasizes Sun's willingness to obediently serve Tang Seng (see fig. 26). The text attempts to show that Mao, with all his superior skills in recognizing demons and fighting them, still remains a truly loyal servant of the Party, devoted to its ultimate goal. Sun Wukong again assumes the leadership of the group, and the pilgrims move toward their ultimate goal with Zhu Bajie inviting the reader/spectator to join them (fig. 16).

Within the story, a didactic purpose is served: The monk (Tang Seng) is instructed—showing, as Mao said, that he "can be instructed" and is not, in essence, a criminal or a demon. This instruction, however, is not in the art of discovering demons and dealing with them. The three transformations of the demon appear in the opera and the picture book at their face value, without any hint as to their essence. Surprisingly, the proofs that supported Monkey's claim in the novel have all been eliminated. The transformations of the demon are so cunning and devious that no eye but the special one of Sun Wukong could ever recognize their demonic core. They seem to be different in appeal, sex, and age; only Monkey is able to discover the true nature of their family link, namely that they are all transformations of the same "revisionist" principle.

What, then, does the picture book teach? First, that only complete reliance and blind belief in Sun Wukong (and his modern counterpart) enables one to discover the demons; second, that the more appealing a proposal or theory may seem, the greater the probability that it is a

Fig. 16. Walking into the Future. Wang Xingbei (text), Zhao Hongben and Qian Xiaodai (illus.), *Sun Wukong sanda baigujing* (Shanghai: Shanghai renmin meishu Press, 1962), p. 110.

demonic device. The art of dealing with the demons is reduced to the single weapon that proves effective against demons: the thousand-jun cudgel of Sun Wukong—in other words, Marxism-Leninism–Mao Zedong Thought.

Both in the picture book and in the opera/film, the best attitude is shown by Monk Sha. Although he fails to recognize the demonic nature of the persons meeting them, he has faith in Sun Wukong and defends him when his master wants to use the Tight-Fillet Spell or send him away. It is with Sha that the reader is to identify.

SUN WUKONG AND THE WHITE-BONE DEMON IN CULTURAL REVOLUTION ICONOGRAPHY

The above analysis, which began as an exercise in interpretation, has already entered the bloody maelstrom of historical action. As it stands, the story is not just a rather amusing little piece of historical symbolism for political purposes. Instead, it provides a powerful image of the period the People's Republic was traversing according to one—the Maoist—interpretation. With the personalities and plot of the *Xiyou ji* widely known among the Chinese public, there was a strong historical resonance with earlier attempts to describe the way to the Western Paradise, and the text provided ample additional material to play on, if times changed.

The forlorn pilgrims accompanying Tang Seng, with their common aspiration to reach the Western Paradise but their varying weaknesses and levels of insight, traverse the uncharted land of transitional society. It is a period of exertion, suffering, and superhuman efforts to reach the goal. No wealthy villages give shelter to the pilgrims. And on the way, apart from hunger, cold, and fatigue, the pilgrims are beset by demons, who cunningly play on their problems. The demons' one and only goal is to eat the flesh of the holy monks, thereby eliminating all hope that anyone will reach the Western Paradise and making the man-eating system all-pervading and eternal. It is only because of the Great Sage Equal to Heaven, Sun Wukong—or, in Guo Moruo's language, the Great Sage Mao—with his magic eye to identify demons and his magic rod to kill them, that there is any chance for the group to make headway toward its distant goal. The opera reduces the demon to a mere concept. Beating down the demon is a spiritual act; no blood flows. This conceptualization of the political opponent as the embodiment of a reactionary ideology was designed to and in fact did remove feelings of fear, ambiguity, and guilt in the political struggles of the succeeding period, when the targets of the Cultural Revolution activists were often rather pitiful elderly people. It was the activists' responsibility and holy duty to beat them down to prevent untold disasters. Toward critics of this procedure, the opera engages in satire and polemics. Those holding the view that in the crisis of the Great Leap one had to focus on the economy and food production and not on ideological and class struggles against revisionism find their lively image in the fat hog Zhu Bajie, who has nothing in mind but banquets and *xiuxi*, rest. In a predictive scenario they are confronted with what the Maoists assumed to be the probable result of the policies of their opponents—entrapment by the revisionist demon. The pinnacle of their ignorance is seen in Tang Seng's claim that even demons can be educated and encouraged to better themselves, that by no means should they be killed at random. As this meant in fact protecting "counterrevolutionaries," the targets of this polemical depiction tried to counter it. There first was the surprising fact that such a highly praised performance did not get a single review in either the *Renmin ribao* or the *Guangming ribao*. After the exchange of poems between Guo and Mao, only the *Xijubao* published an article in December 1961, taking exception to the charge that Tang Seng "protected demons." Like Emperor Gaozong in Guo Moruo's *Wu Zetian*, Tang Seng in our opera is muddleheaded, unable to make out the difference between humans and demons, and likely to listen to Zhu Bajie's ill-advised entreaties—certainly anything but a flattering assessment of the political acumen of the Party at the time. A critic of the Sun Wukong play conceded, on purely historical grounds, that Gaozong and Tang Seng had problems, but he vehemently rejected the charge that Tang Seng protected counterrevolutionary demons. "The criticism of this person [Tang Seng] (a person who is not without his weaknesses) should be based on facts," the critic added.[54] In the opera, however, only Sun's comeback and renewed assumption of leadership could then save the pilgrims, and it was the very Zhu Bajie who had engineered his dismissal who asked him back.

Another historical "text" that strongly resonated with the political situation in China during the mid-sixties was the Taiping rebellion.[55]

---

54. Jiang Shuiping, "'Jiushi yaogui, ye bu zhun da,'" p. 37.

55. The Taipings' progress through endless battles with the "demons" to their New Jerusalem in Nanjing provided some precedent along the lines of the *Xiyou ji*. Poems would refer to revolutionary youths as *tianbing*, "heavenly soldiers," the official name of the Taiping military; cf. "Nahan," in *Tiananmen*

However, although the Taiping rebellion had been included in the national revolutionary pedigree, the resonance with it was not as strong as the one with the lively and familiar imagery of the *Xiyou ji*, which in fact provided many of the terms, images, and precedents for behavior and analysis—in short, much of the "iconography"—of the Cultural Revolution.

My primary concern here is the interpretation of texts; I therefore will not present a detailed account of the actual political and psychological role played by the text under observation. However, history is not alien to the inner structure and the meaning of the text. The text provides a lively metaphor defining the situation, the protagonists, the problem, and the probable historical development. But the reader was not arrested in his perception in the year 1962 or 1963. As long as opera, film, and text with their strong political load were reshown and reprinted, they were read and reread against the changing political realities.

History itself would have to explore the possible interpretations and identify more closely the various elements of character and plot. On the other hand, the text raised the possibility and even the probability that certain things would happen. We will now loosen the brakes on the reader's historical experience that we have artificially fixed at the date of the picture book's publication and try to see what happens to the text when confronting a history for which it had given a predictive scenario. The various applications of the text for the understanding and interpretation of history will also serve as a check of whether my interpretation is the mere brainchild of a scholar or the actual way in which the text was handled where it was most relevant, in China during the years following its publication.

Mao's poem was published in January 1964. Its content and political direction had probably been known and communicated to the authors

---

geming shichao, p. 138, no. 7. They would routinely refer to the beheading of "demons" when describing the struggles; even the anti-demonic *jian* sword of Marxism-Leninism was occasionally alluded to, recalling the sword given to Hong Xiuquan for his battles; cf. "Baitong huawei hantianli," in *Tiananmen shiwenji, xubian*, p. 167, no. 3. The Taipings' internal conflicts were also seen to repeat themselves with Party cadres arrested by the KMT eventually taking the role of Li Xiucheng, a Taiping leader said to have recanted after being captured; cf. *Jinggangshan*, Apr. 20, 1967. About the Taiping vision, see my *Reenacting the Heavenly Vision*.

of the revision before that date. The battle for the orientation of the political leadership had in the meantime heated up. The publication of the text was a part of it. The lines "when today Sun the Great Sage is acclaimed / this is only because demonic vapors are on the rise again" have to be read as a public statement about a development that had already been anticipated by Mao in 1961, as the date of the poem indicates.

The controversy about the agricultural policies that were introduced in 1961, which were seen as a reflection of Khrushchevian goulash communism, was by then in the open, and could be found in the passage of the story about the rural girl with her dumpling. The discussion about the different forms of violence and about humanism had been publicly started by Mao's followers and could be found in the appeal of the old woman for Buddhist compassion. And it would not take long before the male head of this demonic family, who even dared to offer an "armed" challenge to Monkey, would be identified.

The language and fantasy of the Cultural Revolution were strongly influenced by the *Xiyou ji*; enemies were routinely referred to as monsters, demons, or underlings of the White-Bone Demon such as wolves, jackals, tigers, and panthers. The battle was on. The editorial in *Hongqi* quoted above, which in early 1967 welcomed the "January Revolution" in Shanghai, might serve as an example:

PROLETARIAN REVOLUTIONARIES, UNITE!

The Golden Monkey wrathfully swung his massive cudgel and the jade-like firmament was cleared of dust.

Guided by the proletarian revolutionary line represented by Chairman Mao Zedong, the glorious Shanghai working class has formed a million-strong, mighty army of revolutionary rebels. In alliance with other revolutionary organizations, they have been meeting head-on new counterattacks by the bourgeois reactionary line, seizing power from a handful of party persons in authority who are taking the capitalist road, and establishing the new order of the Great Proletarian Cultural Revolution. With an irresistible, sweeping force, they are following this victory and brushing aside the rubbish that stands in the way of the wheel of history.

The Golden Monkey of the poem quoted here refers to Mao, whose "proletarian revolutionary line" is the anti-capitalist and anti-revisionist capacity of his cudgel, which is "massive" because it moves and guides the "million-strong, mighty army of revolutionary rebels" who do the actual fighting against the "bourgeois power-holders."

Nie Yuanzu's poster of May 25, 1966, declared, "Destroy all monsters and all revisionist elements like Khrushchev,"[56] and the *Renmin ribao* published a clarion call for the Cultural Revolution under the title "Sweep Away All Monsters."[57] Another image familiar from the *Xiyou ji* is the "demon-finding mirror" of Mao's thought,[58] the equivalent of the Monkey's eye. The conciliatory text of the opera had located the danger outside of the country, the demon residing in the Soviet Union; in the opera no member of the pilgrim group changes into a demon. With the beginning of the Cultural Revolution, however, revisionist demons were sought in the Party leadership itself, and the Red Guard papers started to redefine the opera and its surrounding texts. Denouncing Wu Han's *Hai Rui baguan*, the Red Guard *Opera Battle Paper* (*Xiju zhanbao*) wrote on June 7, 1967, that this play appeared "exactly at the juncture when dark clouds were rising," referring not to the clouds of Soviet revisionism but to Peng Dehuai's "right-opportunist" criticism of the Great Leap.[59] In the same vein, a cartoon in *Jinggangshan*, the paper of the Jinggangshan faction at Qinghua University, adapted the opera to the situation prevailing in early 1967 (fig. 17). The name of the cartoon's collective author can be translated as the "Fighting Brigade 'Not Afraid of Monsters'" and its title as "Sun Wukong Four Times Beats the White-Bone Demon."[60] In terms of the artistic quality of the drawings and the sophistication of the text, this cartoon certainly is a far cry from the picture book, but we will nonetheless reproduce some drawings for the purpose of documentation. The cartoon appeared under Mao Zedong's "Reply to Comrade Guo Moruo."

The text accompanying the first panel points to one of the few political "weaknesses" of the opera and the *Xiyou ji*, namely, that the journey was to be to the "West," which in 1967 was not a good address, as it was the home of only capitalists and revisionists. It begins: "The tale tells how Tang Seng and his disciples, altogether four people, went to

56. Guillermaz, *The Chinese Communist Party in Power*, p. 381.

57. Ibid., p. 378.

58. See "Revolutionary Big Character Posters Are 'Magic Mirrors' That Show Up All Monsters," in *Peking Review*, June 24, 1966, which says on p. 18 "The [Yanan] talks are a 'magic mirror' to detect demons." *Hongqi* 6, 1966, speaks of the "demon-unmasking mirror of Mao Zedong thought" that discovered the demonic essence of Wu Han.

59. Beijing shi wenlian "Xiang Taiyang" geming zaofan bingtuan "Jinjunhao" zhandoudui, "Jiekai tehao ducao *Hai Rui baguan* de heimu."

60. Bupagui zhandoudui, "Sun Wukong sida baigujing." See for the background to the story Hinton, *Hundred Day War*, pp. 41ff.

Fig. 17. The Demon Redefined as Liu Shaoqi. The first two and the last two rows of illustrations in the Jinggangshan faction's "Sun Wukong Four Times Beats the White-Bone Demon." Bupagui zhandoudui, "Sun Wukong sida baigujing," *Jinggangshan*, Feb. 1, 1967.

the East [*sic*] to get the true scriptures; all along their way they subdued monsters and quelled demons, . . . and had to endure many difficulties and troubles. . . ." One day, it continues, they came to a mountain where there was a "White-Bone Demon," which had "cultivated itself for many years." The term "cultivate" (*xiuyang*) refers to Liu Shaoqi's book *How to Cultivate Oneself to Become a Communist*, but here the *xiu* is read to mean "revisionism" (*xiuzhengzhuyi*), and the compound *xiuyang* to mean "revisionist nurture."

This demon has mastered the art of "transforming itself." It can command the wind and rain and "is very perceptive." Gathering all its under-goblins, it hears that Sun Wukong has cleared all ox-spirits and snake-demons out of his way. In response it changes, in the second panel, into a beautiful woman riding a bicycle and carrying a basket of food. The woman introduces herself as Mrs. Wang, the wife of "Mr. Liu Goodman" (Liu Shanren)—a reference to Wang Guangmei, the wife of Liu Shaoqi. Indicating that her husband is doing good all the time and has specialized in "revisionist nurture," she tells them he has sent her to help them stay there—that is, to stop their trip. Zhu Bajie, who wears an official hat and black clothes, is quickly taken in by her because she gives him special rations. He wants to make her his "model," saying, "With leaders like you, China certainly has a future." He definitely wants to stay and not go to the East for the scriptures. When Sun strikes at her, she pleads, "Slowly now, it will have to be investigated [first] whether I am revolutionary or not." Thus, the cartoon denounces the demand for an investigation as a demonic device. Sun kills her, saying that she specializes in leading wanderers astray. A discussion about her essence follows. Zhu believes she is good, and even if she has faults, she is just an old revolutionary confronted with new problems. And even the working-class Sha states that it has not been established that she is a demon. In its next transformation the demon is middle-aged and male, a high functionary from the Liu mansion. He charges that Sun is in fact a small ox-spirit and snake-demon—in short, a "Trotskyite element that must be severely punished." It will be recalled that one of the charges Khrushchev made against Mao was "Trotskyism," and it was also one of Liu Shaoqi's charges against the first Red Guards. (Since 1978, Hu Yaobang has publicly expressed the opinion that Kang Sheng, the "adviser" to the Cultural Revolution Group and a close associate of Mao Zedong, was a lifelong Trotskyist agent.)[61]

61. See "Problems Concerning the Purge of Kang Sheng."

Helpless, Tang Seng restrains Sun Wukong by reciting the Tight-Fillet Spell: "Revolution is a crime; to rebel is unjustified." His pain notwithstanding, Sun Wukong kills the demon's second incarnation, which represents the early inspection teams sent by Liu Shaoqi to the universities.

Zhu Bajie now shows his real nature. He chastises Sun and proudly refers to his own high birth: "I am a revolutionary from birth; you are just a groom." Thus Zhu is made to represent the group of children from high-ranking cadre families in the elite schools who set up Red Guard groups in the early phase of the Cultural Revolution, and our identification of Zhu as the gluttonous middle- and high-level functionary is confirmed.

Sun now instructs Sha about the true nature of the demon, and together they write a big-character poster, which they paste to the mountain where Liu resides, that is, his headquarters. Another gentleman is then sent by Liu, Wang Guiwai. The pun in his personal name indicates that he "worships things foreign." He is even higher up in Liu's hierarchy, and is a reference to Wang Renzhong, who was accused of having disbanded the early Red Guard groups. Wang demands the punishment of Sun. Sun's headband is again painfully tightened by Tang Seng, while Zhu Bajie openly gloats and tears down the poster, saying "Only I, old Pig, am allowed to rebel." Monkey now tries to engage Wang in debate, but Wang only utters "false and devious words," so Monkey kills him, too. Next Liu Shaoqi himself, armed with a sword to attack Sun, comes along. Monk Sha, who has heretofore been ambivalent, now sides with Sun to defend him and his "revolutionary headquarters," while Tang Seng, upon seeing the white hair of this senior cadre, mumbles "Amida Buddha" (*emituofo*) in shock. Sun strikes Liu, and all that remains is a heap of white bones, with *xiu*, revisionist, inscribed on the spine. Zhu, who has gone away to get reinforcements against Sun, comes back and accuses Sun of being in form "left" but in fact an adherent of a "rightist bourgeois counterrevolutionary line." The monster uses this opportunity to regain his strength and make a last attempt to kill Sun. Sun, however, is warned by Sha and kills the monster. Zhu's quibbling thus detracts from the "main contradiction" and objectively serves the enemy. However, Zhu does not change in nature. True to the original opera and picture book, he stays with Tang Seng after being thoroughly lectured by Sha to reform himself. On they go toward the "East," to seek the true scriptures.

Sun Wukong is not a simple play on Mao Zedong. In the resonance between the two, each retains a certain independence of action. Sun

Wukong has the skill to multiply himself into identical replicas by chewing on his own hairs. It was no sacrilege for young Mao enthusiasts to assume the role of those small replicas. At Peking University there was a powerful group of rebel teachers called "Massive Cudgel,"[62] an allusion to Mao's poem, and at Qinghua University there was a "Sun Wukong" contingent in late 1966.[63] As early as February 28, 1966, the Chairman had called for such local Sun Wukongs. In a conversation with Kang Sheng, he said: "I have always advocated that whenever the Central organs do something wrong, it is necessary to call upon the local authorities to rebel and attack the Central government. The local areas must produce several more Sun Wukongs to vigorously create a disturbance at the Palace of the King of Heaven."[64]

The story in this version tells the experience of the Jinggangshan faction with the work team during the early phase of the Cultural Revolution. The work team was followed by the Preparatory Committee, which pursued the same course; after it came Wang Renzhong, at the time the "adviser" to the first Cultural Revolution Group. As is well known, Mao eventually charged this group with sabotaging the Cultural Revolution. In the cartoon, the young Maoists defeat their opponents. The various manifestations of the White-Bone Demon are now all Chinese and identified with Liu Shaoqi and his adherents. The Buddha transformation does not appear, but since Liu was branded the Chinese Khrushchev, this was not necessary.

Tang Seng and Zhu have familiar meanings, but Sha is still a problem; from this text, it seems that he stands for the "working class" or working-class Party members. The methods of dealing with the demonic enemy that were portrayed in the picture book are also closely followed in this version. Only when the White-Bone Demon is dead does the sign "revisionist" reveal itself on her bones, and only Monkey is able to see through the disguise beforehand. He can expect to be punished by the Party with the new Tight-Fillet Spell, but all suppression notwithstanding he has to kill the demon in the very interest of the Party.

It is well known that in times of turmoil and upheaval old role models lose their power, and rebels must engage in an often-agonizing search for new authenticated forms of behavior. The Red Guards, who

62. See Yue and Wakeman, *To the Storm*, p. 200.
63. Hinton, *Hundred Day War*, p. 76.
64. Mao Zedong, "Down with the Prince of Hell," in *Miscellany of Mao Tse-tung Thought*, vol. 2, p. 382.

had been taught by Chinese schools to be docile and to expect unending disaster if they opposed the "leaders" on any issue, were in desperate need of new codes for their language and clothing, gestures and values. They had to overcome great inhibitions in order to engage in "class struggle" against the very elders to whom they had been taught a few months before to submit in all matters. The depiction of these leaders in the *Sun Wukong sida baigujing* as monsters and avatars of the White-Bone Demon was a radical reversal of their original high standing on the social scale; the brutality of that reversal still bears witness to the fright instilled by the act. Most of the victims of the Cultural Revolution, at least during the early phase, were elderly men, experienced and often knowledgeable, who could easily match any youngster in a public debate. Here opera, film, and picture book came into their own. They eliminated the need for proofs for the demonic nature of the White-Bone Demon and made it clear that only Mao's magic eye could discover the demon's essence. And with vivid illustration and high authority they introduced the appropriate way to deal with the now-Chinese White-Bone Demon; with neither previous investigation nor subsequent vindication, Sun beats down the demon's manifestations with his "thousand-*jun* cudgel of Mao Zedong Thought" (figs. 18–21).

In the minds of children, the fine difference between the big stick of Mao's thought and an actual big stick became easily blurred; beating down the demon of revisionism turned into subjecting the "revisionists" to this very treatment—and beating them all the more severely the more they professed to be good Buddhists. In the iconography of the Cultural Revolution, Monkey's cudgel thus becomes the legitimation for the *da gunzi*, the big stick. After Mao's death, the big stick came to represent all that was evil during the Cultural Revolution. Yao Wenyuan himself was depicted as the "golden cudgel," a direct reference to Sun Wukong's cudgel (fig. 22). The inscription on the club reads "Golden Cudgel"; the smaller characters to the left, "Inscription written by Jiang Qing," make it clear who gave this honorary title to Yao Wenyuan.[65]

In a story written by Wang Meng in 1979, "Youyou cuncao xin" (The Loyal Heart, sometimes translated The Barber's Tale), the big stick appears among the debris in the barber's literary salon left behind by the Cultural Revolution (fig. 23).[66] Charges of "using the big stick"

---

65. "Yao Wenpi yingji" (Photo Album of Yao the Literary Ruffian), in Erling and v. Graeve, *Tigermaske und Knochengespenst*, p. 81, illus. 93.

66. Wang Meng, "Youyou cuncao xin."

Fig. 18. Killing the Young Woman. Killing "goulash communism." Wang Xingbei (text), Zhao Hongben and Qian Xiaodai (illus.), *Sun Wukong sanda baigujing* (Shanghai: Shanghai renmin meishu Press, 1962), p. 25.

were leveled by writers against leaders who tried to silence critical voices, a charge that implied that these leaders were using Cultural Revolution methods.

We will now turn to the next stage of the battle, which required a rereading of the story—in the year 1976. Now, it was Jiang Qing who was identified as the White-Bone Demon. The poems that were deposited at the Heroes' Monument on Tiananmen on April 5, 1976, retain the basic imagery of the Sun Wukong play but propose this new identification. Monster language is used consistently to describe the "enemy," and there are frequent references to Monkey and the White-Bone Demon, the latter obliging here by being in "essence" a female demon, the "White-Bone Lady"; the other members of her group are sometimes depicted as her animal underlings. Here are some examples:

Fig. 19. Killing the Old Woman. Killing "revisionist humanism." Wang Xingbei (text), Zhao Hongben and Qian Xiaodai (illus.), *Sun Wukong sanda baigujing* (Shanghai: Shanghai renmin meishu Press, 1962), p. 35.

The Premier died and left a hero's name, [but] still there are maggots detracting from his rich merits.

> To reject him and uplift themselves a dark wind they raise,
> the ghost of Empress Lü [i.e., Jiang Qing] acts out her lewd designs.
> The demons want to gobble up humans and exude stultifying vapors,
> The pestilential chicken dares shake the majestic roc.
> Prepare to lift the thousand-*jun* cudgel of Marxism-Leninism
> to utterly beat down the White-Bone Chameleon.[67]

The "thousand-*jun* cudgel," of course, is Sun Wukong's weapon. Another poem reads:

> The Premier's last will had not even been acted upon
>   when the national traitors' wild ambitions already rose.

67. *Tiananmen geming shichao*, p. 188.

Fig. 20. Killing the Old Man. Killing the armed male head of the household. Wang Xingbei (text), Zhao Hongben and Qian Xiaodai (illus.), *Sun Wukong sanda baigujing* (Shanghai: Shanghai renmin meishu Press, 1962), p. 56.

> Where the demonic wind of the treacherous and malicious rises
>   the golden cudgel of the Great Sage should not be stored away . . . [68]

The third line quotes the words "treacherous and malicious" from Mao's poem. The golden cudgel has become the property of everyone who has mastered Mao Zedong Thought. The full arsenal of anti-demonic imagery is present in the following paean to Zhou Enlai:

Who says you have already closed your eyes?
No, you always keep open this sharp eye of yours.
It emits the brilliant rays of Marxism-Leninism
and notices the White-Bone Demon in its devious changes;
Like a flying knife, it cut apart Liu Shaoqi's disguise,

68. Ibid., p. 135.

Fig. 21. Killing the White-Bone Demon (Old Version): Sun Alone Beats Down the Demon. Killing the "revisionist demon." Wang Xingbei (text), Zhao Hongben and Qian Xiaodai (illus.), *Sun Wukong sanda baigujing* (Shanghai: Shanghai renmin meishu Press, 1962), p. 107.

and preserved the luminous demon-mirror of Chairman Mao's revolutionary line, striking terror in how many demons' hearts!
Alas! White-Bone Demon:
  Don't get beside yourself with glee,
  Don't get excited.
  Yesterday you found no good end in the Gobi Desert [referring to Lin Biao]
  Don't hope that today you might borrow another body to return to life!
You don't believe? Please turn your head and look:
  the people have already lifted up
  the thousand-*jun* cudgel of Mao Zedong Thought.[69]

69. Ibid., p. 82; cf., in the same volume, pp. 45, 53, 125, 156, 270, 330; and in *Tiananmen shiwen ji*, pp. 297, 302, 26, 234, 156, 165, 182, 207, 240, 248, etc.

Fig. 22. Golden Cudgel Yao Wenyuan. "A
big stick." J. Erling and D. v. Graeve, *Tigermaske und Knochengespenst, die neue
chinesische Karikatur* (Cologne: Prometh
Verlag, 1979), p. 81. By permission of the
publisher.

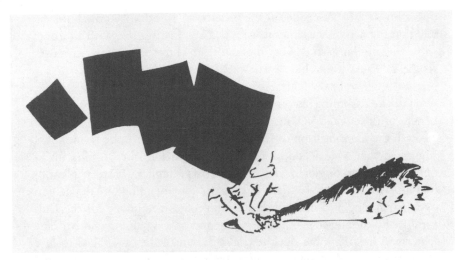

Fig. 23. Big Stick Articles. Caricature, possibly 1979. No further attribution is given. J. Erling and D. v. Graeve, *Tigermaske und Knochengespenst, die neue chinesische Karikatur* (Cologne: Prometh Verlag, 1979), p. 94. By permission of the publisher.

It will be recalled that within traditional Marxist-Leninist doctrine, all deviations are "rightist," even if they are leftist in form. Thus there was no contradiction in attacking Lin Biao and the group around Jiang Qing in the same vein as Liu Shaoqi and Khrushchev. Had not Lin Biao tried to flee to the Soviet Union? After the events of September 1976, the "Gang of Four" was criticized as "revisionist" and "rightist" while the criticism campaign against Deng Xiaoping went on in the same terms. Jiang Qing and her associates were then accused of wanting to restore private farming and capitalism in China.[70]

How was the role of Mao Zedong to be explained under these circumstances? Mao had installed Hua Guofeng, and he was therefore credited with having been instrumental in the demise of the "Gang of Four," a term Mao himself is said to have created for them. One episode within the opera/picture book text thus assumed a richer meaning, namely, when Sun changes into the mother of the demon and acts as part of the demonic family for the purpose of educating Tang Seng and his companions. In the first revised version (1962) the public in the

70. See the fine caricatures on this theme collected by Erling and v. Graeve, p. 105.

opera house and the reader of the picture book did not know until the end that the demon's mother was indeed Sun in disguise. With an ironic smile, the old lady asked her "daughter" to show her various disguises to the pilgrims until they learned their lesson. A new version of the picture book published in 1977, in which we see Sun killing the old woman and assuming her guise, eliminates the dramatic moment for the benefit of the educational meaning.[71]

With the identification of Jiang Qing as the White-Bone Demon it is suggested that Mao Zedong went much further in the "setting up of opposites" than originally described in this chapter. History contributed its own interpretive share so that the control gained by the demon over Tang Seng and his two disciples becomes the image for the Cultural Revolution itself, with Jiang Qing and others gaining control. The Chairman lets them act out the tricks by which they managed to lure Tang Seng and Zhu Bajie into the trap, and he eventually beats the demon down without opposition from a now-instructed Tang Seng. This amounts to the quite surprising explanation of the Cultural Revolution as a "setting up of opposites" for the purposes of ultimate ideological instruction. The yellow cloth wafting down from the sky with the *fozhi*, the "Buddha's directive," also changes its meaning under the new circumstances. The campaigns of the Cultural Revolution were always based on a "directive" from the Chairman. The implication is now that the demon used these "directives" to force the Party to submit and, furthermore, that the Party in fact blindly obeyed, an obedience that only showed how much it was in need of instruction. The thunderstorm in Mao's poem is also enriched by a new layer of meaning. Originally it referred to earlier revolutions; now it becomes a comment on the Cultural Revolution, which "by necessity" will revive the White-Bone Demon, that is, people like Jiang Qing. Post-1976 caricatures routinely depict Jiang as a transformation of the White-Bone Demon (figs. 24 and 25). This characterization is what prompted Ross Terrill to entitle his biography of the Chairman's widow *The White-Boned Demon*.[72]

71. Wang Xingbei, *Sun Wukong sanda baigujing* (1977 ed.), p. 45.
72. Terrill, *The White-Boned Demon*. Surprisingly, Hua Junwu drew a caricature in late 1976 that depicts Jiang Qing as the Monkey stealing the fruits of Mao's thoughts in literature and the arts. The episode, based on Monkey's stealing the peaches from the Heavenly gardens, was an inversion of the traditional identification of Monkey, and was probably designed to encourage the public to form its own second thoughts. The illustration is reproduced in Erling and v. Graeve, p. 94.

Fig. 24. The Demon Redefined as Jiang Qing. Painted by Zhang Ding in the winter of 1976. J. Erling and D. v. Graeve, *Tigermaske und Knochengespenst, die neue chinesische Karikatur* (Cologne: Prometh Verlag, 1979), p. 7. By permission of the publisher.

A flattering reference was also made in the same period to Hua Guofeng as the new Monkey King who beat down the White-Bone Demon,[73] but it was not developed into the full imagery.

The new historical situation after 1976 accordingly necessitated a revision of the original picture book, and the 1977 revision was published with changes in about a third of the pictures and text.[74] First, Monkey's status is raised; he is now called "The Great Sage, Equal to Heaven." Second, some efforts are now made to show that Monkey

73. *Tiananmen shiwen ji*, p. 297: "Guofeng inherited the Party's mandate and struck down the White-Bone Demon. . . ."
74. Wang Xingbei, *Sun Wukong sanda baigujing*.

Fig. 25. Sun Wukong Beats Down Jiang Qing. The battle
between the Monkey King and the White-Bone Demon,
in reverse order. In the top panel, the demon assumes the
form of an old man; when beaten down, she turns out to
have only dunce caps inscribed "Confucian," "Capitalist
Roader," and "Warlord" in her big bag. In the second
transformation, she comes with a Buddhist rosary, chanting
emitofo and promoting herself as a true disciple of the
Chairman, but her prayer beads are really handcuffs.
Finally, she takes the form of a young woman with a book,
and it turns out that she wants to become empress. The
inscriptions of the fringe, the book, and the paper on the
floor are indecipherable in my copy. The sequence purports
to show the historical development of Jiang Qing, who first
slanders the people, then handcuffs them, and finally
sets herself up on the throne. Gao Made, "Sanda baigujing
xinbian," in *Lishi de shenpan—jiepi "Sirenbang" manhua
xuan* (Shanghai: Shanghai renmin meishu Press, 1979).

does indeed do some investigation of the demons. Whereas in the 1962 version he instantly executes the young woman, yelling "impudent demon," the new text says: "With a yell he blocked her way. He sniffed, and noticed demonic vapor; then he looked at this girl with a concentrated gaze, and in the golden pupils of his fire eyes the original form of the White-Bone Demon became visible." He uses a similar technique to investigate the other transformations; the text evidently reflects a reaction to criticisms against unfounded charges made during the Cultural Revolution. Third, after the Chairman's death it seemed possible to eliminate one of the charges against Tang Seng, that of his liberal use of the Tight-Fillet Spell. The pictures of Sun rolling on the ground with a Party-induced headache have all been eliminated. And the status relations between Tang Seng and Sun have been changed too. In order to kill the old man, Sun now has to "push Tang Seng away," an action rich in symbolic meaning; when the demon is finally subdued, Sun no longer falls on his knees to accept the master's thanks and welcome, but stands proudly (figs. 26 and 27).

Fourth, after Tang Seng and Zhu Bajie have criticized themselves for failing to differentiate between men and demons, Sun "warns everybody that on this way to the West there are many more monsters, and one has to watch out." This statement is an indication that even further on, "class struggle" will be the "key link." This political line was not changed until the Third Plenum in December 1978. Fifth, and most important, no longer is it Sun Wukong alone who kills the White-Bone Demon. Sun uses his familiar technique of pulling out some hairs and having them change into smaller replicas of himself. It might be an accident that the number of additional Monkeys thus produced is four. But will be recalled that by 1979, attacks were being made against the "small Gang of Four," meaning Mao's protégés who were instrumental in arresting Jiang Qing and the others but remained anathema for Deng Xiaoping and his group, that is, Hua Guofeng, Wang Dongxing, Wu De, and Ji Denggui. This group might have been behind the change in the picture, which gives credit for beating down the Gang of Four jointly to Mao and four Maoists (fig. 28; cf. fig. 21).

The final credit, however, goes to Sun. The text says: "Out of his mouth, Wukong spat a magical fire, which burned the demon so that its original shape was revealed." This seems be a reference to Mao's criticisms, including his use of the term "Gang of Four," which were greatly publicized after the group's arrest. In addition, Sun's hard criticism of Sha, that he is loyal all right, but "lacks qualification," was also

Fig. 26.   Reaccepted Among the Pilgrims (Old Version): Monkey Bends His Knee and Is Reinstated. Wang Xingbei (text), Zhao Hongben and Qian Xiaodai (illus.), *Sun Wukong sanda baigujing* (Shanghai: Shanghai renmin meishu Press, 1962), p. 108.

Fig. 27. Reaccepted Among the Pilgrims (New Version): Sun Stands Up and Is Reinstated. Wang Xingbei, *Sun Wukong sanda baigujing* (Shanghai: Shanghai renmin meishu Press, 1977). By permission of the Harvard College Library.

Fig. 28. Killing the White-Bone Demon (New Version): Sun with Four Replicas Beats Down the Demon. Wang Xingbei, *Sun Wukong sanda baigujing* (Shanghai: Shanghai renmin meishu Press, 1977). By permission of the Harvard College Library.

eliminated. The addition of pictures showing how Sun assumes the shape of the demon's mother has already been mentioned.

By the time that this revised version appeared, the forces against whom the original version seems to have been directed had made substantial headway. This group pointed to the experience of the Cultural Revolution as proof of the correctness of their own policies. Thus, the anti-demonic language and imagery largely disappeared from public, or perhaps only from publicized, language and fantasy. However, the identifications between the story's characters and their counterparts in contemporary politics were, it seems, so firmly established in the public mind by that time that the changes in their evaluation had also to be expressed in terms of the characters and events of the *Xiyou ji*.

SUN WUKONG AFTER
THE CULTURAL REVOLUTION:
THE TRUE AND THE FAKE MONKEY

Wu Han's *Hai Rui Dismissed from Office* might have originally addressed much broader issues than the dismissal of Peng Dehuai at the Lushan Plenum in 1959. After Mao had made the link between Hai Rui and Peng, however, the resonance between the two characters became so strong in the public mind that Peng's posthumous rehabilitation had indeed to be preceded by that of Hai Rui and the play about his deeds. There was an official proclamation in 1979 that *Hai Rui Dismissed from Office* had been falsely charged with being a *pièce à clef*, and that in truth it had been pure literature about an upright historical figure. This only added an ironic touch to the affair, because any experienced China-watcher could predict from the rehabilitation of Hai Rui that Peng Dehuai's name would be restored soon.

A similar phenomenon occurred in our case, with regard to both Zhu Bajie and Sun Wukong. In 1962, the editions of the opera, the picture book, and the film all contained a lively image of the weaknesses of Zhu Bajie and the disastrous political results they were supposed to have. There were also efforts to counter this attack, presumably by the faction that saw itself attacked in the not-too-flattering picture of Pigsy. The identification of banquet-loving, rest-prone leading cadres with Zhu Bajie, however, was already so firmly rooted that any restoration of these cadres' standing had to entail a rewriting of Zhu's character.

Thus, in 1962, a book had appeared under the title *Zhu Bajie xinzhuan* (New Biography of Zhu Bajie). The anecdotes and stories it con-

tained were not in the *Xiyou ji*; they were seemingly invented for the
above-stated purpose of enhancing Zhu's standing.[75] The author also
collaborated on an opera written for the same purpose, *Zhu Bajie xue
benling* (Zhu Bajie Acquires a Qualification), which showed Zhu as
someone with a solid professional education.[76] The *New Biography of
Zhu Bajie* was duly reprinted in 1978, along with articles explaining
that the Gang of Four had greatly slandered Zhu Bajie, who in fact was
greatly loved by the Chinese people. By 1978 the leaders who might
have felt themselves attacked by the opera in 1961 were making their
comeback.

More important, however, was the question of Sun Wukong. The
political leadership in its new composition decided to introduce a leftist
deviation without quotation marks in order to account for the Cultural
Revolution and the Great Leap Forward. This made it possible to separate the issues of Liu Shaoqi and others like him from the case of Lin
Biao and the Gang of Four. It was now possible to say that the attacks
against the former were only a product of the ultra-leftist deviation of
the latter. This, however, resulted in the breakdown of the unified field
of the interpretation of our story. Sun Wukong's role now had to be
reinterpreted, and the same was true for the thunderstorm that had
arrived on earth, the Cultural Revolution.

In about 1980, a new opera was staged in China, which again took
up the Sun Wukong theme, *Liangxin dou* (The Struggle between Two
Minds) or *Zhenjia Sun Wukong* (The True and the Fake Monkey). A
traditional Peking opera, it is based on chapters 56 through 58 of the
Xiyou ji, which it adheres to very closely. In due time a picture book
also came out, and again we will use the picture book as the basis of our
analysis.[77] The change in the *Xiyou ji* reference argued, in short, that
the Cultural Revolution happened in a different chapter of the *Xiyou ji*
than was assumed in the *Sanda baigujing* .

I will first briefly summarize the plot. Zhu, who is hungry, complains
that Tang's horse is too slow. Monkey waves his rod and the horse
dashes forward—only to land Tang in the midst of robbers who want
to deprive him of his last farthing. Monkey tries to solve the problem by
killing the robbers, but this enrages Tang, who intones the spell and

75. Bao Lei, *Zhu Bajie xinzhuan.*
76. Bao Lei and Sun Yi, "Zhu Bajie xue benling," pp. 53ff.
77. I have only the English translation in hand: Zhang Cheng, ed., *The Real
and the Fake Monkey*. A videotape of the opera performance of the Fujian
Province Peking Opera Troupe is available from Zhongguo dianshi, Peking.

Fig. 29. A Complete but Fake Party. Zhang Cheng (ed.), Zheng Jiasheng (illus.), *The Real and the Fake Monkey* (Beijing: Zhaohua Publishing House, 1983).

sends Monkey away. Monkey goes to complain to the compassionate protectress of the group, the Bodhisattva Guanyin. Meanwhile, "another" Monkey beats up Tang and steals his travel documents. When Sha goes to the Flower-Fruit Mountain to get the documents back, he sees the other Monkey there reading them. This Monkey has set up his own pilgrim group with transformed monkeys acting as Tang, Zhu, Sha, and even the horse, "entirely indistinguishable from the real ones" (fig. 29). Sha goes to complain to Guanyin, but finds Monkey has been there with her for the last four days, so he realizes that there must be two. Both Sha and this Monkey go back to Flower-Fruit Mountain, and a wild battle ensues between the two identical Monkeys, who also

Fig. 30.   Two Identical Monkeys in Battle. The "true" and the "fake" Monkey, battling each other. Zhang Cheng (ed.), Zheng Jiasheng (illus.), *The Real and the Fake Monkey* (Beijing: Zhaohua Publishing House, 1983).

say the same things (fig. 30). Both Monkeys tour the worlds to get a judgment as to who is the true Monkey, but neither the heavenly guardians nor the Jade Emperor nor Bodhisattva Guanyin nor the lord of the netherworld can tell them apart. When they are finally brought before the Demon-reflecting Mirror, where their difference should show up, the assembled heavenly worthies of the Party leadership discover that the two still appear to be exactly alike (fig. 31). Finally, the matter is referred to the Buddha himself, who reveals that one of the two is the true Monkey while the other is a "six-eared macaque" with special abilities. He says: "When Tripitaka and his disciples weren't paying attention, he started playing his dirty tricks." The true Monkey then kills his impostor alter ego. Guanyin accompanies him back to his master, who accepts him again. Guanyin exhorts him: "Take Monkey back, for the evil influences along the road to India have not been entirely dispersed. Let Monkey protect you, for only in that way will you be able to obtain the scriptures from the Magic Mountain." Pigsy meanwhile returns

Fig. 31. The Gods Figure Out the True Monkey. The politburo of heavenly authorities looking at the two Monkeys in the mirror in an attempt to determine which is the true Mao Zedong. Zhang Cheng (ed.), Zheng Jiasheng (illus.), *The Real and the Fake Monkey* (Beijing: Zhaohua Publishing House, 1983).

with the travel documents. The last page reads: "So Tripitaka once again accepted Monkey as his disciple. Having learned a rather painful lesson, the master and his disciples continued on their journey to the West with a renewed sense of purpose." An additional lesson is provided by the book's Publisher's Note, which ends: "Finally Tathagata reminds Monkey that the only way to prevent similar diabolic manifestations from occurring is to maintain a harmonious relationship with his master, Tripitaka."

We turn now to the analysis. Monkey is appalled at being dismissed for killing the "robbers" (fig. 32). The robbers might be read as the "right opportunists" who opposed the Great Leap. True, by the time

Fig. 32.   Monkey Resentful of Bad Treatment. Monkey's resentment at being
"dismissed" by the Party. Zhang Cheng (ed.), Zheng Jiasheng (illus.), *The Real
and the Fake Monkey* (Beijing: Zhaohua Publishing House, 1983).

that this text appeared, Peng Dehuai had been rehabilitated, but there
had been no official denunciation of either the Anti-Rightist campaign
of 1957–58 or the Anti-Right-Opportunist campaign that followed the
Lushan Plenum. Tang Seng sees Monkey's treatment of the robbers
as overly harsh, and he sends Monkey away, reflecting Mao's loss of
power in the early sixties. From now on, Monkey's inner ambiguity is
externalized by having two all-too-similar personalities challenging
each other's authenticity. One of them beats the Party unconscious and
makes off with the documents (fig. 33).

   This Monkey, "true" or "fake," sets up a new "Party," which is not
only indistinguishable from the real thing but even has all the credentials. In allegorical form we find here the violent elimination of the old

Fig. 33.   Monkey Beats Down Tang Seng. The "fake" Monkey hits the "real" Tang/*dang*. Zhang Cheng (ed.), Zheng Jiasheng (illus.), *The Real and the Fake Monkey* (Beijing: Zhaohua Publishing House, 1983).

Party organization during the Cultural Revolution and the setting up of a "new" Party recruited from among the "rebels," a process described in many works (e.g., Liu Binyan's "Renyao zhi jian") after the Third Plenum, that is, after early 1979. This indeed was the "official" Party; it was led by Mao and had all the proper credentials. In the opera *Liang-xin dou*, which has been widely staged since 1980, this "real Party" of the Cultural Revolution is a six-eared macaque that has acquired some political tricks. One of the two stays loyal to Guanyin and the "real" Tang Seng, however, while the other sets up a fake organization, with the real credentials. The battle between the two is a battle between two mutually opposed tendencies of the "mind," or Sun.

The story thus attempts to analyze Mao Zedong and his attitude

Fig. 34.   The Greap Leap Downward. Zhang Cheng (ed.), Zheng Jiasheng (illus.), *The Real and the Fake Monkey* (Beijing: Zhaohua Publishing House, 1983).

during the Cultural Revolution. Sun/Mao is angry at the Party. The problem started with his forcing Tang/*dang* into a kind of Great Leap Forward by means of his magic rod, to enable them to reach a place where there would be enough food sooner. In the *Xiyou ji*, Tang Seng races "on level ground," but in *Liangxin dou* the stampede is downhill, a comment on the direction the Great Leap Forward took (fig. 34).

The other side of Sun/Mao in this interpretation is his ongoing loyalty to Tang/*dang* even when they are having trouble with each other, and especially his loyalty to Tang's ultimate goal, the Western Heaven. The Monkeys do desperate battle with each other, and there are passages in which neither of them seems to know which in fact is the real Monkey and which is the fake. To solve this quandary is beyond everyone else's capacity as well; therefore, no one is really to blame for failing to recognize the true and the false at the time. The Cultural Revolution is thus the battle within Mao himself; there is no outside demonic enemy. The differences between true and fake Maoism are hard to fathom. Only the Tathagata himself is capable in the end of bringing out the essential difference. He is sitting in the very Western Paradise to which Tang Seng and his party are journeying, and he is thus intimately familiar with the ultimate goal of the pilgrims (which is now defined as the achievement of the Four Modernizations). From this perspective, the Buddha is able to distinguish the true Monkey from the six-eared macaque, the pseudo-Party of the Cultural Revolution. Well in tune with the Resolution of the Third Plenum of the Central Committee of the Communist Party of China in December 1978, the Buddha decides that the true Monkey is to protect Tang Seng during the further stages of the journey. It will be recalled that the Party to this day has not dissociated itself from Mao; indeed, some public criticism of his policies especially during the Cultural Revolution notwithstanding, the Party has even made a point of stressing his great contributions. Within *Liangxin dou*, it is none other than the true Monkey who beats down his alter ego. Guanyin recommends Monkey as a specialist in anti-demonic class struggle, saying "the evil influences along the road to India have not been entirely dispersed. Let Monkey protect you, for only in that way will you be able to obtain the scriptures from the Magic Mountain." In this, Guanyin toes the line of the Third Plenum, according to which the emphasis was now to shift from "class struggle" to "production." It maintained, however, that even in the future class enemies might pop up.[78]

After the "painful lesson" of the Cultural Revolution and the elimination of the pseudo-Mao macaque, the "master and his disciples continued on their journey to the West with a renewed sense of purpose," as stressed by the new leadership under Deng, which, ironically in the person of Zhu Bajie, brings the legitimizing documents back into the proper hands.

78. "Communique of the Third Plenum," p. 11: "There is still in our country today a small handful of counter-revolutionary elements and criminals who hate our socialist modernization and try to undermine it. We must not relax our class struggle against them, nor can we relax the dictatorship of the proletariat." This phrase comes after an assurance that the main emphasis in now on production, and should have been so since the early fifties.

It certainly has to be kept in mind that the above represents just one, and a highly authoritative, use of the Sun Wukong image. Using the same metaphor, entire groups could link themselves to the spirit of Sun, just as he could replicate himself by chewing on his hairs. The members of the Li-Yi-Zhe group, who in 1974 came out with big-character posters opposing the "Lin Biao system" and advocating legal guarantees for the citizens, freely called on the Sun Wukong image in referring to themselves as (at the time they saw themselves in this way) Mao's loyal disciples. They charged Lin Biao and his group with "chanting the 'Tight Fillet' incantation" around the heads of the "slaves" and emphasized the rebellious spirit of Sun.[79] A short article in 1979 in the *Tianjin ribao* even made direct reference to the Sun of *Sun Wukong sanda baigujing* to emphasize that "Tang Seng" (that is, many of the Party leaders) were "undemocratic" and in their stubbornness got themselves and the country into one mess after the other. The article argued that if "Sun Wukong" (that is, innovative, daring young people) were not given democratic leeway, the Four Modernizations could not be achieved.[80] In 1979, a caricature by Ding Cong followed a similar train of thought (fig. 35).

In the cartoon Jiang Qing as the White-Bone Demon ties the feet of Tang Seng's horse with the fetters of "ultra-leftist thinking." The Party is dressed in cape that looks like a brick wall and engaged in *benben zhuyi*, doing everything according to the prescriptions of the Marxist classics. Zhu Bajie is again in the garb of a glutton, unconcerned with the pilgrims' progress. Sha, who wears glasses, has thus been changed into an intellectual—representing the teachers, doctors, and engineers who, according to many stories of this year, were in fact carrying the heavy burden of the country's modernization. Sun Wukong now is a critic, his cudgel changed into a bamboo writing brush, and is helpless against this combination of circumstances.

A year later, in 1980, an article by Gu Ertan entitled "Thoughts Evoked by the *Xiyou ji*" argued that "Tang Seng's journey to the West to get the scriptures evokes our New Long March. His going to the West for the scriptures is endowed with a new meaning, namely, to go to search for truth in a direction that has already been determined. . . . The way lying ahead of us is, I am afraid, not as smooth as the one traversed by Tang Seng and his disciples, and we are very much in need

79. Chan and Unger, *The Case of Li I-che*, p. 31.
80. Shi Gandang, "Tang Seng he minzhu."

Fig. 35.   The Journey to the West Stalled. Ding Cong, "Xiyou xinji" (1979), in his *Zuotian de shiqing* (Beijing: Sanlian, 1987), p. 57. By permission of the Harvard College Library.

of courageous and steadfast Sun Wukongs with a high level of skills in the military arts." Gu adds that Tang Seng, however, is not exactly even-handed in the treatment of his disciples. Although Sun defends Tang and leads him, and "never hits his own people [*zijiaren*]," Tang invokes the Tight-Fillet Spell against him. On the other hand, there is Zhu Bajie, who "quite apart from his devotion to food and his laziness wants to store bits of silver in his ears in order to get some private treasure, and even fools around with women." Zhu also constantly bad-mouths Sun and reports on him to Tang, but for this he is never punished. Having described the general situation of the Party's attitude toward the more daring, innovative, and "fearless" Sun Wukongs and the gluttonous, lazy, corrupt Zhu Bajies with their little reports (*xiao baogao*) to the higher-ups, the author applies these lessons to literature, where daring, truth-seeking authors and texts slip into Sun's role, while "some comrades" block and bad-mouth them. He adds: "Some directives from the leaders in the Center concerning literature and the arts, even the social effects proposal, are supposed to create in our ranks a great number of Sun Wukongs with real knowledge and deep insight, high artistic standards and great outspokenness." These comrades, however, "mistake [these directives] for Tight-Fillet Spells and secretly gloat," as Zhu did when Sun suffered from Tang's invoking the spell.[81] The "social effects proposal" refers to an article by Feng Mu in the *Wenyi bao* of January 1980 enjoining writers to keep the possible negative social effects of their writings in mind. Feng Mu had otherwise come out in support of critical texts, but this article was used to silence many others.

Since the Third Plenum, Monkey has also resumed on occasion another role that he had played in 1956–57: with his irreverent attitude, his daring, and his wit as well as his great feats he is a symbol for the best that China can muster on its long way to the West—that is, toward technical modernization. In illustrations in science fiction, he is sometimes shown as the Chinese spirit of technical innovation and progress.

In the more politically minded parts of the press, however, a different member of the group of pilgrims—Zhu Bajie—assumed the role of the technical innovator. Even in the early sixties, attempts were made to elevate his stature by assigning professional skills to him. In a recent picture book, Zhu Bajie is portrayed as the real hero of the new political line. Monkey brags about his great feats, which are shown as being quite ridiculous when compared to the achievements of the modern age with robots and computers. Monkey not only totally fails to understand them, but even refuses to take them seriously, an implied criticism of Mao's attitude toward modern technology. Zhu Bajie then enters the stage, a bulging, contented farmer who manages a pig farm with the most modern methods, consummating the triumph of Zhu's point of view that food, and animal protein at that, deserves highest priority (fig. 36). The future belongs to Zhu, we are told. Sun Wukong finally submits to the spirit of modern technology, the robot (fig. 37); he gives up his traditional arrogance toward technology, and a new laser-type instrument is used to fill his head with modern knowledge.

CONCLUSIONS

a. The various media through which *Sun Wukong sanda baigujing* has appeared before the public since 1961 have contributed to a body of literary attempts to present what might be called the Maoist vision of the role of the Party and its segments, and the interaction between

81. Gu Ertan, "Cong *Xiyou ji* suo xiangqide," pp. 23f.

Fig. 36. Pigsy, the Stalwart of the Scientific Technical Revolution. Zhu Bajie, master of modern scientific farming. Chai Liyang and Li Ganxing (text), Han Wu and Jiang Xiangnian (illus.), *Sun Wukong xinlixian ji* (Changsha: Hunan renmin Press, 1982). From the private collection of David Plaks.

Fig. 37. Monkey's Arrogance Overcome by the Robot. Sun Wukong submits to the spirit of the Four Modernizations. Chai Liyang and Li Ganxing (text), Han Wu and Jiang Xiangnian (illus.), *Sun Wukong xinlixian ji* (Changsha: Hunan renmin Press, 1982). From the private collection of David Plaks.

"foreign" revisionists and the inter-Party struggle. Guo Moruo's *Wu Zetian*, the fourth volume of Mao's works, and the polemic with the Soviet Union and Yugoslavia belong to the same group. Guo's play and the Sun Wukong opera set out to counter the strongly critical statements made in texts of what might be called the Hai Rui group and present their definition of the problem, the avenues for their solution, and the hero who was to bring about this solution. Both groups engaged in open polemics with each other through their texts. Tian Han puts the Maoist "class struggle" approach into the mouths of his two chief villains, who use this set of definitions only for the purpose of protecting their own privileges. The Sun Wukong opera puts the "economy" definition into the mouth of Zhu Bajie and shows to what dire results it would lead if it were followed. Both sides play on the theme of their hero's dismissal.

b. Both factions made use of the form of the historical play or opera extensively to discuss, by implication, actual political problems and to propagate their own views. Each was keenly aware of the importance of literary works for the formation of the public mind and public opinion. At the time, the dissension between the two factions was not in the open; therefore, this instrument was used to lead a public debate about a topic that officially did not exist. Later, shortly before and during the Cultural Revolution, many of the texts were "translated" into direct discourse; this is true for both *Hai Rui baguan* and the Sun Wukong theme, in the latter case through the Jinggangshan adaptation.

Although such translation occurred, although it can be assumed that the more sophisticated readers and operagoers would get the message, and although my own analysis has tried to isolate the translatable elements and to show how far the text sustains such translation, it must be pointed out that the historical drama can fulfill its contemporary political role only when and insofar as the historical screen retains its own logic and integrity. The identification of Mao with Sun operates through a third medium; the traditional characteristics of Sun—his irreverence, daring, and acute analytical powers—have to correspond in the public mind to some key characteristics of Mao to make the identification credible and prevent it from becoming trite propaganda. And Sun has to be a credible character within the context of the story itself to become a powerful image of the Chairman. The same is true for the other characters and for the plot. *Sun Wukong sanda baigujing*—as an opera, as a puppet play, as a film, and as a picture book—retains a high degree of artistic integrity and simple quality, resulting in enjoyable performances that "work" whether the political innuendo is fully understood or not.

c. *Sun Wukong sanda baigujing* contains propositions not explicitly made in other contemporary published materials. These include polemics about eating or being eaten; Khrushchevian revisionism as a man-eating demon beleaguering the pilgrims on their way toward Communism; the transition society as a barren land to be traversed through constant struggle; the Party as a muddleheaded body, unable to recognize the danger to it and willing to follow Zhu Bajie instead of Mao; and Sun Wukong, the tragic, misunderstood hero who protects the Party from deadly dangers but is dismissed from his leadership function, until through the "setting up of opposites" he is finally able to "instruct" Tang Seng and can again lead the Party. These elements together form, in symbolical guise, a coherent body of doctrine that surfaced in explicit political language only years later. When we compare the propositions of this text with those from the Hai Rui group, and also with others hailing from the same political orientation such as *Wu Zetian*, we discover that a lively and bitter polemic was raging at this critical juncture. The leadership was divided between those who saw the country threatened from within by a devastating famine, and those who saw it threatened from without by Soviet revisionism. Both sides in these underground polemics on the stage gave no quarter. The demons are as routinely killed in *Sun Wukong sanda baigujing* as the villains are assassinated or executed in *Guan Hanqing, Hai Rui baguan,* and *Xie Yaohuan.* The harsh language of enemies and friends is contrasted in the Sun Wukong opera by a conciliatory treatment of Tang Seng and, especially, Zhu Bajie, which corresponded to the "mild" language of Mao's poem. With the sharpening of contradictions and the redefinition of the conflict in terms of intra-Chinese struggle, the White-Bone Demon was eventually reidentified. Traces of the old definition still showed on the explicit level in the description of Liu Shaoqi as China's Khrushchev and the basically conciliatory treatment, even in its sharp accusation, of Zhu Bajie.

d. The link between the *Xiyou ji* theme and transition society had been so firmly established that any change in the doctrine about the latter had to be prefigured, accompanied, or expressed through a change in the former. This process is evident not only in the various versions of the Sun Wukong text itself but also in the various adaptations of the theme to contemporary reality, in the efforts to rehabilitate Zhu Bajie, and finally in the explanation of the Cultural Revolution in terms of the ambivalence of Mao's attitude toward the Party. All of the different adaptations and applications, however, agreed in accepting the *Xiyou ji* as a valid paradigm for PRC history.

e. The dense texture of characters and plot and explicit and silent argument that characterizes the opera *Sun Wukong sanda baigujing* makes it a fairly concrete and specific statement and analysis, more vivacious, richer, and infinitely more effective in terms of feeding and instructing the public fantasy than any of the existing explicitly political texts. The opera reveals its deeper layers when we reconstruct the horizon within which the reader or spectator perceived the work at the time. The elements of that horizon would seem to consist of the *Xiyou ji*, the earlier applications of this text to PRC reality, other historical dramas following the same line of argument, other historical dramas against which the opera engages in a polemic, attempts to influence or "correct" the depiction of protagonists of the plot, the social reality of the time, and political battles both in the center and internationally. The horizon of perception changes with a change in any one of these elements, and the perception of the text may be appropriately adjusted.

f. It seems that any movement about to make a radical change needs a prospective scenario to envisage how things will develop. This scenario will define the problems for the participants in the movement, identify their role and promise, as well as offer a picture of their eventual success: the Western Paradise, the Heavenly City, Jerusalem. To a substantial degree, the success of a movement in capturing the public mind and in convincing its activists to contribute their lives and fates to the cause depends on the authority, analytical capacity, and concreteness of this scenario. Marxism-Leninism does provide such a scenario for the revolution, but not for the period of socialist transition. It is one of the strengths of Mao as a political leader to have time and again provided such grand vistas and general models. The story of the Foolish Old Man Who Moves the Mountain, studied elsewhere,[82] is one such myth, spelled out on the eve of the victory over Japan. It has permeated the language and fantasy of Party members and common people in China, providing a prospect of future development. The Sun Wukong theme is another. Focusing on the "necessity" for ongoing "class struggle" in China, it caught the imagination particularly of educated youths in the cities and became the quarry from which materials for the verbal

82. See my "Rewriting the PRC's Foundation Myth: Gao Xiaosheng's 'Li Shunda Builds the House,'" in Wagner, *Inside the Service Trade*.

edifices of the Cultural Revolution were taken. It provided legitimacy, precedent, depth, and grandeur for the enterprise, as well as behavioral models down to such details as the fearsome big stick of anti-demonic criticism. Certainly one of the weaknesses of the opposing faction was that its more pedestrian and "realistic" goals were hard put to match this more radical scenario of Mao at the level of political imagination. Thus the opposing faction resigned itself to either stating its case within the framework set up by its opponent or trivializing weighty political matter to become stories for small children.

The Politics of the Historical Drama

In the political struggles that preceded the Cultural Revolution during the years 1958 through 1966, the stage became a hotly contested battleground. A number of historical plays appeared. Some of them were apparent attacks both on members of the Party leadership including the Chairman and on policies advocated during the Great Leap Forward, whereas others supported these very leaders and policies. Jiang Qing, ending the ban on political activity imposed on her by the Central Committee in 1939 in Yan'an, linked up with Kang Sheng, Lin Biao, and the military propaganda department, as well as with Ke Qingzhi and Zhang Chunqiao from Shanghai to gain control over the stage through introducing her "revolutionary model operas" and the organizing of criticism of the plays of her opponents. Yao Wenyuan's attack against Wu Han's *Hai Rui baguan* is often quoted as the opening shot of the Cultural Revolution. The writing of the text had been organized by Kang Sheng, Jiang Qing, and Zhang Chunqiao in many months of revision. We are thus forced to assume that writers of historical dramas and their critics, leaders, readers, and public cannot have been oblivious to the implications of these texts, and that the politics of these texts were crafted, read, and studied with much energy and acumen by all sides concerned.

The rich scholarly literature on the political history of this period has recognized the importance of these plays, and two English translations of *Hai Rui baguan* have been published.[1] However, scholars have shirked the unfamiliar territory of dramatic symbolical expression, and have for the most part concentrated on nonliterary texts like Wu Han's articles on Hai Rui,[2] Deng Tuo's *Evening Chats at Yanshan*,[3] prefaces to literary works, and the blunt language of the criticism of many of these pieces in the wake of the Cultural Revolution. Even many of the nonliterary sources like the Red Guard materials and the rich memoir literature of the post-1979 period still await more detailed study. Both types of materials, as a rule, comfortably supplement each other in terms of their factual statements while retaining an assessment of the facts which could not have been further apart. The social history of the Great Leap and the years thereafter is still a dark chapter, although important demographic data have recently become available. To this day, however, the richest data still come from literary sources, to the point that short stories have been used in a recent article as important evidence for the study of the Great Leap famine.[4]

This final chapter will try to generalize the results gained from the close study of some of the historical plays to arrive at a broader view of the period and the role of the historical drama within it. I do not intend to include every historical drama written during this period. Nor do I include all the debates in the field of historical study, which ran parallel to the drama debate, or take into account here the equally controversial plays dealing with "revolutionary history," that is, with the period immediately preceding the establishment of the People's Republic in 1949. This chapter thus is less intended as a summary of all the available evidence than as an exploration of potential avenues of inquiry that might stimulate others to join in the endeavor.

THE IMPLIED ASSUMPTIONS OF THE HISTORICAL DRAMA

With the advent of the Anti-Rightist movement in June 1957, the group of younger writers who had written the most important stories of the Hundred Flowers period disappeared from the literary scene; among this group were Liu Binyan, Wang Meng, Liu Shaotang, Deng Youmei,

---

1. Wu Han, *Hai Rui baguan*. It was translated by C. C. Huang as *Hai Jui Dismissed from Office*; and by C. Ansley as *Hai Jui's Dismissal*.
2. See Pusey, *Wu Han*. Many authors have taken up his arguments; see the bibliography in Fisher, " 'The Play's the Thing,' " p. 27, n. 6.
3. See the introduction in Glaubitz, *Opposition gegen Mao*.
4. See chapter 2, nn. 44–47.

Gao Xiaosheng, and others. The two literary genres employed by this group, literary reportage (*texie*) and the short story (*duanpian xiaoshuo*), can both be traced back to the social novel, not the political novel.[5] Both genres, as defined in their socialist context, focused on the life of the common people, the *texie* more on its social and political aspects, the short story more on its emotional aspects. Within the confines of both genres, an unquestionably important aspect of Chinese reality, to wit, the top political level of the country and the policies set there, could not be handled. The choice of these genres also indicated a self-restriction on the part of the authors, attributable to the political risks associated with handling such sensitive issues.[6] The Party and its organizations were very much in control, and the influence even of the individual personalities of the leaders was felt throughout the country. Furthermore, both genres are eminently modern, inpregnated with the spirit of cool, fact-oriented *Sachlichkeit* even where they are emotional. They are not genres of big words, no one reviles Heaven and Earth in a *texie*, and Achilles raping Penthesilea, dead, on the battlefield,[7] has no place in a short story. The socialist world with its "scientific socialism" seems ideally suited for these genres, as they imply the utter rationality and modernity of their inmates.

However, the actual social climate developed quite independent of the official words used to describe it. Already in some stories and caricatures of the years 1956 and 1957 there is a level of aggressiveness against the bureaucrat and fat-cat official that seems to confirm Liu Binyan's description of a growing discontent of the young with their leadership. A short passage in Wang Meng's "Young Man..." that expressed this feeling instantly became a national scandal precisely because younger readers found in these few lines an expression of their own frustration.[8] Even there, however, the frustration was very personal, and no hard words against bureaucrats were ever used.

The Anti-Rightist movement, which began in the middle of 1957, removed these younger writers. They had been operating under the umbrella of high-level cultural leaders like Hu Yaobang, the head of the Youth League, and Deng Tuo, the vice-editor of the *Renmin ribao*. The Anti-Rightist movement hit several hundred thousand people, a large

5. See my "Liu Binyan and the *texie*."
6. See for detailed studies of some relevant works from the Hundred Flowers period my "The Cog and the Scout."
7. As in Wolf, *Kassandra*.
8. See Wagner, "The Cog and the Scout," pp. 366ff.

majority of them non-Party intellectuals and young intellectuals in the lower reaches of the Party and its mass organizations. The senior leaders, many of whom had also made bold statements during the Hundred Flowers period, remained in office, although they lost their "horses."[9] They were willing to come out hard against the non-Party intellectuals, but they were adamantly opposed to pursuing the kind of inner-Party rectification that Mao proposed at the time. Tian Han, head of the Dramatists' Association as well as its Party secretary, for example, was willing to use harsh words against his old friend Wu Zuguang, who was sent to Heilongjiang for reeducation. Shortly thereafter, he wrote *Guan Hanqing*, which takes up Wu's demands for greater artistic and political autonomy, and may even allude to Wu.[10] Another example was Wu Han, Beijing's vice-mayor. He first mounted a harsh attack against the "bourgeois rightists,"[11] but eventually came out with an even more scathing attack against Great Leap policies. There seems to be more a political than a moral motive at work among these senior leaders. They seem to have been willing to engage in fierce factional battles within the leadership, but were reluctant to have youngsters and outsiders join in such intricate business. The authors of the new historical dramas were not young Party intellectuals or non-Party writers of earlier renown, but high-ranking political and cultural leaders within the Party. Their use of the historical drama as the main platform for ideological and political contention in the public sphere after 1958 had a number of important implications in terms of both the writer's perception of society, and of his work.

A CHANGE IN THE RESONANCE BOARD FOR THE PRESENT

The realist writings of the Hundred Flowers period had used the ideal of a future socialist society as the resonance board for the present, and they had measured the present problems of "irrational" and "unscientific" bureaucratic behavior with the yardstick of the futuristic ideal of "scientific socialism." By implication, they accepted the claim that new China was something radically new and unprecedented—a claim encoded in the extraordinary renaming of all aspects of social reality. The

9. The metaphor is Wu Han's. "Going to battle to shoot men, one first shoots at their horses," says Hai Rui. See *Hai Rui baguan*, p. 22.

10. See chapter 3.

11. Wu Han, "Wo fenhen, wo kongsu," 1957. Cf. MacFarquhar, *Origins*, vol. 1, pp. 270ff.

basic assumption of the historical drama, however, is continuity in change. The resonance board of the present thus is historical experience. The writer attempts to keep this experience alive by putting on stage the phases, constellations, and conflicts in history that resonate with the present, distributing, retroactively, praise and blame, and thus maintaining the "educative" function associated with literature. There is much leeway in the term resonance (which I take here from Benjamin Schwartz), and consciously so. As a metaphor it indicates a two-way interaction: the present imposes itself on the past, occasionally deforming it completely; and the past imposes itself on the present, defining the conflicts, setting up role models, naming the heroes, and predicting the outcome, occasionally forcing the present into a gruesome mimicking of past disasters. Within this general dynamics of resonance, there might be anything from *ad personam* innuendo to vague parallelisms in constellation, from role patterning to base flattery. Nevertheless, the historical drama in socialism flouts the fundamental assumptions built into the definitions of the modern genres in socialist states. The use of the historical drama may be a tactical step; in times of patriotic fervor in defense of the fatherland, historical plays might be written to mobilize the great heroes of the past for the present cause, abandoning for the moment the literary themes and genres associated with socialism. But the late fifties and early sixties were no such time. Then it is a strategic step attesting to the insight that the radical revolution and renaming has only obfuscated the continuity of the past. This again changes the perception of the past. Defined as the feudal past it is the period of repression and desperate resistance, getting ever darker as the present lights up. The ruling class is cruel and bad, the common people are the heroes, and the reformers in the ranks of the ruling class at best obfuscate the fundamental antagonism. This had been the argument in the early fifties against films dealing with the late Qing. In this reading, the present suffers from the past, from the birthmarks of the past as Marx called them, from bureaucratism, backwardness, superstition, and low productivity. Thus the battle with the past continues, and the past is evoked only in order to more radically obliterate it. In the new historical drama of this period, history regains its ambivalence and a degree of its complexity.

There are notoriously bad characters among officials, but also some good ones; history is not only propelled by heroic, halberd-wielding masses, there are not only warts to be inherited, but honesty, justice, respect for law, devotion to public welfare, and, above all, *Heldenmut vor Fürstenthronen*, or heroes' courage to confront the mighty. The past becomes a source of inspiration to understand the present and to deal with it. And the new historical drama becomes the music played on the strings of the present, but receiving its richness and depth through resonance with the past.

A CHANGE IN THE SOCIAL REALM OF THE TEXT

The narrative prose of the preceding years dealt with "the people." Protagonists typically were common folk, either benign (poor and lower middle peasants, workers, and young intellectuals linked to these two) or malicious (landlords, capitalists, and their intellectual lackeys). The theme was thus social conflict.

The new historical drama inherits from the traditional drama its protagonists. It specializes in dealing with "emperors and ministers." There was also in traditional drama a "talented scholar and virtuous beauty" tradition, but this was not followed by the new historical drama. This was no time of love; more pressing themes required attention. The most talked-about new historical dramas take place among the highest ranks of society, often directly at court. Their protagonists are differentiated not just by intrinsic character but by their attitudes toward the "interests of the people" broadly defined. They make great use of the elements of traditional intrigue to show the circuitous ways by which heroes must sometimes travel in order to benefit the people and the nation. This is a radical shift of focus. The historical drama takes upon itself to deal with the national leadership, the political intrigues and battles going on at this level, and the policies upheld by the opposing factions.

Employing the dramatic elements from the old opera, the intrigue, the confrontation of vile official with upright judge and the like, it indicated the continuity of these constellations under the present conditions.

A CHANGE IN THE STRUCTURE OF THE PROBLEM

There had been criticism of bureaucracy in the Hundred Flowers texts, but the controversy centered on the issues of economic and social progress. Rational arguments were advanced, and the opponents' objections, motives, and historical experiences were spelled out. Opponents were not just "dogs" or villains, but were seen as old revolutionaries who had become rigidified in their habits, or had failed to manage the transition from a wartime emphasis on command structure and discipline to a civilian economy in which different types of specialists interacted. In the new historical drama, the emphasis on rationality, implied in the earlier prose texts as the binding code for all, has disappeared. In its view, the political center is occupied by politicians who spend their lives in power intrigues. The heroes entering this dark realm have to deal with its intricacies. Characters no longer change in the new historical drama; they constantly say and act out their very essence. If they are villains, they are so throughout, and the same is true for the heroes, the weaklings, the emperors. They are engaged in a power battle where no one is ever convinced by facts and arguments. Instead, the opponent is routinely executed, tortured, poisoned, slaughtered, or helped to the other world by some other means. This implies that the inherent Marxism of the authorial voice is abandoned as being inappropriate for the handling of both the very dark and the very bright sides of human behavior. It also means that the common argumentative code and institutional structure that Marxism-Leninism and the Leninist party doctrine had imparted to protagonists in earlier texts have disappeared.

There is no value left that is cherished by both factions; consequently, there is no basis for even minimal mutual respect.

AN INCREASE IN THE TEXTUAL PITCH

The historical drama is generically linked to the opera, and in many cases the pieces were directly written as operas or are spoken dramas adapted to opera later. The speed with which those written as *huaju* or spoken drama such as Tian Han's *Guan Hanqing* were transformed by prominent opera companies demonstrates their intrinsic affinity. The *huaju* in China is a modern genre, linked to the values of modern city intellectuals, who represented its chief audience. In the tradition of the old opera in its various styles, the *huaju's* language and the action on the stage are characterized by their intensity. The vile official is vile to the core: he habitually rapes women and plunders the people, and his language is one of debauchery and violence, of unabashedly brutal power. The upright official is his match on the opposite end of the scale, and the poor wretches from the people combine utmost moral purity with perfect helplessness. Eyes are gouged out on stage, bureaucrats are beheaded, Heaven and Earth are reviled or implored, vengeance is demanded in the bloodiest terms, and protagonists assure each other that they only regret that they cannot eat the other's flesh. In language and deed, neither side gives the other quarter.

This increase in pitch in part is due to the change in genre from short story to theater, with the stage requiring a theatrical exaggeration of word, gesture, and action. Of course, the public will not necessarily feel called upon to proceed to "skin alive those vile officials" in the real world if the hero demands this on stage. Nevertheless, the sudden increase in intensity of language that accompanied the genre change from short story to historical drama is indicative of the authors' perception that this new language would better suit the type and level of controversy that had come to prevail than the sedate *Sachlichkeit* prose. The impact of this change was soon to be felt within literary and political prose as well. The literary and political language of the Cultural Revolution and the period immediately preceding it adopted much of the grand pose and crass imagery of the language of the historical drama.

A CHANGE IN PUBLIC

The Hundred Flowers prose was addressed to the modernist coalition of progress, the young production enthusiasts, the enlightened top leaders, and, in particular, to open-minded middle-level city intellectuals. Hundred Flowers texts were widely accessible, easy to read, and used the common cadre language of the day without infusions of either classical Chinese (*wenyan*) or local dialect. They were marked also by a complete absence of the rich texture of historical allusion that makes classical texts often such absorbing and difficult reading.

In contrast, the new historical play was performed only in the key cities of the country and it appeared in obscure periodicals like *Juben* or *Beijing wenyi*. It was fraught with historical weight, and if one failed to understand the historical references one would also fail to grasp the contemporary "meaning." Finally, it contained many *wenyan* elements from its historical sources; Meng Chao's *Li Huiniang* was even outright written in *wenyan*. Traditional plays were often understandable to an illiterate audience because the plot and texts were known, and many knew them by heart, but the new historical plays were either "adaptations" of unknown and obscure texts or were entirely new. Apart from general historical knowledge, the public had nothing to go by but the singing and speaking and the lines that were projected on a screen at both sides of the stage. The traditional opera public from the lower order was therewith in fact excluded; the young in most cases were unfamiliar with these "traditional" ways, which they felt to be outmoded. Thus the public for these plays seems to have consisted of the older generation of intellectuals in the cultural and political leadership of the capital and other larger cities. A list of the actual participants in the discussions and battles around these plays, all of whom evidently attended performances, does indeed read like a blue book of New China. Through the choice of this genre and medium the literary discussion about the national leadership, national policies, and conflicts was in fact restricted to the senior members of the political class, who were in fact the essential protagonists, both on stage and in real life.

Public performances thus had a special meaning, giving the different factions and groupings a chance to voice their feelings openly and publicly in the very face of their opponents. The battle for the public mind was in fact a battle for the minds of a small group of members of the political class. The forum provided by the theater, with its restriction to the major urban centers and its many private performances for national or provincial leaders, proved to be optimal because it established a language—the historical medium—in whose terms the most unutterable issues of the present could be legitimately discussed.

A CHANGE IN AUTHORIAL STANCE AND PERSPECTIVE

In the prose of the preceding period, the values upheld by the heroes and the authorial voice were rational and modern. An emphasis on the development of production, the development of a social climate that would promote the full use of each individual's capacity, enthusiasm for the great goals of communism, and a relentless rejection of things traditional as backward and bad characterized these texts. In the new historical plays, the values of economic production and modernity have completely disappeared. Their heroic protagonists embody traditional values of honor, uprightness, justice, benevolence, public interest, personal obligation, and patriotism. Adherence to these values gives the protagonists the strength and self-righteousness that enable them to dare to stand up to the mighty. This point is made quite explicitly by Wu Han, who advocated that one should emulate the moral values of traditional heroes such as Hai Rui or Judge Bao. The measuring rod for the negative characters has also changed. Their bureaucratic power wielding is bad not because it obstructs the development of the productive forces, but because it contravenes human values shared by every decent human being in the play. Again, this moral stance is encoded in the tradition of the genre, but this very fact made the genre attractive.

A CHANGE IN DEPTH

The flat characters and actions of the *texie* and *xiaoshuo* of the Hundred Flowers period reflected a Marxist assumption about the simplicity of truth and of human motives. With the new historical drama, the resonance between the past as it is portrayed on stage and the present as it exists in the viewers' minds greatly increases the depth of both characters and actions. If depth is described as the volume and diversity of silent text created by a literary work in the process of being read or performed to an audience, the very remoteness of the historical action, which in most cases does not permit direct translation into the present, greatly challenges the readers' or spectators' associative powers without offering any simple or flat solutions. True, the historical play most frequently adopts the neat distribution of villainy and virtue that in the traditional opera is emphasized by the characters' appearing in stock masks. In most cases, the greater depth is not inherent in the play itself, but results from the play's resonance with the present.

A REDEFINITION OF THE PRESENT PERIOD

Inevitably, the use of the historical play in the late fifties and early sixties will bring to mind other uses of this genre in earlier times. For most of the authors who wrote such plays in the late fifties and early sixties, it was by no means the first time to do so. They had written historical plays during the thirties and forties in order both to achieve a high patriotic pitch and to allow an indirect avenue of criticism to counteract the often-ruthless government censorship of the Guomindang. By tradition, even ruthless rulers have permitted historical dramas to be staged. The Empress Dowager Ci Xi for instance had a Peking opera on Empress Lü performed for her, although quite obviously it was she herself who was being indirectly attacked. Guo Moruo's *Qu Yuan* was allowed to be performed in Chongqing under the Guomindang Secret Service Chief Dai Li's eyes and with Zhou Enlai's guidance. The historical drama is thus the ultimate genre to which a writer will have recourse at a time of crisis, and the critical historical play tends to appear when a crisis is combined with or caused by severe repression that effectively closes all direct avenues of remonstrance. By again using the historical play in a critical fashion in 1958–1962, writers were implying that the control of the public sphere was now as tight and reckless as it had been under Dai Li, that the internal crisis of the land impelled them to speak, and that they only could do it through the time-honored and relatively immune genre of the historical play.

Most of these points would seem to apply quite independently of the specific ideological stance an author would take with a play, although the momentum for using the genre of historical drama was provided by the plays with a critical stance and other authors only responded in the same medium. The implications of the use of the historical drama at this time which I have spelled out above were not necessarily explicitly present in everbody's mind. There is no question that authors, censors, and audience shared the assumption that the plays played on the present. By adopting the genre of historical drama in the opera tradition, however, a writer also adopted a certain role and stance. The genre brings certain words and plots to his or her mind and leads to the adoption of opinions that otherwise might not have occurred to him or her. To a certain degree, the adoption of the genre informs the "thinking in images," which has its own dynamics, and often disastrously so, leading an author against all better counsel right into the bullpen or into Kang Sheng's prison.

The dramatic shift involved in the adoption of the historical drama as the main form of literary expression coincides with similar changes in related fields, to wit, the adoption of *zawen* in prose and the resurgence of political debate through the medium of historical scholarship centered around the proper evaluation of such figures as Cao Cao, Wu Zetian, Wei Zheng, and Hai Rui.

THE POLITICS OF THE HISTORICAL DRAMA: A NARRATIVE HISTORY

INTRODUCTION

Most of the material related to the historical drama is not available in translation, nor has it been dealt with in specialized scholarly studies. Therefore it may be helpful at this point to give a short *histoire raisonné*, including plot summaries and accounts of subsequent changes in plots, literary debates, and political interventions. This not an entirely gratuitous exercise as most of the nation's top leadership as well as its cultural luminaries were involved in the history of this genre. In a second step, we will study the same material in terms of its structural and literary *topoi*.

TIAN HAN'S GUAN HANQING

Tian Han's *Guan Hanqing* (see chap. 1) set the stage for the new historical drama. It developed the basic techniques of writing such plays, understanding them, and using them in the public sphere. It focused on the political center, and differentiated between two factions at court, of which one, forming a network, was "in favor" and utterly depraved; the other, consisting of individuals, was out of favor, and relatively acceptable. The play created a symbol for the self-perpetuating small ruling group versus the "masses" with the image of the Mongol and Semu versus the Han Chinese. It defined personal favoritism of the emperor as the cause for the rise of the villains to power, and political rather than economic power as the fundament of their might, thus rejecting the traditional class-analysis approach. It revived the symbol of the pure, upright female for the people, showed the hero to be an intellectual in the lowest reaches of the imperial ranking order, and defined absence of legal protection and the prevalence of tyranny in the public sphere as the main problems; it described the historical "present" as a time of social crisis, which propels and forces the hero to speak out. *Guan Hanqing* set the high pitch of big words, grand slogans, and crass actions as the standard, and introduced the theme of *ma*, cursing the villain, which soon was to change into *ma huang*, cursing the emperor. In terms of reaching the public it was well timed and done with strategic genius. Tian Han himself saw the play interacting with the later historical dramas, and advocated a restaging, which took place in 1963 with top actors like Lan Tianye as Guan Hanqing and Di Xinshi as Zhu Lianxiu. As Zhou Enlai and Chen Yi had been among the promoters of the piece, and Zhou Enlai had even had the end changed, the play remained long immune from extensive criticism, but from the beginning of the Cultural Revolution it was listed as a "poisonous weed" together with *Xie Yaohuan*, whereas other pieces by Tian Han such as *Princess Wenzheng* seem to have remained unscathed.

GUO MORUO'S CAI WENJI

Guo Moruo's *Cai Wenji*,[12] the first draft of which was written in early February 1959, was in many respects a response to the challenge of *Guan Hanqing*. This too is a historical drama, with a writer, in this case

12. Guo Moruo, *Cai Wenji*.

a woman writer, as the main protagonist. The play shows the interaction of her real life with her poetry, the moving *Hujia shiba pai*. Within this common framework, however, Guo Moruo adopts a completely different stance. Whereas Tian's hero Guan Hanqing vilifies the corrupt officials, Guo's heroine Cai Wenji learns to praise Cao Cao, a man who had been traditionally vilified both in the histories and in popular tradition. The play was to serve, said Guo himself, to restore Cao Cao's name (*fan Cao Cao*).[13]

Cai Wenji, the daughter of the famous poet Cai Rong, flees the turmoil of the capital at the end of the Later Han and after the death of her father. She and her amah are saved by a Hun prince. The prince takes them to this home, marries Cai, and has two children with her. Once Cao Cao has established control over north China, he sends a delegation with rich presents to buy her return. Both the Huns and Cai Wenji are suspicious about Cao Cao's intentions. The Huns believe that on the heels of the envoy is a big army, but this suspicion is based solely on the bragging of a subaltern in the delegation whose high-sounding title is misunderstood by the Huns.

Cai Wenji, for all her nostalgia for her original home, suspects Cao's motives, fearing he wants to use her knowledge of the Huns to spy on them. In fact, however, Cao only wants to further culture, and hopes she might restore some of her father's lost writings from the debris. The envoy is a childhood friend of Cai's, the two having grown up together. When her husband listens in on her conversation with the envoy, he becomes convinced of Cao's good intentions, and instantly swears a vow of brotherhood with the envoy. Cai is allowed to return, leaving her children behind. Saddened by her separation from her husband and her children but also anticipating her return, Cai spends sleepless nights composing the eighteen songs she entitles *Hujia shiba pai* (Eighteen Pai for the Hujia). In a dazzling flashback reminiscent of film, she recalls her flight from the capital and questions the widsom of her decision to leave. The envoy criticizes her individualism. Some years ago, he says, when there were refugees and many people were separated, she did not pity them. Now she herself is in such a situation and she is sad. However, for the people at large the former situation, "a thousand *li*, no chicken," has changed into bountiful times, with "dishes of food and jugs of beverage to greet the king." She is called upon to make the joy of

13. Ibid., p. 1. Cf. Guo Moruo and Jian Bozan, *Cao Cao lunji.*

the land her own and, under the motto that Huns and Hans are now one family, to see all children as her own. This challenge to her "narrow-mindedness" in the envoy's frank heart-to-heart talk affects her like a life-saving medicine; she begins to rejoice, and stops writing poetry.

The real hero enters only in act four. We have been informed about the false charges against Cao Cao and have heard the subaltern brag that Cao "sharply thinks every second" to the point of becoming "dizzy," that he has an excess of talents, writing poetry, doing calligraphy, being able to write and shoot, guiding men so that each develops his capacities to the fullest. Everybody loves him and fears him. He makes prompt decisions, enforces the law strictly. The envoy himself had said that Cao cares for the people, that he uses the military only when unavoidable, that he has introduced a system of military agricultural colonies (*tuntian*) for the purpose of easing logistic problems and reducing expenditure and has settled refugees and secured the borders.

We find Cao Cao informal and simple at home, reading Cai Wenji's poems while his wife tries to repair a tattered ten-year-old quilt for him—a true Communist leader. He and his wife discuss why Cai's father had allowed himself to be pressed into the service of the infamous Dong Zhuo, who presided over the collapse of the Han. Cao Cao remarks that the trouble with intellectuals is that they think about running away (to Yan'an in the more recent past) but then don't do it.

A crisis develops when Cao Cao, misinformed about the actions of the envoy, thinks the latter entered into secret doings with the Huns and orders his suicide. Cao's rash temper, however, is moderated by his brother, who acts as a kind of prime minister and secretary to the genius. Cao is also willing to listen to criticism based on facts, coming here from Cai Wenji. Cao Cao apologizes for his mistake and the envoy is promoted. Some years later the envoy marries Cai Wenji, who now tries to refashion her poetic craft. From singing about her former sufferings she has gone to singing the glories of the bumper harvests secured by Cao Cao's rule.

Even as depicted by Guo Moruo, Cao Cao has his weaknesses. He fails to see his bureaucratic and chauvinistic subaltern envoy for what he is, and he believes him to the point of ordering the suicide of the leader of the delegation. In this situation, he needs the writer. Cai dares confront him with the facts and prevents him from a grave mistake. Cao Cao, who surrounds himself with writers, had detected Cai's bravery.

Referring to a poem by Cai Wenji, Cao Cao's brother Cao Pei remarks: "Her daring is great indeed. Heaven and Earth and all the spirits and gods she curses." Cao Cao answers: "I esteem her for these very passages, but I am afraid others might blame her exactly for these lines."

The reference in this passage to *Guan Hanqing*, in which Dou E curses Heaven, Earth, and the spirits, is evident; in fact, the entire play silently refutes the assumptions built into *Guan Hanqing*. The people do not cry out against injustice but are prosperous and happy. Those in power are not villains, although some bureaucrats create problems. The bureaucrats are not the personal favorites of the emperor, and they wield no real power. The emperor does not shield himself from criticism but actively invites it—the straighter and more "daring," the better. In answer to Tian's allusion to Mao in the image of Khubilai Khan, Guo Moruo proceeds to rehabilitate the maligned Chairman. Despite rumors of his ruthlessness, cunning, and brutal ways, in fact he sleeps under a tattered quilt, loves poetry, and does all he can to promote Chinese culture. Tian Han was seen as describing himself in the person of Guan Hanqing. Guo Moruo in his preface quotes Flaubert's "Madame Bovary, c'est moi," arguing that Madame Bovary was entirely Flaubert's creation. Guo had lived in Japan for many years, had married a Japanese woman there and had had children who stayed behind when he returned to become a poet closely associated with Mao Zedong. In this sense he wrote, "Cai Wenji, that is I—she is described according to myself." In Tian's play, Ahmad owes his position to the favoritism of the Chairman. Guo, in his play, admits that the Chairman may too easily believe slander he hears from shady characters. However, he is a superhuman, and his mistakes are easily corrected by those who sing his praise, while those who denounce him are at best victims of unfounded rumors. Tian Han proceeds to "reverse a verdict"—according to my interpretation, the verdict against the countless intellectuals victimized during the Anti-Rightist campaign. Guo Moruo, too, reverses a verdict—one that has prevailed in scholarship and popular tradition: that Cao Cao and Mao Zedong, his modern counterpart, are tyrants.

When Cai Wenji directly confronts Cao Cao to plead for the condemned man, one can sense in the background the impact of a political discussion that would soon lift historical drama to both prominence and notoriety. In the preface to *Cai Wenji*, written on May 1, 1959, Guo states that in recent days, important changes had been made. By then, Mao Zedong had made his recommendations about "learning from Hai Rui."

PLAYS ON THE HAI RUI THEME

In 1962, Tao Zhu was quoted as saying that the Party had behaved "tyrannically" during the Great Leap;[14] as early as 1959, Zhou Yang protested that no one dared to speak up.[15] The result of this failure to speak up was costly. Base-level cadres, not daring to present realistic assessments of current and predicted harvests, submitted grotesquely inflated figures. Since state procurement was based on these figures, a famine resulted, and no relief work had even been organized. It is claimed that remarks made by Mao Zedong at the Second Zhengzhou Plenum in early March of 1959 were instrumental in creating the conditions for the new historical drama to emerge. While his remarks were indeed instrumental, by the time when they were made the theme of remonstrance with the emperor and of daring to speak out to the mighty was already well established.

The Ming dynasty official Hai Rui (1540–87) achieved renown as an upright judge, and as the author of a daring memorial to the Jiaqing emperor in which he bluntly accused the emperor of dereliction of his duties. These qualities made him an ideal Hundred Flowers character. The same was true for Guan Hanqing, whose play *Dou E yuan* had been rewritten with Hai Rui entering at the end to solve the case of the injustice done to Dou E. A book-length biography of Hai Rui by Jiang Xingyu appeared in Shanghai in September 1957.[16] Hai Rui was present on stage in the revised *Dou E yuan*, and in a number of other plays, daringly speaking out against powerful villains. At the same time, Tian Han's *Guan Hanqing* had been staged in mid-1958, many months

14. A generally well informed Red Guard source, *Xiju zhanbao*, attributes the following statement to Tao Zhu at the Guangzhou meeting in March 1962: "During the last two or three years . . . people have been subjected to some spiritual tyranny [*nüedai*]." He spoke of the PRC as an "autocratic monarchy," *zhuanzhi wangguo*, and said that the "atmosphere for killing and purging has been too strong." Cf. Zhongguo juxie geming zaofantuan, Zhongguo juxie, "Yige chumu jingxin de fangeming fubi shijian," pp. 2f.

15. In April 1959, Zhou Yang is quoted to have said at the Conference of Shanghai Literature and Art Circles, "in feudal society there also were high personalities possessing loyalty and full of upright feelings. Hai Rui is an indomitable personality, he certainly is not inferior to Judge Bao. . . . Presently there are some people with little daring; their criticism is confined to the realm of base level cadres like office chiefs, but they don't dare to go higher." See the Red Guard source *Hongse pipanzhe*, May 24, 1967, p. 4.

16. Jiang Xingyu, *Hai Rui*.

before Mao's statement. Mao made his statement about Hai Rui after having seen such a Hai Rui play on January 16 or 17, 1959, in the capital. The Opera Art Ensemble of Mao's home province of Hunan gave two plays, one of which dealt with Hai Rui. Entitled *Shengsi pai* (Tablets of Life and Death), it was an opera in the *huagu* style of Yiyang county.[17] The earthy simplicity of the acting in this very deft local style was well in tune with the emphasis being given the people's creativity during the Great Leap.

In the story, the son of He Zongbing, who himself was linked to the vile faction of a powerful, brutal minister of the Ming emperor Shizong, tries to do violence to a young woman, Wang Yuhuai. In the process, he falls into a river and drowns. He Zongbing then accuses Wang of killing his son and demands her execution from the district magistrate, Huang Boxian, threatening "if you do not pass this judgment, this will be the end of your being district magistrate of the seventh rank, and in fact a death sentence might be given to you; at the least, everyone in your family will be sentenced to punishment." Afraid to oppose this tyrant, Huang advises Wang Yuhuai to flee, but she declines because she does not want to bring trouble to her family. Her father, who is serving on the front, had saved magistrate Huang's life on an earlier occasion. Desperate, Huang decides to sacrifice his own daughter instead of executing Wang. However, his adopted daughter steps forth to be killed instead, in order to show her gratitude to her stepparents, and Wang herself does not want any of the others to die for her. The three young women decide to inscribe three tablets, one with the character meaning "death," and the others with that meaning "life." Then, on a darkened stage they desperately grapple for the death tablet, each trying to sacrifice her own life for the others. Describing this scene, a *Wenhui-bao* comment emphasized to the public that "it is a play with educational meaning." Eventually, the magistrate's daughter gets hold of the death tablet, and her father has to lead her to the execution ground, where he will supervise the procedures himself under the eyes of He Zongbing. Happily, however, Hai Rui, who is provincial governor there at the time, arrives. In civilian clothes, he bravely confronts He Zongbing. Hai Rui points out the simple fact that a weak young woman

17. Guo Xinghua, "*Hai Rui baguan*," p. 112, mentions Mao's seeing this play. The dates of the performance are taken from the advertisement in *Guangming ribao* on the days preceding.

would have a hard time drowning a stout young man, drags out the truth, and dares send He Zongbing to prison.[18]

The play was probably performed in a rewritten form that was published later in 1959, but I have seen no original text.[19] I can only assume that the rewriting put it more in tune with a trend already established in *Guan Hanqing*. Although the play has a provincial setting, its villain is part of a network of villains who are in power in the center and use that power ruthlessly. Its central theme is the reversal of an unjust verdict. The three virtuous and upright young females represent the people, and Hai Rui as a character to emulate sends the villain to prison, regardless of the consequences for himself. The evening of its performance was quite an event, with Mei Lanfang, Tian Han, Li Chao and other luminaries attending besides the Chairman and probably Zhou Yang. The performance was reported by the Xinhua News Agency,[20] and Mei Lanfang wrote a long review of the play for *Renmin ribao*.[21] It was followed by another long review by Tian Han of the second play performed that night, *Wang Shaojun*.[22] The *Guangming ribao* devoted half a page to a review of the play,[23] and the *Wenhuibao* in Shanghai even added a photograph to the summary,[24] all of which attested to the importance of the event and the high status accorded to the performance. Attendance, in socialist

18. I take this to be the plot from the reviews, see below, nn. 21 and 22, and an illustrated narrative of the entire text, but based on a revision; cf. Wu Shao-qiang, adapt., *Shengsi pai*.

19. *Shengsi pai*, adapt. Weng Ouhong (Beijing: Zhongguo xiju Press, 1959). This reference is from *Jianguo yilai wenyi zuopin zhuanti shumu*, p. 216.

20. Xinhua brought out a press release on Jan. 17, 1959, which was quoted in the *Wenyibao* of Jan. 18, on p. 3.

21. Mei Lanfang, "Chuantong daode liliang shanshuozhe guanghui," p. 8.

22. Tian Han, "Tan *Wang Shaojun* de suozao."

23. Li Chao, "Zhongshi chuantongju de jinghua."

24. "Hunan huaguju *Shengsi pai* zai Beijing yanchu shoudao haoping," p. 3. A month later, in February, the *Xijubao* carried a long article, and on June 30, Chen Xi, the head of the Cultural Bureau of Hunan Province, wrote another article in *Renmin ribao*; it mentions that a further rewriting of the play into another local opera form, *Huaiju*, was under way and that the play was being filmed in the Haiyan Film Studio in Shanghai. See Chen Xi, "*Shengsi pai* ji qi luncheng." The film was released in black and white in 1959 under the directorship of Zhang Tianxi; see Zhongguo dianying ziliaoguan and Zhongguo yishu yanjiuyuan dianying yanjiusuo, *Zhongguo yishu yingpian bianmu*, vol. 1, p. 510.

states, of the highest leaders at theater performances is no rarity. It provides the public in these states, with their narrowly controlled public sphere, with a unique opportunity to express their feelings to their temporal masters through applause, sighs, laughter, manifest boredom, or other signals of moderate risk. In terms of printed matter, we only have the reviews to tell us of audience reaction. About Hai Rui's appearance on stage, Mei Lanfang wrote: "His arrival reverses this unjust verdict. When on stage the upright forces have overcome the vile forces, the spectators heaved a sigh of relief in unbounded satisfaction. Sun Yangsheng played the part of Hai Rui. His singing was very moving with his resounding voice, and it was impressive how each of his movements expressed the stature of this governor who in simple clothing is on a private visit." The audience's sigh of relief when Hai Rui dares confront the vile official, reverse the unjust verdict, and put the said official to jail, coming as it did amidst widespread charges of ruthless and tyrannical behavior of leading cadres and the banishment without trial of hundreds of thousands of intellectuals, might have been such a signal.

It appears, in other words, that the Chairman was reacting to an existing climate of public opinion, which was manifest in the Hai Rui pieces, Guan Hanqing's *Dou E yuan* and his frequently staged pieces about the upright Judge Di, and Tian Han's *Guan Hanqing*. The over-reporting of the *Shengsi pai* performance would seem to support the proposition that elements within the political and cultural leadership considered it useful to allow a degree of public emulation of characters like Hai Rui and a degree of cursing (*ma*) of high government villains on stage. This may have something to do with actual public opinion, but in itself certainly is no indicator. A curious opera that appeared in *Juben* as early as April 1959 would support the proposition that the Hai Rui wind was blowing long before the Chairman decided to blow in the same direction.

The piece is entitled *Da Qianlong* (Trouncing the Qianlong Emperor). A product of the Peking opera company of the city of Zhenjiang in Jiangsu province written collectively with Zhao Wanpeng "holding the pen," it had been revised by the Zhenjiang branch of the province's Opera Work Committee, a process that must have taken several months before the eventual national publication.[25] The play had

25. Zhao Wanpeng, *Da Qianlong*.

moved, as the title indicates, from the more modest "cursing" (*ma*) of the villain (and then emperor) to "trouncing" (*da*) the emperor.

The Zhenjiang magistrate is informed by the Qianlong emperor's majordomo that his majesty will soon arrive on an impromptu *nanxun*, a southern inspection trip. The magistrate instantly orders the citizens to hand over two strings of copper coins per head for expenses, to resurface the streets, to erect altars in front of the houses, and not to dare to weep and wail. The emperor arrives in his *xinggong*, travel palace, and, seeing the town so trim and proper, he rejoices at the evidence of his virtue: "As the Lord of the Great Qing has the Way, all within the four seas is at peace," he sings. Having informed himself perfunctorily about the local situation, he decides to make an incognito outing to a nearby scenic spot.

Under the title of "People's Resentment," the third act introduces two young women, one of whom is named Wu Fengzhao. The area has been afflicted by natural disasters, there has been a drought, and people are going hungry. The imperial visit does not bring rain and is a burdensome expense. The young women are even prevented by it from watering their vegetables, whose leaves have turned yellow. Talking among themselves, they lustily curse his majesty, saying, "He knows nothing about the drought here and the terrible harvests," "He does not care for the people's suffering," "Since he is the emperor, why doesn't he take care of our problems?" "He just wanders in the mountains and enjoys himself near the water." In short, they "resent this imperial tour to Zhenjiang." One of the young women, Wu Fengzhao, says she could simply "kill him for it." The visit of the emperor does not bring happiness but *huiqi*, unhappiness. Then the grandfather of one of the women comes by. Although he is an intellectual, a *xiucai*, he has to contribute to his family's survival by selling bean curd. Showing him the yellowing leaves of the vegetables, the women tell him that they have "cursed this emperor who lacks in virtue" for what has happened. "What is the use of cursing him," he asks. "Whether or not it is of any use, calling him a name or two is a good way to let off steam," they answer.

Upon the emperor's return from the outing, the emperor's majordomo suggests that he may want to choose some local women for his inner chambers, as they are famed for their beauty. Then, he says, his majesty could have a "southern inspection tour" right at home without having to go through the trouble of climbing mountains and crossing rivers. They encounter Wu Fengzhao, and in a little farce the emperor (in common clothes) tries to trap and grab her. She threatens to call the police, and the emperor claims they have no say over him. She curses him as a robber and bandit, and he says "the imperial law does not apply to me." Eventually he reveals his identity, but she answers that she could not care less. She finally says: "You say you're the Qianlong emperor; well then, I'll trounce you, you lecherous lord who does not have the Way," and she slaps his face. She runs into her house, and the emperor sees that it has a "seven star stone" affixed over the door. Incensed, the emperor orders the magistrate to arrest such "preposterous people who offend the emperor and deceive the authorities," who, in the magistrate's words, turn to *caofan* (rebellion) and dare to "trounce the emperor." As his majesty is embarrassed by his own action, he does not want to admit that he has been trounced by a young woman, and, when pressed for information about the criminal, he awkwardly describes "him" as *baixing*, the people. That the young woman is to stand for "the people" is not surprising; the symbolism is further emphasized by the seven star stone. Many houses in fact had such stones (sometimes they are simple slips of paper) adorned with the *beitou* constellation (Ursa Major), which was supposed to be protective. Here, the pun is on the Chinese flag with its five stars, of which four represent workers, peasants, soldiers, and national bourgeoisie, and the fifth, the Party. The number seven here might indicate that significant groups have been left off the flag (like intellectuals and minorities). To prevent the arrest of the young woman, her grandfather the intellectual bean-curd seller devises a strategy: During the night all the houses along the lane will put up seven star stones so that on the next day all will be arrested and brought before the emperor. What the grandfather, the intellectual, sells is "white and spicy" bean curd, a fitting symbol for his clean and sharp-witted criticism. Making use of the emperor's embarrassment, and pretending to flatter him as *youdao*, having the Way, the people of the lane eventually force the emperor to say that he will protect them against all sorts of villains. Then Wu Fengzhao tells of being molested by a man and asks for the emperor's punishment. The emperor leaves in a huff. Having cursed the emperor (*mahuang*), slapped him in the face (*dahuang*), poked fun at him (*chaonong huang*), and eventually forced him into a shameful retreat (*xiuzou*), the people of the seven stars rejoice. In a rapid exchange of jubilant phrases, the piece ends:

WU: He lost face.
XIE: He made a fool of himself.

WU: He gave us something to laugh about for days on end.

XIE: Emperor Qianlong,

WU: with his pompous air,

XIE: The seven star stone

WU: is like Mount Tai,
         if the multitude of men are united in their hearts, there's
         nothing he can do,

XIE: even his thousand armies and ten thousand horses prove futile.

MASSES: (in chorus) Ha!
         the girl's courage is as high as heaven,

WU: even with courage one still needs you all to rely on,

XIE: We risked our bodies' being cut to pieces!

MASSES: (in chorus) We pulled that old emperor from his high horse!

The little piece is a satire on the Chairman's inspection trips. The real situation has been embellished by the local cadres, and he is not really interested in seeing more than would confirm the heavenly mandate. In the form of a historical play, the criticism that he molested the people could be allegorically expressed by having Qianlong molest the young woman. The play emphasizes the utter ignorance of the top leader of the real plight of the country. He is vengeful, furthermore, and sees opposition to his molesting the young woman as the political crime of rebellion. But again, the play never utters the thought that the emperor should be overthrown (which would have been "counterrevolutionary" in contemporary parlance). He is and will remain the emperor, and the people find relief for their frustration through symbolical action. They curse him, beat him, make fun of him, and unhorse him. The audience is invited to rejoice in these activities at the second level of symbolical action, the performance of these activities on stage. Nor is there any doubt about the contemporary meaning of unhorsing the emperor; it is a quote from the Chairman himself, who in a speech at the Conference on Propaganda Work in March 1957 emphasized that "during the period of the struggle for socialism and communism" there would be a need for people with integrity and lofty ideals (zhishi renren), and a need for a daring spirit to speak up, even to the highest authorities. He added: "He who is not afraid of being cut to pieces, dares to unhorse even the emperor."[26] This Hundred Flowers slogan had come straight from the *Honglou meng*, and *Da Qianlong* proceeded to act it out on

26. Mao Zedong, "Zai quanguo Gongchandang xuanzhuan gongzuo-huiyishang de jianghua," p. 442.

stage with the emperor being literally pulled from his high horse at the end.

As this play was quite certainly written before Mao made his statements on Hai Rui and the Hai Rui spirit, it seems clear that there was already a climate of opposition to the "unjust verdicts," the strangulation of public criticism, and the Chairman's negligence of the actual problems of the country. Mao Zedong had been sharply criticized for his handling of the center and for his responsibility in launching the Great Leap at the Party plena in early 1959. Whether he intended to drag these critics into the open for the purpose of "unmasking" them and beating them down, or whether he was serious in his avowed desire to open the avenues through which realistic reports and proposals could reach him, must remain an open question. We do know that at this time Mao was developing the theory that it is necessary to "set up opposites" if they are not spontaneously forthcoming, because otherwise the lessons cannot be publicly drawn.

Mao took up the Hai Rui theme at the Second Zhengzhou Plenum in late February and early March of 1959. Of the eight points that he laid down there, the last two deal with "speaking up." Echoing the threats of *Shengsi pai*'s He Zongbing, he said: "There ought to be created within the Party an atmosphere of speaking out and of correcting shortcomings. Criticizing is sometimes rather painful, but so long as criticism results in correction it is all right. When people don't dare speak out, it is for one of six reasons: fear of admonition, fear of demotion, fear of loss of prestige, fear of dismissal from the Party, fear of execution, fear of divorce. It was only after his execution that Yue Fei became famous. Speaking out should involve no penalty, and according to Party regulations people are entitled to their own opinions. In the past under the court system I don't know how many people were put to death; but there were still many who braved death to oppose the court."[27]

Mao is not speaking of the past, but of the present. Although he says that no penalty *should* apply to critics, he makes it clear that in fact people might get hurt; but even if they die, they might make it to fame. This implies a division of labor; the leadership would play its role by hitting critics over the head, and the critics would find their satisfaction in cursing the leadership and pointing out mistakes, perhaps even being killed in the process, but certainly dying as popular heroes. There is no evidence that he specifically mentioned Hai Rui on this occasion. Offi-

27. *Miscellany of Mao Tse-tung Thought*, vol. 1, p. 176.

cial PRC sources claim that he mentioned Hai Rui for the first time at the Shanghai Work conference (March 24 to April 4, 1959).[28] But early in March, Zhou Yang had already come to Shanghai and "transmitted" to the celebrated Peking opera actor Zhou Xinfang "a commission for a work" to be "performed on the occasion of the tenth anniversary of the People's Republic," and said to him: "Since the Anti-Rightist [campaign] no one dares to speak out. Writing Hai Rui plays will encourage everyone to dare say the truth."[29] Immediately in March a group was formed in Zhou Xinfang's company to set about writing the play and they finished the first draft in the beginning of April. The group entered into contract with Jiang Xingyu, who had written a biography of Hai Rui in late 1957.[30] Zhou Yang had acted in 1958 as Mao's spokesman in literary matters, and he and Guo Moruo had shared in the honor of detailing Mao's thoughts on folk songs and on "combining revolutionary realism with revolutionary romanticism." Thus, he may have acted on the Chairman's orders, as the decision to perform a Hai Rui play on the grand festivities of the tenth anniversary would have to be made at a rather high level. But many leaders had in "early 1959" begun to advocate "daring to keep the truth and daring to speak," and "someone" (not the Chairman) had "called this the 'Hai Rui Spirit.'" This "someone" (*youren*) was a "leading comrade," probably the vice-minister of culture, Qian Junrui.[31]

Mao decided to promote this theme. The most detailed report about his remarks is by Guo Xinghua, who writes:

> Propagating Hai Rui has been recommended by Chairman Mao. In April 1959 at the time of the Shanghai Conference, many comrades spoke about the need to promote daring to speak out, daring to speak the truth. This was because after 1958 many problems showed up in the work, and Chairman Mao was very much concerned. Once, Chairman Mao had seen the Hunan opera *Tablets of Life and Death* where Hai Rui shows up in the last act; thereupon he took out the "Biography of Hai Rui" in the *Mingshi* to have a look, and he spoke about one of the Hai Rui stories. The Chairman said [in substance, as there are no quotation marks]: This man's cursing of the emperor was quite devastating. [Hai Rui] said [the emperor's reign name] Jiajing meant "house for house all emptied out"; he even wrote this phrase in a memorial to the emperor. Thereafter, he was imprisoned. One day they

28. *Peng Dehuai zishu*, p. 300.
29. Xu Siyan, "Wei *Hai Rui shangshu*," pp. 81f.
30. Jiang Xingyu, "Hai Rui," p. 89. Jiang was also the author of the article "Nan Bao Gong—Hai Rui."
31. Guo Xinghua, "*Hai Rui baguan*," p. 112.

suddenly brought wine and food for him, and he was quite intrigued, and asked to see the prison director. But as soon as [Hai] learned that the Jiajing emperor had died, he loudly wailed, and spat out all the things he had just eaten. Chairman Mao said, although Hai Rui had attacked the emperor quite devastatingly, his heart was loyally devoted to the emperor.[32]

At this meeting, Peng Dehuai had been sharply critical of the Chairman, Red Guards would later charge. He was claimed to have "voiced opposition to Chairman Mao's assuming command in person," which "meant discarding the Standing Committee of the Politbureau." He "expressed great dissatisfaction with the Chairman's criticism of him" and called Mao's speech at this meeting *tiaobo*, "instigating discord."[33] By emphasizing Hai Rui's loyalty, Mao seems to have assured even harsh critics like Peng Dehuai that he recognized their basic commitment to him. According to another account, "Chairman Mao first proposed at the Shanghai Work Conference to learn from Hai Rui's spirit of being upright, outspoken, and not fawning."[34]

According to Guo's account, Mao went a step further: "After the Chairman had thus spoken [at the Shanghai Plenum], he gave the *Mingshi* [which contained Hai Rui's biography] to Peng Dehuai for his perusal." This looks very much indeed like "setting up an opposite." "After this affair, comrade Qian Junrui transmitted [supreme approval for propagating Hai Rui] to the comrades responsible for the literary and art circles."[35] According to Professor Wu Xiaoling, Qian also suggested that Wu Han would be the proper man to write an article about Hai Rui.[36]

The different leaders like Zhou Yang and Hu Qiaomu thus had full authority to organize the propaganda campaign on Hai Rui. Zhou Yang sent further materials to Zhou Xinfang. Also in April, Zhou Yang stated at a Conference of Shanghai Literature and Art Circles: "In feudal society there were also high personalities with loyalty and full of

32. Jiang Xingyu, "Hai Rui," p. 89, writes that "the responsible comrade from the center advocated 'the spirit of Hai Rui.'"

33. Union Research Institute, *The Case of P'eng Te-huai*, p. 204.

34. Hu Yuzhi and Li Wenyi, "Kuairen kuaiyu gandan zhaoren, shenqie huainian Wu Han tongzhi." The latter characteristic was first stressed in a May 13, 1959, article by the senior editor of *Wenhuibao*, Wen Yibu, "Bao Gong yu Hai Rui."

35. Guo Xinghua, "*Hai Rui baguan*," p. 113.

36. Wu Xiaoling, handout for his talk "The Story of Hai Rui," Center for Chinese Studies, University of California, Berkeley, November 1985.

upright feelings. Hai Rui is an indomitable personality, and certainly not inferior to [the famous incorruptible Song dynasty] Judge Bao. Presently there are some people who have little daring. Their criticism remains confined to the lowest-level cadres like office heads, but they don't dare go higher."[37] Staying within his comparison to Judge Bao, who hailed from the north, Jiang Xingyu published his "Hai Rui—the Judge Bao of the South" on April 17 in *Jiefang ribao*, and an editorial on Hai Rui by Wen Yibu, the paper's senior editor, was carried in the Shanghai *Wenhuibao* on May 13. Wen stressed Hai Rui's indomitable spirit (*gang*). The times of Hai, he said, were such that "he who spoke out was criminalized," while now "we have already a great time where he who speaks out is without guilt," a surprising statement to make in the summer of 1959. People are nonetheless afraid of possible consequences, he added, but this is like being afraid of ghosts. They only exist in your head. "Nonetheless, there are still a great number of people around who are afraid of ghosts. This style [of speaking the truth] is indeed not much developed. Therefore to see plays on Judge Bao or Hai Rui has a practical educational meaning."[38] In June, Hu Qiaomu had Wu Han write his *Hai Rui ma huangdi* (Hai Rui Upbraids the Emperor) to make it clear that criticism was not to stop at some lower level but would have to reach as high as the Chairman himself.

We are thus dealing with organized Party propaganda activity where the intentions of the promoters, the motives of those who fell in line, the aspirations of the historians, playwrights, and actors, and the feelings of the general public in this hysterical year formed a web of exceedingly intricate relationships from which even a Hai Rui would have had trouble extricating himself. We have to go by the sources at our disposal, and these are the plays and some reports of plays. A "Hai Rui industry" sprang up in Shanghai. The Huangpu Peking Opera Company produced *Hai Rui Fights Zhang Zhibo with Astuteness*; it was then revised to sharpen the conflict. At the same time, work on a second Hai Rui play was promoted; it dealt with Hai Rui's criticism of the Jiajing emperor. There was also a third Hai Rui play. The Shanghai Zhicheng Huai Opera Troupe wanted to stage a dance drama on Hai Rui, and the People's Pingtan Troupe, which performed ballads in the Suzhou dialect with musical accompaniment, staged two older Hai Rui

37. *Hongse pipanzhe*, May 24, 1967, p. 4.
38. Jiang Xingyu, "Nan Baogong—Hai Rui," *Jiefang ribao*, April 17, 1959.

plays, and produced a new one, *Hai Rui beiqian* (Hai Rui Pulls the Rope), to which we will return later. All these activities were on by mid-May 1959. The general ideological guideline that they followed was contained in the slogan "the spirit of daring to hold on to the truth of this historical personality should be propagated."[39]

The writers of these plays were not left alone with their orders, but were closely guided. Hu Qiaomu guided Wu Han's hand; Tao Xiong, the vice-director of the Shanghai Peking Opera Theater, wrote in late 1959 that *Hai Rui shangshu* "was written under the eager solicitude of top-level leaders, and with the warm support of historians and literary specialists."[40]

This writing group with Xu Siyan "holding the pen" first drowned in the abundance of material on Hai Rui. It had set out to write a Hai Rui play based on traditional lore (*zhuanshuo*) to celebrate Hai Rui's "incorruptibility and purity" and the "Five Not-Afraids" of Mao, but the wealth of historical material changed it into a historical play (*lishiju*). As for the play's focus, a "leader" proposed that it be on Hai Rui remonstrating with the Jiajing emperor, a theme not dealt with in *Tablets of Life and Death*, the play seen by Mao or otherwise in popular tradition. Another "leading comrade," also from Shanghai, further suggested that Hai and the emperor should meet face to face (although this was not historically accurate), since such a confrontation would strongly heighten the dramatic effect. Both suggestions, needless to say, were accepted by everyone.[41] Zhou Xinfang, who had just joined the Party,[42] took no part in writing the earlier drafts, but he and Xu Siyan spent a month finalizing the text in July and August. Well aware of the kind of language to be used in this genre, Zhou Xinfang proposed to include the phrase already used in *Trouncing Qianlong* from Mao's 1957 speech about unhorsing the emperor. The process of a gradual darkening of the plot, which we observed in the *Guan Hanqing* play, is equally visible here. In addition to fixing the theme on Hai Rui's memorial and the direct confrontation between Hai and the emperor, the image of the emperor himself is also changed. Hai Rui's memorial as recorded in the *Mingshi* had praised the emperor as an enlightened ruler; now he is characterized as an "extremely tyrannical ruler" (*zuizuibaode jun*). The characterization is then changed to "licentious" and "imperious and

39. "Shanghai xijujie chuangzuo Hai Rui jumu."
40. Tao Xiong, "Chenyuan shierzai de wenziyu," pp. 76f.
41. Xu Siyan, "Wei *Hai Rui shangshu*," p. 82.
42. Zhou Xinfang, "Yongyuan wangbuliao zhe zhuangyan de shike."

violent," the term *bao* (tyrannical) frequently recurring. Zhou Xinfang, who had helped revise the text, directed the play and played the lead. By now, history had already identified the play's roles with the real-world figures. Peng Dehuai had accepted Mao's offer to become the Hai Rui, and be set up as the opposite, with the danger of being cut to pieces and the hope of being thereby immortalized. Both danger and hope were fulfilled in due order.

At the Lushan Plenum, which had ended in August, Peng had compared himself to Hai Rui and attempted to bring the facts about the Great Leap and about the climate of public opinion to the attention of the leadership. Playing his historical role, he spoke out right to Mao's face, and he laid much of the blame to his door. And Mao, cast in the role of the Jiajing emperor, played his part in pointing to a rightist conspiracy behind Peng's criticisms. The danger of "revisionism" was now uppermost in the Chairman's mind, and Peng, in both his political opinions and his close contacts with the Soviet leadership, was in Mao's eyes the clear representative of that current. Peng Dehuai, he argued, was a mere "rightist" Hai Rui, a man who was politically on the wrong side and only donned the prestigious cap of the Ming official. With this line he implied that he would tolerate further activities to promote Hai Rui, while resolutely beating the "rightist" Hai Rui over the head. Whatever the original intentions that prompted the promotional activities may have been, it was now clear that whenever Hai Rui was mentioned together with the emperor, "emperor" would be a reference to the Chairman. The fact that Zhou Yang, Hu Qiaomu, and Qian Junrui continued to promote Hai Rui texts after the Lushan Plenum would indicate that Mao himself advocated this continued promotion; Hu was at the time something like Mao's secretary, Zhou Yang Mao's literary spokesman, and Qian had made Mao's remarks at the Shanghai Conference a matter of top priority for the Propaganda Department. The "opposite," it seems, was in reality much larger, and had to be given more leeway to come out on stage. A month after the end of the Lushan Plenum and in the middle of an "Anti-Right-Opportunist" campaign, Zhou Xinfang's *Hai Rui Sends up a Memorial* was performed on the occasion of the tenth anniversary of the founding of the Republic, an occasion that by definition assured it maximum attention.

The first act of the play,[43] entitled "Striving to Become an Immortal,

43. Shanghai jingjuyuan, with Xu Siyan holding the pen, *Hai Rui shangshu*. This is based on revisions made in 1961. The original text appeared in *Shanghai xiju* 1959.2. I will not deal here in detail with the changes.

Letting the Government Go to Rot," shows the Jiajing emperor in Taoist cap and monk's garb and surrounded by Taoist magicians; he is cooking cinnabar (appropriately red in color) on a special stove under the image of Laozi, the all-too evocative white-bearded Sage. All kinds of extraordinary wonders are constantly performed or promised, and rare plants with magic powers are constantly brought in. The emperor has already 769 plants at his disposal, all of which secure immortality. He is not quite sure whether to believe in these airy promises and wonders, but eventually is so much drawn in by the promise of immortality that he goes along. By hoax, one of the magicians makes a flowering branch suddenly appear on the Laozi altar, evidently to indicate that the emperor (the Chairman) had been favored with the gift of a new, flowering branch of this old learning (a new contribution to Marxism-Leninism). The emperor decides to celebrate the occasion by making a sacrifice to Heaven; this, the highest of sacrifices, is performed only at times of assured dynastic glory and triumph. The prime minister, Xu Jie, enters and in good operatic fashion introduces himself to the public and explains his mask:

> I am Xu Jie, the highest-ranking minister, well-versed in adapting to
>   circumstances;
> firmly keeping my mouth shut, avoiding judgment of right or wrong,
>   I put caution first.

When informed about the miracle of the flowering branch, he sings:

> Of course, I know that these miracles are all concocted and invented,
> but if I reveal it, I fear to offend the Dragon's mien.
> I have only to hoist the flag of going with the wind—
> my master's happiness lies in greatly extending his years.

Sung on the eve of the huge celebrations for National Day 1959, the opera's resonances were quite deafening. In the next act, while the emperor is being given concocted reports about the dreamy world of immortals, the ministers crowd outside the palace with reports of inundations, incursions, and famine. When they are not admitted into the emperor's presence, some of them imitate Xu Jie by being "tactful" and withdrawing (zhique), but not so Liang Cai, whose name announces him as a talent of high caliber. When the bearer of another miracle is instantly admitted, Liang explodes. Notwithstanding the entreaties of his companion that he should go by the proverb "close your mouth and hide the tongue, and your security is guaranteed forever," he proclaims that he is "itching to submit a memorial for the complete expulsion of these foxish immortals and demonic Taoists." His companion warns him that previously, under Yan Song, Yang Cui had done exactly this and had paid for it with his life. Criticizing the abuses of leaders will end in disaster. Liang Cai comes from the department of revenue, which is Hai Rui's yamen; our introduction to Hai Rui thus is through Liang, a man influenced by his spirit. For his criticism, Liang is instantly sentenced to sixty strokes and banished to a distant region.

Xu Jie, who witnesses the scene, resigns himself to the fact that he can do nothing, and the scene ends with a duet by him and Li, Liang's companion.

LI: Close the door and push out the moon before the window.

XU: Let the plum blossoms come forth on their own.

LI: Let us go submit Taoist charms and congratulatory messages [for the sacrifice].

XU: (sighs) Ai!

In the third act, entitled "The Ears Hear and the Eyes See," the hero enters. The emperor has sent a Taoist to build a garden for his many plants of immortality. The garden is to be built, however, in a slum where many poor people live. The Taoist evicts them, as snow falls, showing Heaven's rage. Hai Rui enters the stage. He is protected by an umbrella, which will take on rich meaning as the play goes on, and hears a man singing *Jiajing Jiajing Jiajiahuhu ganganjingjing*, a pun that plays on the emperor's reign title and can be translated as "house by house, completely emptied out." (Wu Han had brought this pun to public attention in his article entitled "Hai Rui ma huangdi.")

Hai inquires into the cause of the singer's distress, promises his support, and gives it symbolically by providing his umbrella to the singer's freezing wife. Hai Rui forces the Taoist, who in classical bureaucratic manner warns him not to overstep his jurisdiction, to make a temporary retreat by proving that the Taoist has pocketed the money assigned to the people as compensation. Not mincing his words, Hai calls the Taoists "ox-demons and snake-specters" and sings that "boundless hatred is in my heart." To his companion, he points out that "if the upper beam is not right, the lower ones will be askance," thus laying the blame at the emperor's door. But he feels the high officials are also to blame; as Mao had said, "to preserve their families and save their lives," they don't "speak loyal words." At this moment, Liang is dragged past, on his way to exile, giving occasion for Hai to say that "there are still

those who are militant and bold, and dare contradict the emperor"—
but evidently such people will be banished to the countryside.

Act four, set in Xu Jie's study, confronts the prime minister with Hai
Rui. Xu sings:

For days I have been sitting in my study writing congratulatory epistles,
wracking my dried-out brain for nothing but jubilations for the present dynasty,
quite some time of my life has been wasted for nothing.

When Hai is announced, he quickly hides his charms and paeans.
They are too embarrassing. There are some very stiff formalities, which
recall the historical Hai Rui's obsession with such matters, and then Hai
Rui takes up a metaphor from Tian Han's *Guan Hanqing*, charging
that the high officials of the court who see the transgressions of the
emperor but do not remonstrate are just "licorice root," a term that is a
catchphrase of the new historical drama.

I have a comparison for them: the licorice root among the medicaments. . . .
Simply said, words that grate the ear are bitter like *huanglian* [a plant used
for medicine, *coptis chinensis*], praises that accommodate the heart are not
different from the sweet taste of licorice root [*gancao*]. The emperor loves
the sweet and hates the bitter; therefore, the great ministers at this present
court, when they are with him, come forth with sweet words and honeyed
phrases. If that is not licorice root, what is it? . . . Regrettably the Holy
Emperor strives for immortality and goes after the Tao. For more than
twenty years he has not ascended to the court to take care of the government.
This has led to internal disasters and external catastrophes, and the people
can no longer sustain this life. As for the great ministers, they have to speak
straightforwardly and remonstrate with the emperor; only then can order
be established. But instead, they just adapt to his tastes; in a word, they
are hypocrites [*xiangyuan*].

Hai Rui then proceeds to compare the present court with the one
that preceded it, when Yan Song reigned supreme. "In earlier times
the crimes of Yan Song's dictatorship rose to Heaven; when he looked
for people's qualifications, the criterion was whether they would cringe
and smile obsequiously [*xiejian chanxiao*] and be docile and obedient
[*fushou tie'er*]. When the emperor did something wrong, they did not
challenge him." Then he directly challenges Xu Jie: "If you shut your
mouth and don't speak up, people will say that you are no different
from Yan Song," and when Xu points to the emperor's long-standing
obsession with immortality, Hai proceeds to prescribe the "proper"
recipe: "There is a saying, 'a violent disease requires violent medicine,'
and I have an excellent recipe. . . . The emperor has eaten licorice root
for quite a few decades, to the extent that the disease has even entered

the vital region between the heart and diaphragm [indicating that his case is nearly hopeless]. Therefore one must now use [the bitter herbs] Dahuang and Badou so that the emperor's bowels will move and so that his entrails will be cleaned out thoroughly. Only then will it be possible to return the dead to the living." Then he sings:

> Dahuang and Badou can bring the desired result. Against the disease give the [proper] medicine, and the hundred symptoms will disappear. First: Demolish the immortality platform and chase out the demonic Taoists. Second: No sacrifice to Heaven, no fasting, no concocting of cinnabar drugs. Third: Open wide the avenues of talk, turn around as early as possible, instantly release the innocent ministers from the imperial prison. Giving a new beginning to the people, the enlightened emperor has the Way; ascend the throne, receive the ministers, approve memorials and edicts, hold court every day.

Xu hears this passionate plea for orderly and regular government, but responds that the drug is much too violent, and proposes milder remedies. "You probably know that a body that has been sick for a long while is completely exhausted. One must use mild drugs and cure slowly; only then will one have the desired effect." But Hai Rui now points to the crisis that the country faces, and he argues that there is no time to be lost, for "the black-haired people in the land find themselves between deep water and scorching fire, and cannot wait another day." In a dramatic exchange with the minister, he drives home the point:

XU:	The gentleman waits for the right moment and then acts; he is not rash.
HAI:	When the urgency is such that your eyebrows are already scorched [by the fire], better not wait.
XU:	Knowing what is possible at the time is what makes a hero.
HAI:	But have you seen . . . ?
XU:	Seen what?
HAI:	The people—they look famished [*mian you caise*]!
XU:	Eh?
HAI:	You, have you heard . . . ?
XU:	Heard what?
HAI:	Their complaints, which fill the roads. Each man curses the present!
XU:	Stop it! Stop!
HAI:	If we wait any longer, the people will have nothing left to eat!
XU (holding his hands to his ears):	You scare me, you scare me to death.

Xu, agitated, draws near Hai Rui, pointing accusingly at him but speechless. Hai Rui is now also extremely agitated.

XU (screaming):   Hai Rui, Hai Gangfeng [Hai's *hao*, or sobriquet]! (Sternly) You are mad. With each phrase you slander the court, denounce his Holy Majesty. Even if your body were cut into ten thousand pieces, you could not atone for your crime...(goes on with a laugh) I think you are upright and honest, and that you have good intentions and no evil designs, don't misunderstand me...[But] you have to keep yourself under control and cherish your future prospects.

Frustrated, Hai leaves him, saying: "What is the use of chatter if the words do not reach their destination?"

In act five, stumbling through the streets after the above exchange, Hai Rui begins to understand why people call Prime Minister Xu the national champion of compromise (*tiaoting guoshou*); he is but a slick maneuverer (*yuanhua jiqiao*). How could he expect Xu to speak out from a sense of justice (*zhangyi zhi yan*) and follow the slogan "dare to act, dare to get things done." This short wedge act marks the turning point for Hai Rui. Rejecting the temptation to resign from office and retreat into the mountains, he decides to do what the smaller fry like Liang cannot do, and what the high ministers are not willing to do— that is, to use the opportunity of the emperor's sacrifice to Heaven to "pour cold water over [the emperor's] head, to awaken him with a shock from his superstitious dreams."

> To seal one's mouth three times is abominable.
> In offering advice and rectifying the times, the pencil should not make turnabouts.
> I am unwilling to steal my official's salary in peace,
> I would rather have the blood from my neck sprinkled on the steps of the throne.

In act six, Hai Rui has to deal with the fact that he may implicate others. His wife is concerned that he will overreact. But faced with the *weiwei ruoruo*, the yes-men at court, Hai says: "When my eyes see the devastation all around, the anger grows in my heart. It's like a bone in the throat: one does not find rest until one has spat it out." He offers his wife a choice: either flee this very night and be saved, or stay with him and be threatened with death by the emperor's special police. Hesitantly she decides to stay with him. He then orders a coffin to be bought and sets out to write his memorial. His motive is to save the dynasty, and to awaken the emperor to the country's crisis.

In his memorial, he lists the Jiajing emperor's crimes:

He hurts the people by increasing taxes and corvée labor.

He hurts the people so that their means of livelihood are in imminent danger.

He hurts the people so that they are driven to a point where they want to weep but have no tears.

He hurts the people through extravagance and reckless use of power.

He hurts the people so that they become destitute, and drift from place to place.

He hurts the people so that they have no home to which to return.

When he has finished writing, he falls asleep at his desk. In desperation, his wife burns the memorial. Hai leaves in a huff, pushing his wife to the ground.

Act seven confronts Hai Rui with He Yishang, his companion in act three. Hai goes to He seeking a place where he can rewrite his memorial. He Yishang has given up. The officials, he says, are "but gamecocks and running dogs," and he drowns his sorrow in wine. When he reads Hai Rui's statement that "the social fabric is rent asunder" and the reference to the mutterings of discontent, he calls this a deft way of "cursing" the emperor. (The term for cursing, *ma*, is another of the catchwords of this branch of writing.) Hai Rui replies, making a change in the wording of Mao's 1957 remark: "In this our dynasty the emperor is a dim emperor, the ministers are crafty ministers and if this my memorial has the effect of the emperor's reforming himself, and of calling upon the great ministers to fear neither Heaven nor Earth [in their remonstrance], then even if I am cut into a thousand pieces, I will still pull them down from their horses." The "unhorsing" is thus not restricted to the emperor but includes the ministers as well.

The eighth act brings the confrontation of the Taoist charms of the ministers with the memorial of Hai Rui, and of Hai Rui with the emperor. The emperor in introducing himself rejoices at the wisdom of his father who set up the special brocade-clothed police "to subjugate the crowd of officials," and congratulates himself that "everything is calm in the land." The high ministers now proceed to describe the exceeding happiness of the country: "the wind is harmonious, the rain falls in time, the state is in peace and the people are satisfied," sings one; "fields and mulberry trees yield a thousandfold, rice and millet fill the granaries," pipes up the next; and, making complete fools of themselves, the eight top ministers sing the emperor's praises in chorus, perhaps with their hips softly swinging.

> The rivers and mountains are settled and secure for a thousand times a
>   thousand years,
> The altars of the nation are well and reposed for ten thousand and ten
>   thousand years!

Again, the emperor retains a certain ironic distance. He is amazed to hear that the little official Hai Rui has written him a congratulatory message, because he had heard that Hai was incorruptible and without equal. Hai Rui, confronting the emperor, whom he first forces to change from his Taoist garb into proper imperial dress, maintains that the great ministers are deceiving the emperor. He charges that the emperor himself is a "tyrant with little compassion and no sense of justice," and proclaims that his memorial was not sent by any faction, but by the suffering people, who will cease to regard the emperor as emperor if these things go on—a threat in no uncertain terms.

Prime Minister Xu is afraid to be implicated, but at the same time he also wants to protect Hai Rui, with whom he basically agrees. Claiming that an execution would only make of Hai Rui what he wanted to be, a martyr, Xu in fact saves his life. Hai Rui's "potent medicine" has its effect: the emperor vomits blood. Hai Rui is imprisoned and is to be executed. Two short wedge acts follow in which the courtiers reveal themselves as completely passive; meanwhile, the dark clouds of popular rebellion are rising.

In the last act the emperor dies. The crown prince, upon Prime Minister Xu's suggestion, releases Hai Rui, saying he is an upright minister who dares to speak out. As Hai leaves the prison, the Taoist magicians are admitted to it. Hai Rui is received by the people as "Hai Blue Sky," their savior. It begins to rain, and the people all try to crowd under Hai's too-small umbrella. During a last song of rejoicing, a huge umbrella appears, and Hai Rui gives everyone on stage shelter under it. The song praises Hai Rui, and seems to contain an oblique allusion that we have also seen in Guo Moruo's poem in another part of this book. Hai Rui, the people sing, "dared to rebel against the emperor, without fright or fear. He eliminated the ills of the age with his superior integrity and great courage. He woke up the dim-sighted and shook the hard-of-hearing, so that the hair and bones of the Son of Heaven were stiff with horror." The last line is *jiuchong tianzi maogu song*! The "*mao*" (hair) after *tianzi*, "son of Heaven," is, of course, ambiguous. The phrase can also be translated "the bones of Mao, the son of Heaven, were stiff with horror."

Hai Rui shangshu is a fine satire on contemporary affairs, much richer in dramatic texture, sharper in satirical exposure, and bolder in political stance than the better-known *Hai Rui baguan*. *Guan Hanqing* had raged against the villain Ahmad, but left the emperor in the background. *Cai Wenji* and *Da Qianlong* had brought the emperor on stage. Now, in *Hai Rui shangshu*, the full attack is on the Chairman himself. Amidst injustice and famine, his only concern is with his own immortality, which he hopes to achieve with the help of Marxist-Leninist magicians who conjure up all kinds of wonders to prove he is the "greatest Marxist-Leninist of our time" and will therefore live for tens of thousands of years. Laozi's picture with the white beard is but a pun on Marx. Kang Sheng as the head of the Party school had thus promoted Mao in 1959.[44] Regular government does not take place; the circle of magicians runs the country. The gardens of immortality plants built for the emperor are reminiscent of the parks and gardens build at the time in anticipation of the wealth to be gained from the Great Leap Forward. The magicians are utterly corrupt. And the emperor has effectively closed the *yanlu*, the way of talk, with his special police; this is a second reference to Kang Sheng, as he was in charge of the special police, which operated beyond any control.[45] The emperor's preoccupation with "ideological issues" prevents him from looking at the realities of the country. He does not really believe all the flatteries, but they are too soothing to hear to be cast off entirely. The climax is reached with the erection of an immortality platform—a reference to the Mao personality cult from which the sacrifice to Heaven is to be made. The powerful first act could be read as but fanciful satire, were it not followed by the depiction of the real situation of the country in subsequent acts. The prime minister, Xu Jie, plays the traditional role of the moderate and even quite honorable prime minister who stays in power in order to prevent the worst; this is a role in which Zhou Enlai had seen himself. The references to the "national champion of compromise," who never contradicts the emperor but tries to secure Hai Rui's release when an

44. Fang Jing, "Dui Kang Sheng," p. 42.
45. Hu Yaobang gave some detail about this system in his talk at the Central Party School in November 1979. See "Problems Concerning the Purge of Kang Sheng," pp. 78 passim.

opportunity offers itself, are nearly too bold to be believed, but they are also too unambiguous to be overlooked. With a gang of ideological magicians in power, with the leaders of the regular government what they are, and with the political and social crisis of the country urgent, the "little official" Hai Rui shakes off the temptation to withdraw to his home and till the fields; he is willing to sacrifice his life to speak out for the people, in the manner of Guan Hanqing. The country's crisis is so urgent as to scorch the eyebrows. The government leaders are mere hypocrites, and it is left to Hai Rui to upbraid the emperor, to confront him with the facts of the land, and to propose reforms, the first of which is the tearing down of the monument of the personality cult. Earlier, Wu Han had written in *Hai Rui ma huangdi* that the Jiajing emperor's greatest error was his pursuit of immortality. Again in *Hai Rui shang-shu*, the play itself becomes the present-day counterpart of Hai Rui's memorial, and the depiction of Hai Rui's later fate contains a specula-tion about the fate of both the writer and his opera troupe. Hai Rui is thrown into prison. The emperor is beyond salvation; even Hai Rui's medicine can no longer cure him. His disease has already entered the region between heart and diaphragm. Although Hai Rui remains fiercely loyal to the emperor (especially in the later version, which introduced into the text Mao's remark about Hai Rui's spitting out the food), only the emperor's death can free him again and make it possible for Xu Jie to secure his release. In helping Hai Rui, Xu Jie is reacting to strong pressures from public opinion, and even the threat of active resistance by the people. The play's ending resembles in its futuristic optimism that of *Guan Hanqing*.

The political problem has undergone further development since *Guan Hanqing*: the Jiajing emperor is no match for a Khubilai Khan, the ideologues have taken over the center to the point where the prime minister, Xu Jie, lacks even the limited leeway of Horikhoson and becomes a hypocrite. The political crisis in the center has by now pro-duced a general social and economic crisis. Only men of Hai Rui's stature can now hold their umbrella over the people and reach true immortality, i.e., become "living Buddhas."

The play uses the same device to get a public hearing that Hai Rui had used for his memorial. The celebration of the tenth anniversary of the People's Republic, with the motto "Successes of Ten Years," was akin to the emperor's ritual of sacrifice to Heaven. The Shanghai Opera Troupe came out with *Hai Rui shangshu* on this very occasion, and the play attracted much attention. The Shanghai papers carried long reviews of it, as did *Xijubao*.[46] They were in part written by members of the troupe itself. As might be expected, the reviews stuck strictly to the historical framework of the play and carefully avoided elaborating on parallels with the present, while maintaining that they existed. A half-page review in *Wenhuibao* by Wei Ming stressed the "crisis situation" that forced Hai Rui to act. It compared him to Judge Bao, who was not only as daring but had "studied many methods of struggle" and was "skillful" in them (as Guan Hanqing had also been, according to Tian Han).

Tao Xiong, writing in *Xijubao*, claimed that the piece was performed in only seven places and had little influence. However, opera companies in Guangzhou, which also had adapted Tian Han's *Guan Hanqing*, in Wenzhou, and in several other places staged it; there were local-opera adaptations of it, and eventually, in the winter of 1961, it was shown in Beijing, at the same time that Wu Han's Hai Rui play was performed. Chen Yi took the occasion to have himself photographed with the leading actor Zhou Xinfang, backstage.[47] In view of the play's political implications, "the leading comrade from the Propaganda Department" suggested two changes, which were immediately adopted. To emphasize Hai Rui's loyalty toward the Jiajing emperor, there was to be a special scene in which Hai weeps upon hearing the news of the emperor's death. In the new, 1961 version, when he hears the news Hai Rui spits out the food and wine he has just consumed, and the official bringing the notice of Hai's release and reinstatement has occasion to affirm that he is a "loyal minister." The second change also concerned the ending. The "leading comrade" maintained that a scene in which the people "kneel with incense and request to be given orders" when Hai Rui is released from prison was too modern and should be made closer to the olden times. Obviously this change would soften the image of Hai Rui triumphant as the spokesman of the people and their protector with the gigantic umbrella (*baohusan*) of his daring and righteousness.[48] Radical critics later had a field day with the play, using the play's violent language and emotions to make formidable quotes about unhorsing the emperor and forcing him to spit blood, thus denouncing the

46. Wei Ming, "Shi ping Zhou Xinfang de xinzuo *Hai Rui shangshu*," in *Wenhuibao*, Oct. 27, 1959; Jian Fu, "Zhou Xinfang chuyan jingju *Hai Rui shangshu*." Further reviews, which are inaccessible to me, are listed by Ding Xuelei, "*Hai Rui shangshu*," p. 96, nn. 1–5. Jian Fu is Tao Xiong's pen name.

47. The photograph is in *Hai Rui shangshu*.

48. Xu Siyan, "Chongban houji," p. 94.

Party and its achievements, and eulogizing a man whose real intention was only to save feudal rule from destruction.[49]

Zhou Xinfang's defense was to say that the people who suggested any similarity between the Jiajing emperor and Mao Zedong were the real detractors of the latter.[50] He was imprisoned during the Cultural Revolution, and refused to recant. The role he had played had changed into his very life, and the scenario he had mapped out was both wrong and right. Zhou Xinfang died in prison, but after Mao's death, on October 23, 1979, both he and the play were rehabilitated, and *Hai Rui shangshu* was restaged.[51]

Hai Rui shangshu was first published in the local opera periodical *Shanghai xiju*, and in late 1959 it was published as a book for national distribution. In January 1960, another play continued with the same theme, although it did not deal specifically with Hai Rui. It was entitled *Sun An dongben*.

SUN AN DONGBEN (SUN AN PUSHES MEMORIALS)

The play, adapted from earlier material by a group of dramatists and actors, was published in January 1960 in *Juben*.[52] The time is the Ming dynasty under the Wanli emperor. Zhang Cong, who rose to power under the old emperor and now completely dominates the young Wanli emperor, is the chief villain. The two ranking ministers have withdrawn from the court, leaving Zhang the control of the center. A minor official, Sun An, has dared to impeach Zhang for embezzling tax grain and trampling on the people. Zhang has him transferred to the capital to be either promoted if he retracts, or destroyed if he does not. In the second act, Sun travels through the countryside toward the capital and is confronted with the social situation of the "present." As it contains one of the most stunning symbolical descriptions of the later Great Leap years, I will quote it at length.

> SUN AN: I am Sun An, a lowly official, the magistrate of Cao-
>   zhou. The abominable Grand Tutor Zhang Cong
>   deceives the emperor and cheats him, bringing suf-
>   ferings to people, that affair of his embezzling two

49. Ding Xuelei, "*Hai Rui shangshu*"; Fang Zesheng, "*Hai Rui shangshu* bixu jixu pipan," pp. 101ff.
50. Quoted by Xu Siyan, "Wei *Hai Rui shangshu*," p. 84.
51. "Youxiu lishiju *Hai Rui shangshu* pingfan."
52. *Sun An dongben*.

hundred thousand piculs of tax grain alone has led in the area around here to (sings)

the young and sturdy leaving their homes and fleeing for their lives
the old and weak falling in the gullies and losing their remaining years
all along the way . . . .
the bodies of the starved fill the streets and the white bones lie openly

(offstage, masses in chorus sing "ai . . .")

cries of the hungry and wailings of the cold,
the land is swarming with people wailing and lamenting,

Voice offstage: The officials do nothing but hurt the people, what do they care if your wife has to leave you and your sons are dispersed,

Masses in chorus: whether you live or die

(From afar, cries of resentment from the people)

SUN AN: Ai! What a shame. (Recites)

When the officials don't take care of the people no wonder voices of hatred rise among them . . . .

Behind the curtain, a
woman's voice: Blue Heaven, Heaven! Injustice, ah!

A carter (offstage): Help! Help!

(Sun An signals to Sun Bao to go and inquire. Bao exits quickly.)

SUN AN: Whence comes this appeal to Heaven and cry of injustice?

SUN BAO (brings the
document describ-
ing the injustice): Sir, a woman from the people threw herself into the river to end her life. She has already been pulled out.

SUN AN: Eh?

SUN BAO: But it was too late; she had stopped breathing and was dead.

SUN AN: Ah!

SUN BAO: She carried eighteen copies of the writ detailing the injustice; please see for yourself.

SUN AN: Be quick, hand it to me!

SUN BAO: Yes, sir.

SUN AN (recites): I accuse the Grand Tutor villain Zhang Cong, for himself he built an imperial palace in Xiang-yang;
my man Wang Yi and my son,

were forcibly enlisted as corvée laborers;
last year in July when the work was ended,
a feast with wine and meats was arranged to cele-
    brate,
the villain in vilest manner broke Heaven's order
and mixed poison into the wine,
to kill the people and eliminate those who knew of
    his doings,
three thousand laborers from the people lost their
    lives, lost their lives!

Can such a thing be? Sun Bao, have this woman
from the people properly buried, let there be no
mistake.

SUN BAO: As you wish, sir.

SUN AN: Aya, but wait! Eighteen copies of the indictment
(examines them) [have gone] from the district to the
circuit, from the province to the capital.
Eighteen offices, why did none of them take up the
case? Ah . . . .
Ah, that's it. (sings)

Embezzling tax grain is no trifle,
the lives of three thousand men even less;
if only I were already near His Majesty's face!
I will investigate and memorialize the court. (Exits.)

In another place, Sun An says: "Ai . . . on my way here [to the capital]
of ten houses, nine were empty! Crying and wailing was heard all over
the countryside. This pitiful sight remains clearly in my memory. All
this I have seen with my own eyes." The last phrase seems to identify
the authorial voice with Sun An, and maintains the authenticity of the
things said on stage for the visible present.

These scenes seem to take off from the dramatic exchange in *Hai Rui
shangshu* between Hai Rui and Xu Jie. *Hai Rui shangshu*, however,
took place in the city, whereas Sun An is traveling through the countryside, where things looked much worse during the famine years.

Sun's father-in-law is a cabinet minister, Huang Yide. From him we
learn that Sun's father had been killed off by Zhang Cong, which the
son does not know, and that in the court a climate of fear prevails,
much stronger than in *Hai Rui shangshu*. Huang Yide slips into the role
played by Horikhoson and Xu Jie. Although his motives are not bad,
his motto is "the ways of the world are unfair; for the time being, it is
best to preserve one's body." He warns Sun to be careful. Taking the

stance of Hai Rui, and using the set of slogans and metaphors already familiar from earlier dramas, Sun states his principles:

> The emperor's favor has transferred me to the capital,
> my heart is sober and calm, sun and moon are bright,
> my frowning brows are set on clearing out the villains.
> If I were but a licorice root on the wall,
> receiving a high salary at the same time,
> would I not be the shame and laughingstock of the ten thousand men of old?
> As long as you yourself are upright and correct,
> why fear that others may blow on you with evil winds?

Sun marches into court and presents his order of impeachment together with the new materials from the drowned woman. Both are instantly rejected. Sun flies into a rage, and pulls out a second memorial whose content is much the same, whereupon he is dismissed from office and threatened with imprisonment. Zhang Cong still wants to win him over, because he knows Sun An has dangerous material against him, so he has Sun restored to office. Sun decides to risk his life by presenting a third impeachment; he is then thrown out of the palace with the threat of being executed should he show up again.

Sun An then reviles Heaven for its blindness, in the style of Dou E.

> Heaven! Blue Heaven with the unseeing eyes!
> In the midst of tragedy, I ask blue Heaven,
> can You bear to see this with your own eyes!
> Right and wrong, crooked and straight have changed their places,
> confused and mixed are the loyal and the wicked.
> What is this, the black-haired people in their innocence are oppressed,
> while the old villain struts about free in front of the jade steps?
> What is this, the emperor only favors the wicked ministers,
> rejects loyal remonstrance, and listens to slanders.
> Heaven, ah Heaven! . . .
> Why do you look on sidelong with hanging sleeves without saying a word?
> How can you reside up in sky and receive incense;
> The world's ways are bumpy and full of dangers,
> standing, a pillar in midstream, here am I, Sun An.

We have a familiar constellation. The villain, a personal favorite of the emperor, is in power, and uses it ruthlessly. The hero receives an unjust verdict, refuses to be "licorice root" and join in the hypocrisy and flattery, and decides to speak out for the people and risk his life to have the villain removed. In the next scene, his wife tries to dissuade him from risking his life—this is another quote from *Hai Rui shang-shu*—and for a moment he is confused.

To serve the state with a loyal heart is all I have ever wished,
but, alas, in this court affairs are chaotic to the extreme;
perhaps one has to admit that a loyal heart indeed serves no purpose...

Then, however, the gruesome scenes from his trip come back to him, with "nine houses out of ten empty" and the "wailing still ringing" in his ears. In the library of his father-in-law, he finds the memorials of seventy-two others who have tried to impeach Zhang Cong before him; all came to naught. "Everywhere the ghosts of the unjustly slain lament." Then he remembers the Guan Yu figure (emulated also by Guan Hanqing and Tian Han), and recalls Guan Yu's statement that though jade may be ground, its white color cannot be changed. He says:

The great man, the real male
is willing to be jade ground to dust, but he will never be a tile, even intact.
For the benefit of the state, I'll eliminate the villain,
if I don't kill this old gangster my heart will find no rest.

Eventually, in his own father's memorial, he reads the charge that the chief villain "privately entered the imperial harem and passed the night in the dragon bed." Affixed to this impeachment is the imperial decision that this is slander and Sun Cunli (Sun An's father) is to be executed. In contrast to *Guan Hanqing* and *Hai Rui shangshu*, here the unjust verdicts that must be reversed date back thirty years, and many were reached under the former emperor.

Outgunning Hai Rui, Sun An buys not one but three coffins to take to court; the two others are for his wife and son. The son first did not burn the memorial, like Hai Rui's wife, but stole his father's writing brush. Eventually, however, he also risks his life. Sun An again quotes Hai Rui, whose mother had encouraged him to dare speak out: My mother brought me up "for the sole purpose of revenging my father, and speaking out for the people." In this way he resolves the conflict between filial piety, which would require him to continue his family lineage, and loyalty. With a quote from the "spirit of righteousness" invoked in a poem by Wen Tianxiang (which was also inserted into *Guan Hanqing*), Sun An and his family put on prison clothes, bind themselves with fetters, and march to court. He repeats his charges, claiming that Zhang Cong's execution would be "a joy for the altars of the nation, and happiness for the ten thousand people." After a desperate plea, he is sent to the execution ground, with a chorus offstage singing the praise of his loyal heart (public opinion being introduced here in the form of the chorus).

Sun's father-in-law, Huang Yide, who had seen things coming this way, is refused permission to retire from office, and feels roused to seek help from two old and powerful men who have temporarily left the court, Xu Long and Shen Li. *Sun An dongben* here develops a theme already touched in *Guan Hanqing*, where under the oppression of Ahmad, the scholars and writers formed something like a private study group, of which Guan was a member. Within that play this theme does not play a major role. Here, however, Xu Long and Shen Li both belong to such a club, which meets privately to discuss affairs of state. Shen is stopped on his way to a club meeting by Huang, who pleads for him to intervene for Sun An, which he promptly does, mimicking Sun An by submitting a second memorial immediately after the rejection of his first. Using the ambiguous wording of a decision of the Wanli emperor, Zhang Cong makes Shen a commoner and bans him from court. Shen gives voice to the elder generation of leaders who are being pushed away from the levers of power:

> High merit and old age count for nothing,
> all meritorious servants of the court are pushed aside.

Eventually, Xu Long has to step in. He comes to court armed with a painting of the emperor's ancestor, the founder of the dynasty, to remind him of his modest origins and the old values. He also brings a bronze hammer that had been given by the founder of the Ming to his own ancestor in recognition of his merits for the founding of the dynasty. When Xu's first memorial is rejected, he instantly draws up another one, and then a third. "You dim emperor must spare [Sun's life] whether you accept my memorial or not! You absolutely must spare him! Definitely spare him! Approve the memorial! Approve the memorial! Approve the memorial!" After being thrice rejected, he has his hammer brought and states, in a scene that plays on a topic established in *Da Qianlong*:

> A bronze hammer in my hand, I go to court,
> the fire of rage in my heart blazing to the ninth heaven.
> If the emperor does not approve my memorial,
> I will first hit the dim lord, and then hit the villain.
> In the mouth of the nine dragons one does not kneel down,
> I'll sit opposite the emperor at the dragon table.

The emperor is a very young man and Xu's disciple; Xu is a senior statesman of a family of long-standing merit: the two match in power. In a short exchange they come to the point:

WANLI:	Imperial Elder Brother.
XU:	Majesty.
WANLI:	Xu Long.
XU:	(Puts his feet on the dragon table) Wanli!
WANLI:	Disobedient minister . . .
XU:	Dim lord, dim lord!
WANLI:	Preposterous! To come to court and not pay respects to the emperor! Why do you sit down opposite me?
XU:	I can sit! I can sit! I can sit! (Sits himself on the dragon table.)
WANLI:	I am the lord of the entire state.
XU:	I am a hereditary *guogong* [member of a family with merits for the founding of the dynasty].
WANLI:	How can a *guogong* be higher than the emperor!
XU:	How can a loyal minister bend the knee before a dim lord!

Xu proceeds to tell the emperor that before his ancestor founded the dynasty he was a cattle thief, and that his generals won the empire for him. Without their exertions he would have come to naught. In view of the merits of Xu's ancestor, the Hongwu emperor had given him this "black tiger bronze hammer" inscribed with the following: "If the prince is not correct, hit the prince. / If the minister is not correct, hit the minister."

WANLI:	I am not guilty of anything, don't hit me.
XU:	Dim lord! You thoughtlessly believe slanders, you don't accept loyal words. . . .

And shortly after, there is this exchange:

XU:	(Holding the hammer, he goes after Wanli, pursuing him and speaking at the same time.) A dim prince like you without loyalty or piety, human feeling or a sense of justice, what use is there in sparing you! (Xu Long lifts the hammer and wants to hit. Wanli crouches. Shen Li stops Xu.)
WANLI:	It's all Zhang Cong's doing.
XU:	Bah! As lord of the state you don't take care of the government. One-sidedly you listen and one-sidedly you trust your favorite, Zhang Cong: With one blow of the hammer I'm going to kill you.

The Wanli emperor is again saved by Shen, and accepts all of Xu's demands. Sun An, whose execution has been postponed through a trick of Shen Li, is brought back to court. The emperor now approves his memorials, and Sun An, now equipped with Xu's hammer, proceeds with the execution, the climactic moment, right in the court, saying:

> Good!
> The bronze hammer has passed into my hands,
> and I am resolved to clean out the villains altogether.
> (Drags out Zhang Cong, who has hidden under a table.)
> Today, revenge has come to you,
> You and the hammer celebrate my first achievement. (Kills Zhang Cong.)

For no apparent reason, the editors printed under this play, on the same page, Lenin's well-known statement about party literature, which opens with the line: "Literature must become party literature."

The pieces we have studied hitherto have already firmly established a set of symbols, characters, and plot devices, all of which are amply used in this piece. The element of the grotesque in this gaudy piece makes it clear that we are dealing with psychological relief work. Not only does it feel good, in such desperate times as 1960, to curse the emperor, beating him up brings even more relief. Needless to say, nothing in the text demands the overthrow of Wanli. The charges are again the same: The emperor has a personal favorite who wields power, and shrinks from neither intrigue nor falsification nor murder of those who have damaging evidence against him. The unnecessary introduction of information about Zhang Cong sleeping in the dragon bed might suggest an *ad personam* criticism. However, as the indications are vague, I will hide the name of the possible candidate in a footnote.[53]

The time is all too familiar, a period of disaster from famine and injustice. A new era has just started, one marked by the youth and helpless ignorance of the Wanli emperor, an indirect reference to the dramatic changes since the "upsurge of socialism in the countryside." The plea is for orderly government and legal guarantees, as well as the elimination of the chief villain. As the play focuses on the court, we don't know whether he is acting alone or controls an entire network. The cabinet minister Huang Yide, in his good will, weakness, and adaptation to circumstances, takes up the role of a Horikhoson. But the older generation from the previous reign—which, within the chronology set up

---

53. Hu Yaobang says in his speech about Kang Sheng: "If exposed, the truth about Chiang Ch'ing's [Jiang Qing's] depravity, degeneration, and promiscuous sexual relations is intolerably repulsive. I don't know how to describe her obscure personal relationship with K'ang Sheng. We all know it, that is enough." "Problems Concerning the Purge of K'ang Sheng," p. 93.

within the play, would refer to the first phase of the Communist endeavor—comes out surprisingly strong in Shen Li and Xu Long. The theme introduced in the second act, the social crisis of the country, remains active as Sun An's motivation, but does not recur in the memorials submitted to the throne. Although *Sun An dongben* shares in much of the sloganeering of the other plays, it is a lively and exciting piece. Sadly, there are no reports available to me on public reactions to its stunning scenes, some of which have been translated above. The piece was regarded as among the major *ducao*, "poisonous weeds," during the Cultural Revolution, but I have seen no detailed criticisms of it.[54]

GUO MORUO'S *WU ZETIAN*

In the summer of 1960, Guo Moruo came out with *Wu Zetian*,[55] a second attempt to stem the tide of historical plays cursing and beating up the emperor. The reversal of verdicts on Wu Zetian and Cao Cao followed, at least in the second case, Mao's having made positive reference to these rulers. Once the discussion of the rulers had begun, however, it ended up contributing to a more nuanced discussion of the Chairman's role. The judgments were reversed, it is true, but most scholars continued to talk about their proportions of good and bad, saying that "in the main" these autocratic, intelligent, and cunning rulers were "good," but problems remained. The question of proportion seems to have been influenced by discussions on Stalin, who was defined by the Chinese leaders as 70 percent good and 30 percent bad, as opposed to the all-out criticisms that they felt Khrushchev had leveled against him. Subsequent to the reevaluation of Stalin, there was a possibility that even the Chairman himself might be judged only "relatively" good. By stressing the "reversal of the unjust verdict" on the two imperial figures, authors could argue that in fact they came out in defense of the Chairman against his detractors and slanderers, while at the same time keeping to "historical truth" by mentioning the facts of the often harsh policies and measures of Cao Cao and Wu Zetian.

Guo Moruo did not join in this exercise. In *Cai Wenji*, he had dismissed every negative comment about Cao Cao' actions as slander, with the single exception of a certain rash act (when Cao orders the

54. It is mentioned as such a "poisonous weed" in Xin Wentong, "Ping Tian Han de yige fangeming celüe," p. 2, col. 1.
55. Guo Moruo, *Wu Zetian*, in *Renmin wenxue* 1960.5. A revised edition is Guo Moruo, *Wu Zetian* (Beijing: Renmin wenxue Press, 1979).

envoy to commit suicide), and proceeded to a complete whitewash, with his persona Cai Wenji eventually breaking into a paean to the Chairman. He uses a similar technique in *Wu Zetian*.

The play's setting is various parts of the palace, the political center of the country. The protagonists are the imperial couple, the ministers, the crown princes, and an old poet and a young poetess; the latter two are directly involved in top-level politics. The first act articulates all the common charges against Wu Zetian, which are voiced by the crown prince, minister Pei Yan, the poet Luo Binwang, and two surviving female members of the Shangguan family, whose progenitors have been sentenced to death by the empress. They revile against the empress's twelve-point plan, which has attracted the women, the peasants and the low-level officials to her side. They are also incensed that qualified officials of low birth may jump stages to gain rapid advancement; as a result, most of the recent appointees are her men. Her critics protest that she has even encouraged denunciation [of conspiracies] (*gaomi*); this especially bothers the group assembled in the crown prince's study, because they plan to topple the empress. Their criticisms betray their own aspirations as a privilege-hungry aristocracy. The crown prince adds some spice when he tries to kiss young Shangguan Wan'er, showing that he is a lecher. The emperor, who is bedridden, has left all power to the empress, who with her lowly origin has nothing better to do than to promote people from her own social level.

The plot of the play is announced through a symbolic device. Before her mother gave birth to the young poetess Shangguan Wan'er, a birth which occurred after both the father and the grandfather of the child had been killed, she dreamed that a giant had given her a scale and had declared that she would give birth to a human being holding the big scale to weigh the empire. Two symbols are combined here, the giant, standing for the people, and the young woman, standing for the people, and they are united by the girl's being mandated as holder of the scale of good and bad for the giant. She is to pass judgment on the empress's rule.

The empress enters. She states, "The more responsibility someone carries, the more he must listen to others. If all in the empire are allowed to open their mouths, the emperor and the officials will make fewer mistakes." She says this, however, to people who are planning a conspiracy; their criticism thus is the result of evil intentions. In a book she had had compiled for the crown prince, the empress finds a poem by Shangguan Wan'er. Although she is incensed about the crown prince's lack of seriousness in his studies, she admires the poem, although she is perfectly aware that it implies a scathing criticism of herself. The poem contrasts nicely crafted but fake paper-cut flowers with real peaches and plums; Li, meaning plum, is the family name of the dynastic clan, the Li. Wu Zetian has only married into the Li family, and thus her fake imperial ambitions are a sorry contrast to the real Li. Questioned by the empress, Shangguan Wan'er is polite but unyielding, and her spirit impresses the empress, who "values such indomitable spirit" because she herself is endowed with it. She recalls that when she was brought to Emperor Taizong's palace at the age of fourteen he had an unruly steed that no one could break. She promised to do it and requested three instruments, a whip of iron, a baton of iron, and a hammer. She then said to the emperor: "'If the horse does not obey, I will use the iron whip to whip it; if it still does not obey, I will use the iron baton to pound it; and if again it does not obey, I will use the hammer to kill it.' The emperor said: 'Good, you are really indomitable. But why do you have to proceed in this manner?' She answered: 'A horse has to work for men. If it is unwilling to do so, it does not act as a horse should and I have to whip it, pound it, or kill it. With men it is the same. If a man does not work well for men, what use is his life?'" Part of the radicalism involved in the rehabilitation of the historical tyrants required that their specific cruelties be denied as slander but their hard hand in dealing with "the enemy" be praised. The empress then defends her killing of Shangguan Wan'er's father and grandfather by saying they sowed discord at court and later plotted to have her removed. This tradition of meritorious ministers rebelling against their emperors, she says, has a long history through the years of turmoil preceding the present dynasty. There are such people today. She feels confident that "as long as I administer the empire well, the people will not oppose me"; this reduces the opposition to the representatives of the magnate clans, the *haozu*. But she herself needs the whip and the hammer to stay in control. And, in full knowledge that Shangguan Wan'er hates her, she invites the young woman to become her attendant and in fact her secretary; on this point the play coincides with history. "If one day I become conceited and harm the people of the empire, look at me as that fierce steed, and use the hammer to kill me." Open and frank talk is thus desirable not because of the crisis in the land and the growing popular resentment, but because of the empress's concern that she, too, might one day fail and need frank remonstrance. In a reversal of the stance adopted by plays like *Guan Hanqing*, *Hai Rui shangshu*, and *Sun An dongben*, with their glorification of *mahuang*, the hero's cursing the dim emperor, in *Wu Zetian* the cursing is done by the villains. It occurs on two occasions. On the first, the crown prince, confronted with the evidence of having hoarded arms in his quarters for an eventual rebellion, puts up a defiant stance and hurls at Wu Zetian all the abuse and slander that have been circulating about her. He is hoping to win over the emperor, who is also present. But the decrepit ruler instead musters his remaining strength to get up from his bed and box his counterrevolutionary son on the ears. The crown prince is not cowed, however. Mimicking the stance of Hai Rui, he refuses to see his mistakes or the utter lack of foundation of his allegations. Guo Moruo is thus saying that those who use the empress's willingness to hear criticism, in fact only abuse it. The crown prince is part of a conspiracy; his criticism does not arise from a good heart. The second occasion for *mahuang* is a public appeal written by the poet Luo Binwang for the rebels. Luo is of lowly origin, but nonetheless, being an impractical intellectual, he sides with the great families, only to be dumped by the chief conspirator, who distrusts him. He, too, curses the empress as part of a conspiracy to unseat her. The empress treats both men with utter magnanimity. She sends her son to her birthplace in Sichuan—sends him down to the countryside—to familiarize him with the life of the common people and reeducate him. But at the same time, it is a place of idyllic beauty and famous sights. There is a bucolic element to banishment here that contrasts to the Hai Rui play, in which banishment is a bitter removal to the poorest regions of the countryside. And Luo Binwang is banned to scenic Hangzhou, recalling the fate of Guan Hanqing, again more a measure to provide him with beauties to describe than a punishment.

Most of the play is devoted to the rebellious intrigues of the scions of the great families; Shangguan Wan'er is the key link. Since a person's class status is determined by that of one's father, Guo Moruo has Wan'er's father executed before she is born. He is thus unable to influence her. In terms of class, she is indefinable; by the dream's prediction she is made the impartial scale of the empire. Whoever wins her wins the country. Instead of becoming the hammer or arsenic that would kill the empress, the girl is won over by the empress and becomes the vital link in the downfall of the rebellious children of the founding fathers. On no occasion during the entire play does the empress commit an injustice or act rashly. One scene in particular merits attention. The emperor is carried on stage, afflicted by not only physical debility but also extreme (and equally symbolical) shortsightedness; wasting his time with the Taoist classic and the writings of the Buddhist Seng Zhao. This looks again like an inverted quote from the Shanghai *Hai Rui shangshu*. The unconventional, astute, literature-loving and outspoken Wu Zetian, notwithstanding her reputation as power-wielding, cunning, and ruthless, takes care of everything. The emperor, despite his debility and weakness, still has the wisdom to entrust the government to her, while he lies in his sickbed reading mystical, impractical classics. Those carrying out the rebellion are people within the center, within the palace and the provincial and military leadership. Within the play there is a clear class line, the representatives of the big, landed families operating through their politicians and intellectuals within the center versus Wu Zetian with her lowly class background and her populist policies that favor the lowly and poor. The original unity of the founding group of the dynasty has disappeared, a new class has risen among these founders, and the main conflict of the drama is to prevent the new magnates from taking over. Their rebellion, utterly lacking in public support, of course fails. The people are rich and happy; in the materials appended to the play, Guo Moruo points proudly to the fact that under Wu Zetian's rule the population nearly doubled.

With *Wu Zetian*, Guo Moruo engages in a running battle with most of the plays studied hitherto. True, there is a crisis in the country, but it is not due to famine, government mismanagement, injustice, or villains wielding power. The people are rich, content, and happy. The problem is that the founding fathers of the dynasty have become a new class of landlords and try to rebel against Wu Zetian's progressive policies. The empress is not "dim" at all, but astute and exceedingly well informed. There is no need to wrest the right of remonstrance from her at the price of one's life; rather, she herself makes Shangguan Wan'er into her spur, whip, and hammer—a clear inversion of the *Sun An dongben* play. Those who remonstrate don't speak for the people but are instead class enemies trying to whip up public opinion in order to promote their own interests. The villains are not government officials who are the personal favorites of the empress but are instead members of the large landlord families, an alien class element in Wu Zetian's proletarian government.

The Horikhoson image badly misrepresents the senior government minister, Guo Moruo charges. Her majesty's policies are utterly correct, and Qian Weidao, through whom Zhou Enlai's role is discussed, is quite right in faithfully executing all her orders and never once contradicting her. The hero of the play is not the remonstrating intellectual but rather Wu Zetian, and through her Mao's role is discussed. She works not for her own good but for the benefit and in the name of the Tang emperor who, with the pun Tang/*dang* (Party) implied in his function and his general role, becomes the counterpart of the Party. Not the empress but the emperor is the one wasting time in studying the classics; it is he who buries himself in these meaningless old books and is so weak that he can hardly stand. If she were not taking care of the government, the Tang dynasty would fall apart. The role of the author's persona, filled in the other plays by the bold and cursing hero, is here taken by Shangguan Wan'er. Her early, mistaken criticisms of the empress stem from her links with alien class elements. In the beginning, she is hesitant to reveal the secrets of the conspiracy, but eventually she sees her mistake. True, the empress has Shangguan Wan'er's face tattooed, but the tattoo does not deface but rather embellishes the girl: The small plum branch tattooed on her forehead shows that she is now, and visibly so, the committed property of the dynastic family of the Tang/*dang*, whose name is Li (plum). Far from becoming the hammer to beat down the empress in Sun An's style or poison her as the conspirators would have it, Shangguan Wan'er comes out in defense of Wu Zetian and eventually manages the downfall of Wu's enemies.

Guo Moruo was apparently in this play the first to react to the Lushan Plenum. The first draft of *Wu Zetian* was finished on January 10, 1960, and *Renmin wenxue* published a later draft in May 1960. The Chairman, Guo argued, had called for criticism, and thus Wu Zetian had made Shangguan Wan'er her hammer. The criticism that the young poet actually proffered, however, was not based on facts, but was slander that served reactionary purposes. The people need Wu Zetian's enlightened policies in order to stay as rich and content as they are; it is for their benefit that Wu Zetian must beat these counterrevolutionaries down. Within the play, she knows what is brewing at an early date, but "sets up the opposite" by letting the conspiracy unfold. Guo Moruo seems to argue that Mao had seriously advocated the "spirit of Hai Rui" just in case the emperor would make the kind of mistakes that would warrant Hai Rui's methods. However, no such case occurred. Instead, the people had bountiful harvests during the Great Leap and were content, and only villains (including the empress's own son) dressed up as fake Hai Ruis.

Wu Zetian used the same cast of characters and the same plot elements as the plays that it countered, but it reevaluated the stance and stature of each of these characters and elements. The play apparently found favor with Zhou Enlai, who had himself photographed with Guo on the occasion of its one-hundredth performance and in recent sources is quoted as having been a supporter of the play at the time. This would coincide with Zhou Enlai's and Guo Moruo's common support of the *Sun Wukong sanda baigujing* play, which took a similar political stance to that of *Wu Zetian*.

Texts often have curious fates and may become vivid images for con- stellations that were in no way anticipated by the authors. *Wu Zetian* is a case in point. At the time it was written, it operated as a criticism of the Hai Rui wave, using the same medium and the same technique of presentation. However, as time went on, the relationship between Wu Zetian and the emperor came more and more to resemble that between Jiang Qing and Mao Zedong during the last years of his life. A number of writers associated with Jiang Qing and her group and publishing under the pen name Liang Xiao came out in 1974 with an article grandly praising Wu Zetian and denouncing the slanders against her as feudal and backward.[56] Then the philosophy study group of the staff of the kindergarten of Qinghua University followed this up with a strong plea for more women in high office, again using the Wu Zetian theme.[57] These texts seem to imply that there was much resentment at the time of Jiang Qing's prominent role and that the Wu Zetian propaganda was used to denounce this attitude.

Sure enough, in 1979 after Jiang Qing's fall from power one author quickly came out with a book entitled *On Wu Zetian*,[58] in which he strikingly proved that Wu Zetian came to power with big landlords as her social base and a conspirational faction at the court as her political instrument. The reference to big landlords must be seen in the context of the time, when Jiang Qing was still accused of wanting to "restore capitalism." When the new leaders around Deng Xiaoping took measures that to many looked indeed as if they were to "restore capi- talism," however, a new deviation was introduced into Communist doctrine to account for Jiang Qing and her group. This was a "left deviation" without quotation marks; in earlier times leftist deviations had quotation marks to indicate that they were in essence rightist. In the main, however, the model for Jiang Qing ceased to be seen as Wu Ze- tian, who was still too much identified with her contemporary equiva- lent of the late fifties and early sixties. Instead, a new empress was called

56. Liang Xiao, "Lun Wu Zetian de lishi diwei."
57. Qinghua daxue zhexue xuexi xiaozu and Beijing daxue zhexuexi, "Lun Wu Zetian de yidian kanfa."
58. Xiong Deji, *Lun Wu Zetian*.

on to represent Jiang Qing: the famous Empress Lü of the Han dynasty.[59]

Guo Moruo's play thus in time unwittingly became a paean to Jiang Qing. Although Guo has been credited by members of the scholarly community with having opposed, as president of the Academy of Sciences, some of Jiang Qing's policies during the last years of the Cultural Revolution, after 1977, his play was buried in painful silence.

One scholar who wanted to restore it to respectability in 1982 used a quote from Guo Moruo as the title of his article: "When reversing a verdict, how can one avoid putting on a bit too much powder." Guo had said this after seeing a performance of Wu Zetian in Kunming. Pointing to Zhou Enlai's support for the play, the author concludes: "For a variety of reasons Wu Zetian has become a forbidden area of literary criticism in contrast to Cai Wenji; the critics all avoid it and do not talk about it. But in fact, Jiang Qing is Jiang Qing, Wu Zetian is Wu Zetian, drama is drama, and the borders between all of them should be clearly drawn." "Ideologically," he adds, "the play is a great achievement."[60] However, a much harsher criticism was made in 1981 in a provocative article by Zeng Liping. Pointing especially to Guo Moruo, Zeng had this to say about the historical drama: "According to the intentions of some leaders or the short-term political necessities of a given time, history became a dough that could be kneaded ad libitum and concocted in the same manner; there were created historical plays with true figures and false acts, looking for support for today's politics and the enactment of policies, proving the new with the old, and praising the new through the old."[61]

Zeng's argument could readily be made about the majority of the new historical dramas. Its criticism of Guo Moruo alone, whose flattery of Mao Zedong has not helped his standing in the intellectual community and who was thus easy to attack, considerably weakens it.

WU HAN'S *HAI RUI BAGUAN*

English translations and specialized studies of Wu Han's *Hai Rui baguan* have appeared, so I believe a short summary and some new in-

---

59. Beijing Qiche zhizaochang gongren lilun yanjiusuo, *Lü hou qiren*; Dian Renlong, Zhou Shaoquan, and Liu Zhongri, *Cuanquan qieguo de Lü hou*; Shi Wei and Li Siyi, *Lü hou cuanquan de gushi*; Zong Gushi, *Dayexinjia Lü hou*.
60. Gao Guoping, "'Fan'an hefang fufen duo,'" p. 22.
61. Zeng Liping, "Ping lishiju chuangzuozhong de fanlishizhuyi qingxiang," p. 7.

formation added here and there might suffice.[62] Wu Han's work as a historian had always had a political connection. His biography of Zhu Yuanzhang, the first Ming emperor, for instance, was intended and read as a criticism of Chiang Kai-shek and his policies. History, he assumed, contained the experience of the past, and seeing parallels with history would allow some prediction to be made as to the probable results of certain measures.

Guided by Qian Junrui and Hu Qiaomu, who ran Mao's secretariat and was concurrently in the Central Committee secretariat, Wu Han had written his *Hai Rui ma huangdi* (Hai Rui Curses [Even] the Emperor) before the 1959 Lushan Plenum. The behavioral model of a Hai Rui, however, had been set up, and, among others, Peng Dehuai started to act out this role. The same might be said of Zhou Xinfang and the authors of *Sun An dongben*. Peng Dehuai used "Hai Rui tactics" when he submitted a memorial to point out the national crisis, a procedure protected by the Party constitution. He detailed some of the mistakes, and proposed some remedies. The language of his letter to Mao is akin to that used by Hai Rui, who, in addition to harshly criticizing the emperor, applauded him as "enlightened." Mao disclaimed the legitimacy of Peng Dehuai's donning the garb of Hai Rui, arguing in the very manner of *Wu Zetian* that Peng was a "fake" and a "right-wing" Hai Rui, not the good, "left-wing" Hai Rui advocated by Mao.[63] This implied that propaganda activities for the "left" Hai Rui should be pursued. Again, various interpretations are possible.

Mao might have felt that other Hai Ruis were still waiting in the wings and should be given leeway to come out into the open. It might also have been that political forces interested in pursuing the Hai Rui theme for the purposes of keeping the avenues of criticism of Mao open used Mao's ambiguous division between "right-wing" and "left-wing" Hai Ruis to vigorously push for keeping the spirit of Hai Rui alive. The Shanghai *Hai Rui shangshu* and the article by Wu Han on Hai Rui, both of which came out in September 1959, were public markers that Hai Rui had not gone down with Peng Dehuai. Wu Han obliged by adding a line against "right-wing" Hai Ruis to this article, and by propagating "left-wing" Hai Ruiism.[64]

62. Pusey, *Wu Han*; Ansley, *The Heresy of Wu Han*; *Wu Han he Hai Rui baguan*; *Wu Han xueshu shengya*; Fisher, "The Play's the Thing"; Huang, trans., *Hai Jui Dismissed from Office*.
63. Guo Xinghua, "*Hai Rui baguan*," p. 113.
64. Wu Han, "Lun Hai Rui."

According to Red Guard sources, the directive to write a Hai Rui play was given to Wu Han again by Hu Qiaomu in late 1959.[65] The great Peking opera star from Beijing, Ma Lianliang, who excelled in much the same roles as his Shanghai competitor Zhou Xinfang, also encouraged him. As a historian, Wu Han was invited to write a plot outline as early as late 1959; only in early 1960 did Ma Lianliang and others press him to actually write a Peking opera.

Throughout the year 1960, there was a Hai Rui lull. The campaign against "right opportunism," as Peng Dehuai's mistake was now called, created an intellectual climate in which people needed even more courage to speak out and had even less hope of being heard. After the Lushan Plenum, the Great Leap frenzy started anew, and the problems of the country took a quick turn for the worse. The fact that during this period Wu Han went through seven revisions of a Hai Rui play on which the Beijing leadership obviously set great store is less innocent than it may look. The public marks of recognition attached to this rather weak piece made it into a political statement, that is, that the spirit of Hai Rui was needed now, as much as in 1959, and that there was support for it among the leadership. By the end of 1960, emergency measures had been taken to restore agricultural production; the publication of Wu Han's article "Hai Rui" in the October/November issue of *Xin jianshe* as well as the publication and performance of the play in early 1961 could be regarded as a self-critical literary statement after the Party leadership had itself made a self-critical reappraisal of its earlier position. While the publication thus seemed well in tune with the times, the preparation and high level of leadership interference during 1960 would indicate that there were political forces making desperate efforts to prevent the Hai Rui theme from being buried along with Peng Dehuai's career.

Wu Han knew the Shanghai *Hai Rui shangshu*. There, the main feature had been the direct remonstrance with the emperor. The crisis was depicted as being due to the lack of courage among the yes-men at court. There was a demand to reverse the unjust verdicts, throw out the magicians, and establish the law in the land. The play's romantic ending heightened but also defused much of its harsh language. Wu Han would have to focus on another issue. He decided to focus on the monopolization of the land by bureaucrats, and to question the Shanghai play's romantic outcome by having Hai Rui dismissed at the end. The first

65. "*Hai Rui baguan* chulong," p. 2.

292	The Politics of the Historical Drama

draft was submitted to Hu Qiaomu, Chen Kehan, and some literary colleagues such as Lao She and Ma Shaobo around March 1960.[66] It should be noted that Guo Moruo is never mentioned in this context; he belonged to another tribe. Around the same time, Deng Xiaoping defused the political issue of the historical drama by issuing a directive that historical dramas should be written for the purpose of popularizing knowledge, saying, "China's entire history should be transformed into historical drama. Make 360 of them, one for each day; then they can be performed the entire year."[67] Deng, who was Wu Han's bridge partner, asked Wu also to compile a handbook of possible topics for such dramas, as a reference for dramatists. This book was compiled in due order.[68]

The first draft of Hai Rui baguan was submitted to Peng Zhen,[69] Politburo member and head of the Beijing Party organization. In the preface to the book edition of Hai Rui baguan, written in August 1961, Wu Han detailed the changes the play underwent.[70]

Originally, he had emphasized the question of returning the land; the "elimination of the bad xiangguan," gentry officials, had been a secondary element. But "a number of friends" pointed out that while it was true that Hai Rui had ordered the return of the land, it was a "reformist" measure "and what would be the meaning of new historical dramas written today and propagating the reformism of history." This advice persuaded him to focus instead on the elimination of the bad gentry. "This was a major change," Wu Han wrote. In fact, it seems that the Beijing vice-mayor, Chen Kehan, visited Wu Han's home at Peng Zhen's request to get him to change the focus, because the emphasis on returning the land would be "reformism." The focus was to be on chuba, eliminating tyrants.[71]

Wu Han had requested permission for a trip already in December 1959. In July 1960, he finally drove off together with Qi Yanming, who as the Party secretary in the Ministry for Culture actually decided things there. They visited Xi'an, Chengdu, Chongqing, Kunming, Guilin, Guangzhou, and Hainan, where they went to Hai Rui's tomb. After ten days, they returned by way of Wuhan.

66. Ibid.
67. Ibid.
68. Beijing shi, "Jiekai."
69. "Hai Rui baguan chulong," p. 2.
70. Translated in Ansley, The Heresy, pp. 3ff.
71. "Hai Rui baguan chulong," p. 3.

Upon his return, Wu Han completed the seventh draft, which was the first to be publicly available. In November, Zhou Yang, acting on Deng Xiaoping's directive, called a conference on historical drama with Wu Han, Jian Bocan, Hou Wailu, and other luminaries attending. This was the occasion for the first internal performance of the play, at the time still called *Hai Rui*. According to Professor Wu Xiaoling, Mao Zedong saw the play at this stage, that is, before public performances started. He is said to have invited Ma Lianliang, who played the part of Hai Rui, to come and discuss the play with him. After the dress rehearsals, the name of the play was changed to *Hai Rui baguan*. In its earlier drafts, it ended with Hai Rui being transferred to another post, but Wu Han felt that this scene lacked dramatic spice. Eventually it was decided to have Hai Rui kill the local villain, regardless of possible consequences for himself, and be immediately dismissed, the play ending at this high dramatic pitch. The title "Hai Rui Dismissed from Office," *Hai Rui baguan*, was proposed by Wu Han's old friend Cai Xitao, who had read the new draft and felt the play was not giving a biography of Hai Rui but relating just one episode in his life.[72]

Each of the earlier versions of the play had been published, and it had been declared a *zhongdian jumu*, a "special emphasis play," by Gao Ge, the vice-head of the Cultural Bureau of Beijing, which meant that all resources were to be concentrated on the piece.[73] When *Hai Rui baguan* was first publicly printed in *Beijing wenyi* in January 1961, it had all the earmarks of high political status. *Beijing wenyi* put the title of the play in boldface in the table of contents and printed it as the first piece in the issue. Furthermore, Wu Han's preface to the play was set in a type rarely used in *Beijing wenyi* called *lao wuhao zi*, "old number five type." A check through earlier and later issues of the journal reveals that this type was used in 1960 for Chen Kehan's keynote article, "On (the Relationship between) Letting a Hundred Flowers Blossom and a Hundred Schools Contend and the Leading Role of Politics," which was reprinted from the theoretical journal of the Beijing Party Committee, *Qianxian* (Frontline); it announced a substantial liberalization in cultural policies.[74] The same typeface was again used in August 1960 for Lu Dingyi's talk at the Third Congress of Cultural and Art Workers,

72. This is first suggested in "*Hai Rui baguan* chulong," and later confirmed by Guo Xinghua, "*Hai Rui baguan*," p. 114.

73. Beijing shi, "Jiekai."

74. Chen Kehan, "Baihua qifang he zhengzhi guashuai."

where he spoke for the Party Central and the State Council, also announcing a liberalization of cultural policies.[75] Zhou Yang's talk at the same occasion was not set in this type, nor the editorials of the periodical itself, nor reprints of important editorials from *Hongqi* a year later. *Lao wuhao zi* is thus a type reserved for key political documents, and it was odd indeed that a preface to a historical play containing a summary of the plot and some comment about the meaning of the characters and conflict should have received such an honor. Although there was and is general agreement that the play has few merits as a Peking opera, it was staged with an all-star cast. Ma Lianliang, who led the Ma school of Peking opera staging, played Hai Rui; the other stars were Qiu Shengrong, Li Duokui, Zhou Hetong, Li Yufang, and Niu Rongliang.[76]

Wu Han left the honor of repeating the charges from Hai Rui's memorial to *Hai Rui shangshu*, which was restaged in Beijing to coincide with the premiere of *Hai Rui baguan*. The latter play merely gives a short summary of this memorial and is otherwise situated later in Hai Rui's life.[77] Now, Xu Jie, who for whatever motives had secured Hai Rui's release after the emperor's death in the Shanghai play, has become the chief of the former high officials (*xiangguan*), who rely on their good contacts (*guanxi*) in the center to control their home areas economically and politically.

The immediate villain is Xu's son Ying. He has ruined the economic base of a family of peasants by arrogating their land but forcing them to go on paying the taxes for it. The male head of the family dies of anger, and his wife, his daughter, and her upright but weak grandfather survive without protection. Xu Ying now proceeds to abduct the daughter, who is bringing flowers to her father's tomb on the occasion of the Qingming festival. The only protection the peasants have is the law, and they go to court against Xu Ying. The judge informs us that he is flooded with charges against the Xu family for forcibly arrogating land, appropriating people's agricultural products, and taking their houses. All this is epitomized in the abduction of the young girl, in a symbolism already too familiar.

Xu Ying bribes the judge and has his bond servant testify that on the

75. "Lu Dingyi tongzhi."
76. Information from Professor Wu Xiaoling.
77. Here I use the edition Wu Han, *Hai Rui baguan*, in *Beijing wenyi* 1961.1.

day in question Xu was in the city studying at another scholar's house; the servant does not fail to mention that he is from the former prime minister's household. Having dismissed the case first because no witnesses had been brought, the judge now dismisses it because of a (fake) alibi, and he has the young woman's grandfather flogged in court for slander. The reversal of this unjust verdict and the punishment of Xu Ying's crime become the focus of the play. Hai Rui has been appointed governor of this Jiangnan area, and he arrives *incognito* in ordinary clothes to get firsthand knowledge. The local officials expect his arrival, and one of them, the Suzhou prefect, speaks approvingly of Hai Rui's memorial to the former emperor; thus, not all officials are portrayed as rotten. The typicality of the Xu family's land-grabbing and tyranny having been asserted earlier, Hai Rui adds, in his first lines on stage, that this area is the richest in the empire. "The land of Jiangnan is rich in fish and rice. It is always said, 'Above there is Heaven, below there are Suzhou and Hangzhou,'" he sings. If things are bad here, and they are, they will be worse elsewhere. "Evil *xiangguan* and greedy officials tyrannize their fellow countrymen. Things have come to such a point as to make people suffer and flee to other areas. The people are already exhausted, wealth has been squandered, the veins of the state are worn out." Shortly after, he learns that the seizing of the lands is at the core of the tyranny. The mother of the abducted woman sings:

> Evil Xu Ying makes use of his power to forcibly occupy fields,
> old men are beaten to death and women abducted. In my utter despair,
>   I implore Heaven . . .

A combination of economic expropriation and legal tyranny have brought things to a crisis, and the "social fabric" is dissolving. Hai Rui spells out his program in the last lines of this act:

> Restoration of the social fabric, annihilation of the bullies and overlords
> so that the ambition of my entire life may be fulfilled.

The term *jigang zhengdun*, restoration of the social fabric, is repeated in Hai Rui's mother's description of her son's achievements during an earlier tenure. There, he had *zhengdun gangwei*, restored the social fabric. Hai Rui, true to the notion established since *Guan Hanqing* that the hero must be not merely upright but also clever in dealing with the real situation, pays a visit to Xu Jie, the former prime minister. Talking about general principles of law, he has Xu agree that the law should be rigorously enforced against the *xiangguan* and the masses alike; thus, he makes it hard for Xu to oppose Hai Rui's prosecution of his son, Xu Ying. Hai solves the case in a manner familiar from many criminal-case plays, and he condemns Xu Ying to death. Although the surface action does deal with eliminating tyrants, the fundamental question remains: the peasants have been deprived of their land. After the judgment, the peasants drive home this point.

> Your Worship's verdict is exceedingly public-minded. It is only that since our fields have been occupied by force [pazhan] by the Xu family and other families of government officials [xiangguan], the fields are gone but the taxes remain. People's lives are hard and bitter and it is hoped that Your Worship will take care of this.

The land-grabbing has been done not only by the Xus; it is a widespread phenomenon. The people are all tenants of the Xu and other xiangguan families; it is thus a "typical" phenomenon. Moreover, they still have to do corvée labor and pay the taxes for the land taken from them. When Hai Rui decides to give the land back, the peasants instantly resolve to put themselves to it with a will; such resolution is familiar from the peasants' exchange at the beginning of the last act of Guan Hanqing. Here, the peasant masses sing in court:

Today our looks go up to blue Heaven [i.e., to Hai Rui]
diligently we shall plow and sow, restoring to order the fields and the gardens.
If we have the land, what worry have we about clothing and food,
a promising future lies before our eyes.

After the land was seized, the fields and gardens naturally fell into chaos so now they must be put back into order.

The families that monopolize the land are not a class of landlords in the terms of traditional Chinese Marxist class analysis. Their power is again bureaucratic; it rests on their political standing and influence. And it is much greater than that of a simple landlord class, because they have influence not just through their wealth, but through their institutional connections, controlling the courts as well as the wealth. The xiangguan families might not care about Xu Ying's execution, but, when ordered to return the land, they conspire to have Hai Rui removed, this act being called a "counterattack." Hai Rui is removed for "savagely oppressing the people and brutally mistreating the xiangguan." He commends his successor to deal severely with the xiangguan, the main problem of the land, and sums up:

> The unjust verdicts are grave, ah grave; they have to be reversed,
> when the fields are returned, then only will the people be at peace.

In a dramatic ending, Hai Rui has Xu Ying executed and then hands over his seal of office. A chorus offstage takes on the role of public opinion, as was done in *Sun An dongben*. The play ends with this note:

> Heaven is cold, the earth is frozen, the wind whistles mournfully,
> lingering thoughts and fond feelings, millions upon millions,
> father Hai returns south and does not remain,
> the ten thousand families burn incense for this living Buddha.

The monopolization of land through collectivization had been a latent theme in *Guan Hanqing*. With *Hai Rui baguan*, Peng Zhen's intervention notwithstanding, it becomes a core theme. Tyranny, injustice, and abuses of power provide most of the dramatic action, however.

The play differs from *Hai Rui shangshu* in a number of important respects. First, it takes place not in the city, but in the countryside, in Jiangnan. Second, it relegates the emperor to the backstage role that he had in *Guan Hanqing*. Third, it ends on a much sourer note. At the end of the play, actual power is in the hands of the *xiangguan*, although the people love Hai Rui.

The situation of the "people" is again summed up in the person of a young woman. The land has been monopolized or collectivized, but the peasants still are forced to do the corvée labor of the Great Leap, and "pay the taxes" in the form of procurement grain. Nevertheless, although the "fields and gardens [i.e., the private plots] are neglected," as was sideline production in the Great Leap, there is no famine. The word "hunger" does not appear, nor do the grisly scenes of *Sun An dongben*. People have fled the area not because they were starving but in order to escape tyranny.

The villains form a network based on their common interests. Besides the essential villainy expressed in their greed and brutality, a new element is introduced in the person of Xu Jie. He is now old and retired, and he protects his offspring. He comes to see Hai Rui, asking him to disregard the law as a favor to the man who once freed him from prison. But true to official admonitions to Communist cadres not to award personal favors, Hai Rui rejects the plea. The *xiangguan*, who control the economy and the courts and have a strong voice in the center, stand against the "people" in the manner of the cadres' relationship with the "masses." The official government organs such as courts of law act mostly in their service but are not identical with them. The distinction made between these two layers of power corresponds to that between the Party and the state organs on the contemporary scene.

The people, represented in the form of the helpless female, set their hopes on Hai Rui. Hai's program does not just involve establishment or restoration of the rule of law and a reversal of the unjust verdicts made before, but also a reform program to eliminate the causes of the distress. Return of the land, *tuitian*, is his slogan, and from his mother we learn that earlier he also abolished sundry other impositions such as corvée labor. He also consolidated the state's demands on the peasants into a single tax, the "single whip tax," so that peasants could no longer be coerced into performing all kinds of services. (The agricultural reforms enacted since 1982, by the way, are a vivid illustration of what Wu Han implied. The land has been returned to the peasants, at least on a contractual basis, sideline production has been greatly developed, state demands on the peasants have been reduced to a single tax, and consequently the levers of power in the hands of the rural cadres have been dramatically weakened and reduced in number.) In bringing up the topic of the "return of the land" to the tillers after the extremely high degree of collectivization imposed with the establishment of the People's Communes during the Great Leap, Wu Han was making a clear reference to the present. Peng Zhen intervened to have this changed because a criticism of the Great Leap for its overzealous collectivization by tyrannical means ran the danger of being perceived as "rightist" or, as he said, "reformist." On the other hand, the emphasis on *chuba*, eliminating tyranny, could be a way to claim that tyrannical abuses of power were a "rightist" thing and should be criticized.

Only after the Party had taken emergency measures to restore production and, as in 1959, again started to advocate closer adherence to the facts, was *Hai Rui baguan* published. Coming as it did after the practical self-criticism of the Party, it did not arrogate the role of the first remonstrator; nevertheless, it was the opening shot of the second round of Hai Rui plays. The silent text of the plot structure and other indicators show that the play did not restrict itself to bringing this self-criticism on stage, in contrast to other plays in which a self-criticism of the emperor after three years of disaster is introduced, together with a reform program.[78] The power situation at the end of *Hai Rui baguan* has the *xiangguan* again in firm control, after they have cooperated smoothly and effectively on all levels to have Hai removed and even censured for suppressing the cadres and masses, the *xiangguan* and the hundred families. *Hai Rui baguan* ends, appropriately, in winter.

78. Cf. Zhongguo pingjuyuan, with An Xi and Gao Chen, eds., *Zhong Li jian*, p. 6.

The emperor appears as the general legitimizing power to whom Hai Rui is loyal. In the end, however, he is "duped" by the *xiangguan*, and Hai Rui is dismissed. This vague portrayal of the center avoids two issues: first, the question of whether power was generally in the hands of some villain, which is nowhere suggested, and second, the treatment of the prime minister, in the Horikhoson tradition. The downward transfer of the action to the provincial level furthermore gave the option of introducing peasants, whose plight in these years was most dramtic, into the text. As for Hai Rui, his situation is much better than that of Hai Rui in *Hai Rui shangshu* or that of Sun An in *Sun An dongben*, both of whom are thrown into prison and threatened with execution. Hai Rui is just dismissed; he is not even expelled from the Party by being made a commoner. Certainly one might discover elements of Peng Dehuai's treatment here, although it seems more credible, as Wu Han claimed in 1964, that the play implied a disclaimer of Peng Dehuai, the attack against "rightist" Hai Ruis being repeated in the preface.[79]

By dealing with affairs in Jiangnan, Wu Han avoided the touchy problems of dealing with the factions in the center. The portrayal of the cadre situation seems more favorable here than in *Hai Rui shangshu* or *Sun An dongben*. In *Hai Rui baguan*, the court assigns Hai Rui to a very high appointment after his daring memorial to the former emperor; he also has a local admirer. In the two other plays, Hai Rui and Sun An are "sesame seed officials," hardly big enough to be seen. On the other hand, although government officials in Wu Han's play are of different kinds, the *xiangguan* now operate as a class, committed, and success- fully so, to maintaining their prerogative of absolute power in all realms of life, and to the reckless and uncontrolled use of that power.

Even after all the revisions, the play lacks dramatic substance. Most things are told rather than acted out. In terms of political acumen and literary skill, it is a far cry from *Hai Rui shangshu*. It attracted attention not as a successful play, but as a political statement by the Beijing Party leadership, and the attacks against Wu Han were really directed against political leaders such as Peng Zhen. It might be due to

---

79. At a meeting of the Democratic League in 1964, someone is said to have applauded Wu Han for speaking out in favor of Peng Dehuai with his play. Informed about this, Wu Han is said to have gone to the meeting and declared that the play rejected Peng. This story is not entirely improbable. The local officials (*xiangguan*) do use in form the same methods and language Hai Rui uses, accusing Hai Rui of "oppressing the *xiangguan* and the hundred families" while in fact defending their own interests. Wu Han could claim that theirs was the "false Hai Rui" attitude. Beijing shi, "Jiekai."

our ignorance of the internal workings of the Chinese Communist government that the degree of top-level Party guidance and influence seems particularly high in this case. Here it is well documented. But it is quite possible that many other literary pieces that were to be presented to the public received, without our knowledge, similar political attention and guidance. When the play was eventually performed publicly, the spectators did their interpretive share, loudly clapping at the words, "reverse the wrong verdicts and eliminate the tyrants."[80] In March of 1961, Liao Mosha wrote in a review in *Beijing wenyi*: "As I watched [the play], my heart beat furiously . . . [and] when I left the theater I was [still] greatly excited. What I was thinking about, I certainly need not explain."[81] Liu Shaoqi saw the play on February 21, 1961, and declared one "could make more such historical plays."[82] Jiang Qing did not see it until July 6, 1961. She then phoned the Beijing Party Committee to have the play stopped. The Red Guard publication *Opera Battle News* put it glowingly: "In this moment when the dark cloud was rolling up [a reference to Mao's poem about the Sun Wukong opera], our beloved Comrade Jiang Qing raised high the mighty banner of Mao Zedong Thought, planting it squarely into the field of literature, and gave battle to the ox-demons and snake-specters. After Comrade Jiang Qing had seen *Hai Rui baguan* in the Yinyuetang on July 6, 1961, she made invincible Mao Zedong Thought into both her microscope and telescope. With one glance she perceived the political conspiracy hidden in *Hai Rui baguan*, and instantly gave the stringent directive: 'This is a bad play; stop performances.'"[83] This was done, but in November, *Hai Rui baguan* came out as a book in Beijing. It was given the highest, i.e., national, distribution status. Also in November, the Shanghai play *Hai Rui shangshu* was given a guest performance in Beijing. The issue remained far from decided. In September 1962, Peng Dehuai again referred to himself as a Hai Rui and submitted a long report on his findings concerning the Great Leap. Shortly thereafter, Zhou Enlai remarked, upon a suggestion by Jiang Qing, that *Hai Rui baguan* "indirectly points at present-day reality and coincides with a wind to reverse correct judgments."[84] In the summer of 1964 at the Beijing theater festival, when the new "contemporary theme" plays fostered by Jiang Qing

80. Du Renzhi, "Huainian geming shixuejia Wu Han tongzhi," p. 29.
81. Quoted in Pusey, *Wu Han*, p. 37.
82. Tie Qi, "Liu Shaoqi ai shenmeyang de dianying xiju?" p. 4, col. 3.
83. Beijing shi, "Jiekai."
84. "*Hai Rui baguan* chulong."

were shown to the assembled leadership, Kang Sheng made an "important" but unpublished speech; in it, *Hai Rui baguan*, together with two other pieces, figured as a counterrevolutionary "poisonous weed." Wu Han's name, however, was taken off the list of people to be investigated for the Hai Rui "problem" in the course of the rectification movement of that year, after both the Beijing Party and the Association of Literary and Arts Workers vouched that he was "left-wing."[85] In a manner quite similar to the way in which *Hai Rui baguan* was written and rewritten during 1960, Kang Sheng, Jiang Qing, and Zhang Chunqiao supervised the writing of Yao Wenyuan's article against *Hai Rui baguan*, which also went through a dozen revisions. Jiang Qing revealed in a Cultural Revolution speech that the latest revision was recorded at the end of a tape of innocuous material, and was sent by plane from Shanghai to Beijing.[86]

In October 1965, Mao Zedong gave the directive to criticize Wu Han, and in November the much-revised article appeared. As is well known, Mao Zedong took issue with the article for the way it focused only on the criticism of Great Leap policies implicit in the play—namely the question of "returning the land"—and argued that Hai Rui is "also" Peng Dehuai; it is now claimed, however, that this discovery was not Mao's. Rather, "according to a discovery made very recently, the first person to point out that the main crime of *Hai Rui baguan* was the dismissal [*baguan*]" was Kang Sheng.[87] Two articles by Guan Feng and by Ji Benyu in the spring of 1966 that argued along these lines were directly approved by Kang Sheng.[88] Although it is evident that post-1978 efforts were made to exculpate the Chairman from the charge of mistreating literature—another case is adduced elsewhere[89]—and blame Kang Sheng for their instigation, these charges against Kang Sheng have a great deal of credibility. Wu Han's eventual imprisonment and death were due to a further intervention by Kang Sheng in 1968. When no charges of treason could be proved against Wu Han, Kang Sheng reportedly said: "If Wu Han does not have the problem of

85. Beijing shi, "Jiekai."
86. Quoted in Yu Ming, "Kang Sheng yu Jiang Qing," p. 36.
87. Kang Sheng is quoted as having said on August 11, 1967, at the Eleventh Plenum, "In 1964 I said to the Chairman that there was a link between Wu Han's *Hai Rui baguan* and the Lushan Plenum." Quoted with other evidence in ibid., p. 36. Cf. *Wu Han he Hai Rui baguan*, pp. 6ff.
88. *Wu Han he Hai Rui baguan*, pp. 8ff.
89. Cf. p. 318.

being a traitor, he still has a problem of being an agent. Investigate."[90]
Wu Han was arrested, and he died on October 11, 1968, after being
hospitalized. But now, let us return to the situation in 1961 and pursue
our narrative with another Hai Rui play, *Hai Rui beiqian*.

HAI RUI BEIQIAN

The text of *Hai Rui beiqian* (Hai Rui Pulls the Rope) was published in
Juben in its issue of February/March 1961.[91] The play had been written
in 1959, during the first Hai Rui wave.[92] But not until 1961, when the
second wave had started, was it published. It is nicely set in the year
1561, and Hai Rui is a magistrate in Chun'an. An imperial inspector
(*xun'an*) is sent to investigate corruption among officials, but uses the
opportunity to bag as much as possible for himself. He carries the imperial sword and has the right to execute recalcitrants without prior clear-
ance from the center. Ironically, he comes with the same title given Hai
Rui in *Hai Rui baguan*. The official, Zhang Biao, decides to teach all the
officials a lesson by forcing Hai Rui to come up with a huge number of
people to pull his boat and carry his things.

In the second act, Hai Rui's praises are sung by two of his attendants.
Hai's reforms, they say, include the setting of clear demarcation lines
for the land and the reduction of taxes. Hai Rui eats like the common
people, and there is little to eat. The situation of the country is described:

> Lately there has been year after year of drought and inundation; only
> think of it, at the court Yan Song monopolizes power, and my lord [i.e., the
> emperor] strives after the Tao with all his heart. How should he know a
> thing about the bitter sufferings of the people?

Hai Rui's measures have partly restored production in his district.
Refugees who had fled exorbitant taxes are coming back, and there is
hope that after a good autumn harvest (the scene is set in autumn)
"hunger and cold can be avoided." But there is still drought, and people
are forced to eat wild herbs. The emissary of Zhang Biao enters this
scene. He demands tea of a woman who has just described her plight,
and when she has only water to offer him, he beats her, a familiar symbolical action. The poverty of the people is shared by the yamen, and

90. Ibid., p. 15.
91. Xi Wen, Yang Zhixun, and Xu Juhua, *Hai Rui beiqian*.
92. Cf. "Shanghai xijujie chuangzuo Hai Rui jumu."

when the emissary goes there to complain about the woman's refusal, Hai Rui takes bold action although he is warned of Zhang Biao's ruthless use of power. His servant, Hai An, tells him what people think of the situation in the center:

> Today, Yan Song monopolizes the power, the emperor trusts and favors him completely, and everyone among the hundred families of the empire says: "The son of Heaven highly esteems the mighty and ruthless; whoever says a word meets disaster. They are all just low grade; every one of them just flatters those in high office."

Hai Rui, informed about the misdoings of the emissary, has him flogged, and takes him in shackles to receive his master. Zhang Biao immediately charges Hai Rui with two crimes: inciting public opinion by bringing his emissary in shackles and contravening the emperor by not properly receiving Zhang Biao, an imperial inspector. True to his reputation as astute and witty, Hai Rui manages to put Zhang on the defensive. Then, before Zhang's very eyes, he pulls out an abacus to add up the profits made by the inspector during his trip.

In order to get back at Hai Rui, Zhang has notices posted that anyone claiming that an injustice has been done to him should present his case to the imperial envoy. Eventually, a man presents himself with the cry "injustice, injustice"; he is the grandfather of the young woman who was beaten in the second act. Zhang is forced to punish his own underling and recompense the grandfather for the damage. In a huff, Zhang decides to leave, and asks for four hundred people to pull his transport ships next morning. Hai Rui and his attendants alone show up and start pulling the ropes, arguing that it is harvest time and people have not a minute to spare. When Zhang's secretary advises him that it would look bad if it were reported that Zhang had his boat pulled by a magistrate, Zhang suddenly discovers a favorable wind, and, asking Hai Rui to return to the shore, he sails off.

Hai Rui beiqian is skillfully written in terms of drama. The action is acted out rather than being narrated, and, while Hai Rui retains his high moral stature in the piece, it spares him the pain of himself pompously stating his principles by having his underlings chat about him. The play has the same core elements of political and social situation as *Guan Hanqing* and *Sun An dongben*. There is famine, caused by a mixture of natural and political disasters, the latter in the form of "exorbitant taxes," the standard reference to the grain purchases during the Great Leap. The emperor, as in *Hai Rui shangshu*, dreams only about reaching the Way and becoming immortal, but, while in the Shanghai play only Taoist magicians run the court and no chief villain is to be seen controlling the country, here Yan Song, who monopolizes power at the court, is mentioned. The play does not make it clear how Zhang Biao and Yan Song are linked in terms of faction, but the arrival of Zhang is immediately associated with Yan Song's power at court.

The focus is on tyranny, wanton abuse of the law, and systematical graft accompanied by high-sounding words about Zhang's mandate to weed out corrupt officials and reverse unjust verdicts. The representative of the villains' faction is depicted in a crudely polemical manner. Zhang Biao comes in as the caricature of a radical. He says he is going to investigate graft and corruption, but the only really corrupt person around is he. He says he is going to reverse unjust verdicts handed down by the local officials and has signs posted that people should tell him their grievances, but in fact he only wants to collect material against the local official Hai Rui, who is much loved by the people. The polemics against the Gang of Four after 1976 made the same charge: that the Four proclaimed proletarian virtues while they themselves were unabashedly wallowing in a bourgeois lifestyle.

The plot is again loosely structured around the victimization of the young female, and her eventual vindication. The play does not waste its time repeating Hai Rui's grand principles, but shows that he is a man of tactical wit, able to outmaneuver even a vicious old fox like Zhang Biao. The people remain passive and sympathetic during the action, although they have an influence as "public opinion." Zhang Biao introduces a new accusation, charging Hai Rui with detracting from Zhang's imperial authority by dragging Zhang's underling in shackles through the fields in view of the public.

The play is modest in its aspirations. Zhang Biao, it is true, wields the imperial execution sword, and Hai Rui's life is indeed threatened. Nevertheless, Hai's realistic endeavor is to get Zhang out of his district without paying the enormous bribes the man demands and thus to protect the people under his jurisdiction. Zhang's head is neither cut off nor cracked with a hammer; nor does Hai Rui dream about such action. Much in the style of *Da Qianlong*, the relief provided to the spectator through the play is symbolic, in the form of first cursing (or hitting) the mighty, and then outwitting them when they want their revenge.

The second wave of Hai Rui plays seems to have created a symbol of identification. Peng Dehuai had used this symbol, but Peng was only one of the possible incarnations of Hai Rui, and his fall was probably more due to his friendly links with the Soviet leadership than to his bringing the facts to the attention of the Chairman. From the record, it would seem that there were three centers for the Hai Rui fashion: Shanghai, which was the center in 1959 but did little during or after 1961, Beijing, which became the center in 1961, and Canton, where *Guan Hanqing* and *Hai Rui shangshu* were staged and *Liu Mingzhu*, a Hai Rui play, was given. In Hainan, from February 1960 through 1962 a local opera entitled *Hai Rui Returns to Court* (*Hai Rui huichao*) was performed in every district; it was also made into a spoken drama entitled *The Tale of Knocking Out Teeth* (*Qiaoya ji*). The theme moved one rank higher with the shooting of a film entitled *Inspector Hai Rui* (*Hai Rui chuxun*) at Canton's Pearl River Studio. In 1963, Tao Zhu, the first secretary of the Party's Central-South Bureau and party secretary of Guangdong Province, assembled a group of high-ranking political leaders to have their picture taken in front of props for this film. It would seem that the assembled leaders were making a statement that they saw themselves as Hai Rui. The photograph was published during the Cultural Revolution. Besides Tao Zhu, the leaders are Wang Renzhong (first secretary, Hubei), Wu Yiguo (secretary, Central-South Office of Culture and Education), Song Kanfu (first secretary, Wuhan), Zhang Pinghua (second secretary, Hubei), Wei Guoqing (first secretary, Guangxi), and Yong Wenshou.[93] The role traditionally assigned to literature in the socialist order of things had been to set up role models of behavior for the reader and the spectator. Whatever may have been the motives of the various factions of the leadership in promoting the Hai Rui role, it provided substantial status and bearing to those who adopted it, and they had been educated in the risks and promises involved through the fate of Hai Rui himself.

SUN WUKONG SANDA BAIGUJING

This play has been studied in detail in chapter 3 of this volume. Fostered by Guo Moruo, Zhou Enlai, and Mao Zedong, it proposed a definition of the problems facing the country, a depiction of the struggles at the center, and a solution to these problems radically different from those of historical dramas in the Hai Rui tradition; it shared many of the assumptions of Guo Moruo's *Wu Zetian*.

93. Beijing shi, "Jiekai"; "Qiongju 'Hai Rui huichao' shi zhu da ducao"; the photo is published in *Zhandou bao* Mar. 10, 1967, p. 4.

It made use of the character of Zhu Bajie to reject the assumption that remonstrance à la Hai Rui is necessary and justified. Zhu does remonstrate with Monkey, in fact has him "dismissed from office," but he is a revisionist, a "right-wing" Hai Rui.

In terms of influencing public opinion and public perception of problems, this play alone may have been more powerful than all the Hai Rui plays taken together, as it was very widely shown as a film, was used as a textbook in the schools, and was a constant source of reference in the education of the young. With its easy access and lively and familiar imagery, it could reach a much more diversified and broader public than the new historical drama and opera, which remained restricted to the political class.

TIAN HAN'S *XIE YAOHUAN*

This play has also been treated in a separate study (see chapter 2). It took up the challenge of Guo Moruo's *Wu Zetian*, and redefined the situation of the country and the problems it faced in a quite radical manner. Combining the familiar themes of injustice and land-grabbing in the case of the victimized female, it provided a much darker perspective for the "hero," the "palace lady" of literature disguised in men's clothing, Xie Yaohuan. After she dares to execute the local villain, she is tortured and killed, in a scene in which Tian Han takes issue with the ending of *Hai Rui baguan*. Even the intervention of the empress herself in the end does not repair the badly torn social fabric. The male lead, Yuan Xingjian, skeptical of a fundamental change at the center, joins the people who have assembled at the "lakes and marshes" to put a latent "public opinion" pressure on the empress.

MENG CHAO'S *LI HUINIANG*

Meng Chao, like Tian Han, is a senior writer of drama, and he took part in the discussions about *Hai Rui baguan*. His *kunqu* opera (a form specializing in ghost themes) *Li Huiniang* came out in July/August 1961, in the same issue of *Juben* as *Xie Yaohuan*.[94] The play is based on

---

94. Meng Chao, *Li Huiniang*. Some of the relevant material may be listed: Feng Qiyong, "Cong *Lüyi ren zhuan* dao *Li Huiniang*"; Zhang Zhen, "Kan kunqu xinfan *Li Huiniang*"; Yang Xianyi, "*Hongmei* jiuqu xi xinfan—kunqu *Li Huiniang* guanhou gan."

an opera classic, *Hongmeiji*, but in this brief synopsis we will dispense
with a comparison and go by the eventual outcome. The text had mostly
been written in 1959 during the first Hai Rui wave, and had benefited
from the advice of an aficionado of ghost plays, Kang Sheng. Kang
helped write the play, gave advice on its staging, and wrote a letter
praising it to Meng Chao after the premiere. He also had it banned on
Jiang Qing's advice in the autumn of 1962 and described it as an "anti-
Party, anti-socialist poisonous weed" in his important talk in Beijing in
June 1964.[95]

The play opens with an introductory song, in which the author states
his intention:

Crossing the Changjiang southward, the mountains become rugged,
debauchery has taken hold of Jian'an.
Fond of reading, in a bamboo-covered hut, "discourses on ghosts,"
my will and spirit link up to a long rainbow,
and I wield my brush to exterminate the traitors in power.
Drawing on the insights of the forefathers,
I lay down my own opinions.
To the old play *Hongmei* I have given a new turn.
Having studied the tender feelings of young lovers and personal resentment [as
    described in the old play]
I write about flourishing dreams being cut off,
write about northern horses neighing at the banks of the Qiantang.
Jia Sidao harms the state and hurts the people; there's playing and singing at
    nightly banquets,
In his laughter is hidden the dagger, and occasion for murder comes;
Pei Shunqing, groaning with anger, speaks straight words and meets his ruin;
satisfying people's minds, extending righteous justice,
Li Huiniang's heroic spirit avenges injustice after her death.

I am not quite clear what the allusion to the rainbow means; I assume
that it refers to the link between the present and the "discourses on
ghosts" that the poet read.

The play is set in around 1275, in the fall. The first act takes place in
Prime Minister Jia Sidao's home, where a birthday party is being prepared for him. The outside world, visible through the windows, is in the
decay of autumn, with leaves falling, while inside, in center stage, a large
arrangement of candelabra and flowers surrounds the character *shou*,
meaning long life. Jia is introduced through the reaction of his servants,
who "tremble with fright." The young Li Huiniang was pressed into the
minister's service as a concubine some years before; in the symbolical

95. Yu Ming, "Kang Sheng yu Jiang Qing," p. 35.

role of the victimized female, she is consumed by hatred of this tyrant
but helpless in his face. Jia Sidao enters. He has just been greatly
honored by the emperor, but the students in the Southern Song capital
of Hangzhou (Jian'an) set upon him with satirical poems. While the
Yuan army is attacking from the north and he is whiling his time away
in debauchery, they charge.

The prime minister is in effective control of the country (i.e., southern China), with his "office controlling the network of the dynasty, and
his power dominating all [within the] four seas." He cares only for
pleasure, singing "let the country go to pieces." Pei Shunqing, a student,
uses the opportunity of the birthday party to send Jia a satirical poem
critical of his inactivity with regard to the country's defense. Li
Huiniang hears the poem and sympathizes. Jia sends his majordomo to
persecute the student.

The second act confronts the students with the prime minister on
West Lake. Pei introduces himself:

Those with book and sword drift listlessly about,
therefore the state is ravaged and fragmented.
I am sad and concerned
that this official [Jia Sidao] will not go to [embattled] Xinting.
Anger fills my breast, and strong is the memory of past heroes,
around the tombs of the upright and loyal [of the past], there is wild grass and
    desolation.
The great lords who came over the Changjiang obfuscated those of the south.
Did [Jia Sidao's] Confucian cap ever fool me?
The rise and fall [of the nation] are great affairs,
Why be afraid of being cut by his knife, boiled in his cauldron, or accused by
    him of forming a party?

He sets out to imitate earlier student leaders of the Han and Song who
had protested against ministers damaging the nation. In a familiar turn,
Pei continues, "At this moment the country is about to change color,
and the government is on the verge of collapse, when externally the
Yuan armies rage, and internally the villains in power indulge in wanton persecution." He has set out, together with other students, to write
a public appeal, a placard, and a memorial to the emperor denouncing
Jia Sidao. The appeal is to be circulated among the students and the
people in general. He stands at the tomb of Yue Fei (whom Mao had
mentioned in 1958 as a Hai Rui figure) and reminisces about Yue's
"cursing" (*ma*) his adversary, Qin Gui, who had then had Yue killed,
"to let out some of the anger in [his] breast." Taking up the *Guan*

Hanqing metaphor of the "sword of the brush," Pei and his friends set out to write a sharply worded manifesto. The confrontation, however, comes directly. Jia goes for an outing on the West Lake. True to the habits of the People's Republic, the area is cordoned off for this "important personality." The students persist, and Pei engages in cursing Jia Sidao:

I'll ask you:
Why are you plundering the people's salt, and practicing usury with double
    profits?
Why are you monopolizing the people's fields, oppressing and plundering them?
Why are you increasing taxes, and collecting them so brutally?
Why are you wantonly using laws and punishments, lining up all the good
    people and killing them like flies? . . .
I say straight to your face that under this great Song dynasty,
wailing fills the fields, and the black-haired people have no place to turn to.

Jia charges Pei with "rebelling against the authorities with wild words," and promises to go after him with all the powers he possesses. In a quote from the *Hongmeiji*, Li Huiniang, who has followed the exchange, murmurs "beautiful, this young man," a phrase that was later changed on Kang Sheng's suggestion to "how strong, this young man," to eliminate the sensual element of the young concubine of an old lecher looking longingly at this strapping youth. Jia hears her sigh, and in the next act he takes vengeance on her.

To hear her out, he slyly proposes she should marry this young man. When the scheme fails, he assails her as a "vile whore" who has had illicit relations with Pei. Li Huiniang, inspired by Pei's daring attitude, also makes a stand and now talks back angrily:

When your Lordship wants to kill me,
how would I dare be afraid?
The threat of evil power is coming from you!

Jia strikes her with his sword and, dying, she yells at him (in the style of Sai Lianxiu when her eyes were gouged out by Ahmad):

Jia Sidao! With the imperial execution sword girt to your waist, how long do you think you can go on with your crimes? I will not close my eyes when dead; I want to see your downfall.

In the next scene, the ghost of Li Huiniang appears in Jia Sidao's garden. She recalls her fate, and finds that her death has ended her sufferings, singing:

Under Jia Sidao's rule,
there's peace only after death.

With the "ghost step" perfected by some masters of this form, she starts
to dance, "fluttering like a crane's wings, I waft about, looking out for
the opportunity to get revenge for the unjust verdict." Meanwhile, Pei
has been arrested and locked up in Jia Sidao's residence. Li notices him,
and decides to save him with the words:

I will become a ghost Guanyin bodhisattva,
save from suffering, save from trouble,
hurting men is what you [i.e., Jia Sidao] do,
To save them, I come!

She helps Pei to flee from Jia's house, only after the two have con-
fessed to each other their sufferings and their love. Jia Sidao goes on
with his feasting; meanwhile, the country's military situation is worsen-
ing, and ever more memorials against him reach the court. When he has
his servants tortured to find out who set Pei free, Li Huiniang appears to
him: "Although, while living, I had no relationship with him [Pei], I
have just formed a marriage bond with him."

She repeats her charges against Jia: "You have sold the state and hurt
the people. . . . Those unjustly condemned clog the streets, looking at
each other." As she is a ghost, even the awesome powers of the prime
minister no longer frighten her. When Jia cries for help, she blows out
the candles with a ghost wind and magically stops the guards where
they are, singing:

I am Li Huiniang. Living, I was unjustly slain;
dead, I have become an evil spirit. The fire of my
hatred rises three thousand yards, my spirit of
righteousness makes people tremble, I spit blood
over three fathoms, enough to control the life of
villain . . . .
Jia Sidao,
you will know me much better still,
wait until I thrust my bloodied head into your chest!
You should know,
Li Huiniang was wronged while alive, and thus became strong after death.

Jia Sidao then stumbles backward, waving his arms, and Li Huiniang
pushes him with her head. Jia falls to the floor, unconscious. Huiniang
jumps on the book table, laughing loudly three times. Then she
continues:

The age-old spirit of righteous rises again among the Han—
I, Li Huiniang, whom you should not believe dead, the invincible living caretaker.

The historical drama has come full circle with this piece. *Guan Hanqing* had translated Dou E's ghost into public opinion, and here the aspirations of the people come back as a ghost. The theme of the ghost of the unjustly slain coming back to take revenge appeared in *Guan Hanqing*, when Zhu Lianxiu and Guan Hanqing promised each other to take their revenge as ghosts if they were slain.[96] In *Sun An dongben*, "all over, the ghosts of the unjustly slain lament."[97] *Xie Yaohuan* and *Li Huiniang* both take up the theme. Xie Yaohuan promises Lai Junchen to take revenge on him as an evil spirit if she is tortured to death. In *Li Huiniang*, finally, the symbol is broadly developed. The unjustly slain—the victims of injustice, persecution, and oppression—come back on stage as the ghosts to take their revenge. From the time when the play was originally written until its final revision, much had happened. There had been a famine, and another compaign. The victims come back in the gruesome face of Li Huiniang, with her bloodied head.

The play, which retains much of the lyricism of its antecedent, operates with the familiar symbols. A villain is in power, the emperor showers him with favors but is not attacked in institutional terms. Land-grabbing, high taxation, and injustice prevail, to which now foreign aggression from the north has been added (a first reference, it seems, to the dispute with the Soviet Union that became an important theme a year later). The hero is a young student (straight from the Hundred Flowers idealism), and he "marries" the young female (as an indication of a permanent union between the intellectual leftist patriots and "the people"). All elements of carnal love have been eliminated in order to demonstrate the disinterested purity of the relationship. As in *Xie Yaohuan*, the heroine is killed; the milder solutions of the Hai Rui plays no longer seem acceptable to the author. The vengeance at the end does not come through a decision at the court, but through the young female, the embodiment of the people's hatred and resentment. The conservative values that dominate the historical drama are again reiterated, with a reference to Wen Tianxiang's poem "Song of Righteousness Prevailing" (a fashion started by Tian Han in *Guan Hanqing*).

96. Tian Han, *Guan Hanqing*, *Juben* ed., p. 23: "We will transform into evil spirits, and eliminate the villains."
97. *Sun An dongben*, p. 65.

By now, Tian Han had been identified with Guan Hanqing; Guo
Moruo had declared "Cai Wenji—that is I"; Wu Han had stated in the
preface to *Hai Rui baguan* that he himself was "a Hai Rui"; thus, it
comes as no surprise that Meng Chao stated "Li Huiniang, that is I; I
have given her my heart's blood. I have also given my feelings to Pei;
therefore I am also student Pei."[98]

Li Huiniang received favorable notice. Peng Zhen went to see it twice
and had himself photographed with the actors; Xia Yan proposed to
change the color of Li's ghost dress from blue to black;[99] and Kang
Sheng proposed red instead.[100] The play came out in a book edition,
which involved a high-level decision. Tian Han is quoted as having said
"A *xiqu* [opera] must be *qu* [bent, indirect]; your text is still too
direct."[101]

The Shanghai *Wenhuibao* carried an article by Liang Bihui criticizing
Li Huiniang and the ghost plays in general. Feng Mu, then assistant
editor of the paper, told Meng that the article came from "an authoritative side" and that he should not reply. Indeed, the article had been
organized by Ke Qingshi on Jiang Qing's request.[102] In June 1964,
Kang Sheng defined the piece as "counterrevolutionary"; in January
1965, it was the first play to be publicly attacked under this label.[103]
The play and the author were both rehabilitated after 1978, and the
play has been restaged, with history obliging by adding yet another
group to those who were seen in 1961 to emerge in Li Huiniang's ghost
to demand revenge.

HUA DA CHAO

Hua da chao is a *yuju*, a Henan opera. Its sharp, biting satire and
boisterous scenes had been "adapted" by He Lingyun, and the play was
published in *Juben* in February 1962.[104] The *hua* in the title stands for

98. Quoted in Renmin wenxue, "Fandang."
99. Ibid.
100. Yu Ming, "Kang Sheng yu Jiang Qing," p. 35.
101. Quoted in Renmin wenxue, "Fandang."
102. Ibid. Liang Bihui, "'Yougui wuhai' lun."
103. Qi Xiangjun, "Chongping Meng Chao xinbian *Li Huiniang*." The article was printed under an editorial note that defined *Li Huiniang* as "anti-party,
anti-socialist poisonous weed." Ibid., p. 2.
104. He Lingyun, *Hua da chao*.

huadan, a female role played by a male; *da* is the familiar "trouncing" or "beating up"; *chao* is the court, and here more exactly the emperor.

The play does not mention the social situation of the country. The court is controlled by the chief villain, Su Dingfang. The young hero, Luo Tong, defies Su's order to get down from his horse near Su's house, and is then accused of rebellion and of cursing the emperor. Luo then charges that Su came to power by means of his dagger and not his talents. When Su wants his underlings to "unhorse" the hero, the latter beats Su up. In the second act the emperor enters, with the traditional lines about his own great rule and the perfect happiness of the people; then he hears a voice rejoicing in the antechamber, "He beat him up, good; he beat him up, good." Su, in whose plight the other courtiers rejoice, asks the emperor to have Luo arrested, and his request is granted. The men at court are all weaklings, and the high minister, Cheng Jiaojin, is no exception. Cheng's wife, however, advanced in age and with missing teeth, is a formidable character. When the wives of the high ministers decide to do something about the case, they make her their leader. The wives of the eighteen highest officials band together and block the execution ground so that Luo cannot be harmed. Old Lady Cheng is resolved that "if the release of Luo Tong is not granted, I'll start a rumpus at court, and beat up this dim emperor." At her first interview with Su, she eventually kicks him when he does not oblige her. The wives march to court, where "a dim emperor sits on the drag-on throne, and a vicious minister acts like a wolf." The emperor argues that "if today he [Luo] dares to hit the high minister, tomorrow he will dare to hit the emperor himself," and refuses to set Luo free. Lady Cheng declares, "You dim emperor, you exasperate me with your words; bring a chair here so that I may sit opposite him [the emperor]." When the emperor threatens her, she takes the chair to hit him, but he makes off through a back door. Lady Cheng's husband makes a feeble attempt to intervene but is easily won over by a few signs of imperial favor.

Before Lady Cheng can return to court for another discussion with the emperor, the latter hangs up the execution sword at the gate to threaten her. She takes down the sword and breaks it to pieces, saying, "you cannot kill loyal and excellent people anymore." Aware of the risks she takes, she arranges things in case of her death. At the beginning of the dynasty, she claims, things were much better and remon-strance was heard. But when the emperor refuses to give in, even Lady

Cheng's husband is angered. The couple take a seat right on the imperial table, and declare that "he is a dim emperor who mixes up right and wrong," whereupon the young emperor orders their execution. Outside, the people are clamoring that they will tear down the palace, and inside Lady Cheng takes an ax that was given to her husband for his merits to hit this emperor "who believes slander, hurts the loyal and excellent, and lets the government go to rot." She announces that thereafter she will do the same to his minister. The emperor hides behind the table, which is promptly overturned, only to reveal Su Dingfang hiding under it. Threatened by the ax, the emperor finally gives in and sets Luo free; Su is chased from the court with a kick from Lord Cheng. The emperor invites his senior adviser Lord Cheng to a banquet to reestablish their friendship.

The piece takes up the tradition of *Da Qianlong* and *Sun An dongben*, especially the latter, by having the senior government officials trounce the emperor. In an ironic inversion, the "helpless female" character is here a young male hero, and the male savior comes in the shape of Lady Cheng. The depiction of the country's political situation is familiar from many of the other plays, and is evident without having to be repeated.

TANGWANG NA JIAN

Tangwang na jian (The Tang Emperor Accepts Remonstrance) is a play about the early years of the Tang dynasty, when Wei Zheng (A.D. 581–643) was still chief minister to the founding emperor, Taizong. Wei had been with the emperor for many decades, and their relationship was marked by mutual trust and a rigorous adherence on Wei Zheng's part to his role as a loyal remonstrator. Wei Zheng, it seems, had not been seen as part of the Hai Rui constellation in 1959; he emerged for the first time in 1962, when, on orders of Lu Dingyi, the Wei Zheng biography from the *Tangshu* was reissued with a commentary.[105] The intention was for Wei Zheng to supplement or replace Hai Rui, but the plays about him were written in a similar vein to the Hai Rui plays. The author of the first Hai Rui biography in 1957, Jiang Xingyu, who had advised the authors of the *Hai Rui shangshu*, was eventually commissioned by the Shanghai paper *Jiefang ribao* in 1962 to write the play *Li*

105. Zhao Wu, *Wei Zheng*. It should be mentioned that Wei made an appearance in Tian Han's Tibet play, *Wencheng gongzhu*, in 1960.

Shimin yu Wei Zheng (Li Shimin and Wei Zheng), which as the title indicates focused on the relationship between the Tang founder and his chief minister.[106]

The play, a Peking opera, was written by Wang Xiezhu and first published in June 1962.[107] In the first act, Wei Zheng discovers that the emperor has sent people to the most distant parts of the country to find precious things with which to embellish the trousseau of his daughter, and he instantly decides to intervene. The emperor comes on stage, convinced that he "has the Way" and that the people are happy, proclaiming:

From the bloom of these times and the number of auspicious omens, it is clear
     that I have the Way,
the people are at peace and content, the four seas are untroubled, and the ten
     thousand states come to my court [with tribute],
the crowd of military and civilian officials protect me with loyal hearts,
we celebrate peace and reduce the punishments. The order can be compared to
     that prevailing under Yao and Shun . . . .

This introduction serves only to justify his spending large amounts of money for the trousseau. The empress remonstrates with him about it: "In the beginning, when the dynasty was founded, parsimony and modesty were valued." With the same ambivalent "today" already studied in chapter one, Wei Zheng intervenes. When he notices that the emperor is trying to evade his criticism, he says: "These days, my lord is quite different from earlier times. Your words are evasive. You withhold your opinions. You are not sincere in accepting criticism." Like Sun An in *Sun An dongben*, he threatens to come with a second memorial, should the first not be accepted. His memorial is supported by the other ministers, who bring up other issues like the costly matter of a palace, also for the princess bride. A ditty circulates: "Inside the palace, slim waists are appreciated; outside the city, many die of hunger." Another minister again compares the present with the time of the founding of the dynasty: "Policies as they are now are different from those at the beginning of the reign. The classics are not valued anymore, and big banquets are all too easily given." The emperor denies that the ditty "defines the core ill of the time." He maintains that with all the wealth around, he is entitled to a few extravagances. Thereupon he dismisses Wang Gui, who had quoted the ditty, and impeaches another

106. Jiang Xingyu, "Hai Rui," p. 89.
107. Wang Xiezhu, *Tangwang na jian.*

critic. The emperor expects criticism from Wei Zheng, but Wei maintains that the emperor will revoke his mistake on his own, and he does. After reinstating this official, Wei stubbornly returns to the issue of the trousseau. In a fourth comparison with the time of the beginning of the dynasty, Wei says: "In the beginning of this reign, the opinions of the multitude were collected and policies were reformed daily. Now one is content with order being already established. You are full of conceit, getting more extravagant from day to day, and love more and more to have fun. I serve Your Majesty, and I want to be an excellent minister; don't force me to be a loyal minister." The examples adduced to illustrate the difference between *liang*, excellence, and *zhong*, loyalty, were taken from the times of the notorious "bad last emperors" of antiquity, Jie and Zhou. Wei Zheng admonishes Taizong to take the last emperor of the immediately preceding dynasty, the notorious Yangdi of the Sui, as his "mirror," saying that if this is not done "today," and the emperor accepts remonstrance, there is a danger "that mountains and rivers cannot be kept," that is, of the demise of the dynasty. Whereupon Taizong dismisses Wei Zheng, but he takes it back after the intervention of the others. Wei Zheng then comes back to the issue of the trousseau. The emperor retreats to his chambers, and the empress hears him mumbling something about killing Wei Zheng and then he would have peace. The empress puts on an official court dress, and warmly congratulates the dumbfounded emperor. "Only because you are an enlightened ruler can Wei Zheng be a minister who talks straight and dares to remonstrate." She hands him a memorial detailing this point. The emperor cedes, and accepts Wei Zheng's remonstrance, and in the final moments of the play he is praised by Wei Zheng as an "enlightened ruler who truly has the Way."

Compared to the other pieces studied hitherto, *Tangwang na jian* is the most accommodating in terms of setting the historical screen for the present. We are not under Wanli or Jiajing, we are not under Jia Sidao, or in the last years of Wu Zetian during her new Zhou dynasty; nor are we under Khubilai Khan, either; our ruler is rather Tang Taizong, in the early and glorious years of the Tang dynasty. The play operates again with the pun Tang/*dang* (Party); the heroes who established the Tang with Li Shimin are still there, foremost among them Wei Zheng. They have the responsibility to remonstrate, and they live up to it. The emperor, true, has slipped in the last years; the references comparing the beginnings of the dynasty favorably with the "present" are numerous. The other pieces studied hitherto as a rule cast a low-level official or an intellectual in the role of potential remonstrator, speaking out for the people in general. Here a new candidate enters, the senior government leader from "liberation" times. Although times have indeed greatly improved, there still is hunger, and the danger of losing the empire is constantly present. How mighty seemed the Sui dynasty; it had unified the country and seemed stable enough, but within a few decades it had wasted its energy (a reference to the Chiang Kai-shek government). Wei Zheng does not mince his words; it is his duty to exaggerate, and to bring the problems out. He does indeed imply a comparison between Taizong and the bad last rulers Jie and Zhou, but only to show the possible consequences of wrong policies. The level of the conflict is greatly reduced. There is no villain in power; indeed, there is no villain in the center at all. No females are unjustly killed, and no land is grabbed. The emperor is capricious, it is true, but though he occasionally makes harsh threats, he is easily swayed because he knows the value of Wei Zheng, and his wife supports Wei Zheng's attitude. Remonstrance is reduced from a life-and-death matter to merely harsh words said to a comrade, and the threat of vengeance is rescinded as quickly as it is uttered. In this play, Wei Zheng redefines, defuses, and trivializes the extreme language of some of the earlier plays, especially of Meng Chao's and Tian Han's plays of 1961. The "friendly" ending suggests that things are under control in the center.

EPILOGUE

The Hai Rui theme stayed alive until 1963. But by then the attempts to revive it had already become quite desperate. Although *Guan Hanqing* was again staged and Tao Zhu had a Hai Rui film made, things had rapidly changed since the Tenth Plenum in September 1962 when Mao enjoined the Party to "never forget class struggle." Deng Tuo stopped his satirical *Evening Chats at Yanshan*, and the imitations of it were discontinued. The historical drama moved to the subject of Sino-Soviet relations, drawing on the rich lore of operas dealing with China's northern neighbors. By 1963, the battle for the stage was fought openly. Dramas on "contemporary themes" and glorifying Mao Zedong Thought gained precedence, and "class struggle" moved to the center. The differentiation that had been made for the old ruling classes into villains and Hai Ruis came to be suspect as "reformism" in historical materialist terms, and seen as an attack on the "revolutionary forces" in terms of contemporary politics. Finally, the literary debates moved from the stage, where Guo Moruo and Tian Han could even trade suggestions about each other's plays, to the interrogation centers and prisons. Around September 1962 the draft for Li Jiantong's novel *Liu Zhidan* was finished and submitted to the leadership for publication. Li Jiantong was the wife of Liu Jingyuan, who had been a friend of the book's hero, a guerrilla hero from the early northern Soviet areas. A leading cadre, who had been in the government of the old Shen-Gan Soviet area and had had differences of opinion with Liu Zhidan at the time, objected to the book's publication by the Gongren Press; he told Kang Sheng that the book promoted the reversal of the verdict of Gao Gang, who had been Liu's successor after his death, and had been purged in 1954. Kang Sheng, we learn from a memoir written by Li Jiantong,[108] had "a great deal of power at the time," and Kang decided that the novel was "counterrevolutionary." Kang is now credited with having coined the well-known phrase normally attributed to Mao (in September 1962) according to which "it was a great discovery to use novels to promote anti-Party activities"; the phrase in fact refers to *Liu Zhidan*, which Mao had not read at the time. The Tenth Plenum established a "working group" under Kang Sheng that attacked what was then described as the "Xi-Jia-Liu anti-Party clique." Between 1962 and 1966, large numbers of cadres were brought to Beijing for study classes, thousands of people were interrogated, and one person was executed. The novel criticized both "left" and "right" deviations, and the former was seen as a censure of Mao. With this secret police action against the writer and her informants, who were charged with embellishing themselves through the novel, the political climate froze. After the "contemporary theme" opera had won the political battle in the summer of 1964, the best the historical drama and its authors could do was fight weak defensive battles to limit the actions to be taken against them. Kang Sheng, who might well have recognized himself as candidate for chief villain in all too many pieces, was himself an amateur and connoisseur of the *kunqu* opera; with Jiang Qing, he had seen many plays performed when they were together in Hangzhou during the early sixties. But in the political battle the historical drama and its defenders lost out, and Kang Sheng used his machinery to persecute the critics, often in the very manner that the critics had anticipated in their plays.

108. Li Jiantong, *Liu Zhidan*, preface to vol. 1.

CONCLUSIONS

The plays on both sides of the factional divide share a common set of characters, plot devices, and allusions that enabled them to use a common language for the discussion of controversial problems. The high coincidence among the plays represents not so much a lack of originality as an attempt to make statements in a compatible way. There were, of course, also differences of opinion within each of the two main groups, sometimes depending on the time of writing.

In the Hai Rui group, the emperor is basically affirmed; there never is a demand for his overthrow. Affirmation of the emperor was a necessary ingredient to make the figure operative for the present, as the authors probably did not advocate the overthrow of the Chairman; or if they did, they could not have felt it opportune to say so. The main charges, however, consist of favoritism toward villains, blindness about the real situation of the country, the desire to achieve immortality in the realm of ideology and theory, and, combined with this, the creation of a personality cult. In many cases it will be stated that "earlier," things had been better. This always refers to an "earlier" under the same ruler or within the same dynasty, to match the present situation. The remonstrator, who can prevent the court from degenerating and the country from falling apart, is a social necessity. In Guo Moruo's plays and the Monkey piece, the hero is the leader himself. Criticism is either equated with slander or comes from an alien class or is a product of revisionist thinking. The emperor is the guarantor of prosperity and the guide on the Way.

The villain is in many of the plays depicted as running the country "now." If the plays give the date when the situation deteriorated, it is equivalent not to 1949, but to about 1956. The villain is not a representative of a class, but wields bureaucratic power based on the emperor's favor; mostly he is a rather crude caricature of radical views, a "leftist." The denunciation of the "bourgeois right" and the subsequent absence of legal protection in the People's Republic are shown not within the ideological system from which this attitude receives its legitimation, but denounced as essential and brutal terrorism. The collectivization of land and the transformation of peasants into agricultural laborers are not described in terms of their own rationale, but as "land-grabbing" by political power-holders. If in the Hai Rui group's plays the villain is a caricature of the "leftist," inversely, in Guo's plays the villain is the class enemy who wants to do away with

Wu Zetian's progressive "equal field system." This villain advocates a reduction of state interference in economic and property affairs, and is a "bourgeois rightist." The system of secret agents and political denunciation is described in the plays of the Hai Rui group as part of the villain's machinery, but in *Wu Zetian* as the necessary instrument of the empress to stay informed about the country and to ferret out counterrevolutionaries. Both sides advocate that their opponents should be violently done away with.

In the Hai Rui group, the hero is the remonstrator. Typically, he represents an image of the writer himself, and up until 1962 it seems that he always occupies a low rank. Candidates for the role of Hai Rui are to be found among the lower, and younger, members of the political class. Only with Wei Zheng do older leaders take on the role of remonstrators. The "people" appear in the remonstrator role only once, in *Da Qianlong*, but even there, the leadership is provided by the local *xiucai*, the bean-curd seller. Hypocrisy afflicts the court, even the potentially positive figure, the prime minister. The ministers are cowed by the emperor. The remonstrator, before the Wei Zheng plays, does not become the top leader of the country; rather, he puts enough pressure on the polity to eventually help the moderate prime minister into the saddle. The hero's loyalty is twofold, to the emperor as an institution, on the one hand, and to the "people," on the other—the latter being the primary factor. He is depicted as not merely hard and unbending, but knowing how to handle the real situation, flexible in his words and deeds, unbending in his principles. In Guo's plays, the hero is also the leader. The person appearing in the other plays as the remonstrator, here becomes the panegyrist for the Chairman once having seen the actual achievements of the Chairman's rule. Zhu Bajie, for example, eventually is the one who goes to the Flower-Fruit Mountain to ask Sun Wukong to return.

With the exception of Wei Zheng (and of the old minister Xu Long in *Sun An dongben*), the prime minister is an ambivalent figure in these plays. "The national champion of compromise" is one of the flattering terms used for a prime minister; generally speaking, his values are compatible with those of the hero, but he "knows the affairs of the world." Where the hero is in substance hard, and flexible only in his tactics, the prime minister figure is flexible through and through, sometimes stating that this is a time when one has to think of preserving one's life and position. In Guo Moruo's pieces, the trusted minister never has to contradict the emperor or empress because he or she is always right. He executes the orders of the Chairman, and sometimes softens the hard edges of this great being.

The people are fundamentally set off from the political class, the Party. The Party is variously depicted as an ethnic group, the *xiang-guan*, the officials in general, or the ruling family. The "people" are a passive but virtuous crowd whose role is "public opinion"; there is often a latent threat of armed rebellion from them. Their only hope, however, comes from enlightened members of the ruling group, on whom they heap flattery. It is a part of the polemical nature of these texts that the arrogation, by the villain, of "popular support" in the form of signature umbrellas and the like will be mentioned as a denunciation of the claim of "leftist" policies to have popular support. The people appear regularly in the form of the victimized pure and upright female. The people cannot speak out for themselves; therefore the hero (Hai Rui or the emperor) has to do it for them. Speaking for the people in their distress gives a high degree of legitimacy and urgency to the hero's endeavor.

The way in which respective playwrights assess the present time is reflected in their selection of a historical screen to deal with it. In terms of macro-time, variants range from the Wanli and Jiajing emperors on the one hand to Tang Taizong and Khubilai Khan on the other. In no case is the time of a "bad last emperor" selected, although in fact many remonstrators died in admonishing them. The differing uses of macro-time are most clearly visible in the exchange between Guo Moruo and Tian Han: Guo sets his play in the Tang dynasty at the height of Empress Wu's legitimate influence and power, and Tian responds by charging that "by now" she has in fact set up a new dynasty and her villainous relatives and secret police chiefs are running the country. In terms of seasonal time, the critical plays tend to use the symbolism of winter, late fall, night, and rain. Spring, summer, and brightness dominate in pieces like *Cai Wenji*. The same division can be observed in the authors' respective assessments of the economic situation, where images of famine, drought, refugees, and terror are confronted with benign images of bumper harvests, regular seasons, and contented faces of the people—the conflicting images describing the very same time and reality. Reference to the present is made through the use, on stage, of phrases depicting the desperate (or glorious) situation that prevails "now," with the "now" referring *on stage* to the historical time, but *in the audience* to the present.

The plays in the Hai Rui tradition constantly quote each other in certain images and values. Some examples: The "licorice root," the "hypocrite," "speaking for the people," "eliminating tyrants," "returning the land," "serving the state," "speaking out," "cursing" the villain and the emperor, "hitting" the villain and the emperor. The most compelling image is certainly the latent allusion to the "ghosts of the unjustly slain," which provided an interpretive horizon for Meng Chao's play when it eventually made it on stage. Li Huiniang—wafting through memory with her "ghost-step," immeasurably strengthened by death, and bringing down a mighty Jia Sidao with his sword in his helpless hand—was quite a compelling image. This image was situated within the play, however, in the realm of the ghosts, the anticipation of and speculation about things to come.

The debate between the two camps divides strictly along factional lines. Hai Rui is unabashedly glorified in one group; the remonstrators are vilified in the other. The plays do not address the other camp, but the public, to whom the texts offer both an interpretation of the present situation and a way to solve its problems. The two camps deal with each other with hatred, anger, and threats of physical annihilation. Already by 1958, the temperature of the Chinese body politic had risen to a fever pitch. One might doubt the wisdom and health of a political culture in which the resolution of a dispute can be envisaged only in the form of the opponent's elimination.

Needless to say, with the return to power of Deng Xiaoping and his associates, the authors of the plays criticized in the sixties were rehabilitated and their plays were restaged.[109] Simultaneously, a new series of historical plays began, often continuing in the old vein. For instance, a play entitled *Tang Taizong* focuses on the "internal turmoil of the Tang house" associated with the incident of the Xuanwu gate, in which the emperor's brother set himself up against the emperor, who eventually prevailed because of the recruitment of such luminaries as Wei Zheng.[110] Another play, *Tang Taizong yu Wei Zheng*,[111] also takes

109. See chap. 2, n. 114 for *Xie Yaohuan*, chap. 4, nn. 43 and 51 for *Hai Rui shangshu*, and the special issue of *Beijing Meng xun* devoted to the official ceremonies to commemorate Wu Han in September 1979, "Daonian Wu Huan tongzhi zhuankan." I am deeply grateful to Professor Wu Xiaoling for offering me his copy of this issue.

110. Li Lun, *Tang Taizong*, as reviewed by Guo Hancheng in "Mantan jingju *Tang Taizong*."

111. Li Minsheng and Yang Zhiping, *Tang Taizong yu Wei Zheng*; see also their "Cong lishi shenshi chufa—huaju *Tang Taizong yu Wei Zheng* chuangzuo diandi tihui."

up the theme of the relationship of the emperor with his senior advisers. In *Hai Rui sou gong*,[112] Hai Rui foils a plot by the empress to set up a faction and grab political power. Authors such as Bai Hua have on occasion returned to the use of the historical play, although it seems that time is running out for these plays, as the young seem to lack the knowledge, the sophistication, and the gusto needed for the appreciation of such arcane matters.

112. Zhao Ximing and Li Shiwu, *Hai Rui sou gong*, as reviewed in *Renmin xiju* 1982.2, inside flap.

Glossary

Ahmad 阿合馬
Alihaiya 阿里海牙

badou 巴豆
Baishe 白蛇
baixing 百姓
bangzi ling 棒子嶺
Bao (Judge) 包
bao 暴
Bao Gong'an 包公安
Baoxiang guo 寶象國
batuo 巴豆
Bei 貝
beidou 北斗
Beijing Renmin Yishu Juyuan
　北京人民藝術劇院
benben zhuyi 本本主義
Bo Yan 伯顏
Bozhou 博州
Bufu lao 不俯老

cai (to guess) 猜
cai (talent) 才
Cai Meibiao 蔡美彪
Cai Shaobing 蔡少炳
Cai Wenji 蔡文姬
Cai Xitao 蔡希陶

Cambaluc 大都
Cao Cao 曹操
Cao E 曹娥
Cao Pei 曹丕
Chang'an 長安
chao 朝
chaonong huang 嘲弄皇
chaoting 朝廷
Chen Kehan 陳克寒
Chen Suzhen 陳素眞
Chen Yi 陳毅
Cheng Jiaojin 程咬金
Cheng Yangqiu 程硯秋
chengxiang 丞相
chiren 吃人
chongchen 寵臣
chou 丑
Chu 楚
chuba 除霸
chujia 出家
Chun'an 淳安
ci 詞

da 打
da gunzi 大棍子
da huang (trouncing the
　emperor) 打皇

325

Dade　大德
dahuang (a medicinal herb,
　　laxative)　大黃
Dai Bufan　戴不凡
Danao tiangong　大鬧天宮
dang　黨
danwei　單位
danxiao　胆小
dao　道
dasheng Mao　大聖毛
dayuejin　大躍進
de　德
decai　德才
Deng Tuo　鄧拓
Deng Xiaoping　鄧小平
Deng Youmei　鄧友梅
Di Renjie　狄仁杰
Di Xinshi　狄辛飾
dianpei liuli　顛沛流離
Dong Zhuo　董卓
Donghai　東海
Dou E　竇娥
duoshi　多事

erguang　耳光

Fa Hai　法海
fahuan tian　發還田
fan　反
fan Cao Cao　翻曹操
fanshang　反上
Feng Mu　馮牧
Fengshen yanyi　封神演義
fennu tuoma　憤怒唾罵
fennu zema　憤怒責罵
fozhi　佛旨
fushou tie'er　俯首帖耳

gancao　甘草
gang　剛
ganzuo ganwei　敢作敢為
Gao　高
Gao Gang　高崗
Gao Ge　高戈
Gao Xiaosheng　高曉聲
gaomi　告密
Gaozong　高宗

Ge Biao　葛彪
Gou Jian　勾踐
Guan Hanqing　關漢卿
Guan Yu　關羽
guanxi　關係
gui dongxi　鬼東西
guilian　鬼臉
Guloushan Houwang ji
　　shimo　骷髏山猴王擊屍魔
Guo Moruo　郭沫若
guogong　國公
Guomindang　國民黨

Hai Rui　海瑞
Hai Rui baguan　海瑞罷官
Hai Rui chuxun　海瑞出巡
Hai Rui ma huangdi　海瑞罵皇帝
Hai Rui shangshu　海瑞上疏
Han　漢
Hangzhou　杭州
haoduo haoduo de　好多好多的
haoqiang　豪強
haoren zhuyi　好人主義
He　何
He Long　賀龍
He Yishang　何以尚
He Zongbing　賀總兵
hen　恨
henda de qifa　很大的啓發
Hong Xiannü　紅綫女
Honglou meng　紅樓夢
Hongmei　紅梅
hongnong renshi　弘農人氏
hongqiang　紅墙
Hongwu　洪武
Horikhoson　和禮霍森
Hou Wailu　侯外廬
hou xue ren　猴學人
Hu Qiaomu　胡喬木
Hu Yaobang　胡耀邦
hua　花
Hua Guofeng　華國峰
huadan　花旦
huagu　花鼓
Huai (king)　懷
huaiju　淮劇
huaju　話劇

huan tian 還田

Huang Boxian 黄伯賢

Huang Junyao 黄俊耀

Huang Yide 黄義德

Huangbao guai 黄袍怪

huanglian 黄連

huiqi 晦氣

Hujia shiba pai 胡笳十八排

Ji Dengkui 紀登奎

Jia Sidao 賈似道

Jiajing 嘉靖

Jiajing Jiajing, jiajia huhu,
 gangan jingjing
 嘉靖嘉靖, 家家戶戶, 干干淨淨

jian 劍

Jian Bozan 剪伯贊

Jiang Qing 江青

Jiangnan 江南

jianzei 奸賊

Jiao Juyin 焦菊隱

Jiaru woshi zhende 假如我是眞的

Jie 桀

jigang zhengdun 紀綱整頓

Jinggangshan 井岡山

Jinlun shengshen huangdi
 金輪聖神皇帝

jiyu 寄寓

juben huang 劇本荒

jun 鈞

juntian 均田

kai yanlu 開言路

Kang Sheng 康生

Ke Qingshi 柯慶施

kexi meiyou benling 可惜沒有本領

Koshin 忽辛

Kuhan ting 苦寒廳

kunqu 昆曲

Lai Junchen 來俊臣

laitou 來頭

Lan Tianye 藍天野

Lao Ah 老阿

Lao Can 老殘

Lao Can youji 老殘遊記

lao jiu 老九

Lao She 老舍

Lao Wu 老無

lao wuhao zi 老五號字

laoweng 老翁

laozhang 老長

Laozi 老子

Li 李

Li (Donkey) 李

Li Chao 李超

Li Decai 李得才

Li Duokui 李多奎

Li Fanggui 李芳桂

Li Huiniang 李慧娘

Li Kui 李逵

Li Shimin 李世民

Li Yan 黎彥

Li Yizhe 李義哲

Li Yufang 李毓芳

Li Zhiyan 黎之彥

Liang Cai 梁材

Liang Jinzhi 梁進之

liangjia 良家

Liangshanbo 梁山泊

Liangxin dou 兩心斗

Liao Chengzhi 廖承志

Liao Mosha 廖沫沙

Lin Biao 林彪

Lin Xiling 林希翎

lishi gushi 歷史故事

lishi ju 歷史劇

Liu (Long-life) 劉

Liu (Mrs.) 劉氏

Liu Binyan 劉賓雁

Liu E 劉鶚

Liu Mingzhu 劉明珠

Liu Shanren 劉善人

Liu Shaoqi 劉少奇

Liu Shaotang 劉紹棠

Liu Zhidan 劉志丹

Liu Zhiming 劉芝明

Lü 呂

Lu Dingyi 陸定一

Lu Xun 魯迅

Lu Zhailang 魯齋郎

Lü Zhenyu 呂振羽

luanguo 亂國

Lugou 蘆溝

Luo Binwang　駱賓王
Luo Tong　羅通
Lushan　龐山

ma　罵
mahuang　罵皇
Ma Lianliang　馬連良
Ma Shaobo　馬少波
Ma Shiceng　馬師曾
mama　罵罵
mantou　饅頭
Mao Dun　茅盾
Mao Zedong　毛澤東
Mei Lanfang　梅蘭芳
Meng Yundi　孟雲棣
mian you caise　面有菜色
Mingshi　明史
Mingtang　明堂
Minzu gong　民族宮
mu　畝

nanxun　南巡
neibu　內部
neihang　內行
ni cai de dui　你猜得對
Nie Yuanzu　聶元祖
Niu Rongliang　紐榮亮
Nü xun'an　女巡按
nüedai　虐待

Ouyang Shanzun　歐陽山尊
Ouyang Yuqing　歐陽豫倩

panhuan　盤桓
pazhan　霸佔
Pei Shunqing　裴舜卿
Pei Yan　裴嚴
Peng Dehuai　彭德懷
Peng Zhen　彭眞
Pingding shan　平頂山
pingju　評劇
pola　潑辣

Qi Yanming　齊燕銘
Qian Junrui　錢俊瑞
Qianlong　乾隆
qiaomiao　巧妙

Qin　秦
Qin Gui　秦檜
Qin Xianglian　秦香蓮
qing　清
Qing mei Houwang　請美猴王
qingguan　清官
qitian　齊天
Qitian dasheng　齊天大聖
Qiu Shengrong　裘盛戎
qu　曲
Qu Yuan　屈原

Rao Shushi　饒漱石
ren xue hou　人學猴
Renmin juchang　人民劇場
Renmin yishuyuan　人民藝術院
Renyao zhi jian　人妖之間
ru　儒
Ruan Hua　阮華
ruanhua　軟化

Sa　薩
Sai Lianxiu　賽廉秀
sanda　三打
Sanda baigujing　三打白骨精
Sanguo　三國
Sanguo zhi yanyi　三國志演義
Sanjia cun　三家村
Sanyang　三陽
Sanzang　三藏
seiji shosetsu　政治小說
Semu　色目
Seng Zhao　僧肇
Sha　沙
Shaanxi　陝西
shan yu ren　善于人
Shangguan Wan'er　上官婉兒
Shangguan Yi　上官儀
Shao Quanlin　邵荃麟
Shaoxing　紹興
shehui diaocha　社會調查
Shen Li　沈理
shiyan　失言
Shizong　世宗
shou　壽
Shouan　壽安
Shu Xiuwen　舒綉文

Shuihu zhuan　水湖傳
Song　宋
Song Kanfu　宋侃夫
Su Dingfang　蘇定方
Sun An　孫安
Sun Bao　孫保
Sun Cunli　孫存立
Sun Tianbao　孫天豹
Sun Wukong　孫悟空
Sun Wukong xiangyao fumo
　孫悟空降妖伏魔
Sun Yangsheng　孫陽生
Sun Yat-sen　孫中山

Taiping　太平
Taizong　太宗
Tang　唐
Tang Jiuyuan　唐久遠
Tang Seng　唐僧
Tangshu　唐書
Tao Xiong　陶雄
Tao Zhu　陶鑄
texie　特寫
Tian Han　田漢
tianbing　天兵
Tianshu　天樞
tiaobo　挑撥
tiaoting guoshou　調停國手
tuitian　退田
tuntian　屯田

waihang　外行
Wan Laiming　萬籟鳴
Wang Dongxing　王東興
Wang Guangmei　王光美
Wang Guiwai　王貴外
Wang Mang　王莽
Wang Ming　王明
Wang Renzhong　王任重
Wang Shiwei　王實味
Wang Wenjuan　王文娟
Wang Yi　王義
Wang Yuhuai　王玉環
Wang Zhu　王著
Wanli　萬曆
Wei　魏
Wei (Empress)　韋

Wei Guoqing　韋國清
Wei Zheng　魏徵
weifeng shaqi　威風殺氣
wen　文
Wen Tianxiang　文天祥
wenlian　文聯
Wenxue yichan　文學遺產
wenyan　文言
wo shule　我輸了
Wu (military)　武
Wu (a state)　吳
Wu Chen　吳琛
Wu De　武德
Wu Feng　吳楓
Wu Fengzhao　吳鳳招
Wu Han　吳晗
Wu Hong　武宏
Wu Sansi　武三思
Wu Xiaoling　吳曉鈴
Wu Xun　武訓
Wu Yiguo　吳藝國
Wu Zetian　武則天
Wu Zixu　伍子胥
Wu Zuguang　吳祖光
Wutong　梧桐
wuxin zhengfa　無心正法

Xia Yan　夏衍
xian　縣
xiandaiju　現代劇
xiang dangdang　響噹噹
xiangguan　鄉官
xiangju　湘劇
Xiangyang　襄陽
xiangyuan　鄉願
xiao baogao　小報告
xiao shuo　小說
Xie　謝
Xie Yaohuan　謝瑤環
xiejian chanxiao　脅肩諂笑
xiezi　楔子
Xin　新
Xin Yuanshi　新元史
xinbian lishiju　新編歷史劇
xinggong　行宮
Xingtai　興泰
xiqu　戲曲

xiucai　秀才
xiuxi　休息
xiuyang　修養
xiuzhengzhui　修正主義
xiuzou　羞走
Xiyou ji　西遊記
Xu Jie　徐階
Xu Jingye　徐敬業
Xu Long　徐龍
Xu Tongjian gangmu　續通鑒綱目
Xu Ying　徐瑛
Xu Yougong　徐有功
Xuan Zang　玄奘
xue　血
xueyi　雪意
xun'an　巡按
xunyou　巡游

Yan Song　嚴嵩
Yang (Lord)　楊
Yang Xianzhi　楊顯之
Yang Zui　楊最
Yanshan yehua　燕山夜話
Yao Wenyuan　姚文元
yaohuan　要還
Ye Hefu　葉和甫
yi ba hekui dasheng mao
　　一拔何虧大聖毛
yi gu yu jin　以古喻今
yijian　意見
Yinyuetang　音樂堂
Yiyang　益陽
Yong Wenshou　雍文濤
yongyetian　永業田
yongyue　踴躍
you chengxiang　右丞相
youdao　有道
Yu　禹
Yu Xun　魚訊
Yuan　元
yuan　冤
Yuan Hua　袁華
Yuan Leshan　袁樂山
Yuan Xingjian　袁行健
yuanhua jiqiao　圓滑機巧
Yuanshi　元史
Yue　越

Yue Fei　岳飛
yueju　粵劇
yuju　豫劇

zaju　雜劇
zaofan　造反
zawen　雜文
zetian　則天
Zetian Huangdi　則天皇帝
Zhang Biao　張彪
Zhang Chunqiao　張春橋
Zhang Cong　張從
Zhang Jianzhi　張柬之
Zhang Pinghua　張平化
Zhang Zhibo　張志伯
Zhanguo　戰國
zhangyi zhi yan　仗義執言
Zhao　趙
Zheng Zhenduo　鄭振鐸
zhengchi jigang　整飭紀綱
zhengdan　正旦
zhengdun gangwei　整頓綱維
Zhengqi ge　正氣歌
zhengzhi xiaoshuo　政治小說
Zhengzhou　鄭州
Zhenjiang　鎮江
zhi　旨
zhiqu　知趣
zhishi fenzi　知識分子
zhishi renren　志士仁人
zhongdian jumu　重點劇目
zhongjian pai　中間派
Zhongju　仲舉
zhongju　衆舉
Zhongzong　中宗
Zhou (an emperor's name)　紂
Zhou (a state)　周
Zhou Enlai　周恩來
Zhou Hetong　周和桐
Zhou Xinfang　周信芳
Zhou Xing　周興
Zhou Yang　周揚
Zhou Yibai　周貽白
Zhouyi　周易
Zhu Bajie　猪八戒
Zhu Lianxiu　朱廉秀
Zhu Xiaolan　朱小蘭

Zhu Yuanzhang　朱元章　　　　zhuanzhi wangguo　專制王國
zhuanheng　專橫　　　　　　　zijiaren　自家人
zhuanshuo　傳說　　　　　　　zuizuibaode jun　最最暴的君

Bibliography

Ansley, Clive, trans. *The Heresy of Wu Han: His Play "Hai Rui's Dismissal" and Its Role in China's Cultural Revolution.* Toronto: University of Toronto Press, 1971.

Ashton, B., et al. "Famine in China, 1958–61." *Population and Development Review* 10.4, 1984.

The Australian Journal of Chinese Affairs.

Bai Wei 白危. "Bei weikun de nongzhuang zhuxi" 被圍困的農庄主席 (The Besieged Village Head). *Renmin wenxue* 1957.4.

Ban Gu 班固. *Hanshu* 漢書. Beijing: Zhonghua shuju, 1975.

Bao Lei 包蕾. *Zhu Bajie xinzhuan* 豬八戒新傳 (A New Biography of Zhu Bajie). Shanghai: Shaonian ertong Press, 1962; 1978.

Bao Lei 包蕾 and Sun Yi 孫毅. "Zhu Bajie xue benling" 豬八戒學本領 (Zhu Bajie Acquires a Qualification). *Juben* 1962.7.

Bao Shiyuan 鮑世遠 and Gong Yijiang 龔義江. "Kan Shaoju *Sun Wukong sanda baigujing*" 看紹劇《孫悟空三打白骨精》 (Seeing the Shaoxing Opera "Sun Wukong Three Times Beats the White-Bone Demon"). *Xijubao* 1960.23/24.

Beijing daxue xuebao 北京大學學報 (Journal of Beijing University).

Beijing daxue zhongwenxi lilun jiaoyanshi 北京大學中文系理論教研室, ed. *Wenxue lilun xuexi ziliao* 文學理論學習資料 (Study Materials for Theory of Literature). 2 vols. Beijing: Beijing daxue Press, 1980.

Beijing Meng xun 北京盟訊.

Beijing Qiche zhizaochang gongren lilun yanjiusuo 北京汽車制造廠工人理論研究所. *Lü hou qiren* 呂后其人 (What Kind of Person Was Empress Lü?). Beijing: Zhonghua shuju, 1977.

Beijing Review.

Beijing ribao 北京日報 (Beijing Daily).

Beijing shi wenlian "Xiang Taiyang" geming zaofan bingtuan "Jinjunhao" zhandoudui 北京市文聯《向太陽》革命造反兵團《進軍號》戰鬥隊. "Jiekai tehao ducao *Hai Rui baguan* de heimu" 揭開特號毒草《海瑞罷官》的黑幕 (Opening the Curtain on the Special Poisonous Weed "Hai Rui Dismissed from Office"). *Xiju zhanbao*, June 7, 1967.

Beijing shifan daxue wenyi lilun zu 北京師范大學文藝理論組, ed. *Wenxue lilun xuexi cankao ziliao* 文學理論學習參考資料(Reference Material for the Study of Theory of Literature). Beijing: Gaodeng jiaoyu Press, 1956.

Beijing wenyi 北京文藝 (Beijing Literature and Arts).

Beijing wenyi zhanbao 北京文藝戰報 (Battle News on Beijing Literature and Arts).

"Beitong hua wei hantianli" 悲痛化為撼天力 (Transform Grief into a Power that Moves Heaven). In *Tiananmen shiwenji, xubian*. Beijing: Beijing Press, 1979.

ben Maimon, Moses. *The Guide for the Perplexed*. Trans. Shlomo Peres. Chicago: University of Chicago Press, 1963.

Bernard, Elizabeth Jeannette M. T. "T'ian Han's 'Reactionary Works': 1956–1962." In G. de la Lama, ed. *30th International Congress of Human Sciences in Asia and North Africa, China 1*. Mexico City: Colegio de Mexico, 1982.

Bernstein, Thomas. "Stalinism, Famine, and Chinese Peasants: Grain Procurement during the Great Leap Forward." *Theory and Society* 13.3, 1984.

Boswell, James. "A Tragedy of Good Intentions: Post-Mao Views of the Great Leap Forward." Unpublished manuscript, 1985.

Bupagui zhandoudui 不怕鬼戰鬥隊 (Battle Contingent Not Afraid of Ghosts). "Sun Wukong sida baigujing" 孫悟空四打白骨精 (Sun Wukong Four Times Beats the White-Bone Demon). *Jinggangshan*, Feb. 1, 1967.

Cao Yu 曹禺, Mei Qian 梅阡, and Yu Shizhi 于是之, with Cao Yu "holding the pen." *Danjian pian* 胆劍篇. Beijing: Zhongguo xiju Publ., 1962.

Chai Liyang 柴立揚 and Li Ganxing 黎干行 (text). Han Wu 韓伍 and Jiang Xiangnian 姜幸年 (drawings). *Sun Wukong xinlixian ji* 孫悟空新歷險記 (New Dangers Encountered by Sun Wukong). Changsha: Hunan renmin Press, 1982.

Chan, Anita, and Jonathan Unger, eds. *The Case of Li I-che. Chinese Law and Government* 10.3, 1977.

"Chedi qingsuan Tian Han de fandang zuixing" 徹底清算田漢的反黨罪行 (Thoroughly Expose the Anti-Party Crimes of Tian Han). *Guangming ribao*, Dec. 6, 1966.

Chen Kehan 陳克寒. "Baihua qifang he zhengzhi guashuai" 百花齊放和政治掛帥 (On Letting a Hundred Flowers Bloom and the Leading Role of Politics). *Beijing wenyi* 1960.3. Orig. in *Qianxian* 1960.4.

Chen Xi 陳曦. "*Shengsi pai* ji qi luncheng" 生死牌及其論爭 ("Tablets of Life and Death" and the Discussion about It). *Renmin ribao*, June 30, 1959.

Cheng, L. *The Politics of the Red Army*. Stanford: Stanford University Press, 1966.

Cheng Yangqiu 程硯秋. "Tan Dou E" 談竇娥 (On Dou E). *Xiju luncong* 1958.1.

Chinese Law and Government.

Chinese Literature.

Chongfang de xianhua 重放的鮮花 (Fresh Flowers Released Again). Shanghai: Shanghai renmin Press, 1979.

"Communique of the Third Plenum of the 11th Central Committee of the Chinese Communist Party, Dec. 22, 1978." *Beijing Review* 1978.52.

Comparative Drama.

"Cultural Exchanges between China and other Countries in 1957." *Chinese Literature* 1958.2.

Dai Ping 戴平. "Han Zang ruchao kan jiangpa" 漢藏如潮看蔣葩 *Xiju yishu* 1979.3/4.

Danjian pian. See Cao Yu et al.

"Daonian Wu Han tongzhi zhuankan" 悼念吳晗同志專刊 (Special Issue in Commemoration of Comrade Wu Han). *Beijing Meng xun* 2, Sept. 1979.

Ding Cong 丁聰. "Xiyou xinji" 西遊新記 (1979) (A New Record of a Journey to the West). In Ding Cong 丁聰, *Zuotian de shiqing* 昨天的事情 (Yesterday's Events). Beijing: Sanlian, 1987.

Ding Xuelei 丁學雷. "*Hai Rui shangshu* wei shei xiaolao" 《海瑞上疏》為誰効勞 (To Whom Does "Hai Rui Sends Up a Memorial" Render Service?). In Shanghai jingjuyuan, *Hai Rui shangshu.* Shanghai: Shanghai Wenyi Press, 1979.

Du Renzhi 杜任之. "Huainian geming shixuejia Wu Han tongzhi" 懷念革命史學家吳晗同志 (In Commemoration of the Revolutionary Historian, Comrade Wu Han). In *Wu Han he Hai Rui baguan.* Beijing: Renmin Press, 1979.

Dumas, Alexandre. *Joseph Balsamo.* Translated into English as *Memoirs of a Physician.* London: Routledge and Sons, 1879.

Eberstein, Bernd. *Das Chinesische Theater im 20. Jahrhundert* (The Chinese Theater in the Twentieth Century). Wiesbaden: Harassowitz Publ., 1983.

Erling, Johnny, and Dieter v. Graeve. *Tigermaske und Knochengespenst, die neue chinesische Karikatur* (Tiger Mask and Bony Specter—the New Chinese Caricature). Cologne: Prometh Verlag, 1978.

"Excerpts from P'eng Te-huai's Talk at the Meeting of the Northern Group of the Lushan Meeting." In Union Research Institute, *The Case of P'eng Te-huai 1959–1968.* Hongkong: Union Research Institute, 1968.

Fan Ye 范業. *Hou Hanshu* 後漢書 (History of the Later Han). Kaiming shuju ed.

Fang Jing 方靜. "Dui Kang Sheng de qingsuan yu 'fei Mao hua'" 對康生的清算與《非毛化》(On the Purge of Kang Sheng and "Demaoization"). *Zhonggong yanjiu* 14.9, 1980.

Fang Zesheng 方澤生. "*Hai Rui shangshu* bixu jixu pipan" 《海瑞上疏》必須繼續批判 (Criticism of "Hai Rui Sends Up a Memorial" Has to Be Continued). In Shanghai jingjuyuan, ed., *Hai Rui shangshu.*

Fei Xiaotong 費孝通. "Zhishifenzi de zaochun tianqi" 知識分子的早春天氣 (Early Spring Weather for the Intellectuals). *Renmin ribao,* Mar. 24, 1957.

Feng Qiyong 馮其庸. "Cong *Lüyi ren zhuan* dao *Li Huiniang*" 從《綠衣

人傳》到《李慧娘》(From "The Woman in Green" to "Li Huiniang"). *Beijing wenyi* 1962.11.

Fisher, Tom. "'The Play's the Thing': Wu Han and Hai Rui Revisited." *The Australian Journal of Chinese Affairs* 1982.7.

Fitzgerald, C. P. *The Empress Wu.* London: The Cresset Press, 1968.

Forte, A. *Political Propaganda and Ideology in China at the End of the Seventh Century.* Naples: Instituto Orientale di Napoli, 1976.

Franke, Herbert, ed. *Sung Biographies.* Wiesbaden: Steiner Verlag, 1976–.

Fu Junwen 傅駿文. "Tan yueju *Zetian Huangdi*" 談越劇《則天皇帝》(On the Cantonese Opera "Empress [Wu] Zetian"). *Wenhuibao,* June 14, 1959.

Gan Bao 干寶. *Soushen ji* 搜神記 (Searching for the Gods). Congshu jicheng ed. Shanghai: Commercial Press, 1935–40.

Gao Guoping 高國平. "'Fan'an hefang fufen duo'" 翻案何妨傅粉多 ("When Reversing a Verdict One Cannot Avoid Adding Too Much Rouge"). *Henan Shidaxuebao* 1982.5. Repr. in *Xiju yanjiu* 1982.10.

Gao Made 高馬得. "Sanda baigujing xinbian" 三打白骨精新編 (A New Edition of "Three Times Beating the White-Bone Demon"). In *Lishi de shenpan—jiepi 'Sirenbang' manhua xuan.* Shanghai: Shanghai renmin meishu Press, 1979.

Gao Qili 高濟立. "Cong *Nü xun'an* dao *Xie Yaohuan,* jian tan *Xie Yaohuan* juben gaibian de chengjiu" 從《女巡按》到《謝瑤環》—簡談《謝瑤環》劇本改編的成就 (From "The Inspectress" to "Xie Yaohuan," Notes on the Achievements in Rewriting "Xie Yaohuan"). *Shaanxi ribao,* Dec. 12, 1961. Repr. in Shanghai xiju xueyuan, Xiju wenxue xi, ed., *Tian Han zhuanji,* vol. 2.

Glaubitz, Joachim. *Opposition gegen Mao, Abendgespräche am Yenshan und andere politische Dokumente* (Evening Chats at Yenshan and Other Political Documents). Olten: Walter Verlag, 1969.

Goldman, Merle. "Party Policies toward the Intellectuals: The Unique Blooming and Contending of 1961–62." In John W. Lewis, ed., *Party Leadership and Revolutionary Power in China.* Cambridge: Cambridge University Press, 1970.

Goldman, Merle, ed., with Timothy Cheek and Carol Lee Hamrin. *Chinese Intellectuals and the State: In Search of a New Relationship.* Cambridge, Mass.: Harvard East Asian Monographs, 1987.

de Groot, J. J. M. *Sectarianism and Religious Persecution in China.* Reprint. Taibei: Literature House, 1963.

Gu Ertan 顧爾鐔. "Cong *Xiyou ji* suo xiangqide" 從《西游記》所想起的 (Thoughts Evoked by "The Journey to the West"). *Wenyibao* 1980.6.

Guan Hanqing 關漢卿. *Dandao hui* 單刀會 ([Lord Guan Goes to the] Feast with a Single Sword). In Renmin wenxue bianjibu, ed., *Guan Hanqing juqu xuan.* Beijing: Renmin wenxue Press, 1958.

———. "Doktor Ching und seine Base, oder Der Yadisspiegel" (Doctor Ching and His Niece, or the Jade Mirror). In H. Rüdelsberger, *Altchinesische Liebeskomödien.* Vienna, 1923.

———. "Die Ehen des Fräuleins Schmetterling" (The Marriages of Miss Butterfly). In H. Rüdelsberger, *Altchinesische Liebeskomödien.* Vienna, 1923.

———. *Gantian dongdi Dou E yuan* 感天動地竇娥冤 (The Injustice Done to Dou E Which Moved Heaven and Shook the Earth). In Wu Xiaoling et al., eds., *Da xijujia Guan Hanqing jiezuo ji*. Beijing: Zhongguo xiju Press, 1958.

———. *Guan Zhang shuangfu xishu meng* 關張雙赴西蜀夢 (The Dream of Western Shu). In Wu Xiaoling et al., eds., *Da xijujia Guan Hanqing jiezuo ji*. Beijing: Zhonguo xiju Press, 1958.

———. "Rescued by a Coquette." *Chinese Literature* 1957.1.

———. "Snow in Midsummer." In Yang Hsien-yi and Gladys Yang, trans., *Selected Plays of Kuan Han-ch'ing*. Beijing: Foreign Languages Press, 1958.

"*Guan Hanqing* zai Riben" 關漢卿在日本 (*Guan Hanqing* in Japan). *Yangcheng wanbao* (Yangcheng Evening News). Apr. 4, 1959.

Guangming ribao 光明日報 (Clarté Daily).

"Guanyu lishiju *Cai Wenji* de taolun" 關于歷史劇《蔡文姬》的討論 (The Discussion about the Historical Drama "Cai Wenji"). *Hongyan* 1980.1.

Guillermaz, Jacques. *The Chinese Communist Party in Power 1949–1976*. Trans. A. Destenay. Boulder: Westview Press, 1976.

Guisso, Richard W. L. "The Reigns of the Empress Wu, Chung-tsung, and Jui-tsung (684–712)." In D. Twitchett, ed., *The Cambridge History of China*. Vol. 3, *Sui and T'ang China, 589–906*, Pt. 1. Cambridge: Cambridge University Press, 1979.

———. *Wu Tse-t'ien and the Politics of Legitimation in T'ang China*. Bellingham: Western Washington University, 1978.

Guo Hancheng 郭漢城. "Mantan jingju *Tang Taizong*" 漫談京劇《唐太宗》 (Notes on the Peking Opera "Emperor Tai of the Tang Dynasty"). *Renmin xiju* 1982.12.

Guo Moruo 郭沫若. *Cai Wenji* 蔡文姬. S.l.: Wenwu Publ., 1959.

———. "Guanyu *Guan Hanqing* de tongxin 關於《關漢卿》的通信 (Letter on *Guan Hanqing*). In Shanghai xiju xueyuan, Xiju wenxue xi, ed., *Tian Han zhuanji*.

———. "Kan *Sun Wukong sanda baigujing* shuzeng Zhejiang sheng shaojutuan" 看《孫悟空三打白骨精》書贈浙江省紹劇團 (Seeing "Sun Wukong Three Times Beats the White-Bone Demon"—Written as a Present to the Shaoxing Opera Troupe of Zhejiang Province). *Renmin ribao*, Nov. 1, 1961.

———. *Qu Yuan* 屈原. Orig. 1942; Beijing: Renmin wenxue Publ., 1954.

———. "Wo zenyang xie *Wu Zetian?*" 我怎樣寫《武則天》? (How Did I Write "Wu Zetian")? In Guo Moruo, *Wu Zetian*. Zhongguo xiju ed., 1962.

———. *Wu Zetian* 武則天. *Renmin wenxue* 1960.5.

———. *Wu Zetian* 武則天. Beijing: Zhongguo xiju Publ., 1962; repr. Beijing: Renmin wenxue Publ., 1979.

———. "'Yuyou chengqing wanli ai,' du Mao zhuxi youguan *Sun Wukong sanda baigujing* de yishou qilü" 玉宇澄清萬里埃，讀毛主席有關《孫悟空三打白骨精》的一首七律 (The Jadelike Firmament Is Cleared for Ten Thousand Miles—Reading Chairman Mao's Poem about "Sun Wukong Three Times Beats the White-Bone Demon"). *Guangming ribao*, May 31, 1964.

———. "Zai Kunming kan yanchu huaju *Wu Zetian* 在昆明看演出話劇

《武則天》(Seeing the Spoken Drama "Wu Zetian" in Kunming). In *Dong-fanji*. Quoted in Gao Guoping, "Fan'an hefang fufen duo." *Henan Shida-xuebao* 1982.5.

Guo Moruo 郭沫若 and Jian Bozan 翦伯贊, eds. *Cao Cao lunji* 曹操論集 (Essays on Cao Cao). Shanghai: Sanlian Books, 1959; repr. Hongkong, 1979.

Guo Xinghua 郭星華. "*Hai Rui baguan* shi zenyang xiechulai de" 《海瑞罷官》是怎樣寫出來的 (How "Hai Rui Dismissed from Office" Was Written). In *Wu Han xueshu shengya*. Jiangxi: Jiangxi renmin Press, 1984.

Gutian wenxue chubanshe, ed. *Guan Hanqing yanjiu lunwenji* 關漢卿研究論文集 (Studies on Guan Hanqing). Shanghai: Gutian wenxue Press, 1958.

"*Hai Rui baguan* chulong de qianqian houhou" 《海瑞罷官》出籠的前前後後 (How "Hai Rui Dismissed from Office" Came Out—The Inside Story). *Beijing xinwenyi*, Sept. 21, 1967.

Hai Rui shangshu. See Shanghai jingjuyuan.

He Lingyun 何凌雲, adapt. *Hua da chao* 花打朝 (The Ladies Beat Up the Emperor). *Juben* 1962.2

He Qifang 何其芳. "Ping *Xie Yaohuan*" 評《謝瑤環》(On "Xie Yaohuan"). *Wenxue pinglun* 1966.1.

He Yantai 何寅泰 and Li Dasan 李達三. *Tian Han pingzhuan* 田漢評傳 (Tian Han—A Critical Biography). Changsha: Hunan renmin Publ., 1984.

Henan Shidaxuebao 河南師大学報 (Journal of the Henan Teacher Training College).

Heym, Stefan. *The King David Report*. London: Abacus Publ., 1972.

Hinton, Harold. *The People's Republic of China: A Documentary Survey*. 5 vols. Wilmington: Scholarly Resources Inc., 1980.

Hinton, William. *Hundred Day War: The Cultural Revolution at Tsinghua University*. New York: Monthly Review Press, 1972.

Hongqi 紅旗 (Red Flag).

Hongse pipanzhe 紅色批判者 (The Red Critic).

Hongyan 鴻雁 (The Swan).

Hu Yuzhi 胡愈之 and Li Wenyi 李文宜. "Kuairen kuaiyu gandan zhaoren, shenqie huainian Wu Han tongzhi" 快人快語肝胆照人, 深切懷念吳晗同志 (Sharp Man and Outspoken, Devoted to Enlightening Others, Heartfelt Commemoration for Comrade Wu Han). *Renmin ribao*, Oct. 23, 1979.

Huang, C. C., trans. *Hai Jui Dismissed from Office*. Honolulu: University of Hawaii Press, 1972.

Huber, Horst. "Wen Tien-hsiang." In Herbert Franke, ed., *Sung Biographies*, vol. 3.

"Hunan huaguju *Shengsi pai* zai Beijing yanchu shoudao haoping" 湖南花鼓劇《生死牌》在北京演出受到好評 (Friendly Reception of the Huagu Opera "Tablets of Life and Death" from Hunan Province). *Wenyibao*, Jan. 18, 1959.

Jamison, D., et al. *China: The Health Sector*. Washington, D.C.: The World Bank, 1984.

Jian Bozan 剪伯贊 and Lü Zhenyu 呂振羽. "Lishi de zhenshi yu yishu de zhenshi" 歷史的眞實與藝術的眞實 (Historical and Artistic Truth). *Xijubao* 1959.4.

Jian Fu 健夫 (Tao Xiong). "Zhou Xinfang chuyan jingju *Hai Rui shangshu*" 周信芳出演京劇《海瑞上疏》(Zhou Xinfang Stages Peking Opera "Hai Rui Sends Up a Memorial"). *Xijubao* 1959.19.

Jiang Shuiping 江水平. "'Jiushi yaogui, ye bu zhun da'" 就是妖怪, 也不准打 ("Even If It Is a Demon, Don't Beat Her"). *Xijubao* 1961.23–24.

Jiang Xingyu 蔣星煜. *Hai Rui* 海瑞. Shanghai: Shanghai renmin Press, 1957; repr. Shanghai 1962, 1979.

———. "Hai Rui, Hai Rui ju, Hai Rui jingshen" 海瑞, 海瑞劇, 海瑞精神 (Hai Rui, Hai Rui Plays, the Spirit of Hai Rui). In Shanghai jingjuyuan, *Hai Rui shangshu*. Shanghai: Shanghai wenyi Press, 1979.

———. "Nan Bao Gong—Hai Rui" 南包公—海瑞 (A Judge Bao of the South—Hai Rui). *Jiefang ribao*, Apr. 17, 1959.

Jiangsu sheng Chenjiang shi jingjutuan 江蘇省鎮江市京劇團, with Zhao Wanpeng 趙萬鵬 holding the pen. "Da Qianlong" 打乾隆 (Trouncing [Emperor] Qianlong). *Juben* 1959.4.

Jianguo yilai wenyi zuopin zhuanti shumu 建國以來文藝作品專題書目 (A List of Literary Works in Book Form Published since the Founding of the PRC). Beijing, 1961.

Jiefang ribao 解放日報 (Liberation Daily).

Jinggangshan 井岡山.

Jingju congkan 京劇叢刊 (Peking Opera Collection).

Joffe, Ellis. *Between Two Plenums: China's Intraleadership Conflict, 1959–1962*. Michigan Papers in Chinese Studies, no. 22. Ann Arbor, 1975.

Johnson, David. "Epic and History in Early China: The Matter of Wu Tzu-hsü." *Journal of Asian Studies* 40.2, 1981.

———. "The Wu Tzu-hsü Pien-wen and Its Sources." 2 parts. *Harvard Journal of Asiatic Studies* 40.1, 1980; 40.2, 1980.

Juben 劇本 (Drama).

"Juqu biaoxian xiandai shenghuo de chuantong" 劇曲表現現代生活的傳通 (The Tradition in Drama to Represent Present-Day Life). *Renmin ribao*, June 28, 1958.

"Juqu biaoxian xiandai shenghuo xingcheng zhuliu" 劇曲表現現代生活形成主流 (It Has Already Become the Main Trend for Operas to Represent Present-Day Life). *Renmin ribao*, June 28, 1958.

Ke Qingshi 柯慶施. "Dali fazhan he fanrong shehuizhuyi xiju, genghao di wei shehuizhuyi de jingjijichu fuwu" 大力發展和繁榮社會主義戲劇, 更好地為社會主義的經濟基礎服務 (Vigorously Develop and Enrich Socialist Drama, Serve the Socialist Economic Base Still Better). *Hongqi* 1964.5.

Ke Shaomin 柯劭忞. *Xin Yuanshi* 新元史 (New Yuan History). Ershiwu shi ed.

Klein, D., and A. Clark. *Biographic Dictionary of Chinese Communism, 1921–1965*. Cambridge, Mass.: Harvard University Press, 1971.

Konrad, George. *The Loser*. San Diego: Farrar, Strauss & Giroux, 1982.

Konwicki, Tadeusz. *A Minor Apocalypse*. New York: Farrar, Strauss & Giroux, 1983.

Kubin, Wolfgang, and Rudolf G. Wagner, eds. *Essays in Modern Chinese Literature and Literary Criticism*. Bochum: Brockmeyer Publ., 1982.

Kumari, Ashwini. "China Tribesmen Flee into Burma and India." *The Washington Post*, Dec. 10, 1958.

Lewis, John W., ed. *Party Leadership and Revolutionary Power in China*. Cambridge: Cambridge University Press, 1970.

Leyda, Jay. *Dianying: An Account of Films and the Film Audience in China*. Cambridge, Mass.: MIT Press, 1972.

Li Chao 李超. "*Xie Yaohuan de fusu*"《謝瑤環》的復蘇 (The Resuscitation of "Xie Yaohuan"). *Renmin ribao*, Sept. 17, 1979.

———. "Zhongshi chuantongju de jinghua, ping Hunan huaguju *Shengsi pai*" 重視傳統劇的精華, 評湖南花鼓戲《生死牌》(Paying Attention to the Characteristics of Traditional Drama, on the Huagu Drama "Tablets of Life and Death" from Hunan). *Guangming ribao*, Jan. 18, 1959.

Li Jiantong 李建彤. *Liu Zhidan* 劉志丹 (Liu Zhidan). Beijing: Gongren Press, 1979.

Li Liming 李立明. *Zhongguo xiandai liubai zuojia xiaozhuan* 中國現代六百作家小傳 (Short Biographies of 600 Modern Chinese Authors). Hongkong: Po-wen Publ., 1977.

Li Lun 李綸. *Tang Taizong* 唐太宗 (Emperor Tai of the Tang Dynasty). Reviewed in Guo Hancheng, "Mantan jingju *Tang Taizong*." *Renmin xiju* 1982.12.

Li Minsheng 李民生 and Yang Zhiping 楊志平. "Cong lishi zhenshi chufa—huaju *Tang Taizong yu Wei Zheng* chuangzuo diandi tihui" 從歷史真實出發—話劇《唐太宗與魏徵》創作點滴體會. (Taking Historical Truth as the Point of Departure—Some Experiences in the Writing of "Emperor Tai of the Tang Dynasty and Wei Zheng"). *Shaanxi xiju* 1982.10; repr. *Xiju yanjiu* 1982.11.

Li Shisan 李十三. *Wanfulian* 萬福蓮. In *Shaanxi zhuantong jumu huipian, huaju*, coll. 1. Shaanxi, 1959.

Li Shusi 李束絲. "Guan Hanqing de *Dou E yuan*" 關漢卿底《竇娥冤》(Guan Hanqing's *Dou E yuan*). In Gutian wenxue chubanshe, ed., *Guan Hanqing yanjiu lunwenji*. Shanghai: Gutian wenxue Press, 1958.

Li Yan 黎彥. "Xuexi *Guan Hanqing* juzuo de jidian tihui" 學習《關漢卿》劇作的幾點體會 (Some Experiences in Studying the Play *Guan Hanqing*). *Juben* 1963.9.

Li Zhiyan 黎之彦. "Tian Han chuangzuo *Guan Hanqing* ceji" 田漢創作《關漢卿》側記 (Sidelights on Tian Han's Writing *Guan Hanqing*). *Xiju luncong* 1982.1; repr. in *Xiju yanjiu* 1982.9.

Li Zhiyan 黎之彦 and Qu Xiwen 翟希文, eds. "Tian Han xiju shici jicui" 田漢戲劇詩詞集萃 (A Collation of Tian Han's Poems on Drama). *Juben* 1982.5; repr. in *Xiju yanjiu* 1982.11.

Liang Bihui 梁璧會. "'Yougui wuhai' lun"《有鬼無害》論 (On "Even If There Are Ghosts, It Does Not Matter"). *Wenhuibao* May 6 and 7, 1963.

Liang Xiao 梁效. "Lun Wu Zetian de lishi diwei" 論武則天的歷史地位 (On Wu Zetian's Standing in History). *Beijing daxue xuebao* 1974.4.

Lianhuadong 蓮花洞 (Lotus Cave). In Zhang Bojin, ed., *Guoju daguan*, vol. 6. Taibei: Guofangbu Press, 1970.

Lin Yutang. *Lady Wu—A True Story*. London: Heinemann, 1957.

"Lingren nanwang de *Xie Yaohuan*" 令人難忘的《謝瑤環》 (Unforgettable "Xie Yaohuan"). (Name of author illegible in my copy.) *Xinjiang ribao*, Dec. 17, 1961.

Lishi de shenpan—jiepi "Sirenbang" manhua xuan 歷史的審判—揭批 "四人幫"漫畫選 (The Verdict of History—A Selection of Caricatures Denouncing the "Gang of Four"). Shanghai: Shanghai renmin meishu Press, 1979.

Liu Housheng 劉厚生. "Fandang fanshehuizhuyi gongtongti—*Li Huiniang, Hai Rui baguan, Xie Yaohuan* zonglun" 反黨反社會主義共同體—〈李慧娘〉、〈海瑞罷官〉、〈謝瑤環〉綜論. *Xijubao* 1966.3; trans. as "Co-workers against the Party and Socialism—a General Discussion of *Li Huiniang, Hai Jui Relieved of His Office* and *Hsieh Yao-huan*." *Survey of Chinese Mainland Magzines* no. 528, June 13, 1966.

Liuling Tong 六齡童. "Wo zenyang yǎn *Sun Wukong sanda baigujing* zhong de Sun Wukong" 我怎樣演《孫悟空三打白骨精》中的孫悟空 (How I Played Sun Wukong in "Sun Wukong Three Times Beats the White-Bone Demon"). In Zhejiang sheng wenhuaju *Sun Wukong sanda baigujing* zhengli xiaozu, ed., *Sun Wukong sanda baigujing*. Zhejiang: Zhejiang renmin Press, 1979.

"Long Live Leninism." Original in *Hongqi*, Apr. 16, 1960; trans. in Harold Hinton, *The People's Republic of China: A Documentary Survey*, vol. 2. Wilmington, Scholarly Resources Inc., 1980.

"Lu Dingyi tongzhi daibiao Zhonggong zhongyang he Guowuyuan zai quan-guo wenxue yishu gongzuozhe disanci daibiao dahui shang de zhuci" 陸定一同志代表中共中央和國務院在全國文學藝術工作者第三次代表大會上的祝詞 (Congratulatory Message by Comrade Lu Dingyi Representing the Central Committee of the CCP and the State Council to the Third Congress of Literary and Art Workers). *Beijing wenyi* 1960.8.

Lu Zhizhao 盧之超. "Ping Kang Sheng an zhengzhi sixiang huafen jieji de lishiweixinlun guandian" 評康生按政治思想劃分階級的歷史唯心論觀點 (A Critique of Kang Sheng's Historical Idealism in Separating Classes According to Their Political Ideology). *Renmin ribao* Aug. 4, 1980.

Luo Guanzhong 羅貫中. *Sanguo yanyi* 三國演義 (Romance of the Three Kingdoms). Beijing, 1972.

Ma Chaorong 馬焯榮. "Lun Tian Han bixia de Guan Hanqing xingxiang 論田漢筆下的關漢卿形象(On the Figure of Guan Hanqing as Depicted by Tian Han). *Xiangtan daxue shehuikexue xuebao* 1982.4; repr. in *Xiju yanjiu* 1982.11.

Ma Zhiyuan 馬致遠. *Po youmeng guyan hangong qiu* 破幽夢孤鴈漢宮秋. In Zang Jinshu, ed., *Yuan qu xuan*, vol. 1. Hongkong: Yiwen Press, n.d.

MacFarquhar, Roderick. *The Origins of the Cultural Revolution. Vol. 1, Contradictions among the People 1956–1957*. New York: Columbia University Press, 1974.

———. *The Origins of the Cultural Revolution. Vol. 2, The Great Leap For-*

ward 1958–1960. New York: Columbia University Press, 1983.

Mailla, Joseph-Anne-Marie Mauriac de. *Histoire de l'Empire Chinois.* Paris, 1799.

Mao Dun 茅盾. "Mao Dun tongzhi zhi daoci" 茅盾同志之悼詞 (Memorial Speech [for Tian Han] Sent by Comrade Mao Dun). *Renmin xiju* 1979.5.

Mao Zedong 毛澤東. "Down with the Prince of Hell, Liberate the Little Devil—a Talk with Such Comrades as Kang Sheng." In *Miscellany of Mao Tse-tung Thought,* vol. 2. Arlington: Joint Publication Research Service, 1974. Orig. in *Mao Zedong sixiang wansui,* vol. 2. Hongkong, 1969.

———. "Dui Aerbaniya junshi daibiaotuan de jianghua" 對阿爾巴尼亞軍師代表團的講話 (May 1, 1967) (Talk with the Albanian Military Delegation). In *Mao Zedong sixiang wansui,* vol. 2. Hongkong, 1969. Trans. in *Miscellany of Mao Tse-tung Thought,* vol. 2. Arlington: Joint Publication Research Service, 1974.

———. "Examples of Dialectics." In *Miscellany of Mao Tse-tung Thought,* vol. 1. Arlington: Joint Publication Research Service, 1974.

———. "Guanyu zhengque chuli renmin neibu maodun de wenti" 關于正確處理人民內部矛盾的問題 (On the Correct Handling of Contradictions among the People). *Xuexi wenxuan* 學習文選. S.l., 1967.

———. "Letter to Guo Moruo." Quoted in Guo Moruo, "'Yuyou chengqing wanli ai,' dui Mao zhuxi youguan *Sun Wukong sanda baigujing* di yishou qilü." *Guangming ribao,* May 31, 1964.

———. *Mao zhuxi shici* 毛主席詩詞 (Poems by Chairman Mao). Beijing: Renmin wenxue Press, 1976.

———. "Nian nu jiao" 念奴嬌. In Mao Zedong, *Mao Zhuxi shici.* Beijing: Renmin wenxue Press, 1976.

———. "Qilü, he Guo Moruo tongzhi" 七律, 和郭沫若同志 (Eight-Line Poem with Seven Characters to a Line, Responding to Guo Moruo). *Wenyibao* 1964.1.

———. *Talk at an Enlarged Work Conference Convened by the Central Committee of the Communist Party of China, Jan. 30, 1962.* Beijing: Foreign Languages Press, 1978.

———. "Zai quanguo Gongchandang xuanzhuan gongzuohuiyishang de jianghua" 在全國共產黨宣傳工作會議上的講話(Talk At the National CP Work Conference on Propaganda). In H. Martin, ed., *Mao Zedong Texte.* Vol. 2. Munich: Hanser Verlag, 1979.

"Mao Zedong sixiang de guanghui shengli shehuizhuyi xinjingju xuangao dansheng" 毛澤東思想的光輝勝利社會主義新京劇宣告誕生 (The Light of Mao Zedong Thought Victoriously Declares the Birth of a Socialist New Peking Opera). *Xijubao* 1964.7.

Mao Zedong sixiang wansui 毛澤東思想萬歲 (Long Live Mao Zedong Thought). 1979; repr. Hongkong: Po-wen Press, n.d.

Mao Zedong sixiang wansui, 2 毛澤東思想萬歲 (Long Live Mao Zedong Thought). Hongkong, 1969.

Martin, H. *Mao Zedong Texte.* Munich: Hanser Verlag, 1979–.

Mei Lanfang 梅蘭芳. "Chuantong daode liliang shanshuozhe guanghui"

傳統道德力量閃爍着光輝 (The Force of Traditional Ethics Radiates). *Renmin ribao*, Jan. 15, 1959.

Meng Chao 孟超. *Li Huiniang* 李慧娘 (Li Huiniang). *Juben* 1961.7/8.

Milosz, Czeslaw. *The Captive Mind*. New York: A. Knopf, 1953.

Miscellany of Mao Tse-tung Thought. 2 vols. Arlington: Joint Publication Research Service, 1974.

Monkey Subdues the White-Bone Demon. Beijing: Foreign Languages Press, 1964.

"Nahan" 吶喊 (Battle Cry). In *Tiananmen geming shichao*. Hongkong: Wenhua ziliao gongyingshe, 1978.

Nanguo yuekan 南國月刊 (Southern Monthly).

Nao tiangong 鬧天宮 (Uproar in the Heavenly Palace). In Zhang Bojin, ed., *Guoju daguan*. Vol. 6, pp. 183ff. Taibei: Guofangbu Press, 1970.

Nao tiangong 鬧天宮 (Uproar in the Heavenly Palace). In Zhongguo xiqu yanjiuyuan, ed., *Jingju congkan*. Vol. 8. Shanghai: Xinwenyi Press, 1953.

Peking Review.

Peng Dehuai zishu 彭德懷自述 (Peng Dehuai—An Autobiography). Beijing: Renmin Press, 1981.

Population and Development Review.

"Problems concerning the Purge of K'ang Sheng: Hu Yao-pang's Speech at the Central Party School." *Issues and Studies* June 1980.

Pusey, J. R. *Wu Han: Attacking the Present through the Past*. Cambridge, Mass.: Harvard East Asian Monographs, 1969.

Qi Xiangqun 齊向群. "Chongping Meng Chao xinbian *Li Huiniang*" 重評孟超新編《李慧娘》(Again on Meng Chao's Rewritten "Li Huiniang"). *Xijubao* 1965.1.

Qianxian 前綫 (Front Line).

Qinghua daxue zhexue xuexi xiaozu 青華大學哲學學習小組 and Beijing daxue zhexue xi 北京大學哲學系. "Lun Wu Zetian de yidian kanfa" 論武則天的一點看法 (On a Way of Looking at Wu Zetian). *Beijing daxue xuebao* 1974.4.

"Qiongju 'Hai Rui huichao' shi zhu da ducao" 瓊劇《海瑞回朝》是株大毒草 (The Qiong Style Opera "Hai Rui Returns to Court" Is a Big Poisonous Weed). *Guangming ribao* Dec. 18, 1968.

Qishi niandai 七十年代 (The Seventies).

"Quanguo gedi jinian Guan Hanqing" 全國各地紀念關漢卿 (Different Regions of the Nation Commemorate Guan Hanqing). *Renmin ribao*, June 28, 1958.

"Rang juqu gengduo genghao di fanying xiandai shenghuo" 讓劇曲更多更好地反應現代生活 (Let Drama Reflect Today's Life Even More and Better). *Renmin ribao*, June 28, 1958.

Renmin ribao 人民日報 (People's Daily).

Renmin wenxue 人民文學 (People's Literature).

Renmin xiju 人民戲劇 (People's Drama).

Renmin wenxue chubanshe, bianjibu 人民文學出版社編輯部, ed. *Guan Hanqing juqu xuan* 關漢卿劇曲選 (Guan Hanqing's Plays). Beijing: Renmin wenxue Press, 1958.

Renmin wenxue chubanshe, hongse zaofandui 人民文學出版社, 紅色造反隊. "Fandang guixi *Li Huiniang* chulong qianhou" 反黨鬼戲《李慧娘》出籠 前後 (The Ins and Outs of the Staging of the Anti-Party Ghost Play "Li Huiniang"). *Xiju zhanbao*, July 5, 1967.

"Revolutionary Big Character Posters Are 'Magic Mirrors' That Show Up All Monsters." *Peking Review* 1966.28.

"Riben gedacheng shangyan *Guan Hanqing*" 日本各大城上演《關漢卿》 (A Number of Big Japanese Cities Stage "Guan Hanqing"). *Xijubao* 1959.4.

Rüdelsberger, H. *Altchinesische Liebeskomödien*. Vienna, 1923.

Rudolph, Richard C. "Wu Tzu-hsü, His Life and Posthumous Cult: A Critical Study of Shih Chi 66." Ph.D. diss., University of California at Berkeley, 1942.

Shaanxi xiju 陝西戲劇 (Shaanxi Drama).

Shanghai jingjuyuan 上海京劇院, with Xu Siyan 許思言 holding the pen. *Hai Rui shangshu* 海瑞上疏. (Hai Rui Sends Up a Memorial). Orig. in *Shanghai xiju* 1959.2; rev. ed. Shanghai: Shanghai wenyi Press, 1979.

Shanghai xiju xueyuan, Xiju wenxue xi 上海戲劇學院, 戲劇文學系, ed. *Tian Han zhuanji* 田漢專集 (Tian Han: A Collection [of Texts and Comments]). Vol. 42 of *Zhongguo dangdai wenxue yanjiu ziliao*, 1980.

Shanghai xiju xueyuan xuebao 上海戲劇學院學報 (Journal of the Shanghai Drama Institute).

"Shanghai xijujie chuangzuo Hai Rui jumu" 上海戲劇界創作海瑞劇目 (Hai Rui Plays under Preparation in Shanghai Drama Circles). *Wenhuibao*, May 19, 1959.

Shaonian zhongguo 少年中國 (Young China).

Shi Gandang 石敢當. "Tang Seng he minzhu 唐僧和民主 (Tang Seng and Democracy). *Tianjin ribao*, Aug. 26, 1979.

Shi Wei 史違 and Li Siyi 勵斯貽. *Lü hou cuanquan de gushi* 呂后篡權的故事 (The Story of Empress Lü's Usurpation of Power). Shanghai: Shanghai renmin Press, 1977.

Shi Yansheng 石彥生. "'Wei min qingming' shi Tian Han tongzhi yiguan de fandong sixiang" 為民請命是田漢同志一貫的反動思想 ("To Speak Out for the People" Is a Reactionary Ideology of Tian Han's). *Xijubao* 1966.3.

Shouhuo 收穫 (Harvest).

Song Tan 送炭. "*Xiyou ji* xinbian" 西游記新編 (A New Edition of "The Journey to the West"). *Xin guancha* 1956.22.

Song Zhidi 宋之的. *Song Zhidi juzuo xuan* 宋之的劇作選 (Song Zhidi's Dramatic Works: A Selection). Beijing: Renmin wenxue Press, 1959.

———. *Wu Zetian* 武則天. In *Song Zhidi juzuo xuan*. Beijing: Renmin wenxue Press, 1959.

Song Zhidi 宋之的 and Jin Ren 金人. *Jiujian yi* 九件衣 (Nine Clothes). 2d ed. Shanghai: Shanghai zazhi Press, 1950.

Strauss, Leo. *Persecution and the Art of Writing*. Westport, Conn.: Greenwood Press, 1952.

———. *Thoughts on Machiavelli*, Glencoe, Ill.: The Free Press, 1958.

Sun An dongben. See Zhao Jianqiu et al.

Survey of Chinese Mainland Magazines.

Tan Zhengbi 譚正璧. *Yuandai xijujia Guan Hanqing* 元代戲劇家關漢卿 (The Yuan Playwright Guan Hanqing). Shanghai: Shanghai wenhua Press, 1957.

Tao Junqi 陶君起. *Jingju jumu chutan* 京劇劇目初探 (Peking Opera Repertoire). Beijing, 1963.

Tao Xiong 陶雄 (Jian Fu). "Chenyuan shierzai de wenziyu" 沉冤十二載的文字獄 (Twelve Years of Grief in a Prison House for Literature). In *Shanghai jingjuyuan, Hai Rui shangshu*. Shanghai: Shanghai wenyi Press, 1979.

Ten More Poems of Mao Tse-tung. Hongkong: Eastern Horizon Press, 1967.

Terrill, Ross. *The White-Boned Demon*. New York: William Morrow Publ., 1984.

Tian Han 田漢. "Bixu qieshi guanxin bing gaishan yiren de shenghuo" 必須切實關心並改善藝人的生活 (The Life Circumstances of Artists Have to Be Resolutely Cared for and Improved). *Xijubao* 1956.7.

———. *Guan Hanqing* 關漢卿. *Juben* 1958.5.

———. *Guan Hanqing*. 2nd ed. In *Zhongguo lishiju xuan*. Hongkong: Shanghai Book Co., 1961.

———. *Guan Hanqing* (*Guan Hanqing*, the Canton Opera version). In *Yueju congkan*. Guangzhou: Guangzhou wenhua Press, 1959.

———. "Guanyu *Guan Hanqing* de tongxin 關于《關漢卿》的通信 (Letter to Guo Moruo on *Guan Hanqing* [May 8, 1958]). In Shanghai xiju xuexuan, Xiju wenxue xi, ed., *Tian Han zhuanji*.

———. "Pipan Wu Zuguang de youpai guandian" 批判吳祖光的右派觀點 (A Criticism of Wu Zuguang's Rightist Views). *Xijubao* 1957.14.

———. "Preface" to *Guan Hanqing*. Beijing: Renmin wenxue Press, 1961.

———. "Renmin xuyao zheyang de yanyuan" 人民須要這樣的演員 (The People Need Such Actresses). *Renmin ribao* June 22, 1957.

———. "San kan yueju *Guan Hanqing* tiyong" 三看粵劇《關漢卿》題詠 (A Poem on the Occasion of Having Thrice Seen the Canton Opera *Guan Hanqing*). In Li Zhiyan and Qu Xiwen, eds., "Tian Han xiju shici jicui," in *Juben* 1982.5.

———. *Shalemei* 莎樂美. (Orig. O. Wilde, *Salomé*; a Chinese translation of the English translation of this text), in *Shaonian Zhongguo* 2.9, 1921.

———. "Shisanling shuiku changxiang qu" 十三陵水庫暢想曲 (A Paean to the Ming Tomb Reservoir). *Juben* 1958.8.

———. "Song *Guan Hanqing* fang Chao" 送《關漢卿》訪朝 (Sending *Guan Hanqing* on the Way to Korea). *Renmin ribao*, Aug. 4, 1959.

———. "Tan *Wang Shaojun* de suzao" 談王昭君的塑造 (On Portraying Wang Shaojun). *Renmin ribao*, Jan. 21, 1959.

———. "Tian Han tongzhi laihan" 田漢同志來翰 (Correspondence from Tian Han). *Juben* 1961.12.

———. *Tian Han wenji* 田漢文集 (Tian Han: Works). Beijing: Zhongguo xiju Publ., 1983.

———. "Wei yanyuan de qingchun qingming" 為演員的青春請命 (A Plea for the Spring of the Actors' Life). *Xijubao* 1956.11.

———. "Weida de Yuandai xiju zhanshi Guan Hanqing" 偉大的元代戲劇戰士關漢卿 (Guan Hanqing, the Great Dramatic Fighter of the Yuan Period). *Renmin ribao*, June 28, 1958.

————. *Wencheng gongzhu* 文成公主 (Princess Wencheng). *Juben* 1960.5.

————. "Women de ziji pipan" 我們的自己批判 (Our Self-Criticism). Orig. in *Nanguo yuekan* 2.1, 1930; repr. in *Tian Han zhuanji.*

————. *Wu Zetian* 武則天. In *Tian Han wenji*, vol. 10. Beijing: Zhongguo xiju Publ., 1983.

————. "Wu Zetian zixu" 《武則天》自序 (Preface to "Wu Zetian"). In *Tian Han wenji*, vol. 10. Beijing: Zhongguo xiju Publ., 1983.

————. "Wu Zuguang neng buneng guo shehuizhuyi guan" 吳祖光能不能過 社會主義關 (Will Wu Zugueng Be Able to Pass the Test of Socialism?). *Xijubao* 1957.15.

————. *Xie Yaohuan* 謝瑤環. Xi'an: Dongfang wenyi Publ., 1963.

————. *Xie Yaohuan* 謝瑤環. *Juben* 1961. 7/8.

————. "Zai Shaanxi sheng wenhuaju zhaoji de wenhuayishujie gongzuoren-yuan dahui de baogao" 在陝西省文化局召集的文化藝術界工作人員大會 的報告 (Report Given at the Congress of Workers from Literary and Art Circles Called by the Cultural Affairs Bureau of Shaanxi Province). *Shaanxi ribao*, Apr. 30, 1957.

"Tian Han de xiju zhuzhang wei shei fuwu" 田漢的戲劇主張為誰服務 (Whom Do Tian Han's Propositions about Drama Serve?). *Xijubao* 1966.2.

Tian Han zhuanji. See Shanghai xijuxueyuan xijuwenxuexi.

Tian Renlong 田人隆, Zhou Shaoquan 周紹泉, and Liu Zhongri 劉重日. *Cuanquan qieguo de Lü hou* 篡權竊國的呂后 (On Empress Lü, Who Seized Power and Usurped the Throne). In *Xuedian lishi congshu.* Beijing: Renmin Press, 1977.

Tiananmen geming shichao 天安門革命詩抄 (Revolutionary Poems from Tiananmen). Hongkong: Wenhua ziliao gongyingshe, 1978.

Tiananmen shiwenji, xupian 天安門詩文集, 續扁 (A Collection of Poems from Tiananmen, Supplement). Beijing: Beijing Press, 1979.

Tianjin ribao 天津日報 (Tianjin Daily).

Tie Qi 鐵騎. "Liu Shaoqi ai shenmeyang de dianying xiju?" 劉少奇愛 什麼樣的電影戲劇 (What Kind of Film and Drama Does Liu Shaoqi Like?). *Beijing xinwenyi*, June 8, 1967.

Tung, Constantine. "Lonely Search into the Unknown: T'ien Han's Early Plays 1920–1930." *Comparative Drama* 2.1, 1968.

————. "T'ien Han and the Romantic Ibsen." *Modern Drama* 14.4, 1967.

Unger, Jonathan. *Education under Mao.* New York: Columbia University Press, 1982.

Twitchett, Denis, ed. *The Cambridge History of China.* Vol. 3, *Sui and T'ang China, 589–906*, pt. 1. Cambridge: Cambridge University Press, 1979.

Twitchett, Denis, and Howard Wechsler. "Kao-tsung (reign 649–83) and the Empress Wu: The Inheritor and the Usurper." In D. Twitchett, ed., *The Cambridge History of China.* Vol. 3, *Sui and T'ang China, 589–906*, pt. 1.

Union Research Institute, ed. *The Case of P'eng Te-huai, 1959–1968.* Hong-kong, 1968.

Wagner, Rudolf G. "The Chinese Writer in His Own Mirror: Writer, State and Society—the Literary Evidence." In Merle Goldman, ed., with Timothy Cheek and Carol Lee Hamrin. *China's Intellectuals and the State.* Harvard

Contemporary China Series, no. 3. Cambridge, Mass.: Harvard East Asian
Monographs, 1987.

————. "The Cog and the Scout: Functional Concepts of Literature in Socialist
Political Culture: The Chinese Debate in the Mid-Fifties." In Wolfgang
Kubin and Rudolf G. Wagner, eds., *Essays in Modern Chinese Literature
and Literary Criticism*. Bochum, 1982.

————. *Inside a Service Trade: Studies in Contemporary Chinese Prose*. In
Press.

————. "Liu Binyan and the *texie*." *Modern Chinese Literature* 2.1, Spring
1986.

————. *Reenacting the Heavenly Vision: The Role of Religion in the Taiping
Rebellion*. China Research Monograph 25, Center for Chinese Studies, University of California. Berkeley, 1984.

Wakeman, Frederic, Jr. *History and Will: Philosophical Perspectives of Mao
Tse-tung's Thought*. Berkeley: University of California Press, 1973.

Walker, Richard. *Hunger in China*. New York: The New Leader, n.d. (Originally a supplement to the journal *The New Leader*.)

————. *Letters from the Communes*. New York: The New Leader, 1959 (Originally a supplement to the journal *The New Leader*.)

Wang Guming 王顧明. "Gaibian *Sun Wukong sanda baigujing* de tihui"
改編《孫悟空三打白骨精》的體會 (Experiences in Rewriting "Sun Wukong
Three Times Beats the White-Bone Demon"). In Zhejiang sheng wenhuaju
Sun Wukong sanda baigujing zhengli xiaozu, ed., with Bei Geng holding the
pen, *Sun Wukong sanda baigujing*. Zhejiang: Zhejiang renmin Press, 1979.

Wang Jisi 王季思. "Guan Hanqing he tade zaju" 關漢卿和他的雜劇 (Guan
Hanqing and His *zaju*). In Gutian wenxue chubanshe, ed., *Guan Hanqing
yanjiu lunwenji*. Shanghai: Gutian wenxue Press, 1958.

Wang Meng 王蒙. "Youyou cuncao xin" 悠悠寸草心 (The Loyal Heart).
Shanghai wenxue 1979.9.

Wang Shaoying 汪紹楹, ed. *Soushen ji* 搜神記. Beijing, 1979.

Wang Xiezhu 王頡竹. *Tangwang na jian* 唐王納諫 (The Tang Emperor Accepts
Remonstrance). *Beijing wenyi* 1962.6.

Wang Xingbei 王星北, ed. (Zhao Hongben 超宏本 and Qian Xiaodai 錢笑呆,
drawings). *Sun Wukong sanda baigujing* 孫悟空三打白骨精 (Sun Wukong
Three Times Beats the White-Bone Demon). Shanghai: Shanghai renmin
meishu Press, 1962. Changed ed. 1979.

Wang Yi 王禕. *Yuanshi* 元史 (Yuan History). Ershisi shi ed.

Wei Ming 衛明, "Shi ping Zhou Xinfang de xinzuo *Hai Rui shangshu*"
試評周信芳的新作《海瑞上疏》(A Tentative Assessment of Zhou Xinfang's
New Work "Hai Rui Sends Up a Memorial"). *Wenhuibao* Oct. 27, 1980.

Wei Qixuan 韋啓玄. "Tian Han tongzhi chuangzuo *Guan Hanqing* sanji"
田漢同志創作《關漢卿》散記 (Notes on Comrade Tian Han's Creating *Guan
Hanqing*). *Juben* 1958.5; repr. *Xiju yanjiu* 1982.11.

Wei Qun 韋群. "Tian Han tongzhi yao ba xiju chuangzuo yin xiang hechu?"
田漢同志要把戲劇創作引向何處? (Where Does Comrade Tian Han Want
to Drag Drama Work?). *Xijubao* 1966.3.

Wen Qing 文青. "Cong *Nü xun'an* dao *Xie Yaohuan* de gaibian kan *Xie Yao-*

huan de fandong benzhi" 從《女巡按》到《謝瑤環》的改編看《謝瑤環》的反
動本質 (The Reactionary Nature of "Xie Yaohuan" as Seen from the Rewriting of "The Inspectress" to "Xie Yaohuan"). *Wen shi zhe* 1966.2.

Wen shi zhe 文史哲 (Literature, History, Philosophy).

Wen Siye 文四野. "*Xie Yaohuan* de maotouci xiang nali?" 《謝瑤環》的矛頭
刺向哪里？(What Is the Target of Attack of "Xie Yaohuan"?). *Guangming
ribao*, Mar. 23, 1966.

Wen Tianxiang 文天祥. *Wen Wenshan wenji* 文文山文集 (Wen Tianxiang:
Works). Congshu jicheng ed. Shanghai, 1937.

Wen Yibu 聞亦步. "Bao Gong yu Hai Rui" 包公與海瑞 (Judge Bao and Hai
Rui). *Wenhuibao* May 13, 1959.

Weng Ouhong 翁偶虹, adapt. *Shengsi pai* 生死牌 (Tablets of Life and Death).
Beijing: Zhongguo xiju Press, 1959.

Wenhuibao 文滙報 (Culture News).

Wenxue pinglun 文學評論 (Literary Criticism).

Wenyibao 文藝報 (Literature and Art).

"Wenyijie shierge xiuzhengzhuyi toumu" 文藝界十二個修正主義頭目(Twelve
Revisionist Pieces in the Literary World). *Beijing wenyi zhanbao* July 13,
1967.

Wolf, Christa. *Cassandra: A Novel and Four Essays*. New York: Farrar, Strauss
& Giroux, 1984.

———. *Kassandra*. Darmstadt: Luchterhand Verlag, 1982.

Wu Chengen 吳承恩. *Xiyou ji* 西遊記 (Journey to the West). 2 vols. Beijing:
Zuojia Press, 1954.

Wu Han 吳晗. *Hai Rui baguan* 海瑞罷官 (Hai Rui Dismissed from Office).
Beijing wenyi 1961.1.

———. "Lun Hai Rui" 論海瑞 (On Hai Rui). *Renmin ribao*, Sept. 21, 1959.

———. "Wo fenhen, wo kongsu" 我憤恨，我控訴 (I Hate, I Accuse). *Renmin
ribao* July 7, 1957.

Wu Han he Hai Rui baguan 吳晗和《海瑞罷官》(Wu Han and His "Hai Rui
Dismissed from Office"). Beijing: Renmin Press, 1979.

Wu Han xueshu shengya 吳晗學術生涯 (Wu Han : A Scholar's Life). Jiangxi:
Jiangxi renmin Press, 1984.

Wu Shaoqiang 武耀強, adapt. *Shengsi pai* 生死牌 (Tablets of Life and Death).
Beijing: Renmin meishu Press, 1962.

Wu Xiaoling 吳曉鈴, Li Guoyan 李國炎, and Liu Jian 劉堅, eds. *Guan Hanqing juqu ji* 關漢卿劇曲集(Plays by Guan Hanqing). Beijing: Zhongguo xiju
Press, 1958.

Wu Xiaoling 吳曉鈴, Liu Jian 劉堅, Li Guoyan 李國炎, and Huang Pinlan
黃品蘭, eds. *Da xijujia Guan Hanqing jiezuo ji* 大戲劇家關漢卿傑作集
(Masterworks of the Great Dramatist Guan Hanqing). Beijing: Zhongguo
xiju Press, 1958.

Xi Wen 稀聞, Yang Zhixun 楊之劬, and Xu Juhua 徐菊華. *Hai Rui beiqian*
海瑞背縴 (Hai Rui Pulls the Rope). *Juben* 1961.2–3.

Xia Yan 夏衍. "Daonian Tian Han tongzhi" 悼念田漢同志 (In Commemoration of Comrade Tian Han). *Shouhuo* 1979.4.

———. "Du *Guan Hanqing* zatan lishiju" 讀《關漢卿》雜談歷史劇 (Remarks
upon the Historical Drama on Reading *Guan Hanqing*). *Juben* 1958.6.

Xiangtan daxue shehuikexue xuebao 湘潭大學社會科學學報 (Xiangtan University Social Science Journal).

Xiju luncong 戲劇論叢 (Essays on Drama).

Xiju yanjiu 戲劇研究 (Drama Studies).

Xiju yishu 戲劇藝術 (Drama Arts).

Xiju zhanbao 戲劇戰報 (Drama Battle News).

Xijubao 戲劇報 (Drama News).

Xijubao ziliaoshi 戲劇報資料室 ed. "Dui *Hai Rui baguan*, *Xie Yaohuan* deng de dapipan jixu shenru" 對《海瑞罷官》,《謝瑤環》等的大批判續續深入 (The Great Criticism of "Hai Rui Dismissed from Office", "Xie Yaohuan", and Others Continues and Deepens). *Xijubao* 1966.3.

Xin guancha 新觀察 (New Observer).

Xin Wentong 辛文彤. "Ping Tian Han de yige fangeming celüe" 評田漢的一個反革命策略 (On Tian Han's Counterrevolutionary Strategy). *Renmin ribao* Mar. 2, 1971.

Xiong Deji 熊德基. Lun Wu Zetian 論武則天 (On Wu Zetian). Jilin: Jilin renmin Press, 1979.

Xu Siyan 許思言. "Wei *Hai Rui shangshu* wenziyu bianyuan" 為《海瑞上疏》文字獄辯冤 (For the Release of "Hai Rui Sends Up a Memorial" from the Literary Prison House). In *Hai Rui shangshu*. Shanghai, 1979.

——. "Chongban houji" 重版後記 (Postface to the New Edition). In Shanghai jingjuyuan, *Hai Rui shangshu*. Shanghai, 1979.

Xu Yingshan 徐仰山. "Shitan 'qingguan xi' de duhai" 試談《清官戲》的毒害 (A Note on the Poison Spread by the "Plays on Upright Officials"). *Xijubao* 1966.3.

Xuexi wenxuan 學習文選 (Selection of Materials for Study). N.p., n.d.

Yanagida Izumi 柳田泉. *Seiji shōsetsu kenkyū* 政治小說研究 (Studies on the Political Novel). 3 vols. Tokyo, 1935.

Yang Hsien-yi and Gladys Yang, trans. *Selected Plays of Kuan Han-ch'ing*. Beijing: Foreign Languages Press, 1958.

Yang Xianyi 楊憲益. "*Hongmei* jiuqu xi xinfan—kunqu *Li Huiniang* guanhou gan" 《紅梅》旧曲喜新翻—昆曲《李慧娘》觀後感 (A New Lease on Life for the Old Play "Red Plum"—Impressions After Seeing the Kunqu Opera "Li Huiniang"). *Juben* 1961.10.

Yangcheng wanbao 羊城晚報 (Yangcheng Evening News).

Yin Bing 伊兵. "Manhua *Xie Yaohuan*" 漫話《謝瑤環》 (Desultory Notes on "Xie Yaohuan"). *Xijubao* 1962.3.

Yin Mo 伊默. "*Xie Yaohuan* weishei 'qingming'" 《謝瑤環》為誰請命 (For Whom Is "Xie Yaohuan" "Pleading"). *Wenyibao* 1966.2.

You Lin 有林. "Ping Kang Sheng de pipan 'weishengchanlilun'" 評康生的批判《唯生產力論》 (On Kang Sheng's Criticism of the "Theory of Productive Forces Only"). *Renmin ribao* July 24, 1980.

"Youxiu lishiju *Hai Rui shangshu* pingfan" 优秀歷史劇《海瑞上疏》平反 (The Excellent Historical Drama "Hai Rui Sends Up a Memorial" Rehabilitated). *Renmin ribao* Oct. 23, 1979.

Yu, Anthony C. *The Journey to the West*. 4 vols. Chicago: University of Chicago Press, 1977–.

Yu Ming 羽明. "Kang Sheng yu Jiang Qing" 康生與江青 (Kang Sheng and

Jiang Qing). *Xin guancha* 1981.1–3.

Yue Daiyun and Carolyn Wakeman. *To the Storm: The Odyssey of a Chinese Woman*. Berkeley: University of California Press, 1985.

Yule, Henry, trans. *The Book of Ser Marco Polo, the Venetian, concerning the Kingdoms and Marvels of the East*. 2 vols. London: John Murray, 1871.

Yun Song 雲松. "Tian Han de *Xie Yaohuan* shi yike daducao" 田漢的《謝瑤環》是一棵大毒草 (Tian Han's "Xie Yaohuan" Is a Big Poisonous Weed). *Renmin ribao*, Feb. 1, 1966; *Guangming ribao*, Feb. 2, 1966; and *Juben* 1966.1.

Zang Jinshu 臧晉叔. *Yuan qu xuan* 元曲選 (A Selection of Yuan Plays). Hongkong: Yiwen Press, n.d.

Zeng Liping 曾立平. "Ping lishiju chuangzuo zhong de fanlishizhuyi qiangxiang" 評歷史劇創作中的反歷史主義傾向 (On the Anti-Historical Tendency in the Creation of Historical Drama). *Xiju yishu* 1981.1.

Zhandou bao 戰鬥報 (Battle News).

Zhang Bojin 張伯謹, ed. *Guoju daguan* 國劇大觀 (A Collection of Peking Opera). Taibei: Guofangbu Press, 1970.

Zhang Cheng, ed. Zheng Jiasheng, ill., *The Real and the Fake Monkey*. Beijing: Zhaohua Publ., 1983.

Zhang Tianxi 張天賜 (director). *Shengsi pai* 生死牌 (Tablets of Life and Death). Haiyan and Hunan Studios, 1959. Black and white film.

Zhang Xiangtian 張向天. *Mao zhuxi shici jianzhu* 毛主席詩詞箋注 (Notes and Commentary on the Poems of Chairman Mao). Hongkong: Kunlun Publ., 1971.

Zhang Yigong 張一弓. "Fanren Li Tongzhong de gushi" 犯人李銅鍾的故事 (The Story of Li Tongzhong the Criminal). *Shouhuo* 1980.1.

Zhang Zhen 張眞, "Kan kunqu xinfan *Li Huiniang* 看昆曲新翻《李慧娘》 (Seeing the Redone Kunqu Opera "Li Huiniang"). *Xijubao* 1961.15/16.

Zhao Cong 超聰. *Zhongguo dalu de xiju gaige, 1942–1967* 中國大陸的戲劇改革 (Drama Reform in Mainland China). Hongkong: Zhongwen daxue Publ., 1967.

Zhao Hongben 趙宏本 (illustrator). *Touxiangpai Song Jiang* 投降派宋江 (Song Jiang the Capitulationist). Shanghai: Shanghai renmin Press, 1973.

———. *Xiaodao hui* 小刀会 (The Small Sword Society). Shanghai: Shanghai renmin Press, 1974.

Zhao Jianqiu 趙劍秋, Yuan Jigao 范季高, Yang Hanqing 楊漢卿, Shang Zhisi 尚之四, and Ji Genyin 紀根垠, adapt. *Sun An dongben* 孫安動本 (Sun An Pushes Memorials). *Juben* 1960.1.

Zhao Jingshen 超景深. "Guan Hanqing he tade zaju" 關漢卿和他的雜劇 (Guan Hanqing and His *Zaju*). In Gutian wenxue chubanshe, ed., *Guan Hanqing yanjiu lunwenji*. Shanghai: Gutian wenxue Press, 1958.

Zhao Wanpeng 趙萬鵬. *Da Qianlong* 打乾隆 (Trouncing Qianlong). *Juben* 1959.4.

Zhao Wu 趙武, ed. and comm. *Wei Zheng* 魏徵. Beijing: Zhonghua Books, 1962.

Zhao Ximing 趙錫銘 and Li Shiwu 李士武. *Hai Rui sou gong* 海瑞搜宮 (Hai Rui Investigates the Palace). Reviewed in *Renmin xiju* 1982.2, inside flap.

Zhejiang sheng wenhuaju *Sun Wukong sanda baigujing* zhengli xiaozu 浙江省文化局《孫悟空三打白骨精》整理小組, with Bei Geng 貝庚 holding the pen. *Sun Wukong sanda baigujing* 孫悟空三打白骨精 (Sun Wukong Three Times Beats the White-Bone Demon). Zhejiang: Zhejiang renmin Press, 1979.

Zheng Zhenduo 鄭振鐸. "Guan Hanqing—woguo 13 shiji de weida juqujia" 關漢卿—我國十三世紀的偉大劇曲家 (Guan Hanqing—a Great Thirteenth-Century Dramatist). *Xijubao* 1958.6.

Zhiji mei Houwang 智激美猴王 (Arousing Monkey King with Wit). In *Jingju congkan* 京劇叢刊, no. 33. Beijing: Zhongguo xiju Press, 1958.

Zhong Ju 鍾炬. "Jiechuan Tian Han zhizuo *Xie Yaohuan* de fangeming qitu" 揭穿田漢制作《謝瑤環》的反革命企圖 (The Counterrevolutionary Aims of Tian Han in Writing "Xie Yaohuan" Disclosed). *Guangming ribao*, Dec. 18, 1966.

Zhong Kan 仲侃. *Kang Sheng pingzhuan* 康生評傳 (Kang Sheng. A Critical Biography). Beijing: Hongqi zazhi Press, 1983.

Zhonggong yanjiu 中共研究 (Studies in Chinese Communism).

Zhongguo dangdai wenxue yanjiu ziliao 中國當代文學研究資料 (Materials for the Study of Modern Chinese Literature).

Zhongguo dianying ziliaoguan and Zhongguo yishu yanjiuyuan, dianying yanjiusuo 中國電影資料館, 中國藝術研究院電影研究所, eds. *Zhongguo yishu yingpian bianmu* 中國藝術影片編目 (A List of Chinese Films). 2 vols. Beijing: Wenhua yishu Press, 1981.

Zhongguo juxie geming zaofantuan 中國劇協革命造反團. "Chedi chanchu Tian Han de daducao *Guan Hanqing*" 徹底鏟除田漢的大毒草《關漢卿》 (Root Out Tian Han's Big Poisonous Weed *Guan Hanqing*). *Xiju zhanbao*, June 7, 1967.

Zhongguo juxie geming zaofantuan, Zhongguo juxie 中國劇協革命造反團, 中國劇協. "Yige chumu jingxin de fangeming fubi shijian" 一個觸目驚心的反革命復辟事件 (A Shocking Incident of Counterrevolutionary Restoration). *Xiju zhanbao*, June 24, 1967.

Zhongguo juxie zaofantuan 中國劇協造反團. "Liu Shaoqi shi zenyang baobi Tian Han de daducao *Xie Yaohuan* de" 劉少奇是怎樣包庇田漢的大毒草《謝瑤環》的 (How Liu Shaoqi Protected Tian Han's Poisonous Weed "Xie Yaohuan"). *Xiju zhanbao*, May 13, 1967.

Zhongguo lishiju xuan 中國歷史劇選 (Chinese Historical Drama: A Selection). Hongkong: Shanghai Book Co., 1961.

Zhongguo pingjuyuan 中國評劇院, with An Xi 安西 and Gao Chen 高琛, eds. *Zhong Li jian* 鍾離劍 (Zhong Li's Sword). *Juben* 1961.9.

Zhongguo xiqu yanjiuyuan 中國戲曲研究院, ed. *Jingju congkan* 京劇叢刊 (A Collection of Peking Operas). Shanghai: Xinwenyi Press, 1953.

Zhou Enlai 周恩來. "Guanyu wenyi gongzuo de sanci jianghua" 關於文藝工作的三次講話 (Three Talks On Work in Literature and the Arts). Beijing: Renmin Press, 1979.

———. "Speech at the 22nd Congress of the Communist Party of the Soviet Union, Oct. 19, 1961." In Harold Hinton, *The People's Republic of China: A Documentary Survey*, vol. 2. Wilmington: Scholarly Resources Inc., 1980.

Zhou Xinfang 周信芳. "Yongyuan wangbuliao zhe zhuangyan de shike" 永遠忘不了這莊嚴的時刻 (I Will Never Forget This Grand Moment). *Xijubao* 1959.13.

Zhou Yang 周揚. "The Fighting Task Confronting Workers in Philosophy and the Social Sciences." In Harold Hinton, *The People's Republic of China: A Documentary Survey*, vol. 2. Wilmington, Scholarly Resources Inc., 1980.

———. "Yong liangtiao tui mai xiang xiju de xin jieduan" 用兩條腿邁向戲劇的新階段 (Striding on Both Legs toward a New Phase of the Theater). *Xijubao*, May 31, 1958.

"Zhou zongli jiejian jingju xiandaixi guanmo yanchu renyuan" 周總理接見京劇現代戲觀摩演出人員 (Premier Zhou Received the Actors of the Trial Performances for Peking Operas on Contemporary Themes). *Xijubao* 1964.6.

Zong Gushi 宗谷史, ed. *Dayexinjia Lü hou* 大野心家呂后 (Empress Lü, the Great Careerist). Jilin: Jilin renmin Press, 1977.

"Zuotan Tian Han Xinzuo *Guan Hanqing*" 座談田漢新作《關漢卿》(A Discussion of Tian Han's New Work "Guan Hanqing"). *Xijubao* 1958.9.

"Zuotanhui chaiji" 座談會摘記 (A Summary of the Discussion). *Qishi niandai* 1980.1.

Index

Compositor: Asco Trade Typesetting Ltd.
Text: 10/13 Sabon
Display: Sabon
Printer: Edwards Brothers, Inc.
Binder: Edwards Brothers, Inc.